Prince

life & times

REVISED & UPDATED EDITION

CHARTWELL
BOOKS

jason**draper**

Prince
life & times

Jason Draper

Quarto is the authority on a wide range of topics.
Quarto educates, entertains and enriches the lives of
our readers—enthusiasts and lovers of hands-on living.
www.quartoknows.com

This edition published in 2016 by
CHARTWELL BOOKS
an imprint of Book Sales
a division of Quarto Publishing Group USA Inc.
142 West 36th Street, 4th Floor
New York, New York 10018
USA

This edition published by arrangement with
Outline Press Limited, 3.1D Union Court,
20-22 Union Road, London SW4 6JP,
United Kingdom
www.jawbonepress.com

ISBN-13: 978-0-7858-3497-7

Library of Congress Cataloging-in-Publication Data available upon request.

EDITOR: Tom Seabrook
DESIGN: Paul Cooper Design
COVER: Balley Design

10 9 8 7 6 5 4 3 2

Printed in China

MIX
Paper from
responsible sources
FSC® C017606

CONTENTS

INTRODUCTION

For a notoriously private artist, Prince Rogers Nelson was surprisingly visible. With a relentless work rate that saw him release 39 studio albums in under as many years (and that's not counting his long list of side projects), since the 1978 release of his debut, *For You*, barely a year passed without a major Prince event taking place. His music was ubiquitous: from the enduring classics that still blast out of radios and club speakers ("I got too many hits!" he would declare during concerts) to his obvious influence on the generations that came in his wake.

A master of surprise, Prince himself seemed to be everywhere. Turn on the news, and there he was: sitting courtside at a basketball match. Having been showered with accolades his entire career, he'd start turning up at awards ceremonies, delivering trophies to artists that looked up to him. One night he would be in Minneapolis, seemingly materializing out of nowhere to sit in with a local band for a few minutes, before disappearing just as mysteriously. The following night, he'd pop up in another city – another country altogether – playing a secret show for an invited audience.

Prince was part of the fabric of everyday life – and not just for fans. In the week leading up to his death, he was spotted acting like any other Minneapolis citizen: cycling around the suburbs, dropping in on his local record store, checking out a live performance at a jazz club.

He was intensely private, yet he was omnipresent. Now he is gone, his absence feels all the greater.

Prince seemed to have beamed in from another planet – another galaxy, even – mastering any instrument he chose; dancing and singing better than anyone who would devote their life to just one of those talents. And he could do it all while throwing cues to his band and never missing a beat. His death served to remind us that he was human after all, but that in itself just makes his achievements all the more astounding.

That Prince changed the world is beyond question. That he did so more than once, while remaining steadfastly committed to living life on his own terms, is yet another wonder of his remarkable career. Throughout the 80s, he revolutionized music with what became known as the Minneapolis sound – a bit of a misnomer, since much of the sound accredited to Minneapolis, the hometown where Prince remained for his entire life, came from just this one five-foot-two genius. A genius who couldn't really be credited with just one 'sound,' either, as he could play it all: funk, rock, pop, soul, R&B. He channeled Sly Stone and Jimi Hendrix, Miles Davis and James Brown, George Clinton and Joni Mitchell – often in the same song. And when he'd finished with changing music forever, he set about changing the music industry itself, waging war on his record label, pioneering internet distribution, and fighting a dogged one-man battle for artists' rights. Any self-sufficient artist – any artist at all who has the courage to follow their own creative path – owes no small amount of their creative freedom to Prince.

In 2013, Prince's then manager, Julia Ramadan, told him: "When it comes to your life story, don't let anyone hold the pen." When Prince died, he was in the

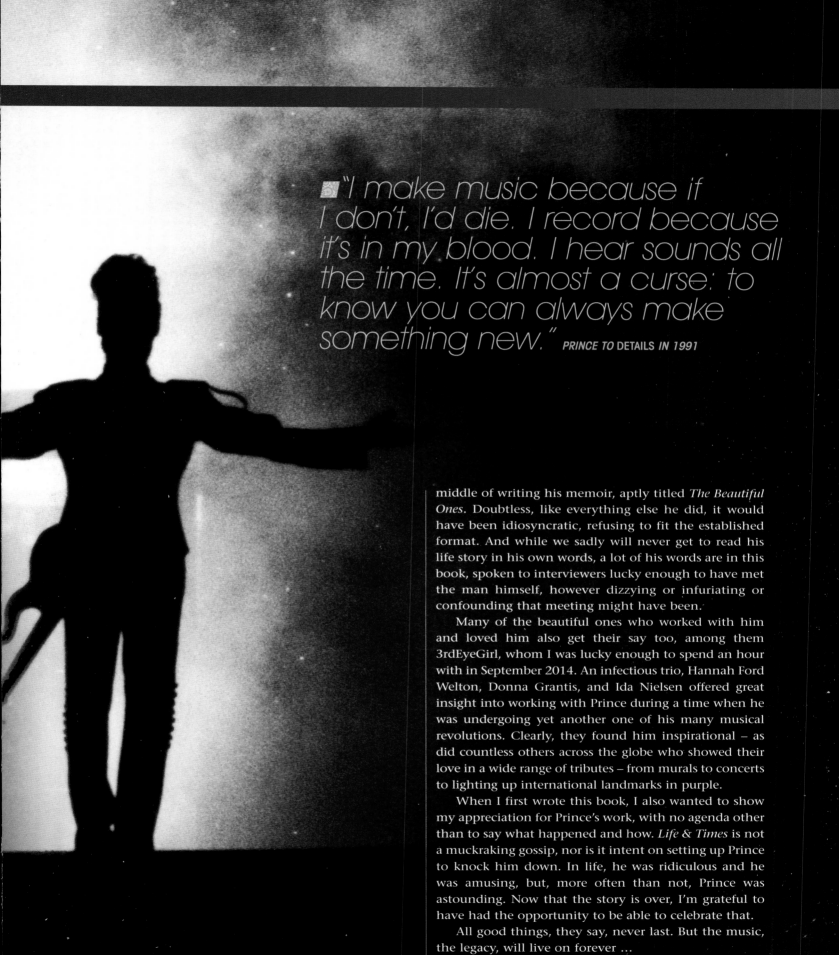

> ■ "I make music because if I don't, I'd die. I record because it's in my blood. I hear sounds all the time. It's almost a curse: to know you can always make something new." *PRINCE TO* DETAILS *IN 1991*

middle of writing his memoir, aptly titled *The Beautiful Ones*. Doubtless, like everything else he did, it would have been idiosyncratic, refusing to fit the established format. And while we sadly will never get to read his life story in his own words, a lot of his words are in this book, spoken to interviewers lucky enough to have met the man himself, however dizzying or infuriating or confounding that meeting might have been.

Many of the beautiful ones who worked with him and loved him also get their say too, among them 3rdEyeGirl, whom I was lucky enough to spend an hour with in September 2014. An infectious trio, Hannah Ford Welton, Donna Grantis, and Ida Nielsen offered great insight into working with Prince during a time when he was undergoing yet another one of his many musical revolutions. Clearly, they found him inspirational – as did countless others across the globe who showed their love in a wide range of tributes – from murals to concerts to lighting up international landmarks in purple.

When I first wrote this book, I also wanted to show my appreciation for Prince's work, with no agenda other than to say what happened and how. *Life & Times* is not a muckraking gossip, nor is it intent on setting up Prince to knock him down. In life, he was ridiculous and he was amusing, but, more often than not, Prince was astounding. Now that the story is over, I'm grateful to have had the opportunity to be able to celebrate that.

All good things, they say, never last. But the music, the legacy, will live on forever ...

JASON DRAPER, London, England, June 2016

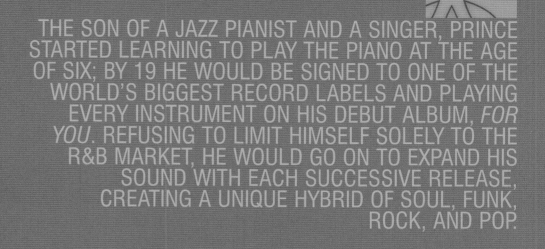

THE SON OF A JAZZ PIANIST AND A SINGER, PRINCE STARTED LEARNING TO PLAY THE PIANO AT THE AGE OF SIX; BY 19 HE WOULD BE SIGNED TO ONE OF THE WORLD'S BIGGEST RECORD LABELS AND PLAYING EVERY INSTRUMENT ON HIS DEBUT ALBUM, *FOR YOU*. REFUSING TO LIMIT HIMSELF SOLELY TO THE R&B MARKET, HE WOULD GO ON TO EXPAND HIS SOUND WITH EACH SUCCESSIVE RELEASE, CREATING A UNIQUE HYBRID OF SOUL, FUNK, ROCK, AND POP.

THE EARLY YEARS
1958–1983

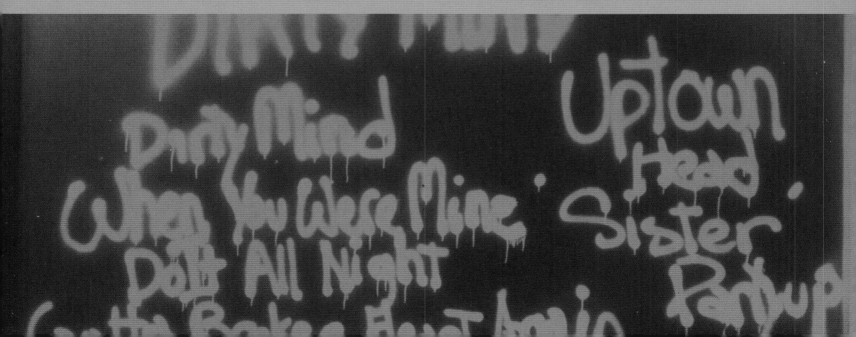

RIGHT FROM THE START OF HIS CAREER, PRINCE HAD TO DEFEND HIMSELF. TO BEGIN WITH, THE QUESTION THAT HE HAD TO ANSWER MOST OFTEN WAS: "IS YOUR NAME REALLY PRINCE?" THE ANSWER WAS SIMPLY, CATEGORICALLY, YES.

Introducing Prince
(1958–1977)

Born on June 7 1958 in Mount Sinai Hospital, Minneapolis, Prince Rogers Nelson was named for the Prince Rogers Trio, the jazz combo led by his father, John L Nelson, who used the stage name Prince Rogers.

Having both struggled in Louisiana, Prince's parents had moved separately to Minnesota earlier in the 50s in search of work in a part of America that was known for its liberal race-relations. Prince would later use his parents' mixed heritage – his father was part Italian, while his mother, Mattie Shaw, had African American, Native American, and white roots – to confuse interviewers who refused to focus on his music alone.

"I named my son Prince because I wanted him to do everything I wanted to do," John Nelson told *A Current Affair* in 1991. "He's done all of it." At the age of five, Prince was taken by his mother (a former jazz singer) to see The Prince Rogers Trio play in a downtown Minneapolis club. The group's mix of jazz standards and original material wasn't earth shattering, but the experience seemed nonetheless to change Prince forever. He watched with interest as his father, decked out in the sharpest of suits, led the band through its repertoire and held sway over the crowd. When a line of dancing girls came out – seemingly also under Nelson's control – Prince had seen all that he needed to see to know that the musician's life was for him.

There are similar echoes in Prince's recollections of seeing James Brown at the age of ten. "[My] stepdad put me on stage with him," he told MTV in 1985, "and I danced a bit until the bodyguard took me off." Like Nelson Sr, Brown would have a lasting effect on the boy. "He inspired me because of the control he had over his band," Prince later revealed, "and because of the beautiful dancing girls he had. I wanted both."

There was a piano in the front room of the Nelson's house, and whenever he wasn't at school or at the local Seventh Day Adventist church the young Prince – nicknamed Skipper by his mom – could be found playing

it. The first pieces he learnt to play were the theme tunes to *Batman* and *The Man From U.N.C.L.E.* By the age of seven he had reportedly written his first song, 'Funkmachine.'

The city of Minneapolis itself was similarly influential on Prince's development. It was one of the few places in America's Midwest where white and black communities weren't so strictly divided, which meant that radio was also less segregated. Whereas big cities such as New York and Chicago had stations that played black music all day, KUXL would only broadcast contemporary funk and soul between 10am and 2pm before reverting to rock'n'roll later in the day, when more listeners would be tuned in. "Listening to white radio was a positive thing that gave [Prince] a real, rounded way of finding out what was going on in music," his first manager, Owen Husney, later recalled, noting that being forced to listen to white pop gave Prince "a real edge."

Music and the radio became a means of escapism for the young Prince as he sought both a way to communicate his innermost thoughts and also a diversion from the physical abuse he suffered at the hands of his father. He has since downplayed this area of his upbringing, telling Larry King that his father was merely "a very strict disciplinarian," but the situation appears to have been rather more serious than that. Prince has reportedly shared stories of real physical abuse with a few close confidantes, and has made reference to it in his work, notably in the semi-autobiographical *Purple Rain* movie and the song 'Papa,' on which he sings: "Don't abuse children, or else they turn out like me."

John L Nelson and Mattie Shaw divorced in 1968, and their ten-year-old son soon began shuffling from home to home. Prince's father left his piano behind, giving the boy free reign to learn the instrument by himself. His mother remarried a couple of years later, but Prince's relationship with his stepfather, Hayward Baker, was fraught. "I disliked him immediately," he recalled. "He would bring us lots of presents all the time, rather than sit down and

talk with us and give us companionship." One direct result of this was that it was left to Prince's mother to teach him about the birds and the bees – which Prince once claimed she did by providing him with an assortment of *Playboy* magazines and erotic literature.

In 1970 Prince enrolled at Bryant Junior High and moved in with his father for a brief spell, during which time he hung out with his much taller and more athletic stepbrother, Duane. This too had quite an effect on the young Prince. "My older brother was a basketball star," he told the *Los Angeles Times* in 1981. "He always had girls around him. I think I must have been on a jealous trip, because I got out of sports." (Prince later referenced Duane – "my brother, handsome and tall" – on *1999*'s 'Lady Cab Driver,' and subsequently hired him first as a bodyguard and then as Head Of Security at Paisley Park.)

Prince didn't stay with his father for very long. In 1972 he moved to Central High, where he began to come into his own. He was still a quiet, shy boy who walked around in denim flares, knitted tank tops, and an Afro, and spent his lunch breaks practicing alone in the music room. But he had also a natural teenage interest in girls, and was reportedly kicked out of his father's house after being caught in bed with one of them. In 1985, while giving *Rolling Stone* journalist Neal Karlan a tour of Minneapolis in the wake of *Purple Rain*'s extraordinary success, Prince pointed out a phone booth as being the one from which "I called my dad and begged him to take me back … he said no, so I called my sister

[Tyka] and begged her to ask him. So she did, and afterward told me all I had to do was call him back, tell him I was sorry, and he'd take me back. So I did, and he still said no. I sat crying at that phone booth for two hours. That's the last time I cried."

Prince had a brief spell living with his aunt Olivia Nelson before moving in with his close school-friend, André Anderson, whose mother became a kind of surrogate mom to Prince, too. Prince initially shared a room with André, but soon grew frustrated at his friend's untidiness and moved into the basement.

By then the boys had already formed a band together – Grand Central, with Prince on guitar, Anderson on bass, and Smith on drums, with André's sister Linda and neighborhood friend Terry Jason joining later – and now had somewhere to practice. Surrounded by musical instruments after rehearsals, Prince continued to practice further in the comfort of isolation. But that wasn't all that went on in the basement. Stories abound of more typical adolescent behavior taking place down there. "Prince and I made music and entertained various local girls," Anderson recalled. "When I first met Prince he was a nice respectable boy. He didn't even cuss. I was the renegade."

Charles Smith had a rather less romanticized view of his time in the basement. "[It] would flood all the time in the spring," he told the BBC documentary *Liquid Assets: Prince's Millions* in 2003. "[Prince] would always cry to me, 'I'm not gonna live like this anymore … When I make it, I ain't ever gonna turn back.'" Smith didn't stay in the group for long, with the other members soon deciding that he was devoting too much time to the school football team. He was replaced in 1974 by another of Prince's school friends, Morris Day, who later went on to front The Time.

The group then became Grand Central Corporation and picked up their first manager in the form of Day's mother, LaVonne Daugherty. She subsequently invited Prince's cousin by marriage Pepé Willie to help oversee the group. Willie had recently moved to Minneapolis from New York, where he had worked as a musician, and had

"His mother basically walked away from him, and his father struggled to raise him and threw in the towel … it certainly doesn't add up to a very secure, well-rounded individual."

ALAN LEEDS (FUTURE TOUR MANAGER AND PRESIDENT OF PAISLEY PARK RECORDS)

often given Prince advice over the phone. His first job was to acquire studio time for the group at the local Cookhouse facility.

At first Willie wasn't sure who the main star of the group was. "Everybody was talented," he later recalled. "But I always, always noticed Prince going over to Linda, the keyboard player, and showing her, 'No, this is what

James Brown, whose command as a bandleader had a big influence on how Prince led his own musicians.

you play.'" Prince would then do the same with Anderson, picking up the bass and showing him what to do, too. Before long Willie had hired Prince as a session player in his own funk band, 94 East. (Several tapes of their collaborations exist, notably 2000's *Prince With 94 East: One Man Jam*.)

On February 13 1977 the *Central High Pioneer* ran Prince's first ever interview. The school paper marveled at his ability to play "several instruments, such as guitar, bass, all keyboards, and drums," noting that he also started to sing but had given up on the saxophone. In the weeks prior to the interview, Prince had been working on a demo with Grand Central Corporation in Minneapolis's ASI Studio (using time paid for by Morris Day's mother). Prince told the *Pioneer* that they hoped to have an album out in the early summer, but conceded that, because of the lack of major studios and record companies, it would be "very hard for a band to make it in this state. … I really feel that if we had lived in Los Angeles or New York or some other big city, we would have gotten over by now." Little did he realize that, in ten years time, he would have turned Minneapolis into a new center of cool, and would be running his own label and hi-tech recording studio out of it.

By the middle of 1976 Grand Central Corporation had renamed themselves Champagne, partly because of the old name's similarity to Sly & The Family Stone bassist Larry Graham's new group, Graham Central Station, and partly because Charles Smith had begun to complain that he had come up with the original name. Champagne began recording at Moonsound Studio, a small recording facility owned by Chris Moon, a local concert promoter who wrote jingles for advertisements. Moon quickly took note of Prince's talent and invited him to collaborate on some songs he had started writing the lyrics to in exchange for as much free recording time as he wanted. Despite suggestions that Isaac Hayes might offer Champagne a recording contract, Prince accepted Moon's offer, and was given the keys to Moonsound just in time for his graduation from Central High on his 18th birthday. Under the Employment heading of his graduation book, Prince simply wrote the word 'music.'

But while he was doing exactly what he wanted – writing and recording his own music around the clock – Prince had yet to find success. "I didn't have any money," he later told *Rolling Stone* magazine, "so I'd just stand outside [McDonald's] and smell stuff. Poverty makes people angry, brings out their worst side. I was very bitter when I was young." Realizing that, in Minneapolis, "we got all the new music and dances three months late," Prince decided to create something of his own. "Anyone who was around then knew what was happening. I was *working*. When they were sleeping, I was *jamming*. When they woke up, I had another groove."

It was around this time that Prince asked Chris Moon to manage him. Moon wasn't interested in doing that, but did make one important suggestion: that Prince drop his surname and perform simply as Prince. In the autumn of 1976 he traveled to New York with a demo tape of four of the 14 songs he had completed at Moonsound. One of them, 'Baby,' was a Prince original that would later show up on his debut album, *For You*. 'Soft & Wet' would, too, but that was a Chris Moon co-write, as were the other two songs, 'Love Is Forever' and 'Aces.'

While staying in New York with his half-sister Sharon,

group of string players were brought in but Prince – keen as ever to dominate his own recordings – preferred to use synthesized sounds that he could control himself.

By the following spring Prince and Husney had completed work on a demo tape. Husney printed up 15 press packs at a cost of $100 each. The two men had decided that the best way to market Prince was with an air of mystery. As such the all-black press packs featured nothing but his name on the outside, with just the tape on the inside. The idea was that Prince could be marketed as a new Stevie Wonder – somebody who demanded total creative control, just as Wonder had.

"I lied my way in everywhere to get him in," Husney later admitted. "Jealously is what makes this business go round." He called Warner Bros Vice President Russ Thyret and told him that CBS was planning to fly Prince out to LA for a meeting. This had the desired effect, as did a similar call to CBS. Soon, as well as securing meetings with the two biggest record labels in America, Husney had also managed to pique the interest of A&M, ABC/Dunhill, and RSO.

Husney's approach to the meetings was similarly clever. He would present the label representatives with the press kit and play them the tape while Prince sat outside in the hallway, in order to maintain an air of intrigue. But while securing the meetings had been easy, getting the right deal would prove rather more complicated. Neither RSO nor ABC was interested in signing Prince, while A&M wouldn't offer anything beyond a standard two-album deal. CBS's representatives were treated to a live, in-studio audition when they watched Prince record 'Just As Long As We're Together' at Village Recorders in Los Angeles on April 8 1977, but still only offered a three-album deal with the added stipulation that Earth, Wind & Fire bassist Verdine White would come onboard as producer.

This, to Prince, was unacceptable, and left only Warner Bros. Once again the offer was for a three-album deal, but at least this label had a reputation for being more artist-friendly. "While everybody was wining and dining," Husney recalled, "Russ [Thyret] took us back to his house, sat on the floor, and talked music with us." Thyret wanted a debut album within six months, and two more by the end of the 70s.

The contract only guaranteed that Prince would be allowed to co-produce his albums, and gave Warner Bros the option of renewing it at the end for either three more albums over two years or two more over one. But it was good enough. On June 25 1977, less than three weeks after his 19th birthday, Prince signed the deal. After returning to Minneapolis he headed straight for Studio 80 to record a new song, 'We Can Work It Out.' It was intended as a symbol of the understanding between label and artist, but the relationship would prove to be rather less harmonious than that.

Prince received an offer from Tiffany Entertainment to buy the publishing rights to the four songs but declined it, aware even at this early stage of the way the music business worked, and that Tiffany would subsequently make all the money from his work. Returning to Minneapolis, he was introduced by Moon to Owen Husney, the head of The Ad Company, an advertising agency that also marketed local musicians. "I thought this group was phenomenal," Husney recalled, "and I said to Chris, 'Who's the group?'" Moon explained that it was just one kid, writing, playing, and singing everything.

Husney was stunned. He was so enthused that he offered to manage Prince, and started gearing the eight million dollars per year that The Ad Company made from its existing clients toward promoting his new charge's interests. With the help of his lawyer, Gary Levinson, Husney raised $50,000 and founded American Artists Inc with the sole purpose of managing Prince. He gave the singer a rehearsal space in his offices, rented him a one-room apartment, and took over from where Chris Moon had left off. "I presented myself as the protector of creativity," Husney recalled. "He was young and a lot of people were going to come at him, and he was vulnerable at the time."

In December 1976 Husney booked Prince into Minneapolis's Sound 80 studios to record a new demo tape with local engineer David Rivkin. (Prince also made some final recordings with 94 East around this time.) Sound 80 was much bigger than Moonsound and gave Prince the opportunity to transfer all that he already knew into a bigger arena, and the chance to take advantage of a wealth of new technology, notably a range of synthesizers such as the Oberheim 4-Voice. To begin with a

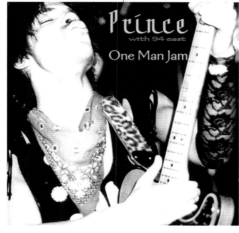

THE NOTE ON THE BACK OF *FOR YOU* SAYS IT ALL: "PRODUCED, COMPOSED, ARRANGED & PERFORMED BY PRINCE." BARRING A CO-WRITING CREDIT FOR CHRIS MOON ('SOFT & WET'), THERE WAS NOTHING MORE TO SAY. HE MIGHT BE A 19-YEAR-OLD BOY FROM MINNEAPOLIS, WHO HAD ONLY SIGNED TO THE LABEL TEN MONTHS BEFORE THE ALBUM WAS RELEASED, BUT IN THAT SHORT TIME PRINCE HAD BECOME THE YOUNGEST PRODUCER WARNER BROS HAS EVER HAD.

For You (JUNE 1977–DECEMBER 1978)

He was also an accomplished multi-instrumentalist, credited with playing 23 different instruments in the album's liner notes, and was hotly tipped to become the 'new' Stevie Wonder.

Warner Bros knew from the start that Prince was a singular talent. The label had beaten three others to secure the signature of a man they all felt had the potential to be one of the most forward-thinking artists of the time. Even so, the hit-making mentality prevailed. Hit records were supposed to have hit producers behind them: a Sam Phillips or a Phil Spector. To the ears of the Warner Bros executives, Prince should be aspiring toward the disco sound of Giorgio Moroder, Nile Rodgers, and Earth, Wind & Fire.

And so it was that the label made provisional arrangements for Maurice White from Earth, Wind & Fire to produce Prince's debut. The trouble with this of course was that Prince had already turned down CBS partly because of its insistence that Maurice's brother Verdine produce his debut. As far as Prince was concerned, the slick, metronomic sound of disco would soon be a thing of the past. Punk had already begun to tear up the rock'n'roll rulebook, and it was only a matter of time, he thought, before a similar change affected the club scene. Giving his debut album the Earth, Wind & Fire treatment could potentially kill it before it even got into stores.

"He didn't want that sound placed on him – he wanted to go forward," Husney recalled. "Prince walked out of the room and said, 'Nobody's producing *my* first album.'" Husney was then left with the task of convincing one of the world's biggest record labels that an unknown teenager with no previous track record should be allowed to produce his own album.

Warner Bros put Prince to the test in much the same way that CBS had a year earlier. After booking him a weekend in Los Angeles's Amigo Studio, a series of top executives came in and out surreptitiously to watch as he recorded 'Just As Long As We're Together' from scratch, all by himself. Prince thought they were janitors and carried on as normal, but the executives were suitably impressed, and agreed to his wish to produce the whole album himself. There was just one catch: somebody more

"He was sort of what we would call an urban legend up in the Minneapolis area. There were these hushed conversations about ... the next Stevie Wonder."

DEZ DICKERSON

experienced would be brought in as the album's executive producer, just in case Prince ran into any difficulties.

The *For You* sessions began in September 1977 at Sound 80 studios in Minneapolis, where Prince had recorded his first proper demo. It was suggested at one point that the engineer of those previous sessions, David Rivkin, might serve as *For You*'s executive producer, but in the end Warner Bros settled on Tommy Vicari, who had previously worked with one of Prince's heroes, Carlos Santana.

Vicari wasn't impressed with the facilities at Studio 80

show, and would roll his eyes whenever Vicari approached the mixing desk. If ever he did deign to ask the producer something, he would push him away as soon as he'd received enough information. By the time the sessions were finished, Husney said, Prince had "absorbed everything he needed out of Tommy Vicari's brain. … Tommy was heartbroken, because he had just been treated like shit."

Having completed work on the basic tracks by the end of December, the *For You* team moved to Los Angeles's Sound Labs studio in January 1978 to begin overdubbing.

"Because I do all the instruments, I'm injecting the joy I feel into all those 'players.' The same exuberant soul speaks through all the instruments." PRINCE

It was here that the pressure seemed to get to Prince. Pushing Vicari away, he spent over a month-and-a-half piling up overdub upon overdub, gradually eroding the spontaneity of the original recordings in a self-conscious bid to prove that he was capable of making the kind of polished, commercial record that Warner Bros wanted. He finally finished the record on February 28, eight months

and suggested decamping to Los Angeles. This worried Husney, who thought his young workaholic might find himself distracted by the city's abundance of sex, drugs, and rock'n'roll. Husney suggested a compromise – the Record Plant in nearby Sausalito – but needn't have worried. As soon as he settled into recording, all Prince wanted to do was work.

After moving out to California in October Prince lodged in a spacious apartment in Mill Valley, overlooking the San Francisco Bay, with Vicari, Husney, and Husney's wife Britt. Their home life was pleasant enough: Husney cooked Prince scrambled eggs, while his wife made the singer's lunch and washed his clothes. Recording was a different matter. Prince made it very clear that this was *his*

after starting work on it. It had cost $170,500 to make – just $500 short of the planned budget for the first three Prince albums – and had turned its creator into a wreck.

Released on April 7 1978, *For You* received largely positive reviews, although most of them were concerned more with the fact that it was the work of a 19-year-old and had little to say about the actual musical content. Prince's local paper, the *St Paul Dispatch*, called the album "a technical marvel and a curiosity" most interesting "because one man did it."

For You is a competent record, and the making of it proved to be a useful learning experience. Prince had got to grips with a wide range of synthesizers, notably the Oberheim, which would characterize much of his early

work. He would not feel comfortable enough with the idea of using real brass instruments on record – in the way that James Brown and George Clinton had before him – until the mid 80s. Anxious to avoid replicating the sound of contemporary disco, Prince went for something totally different, creating his own 'horn section' by multi-tracking synthesizer and guitar lines.

Another important characteristic of *For You* is Prince's reliance on high-pitched vocals on both the suggestive, up-tempo material ('Soft & Wet,' the album's only minor hit) and the lovelorn, acoustic ballads ('Crazy You'). The whole thing seemed to be aimed squarely at the young, female R&B market, right down to the softly airbrushed sleeve art of the Afro-haired singer. Only the final track seemed to suggest something else. With its frenzied, finger-tapping solos and similarly showy bass-playing, 'I'm Yours' seems closer to the MOR rock of Journey than Santana, and a firm reminder of the fact that Prince wanted to reach beyond the black audience.

Genuine mainstream success was still some way off, however. As impressive as *For You* might have been, it still bore the hallmarks of overproduction – the opening title track has over 40 layers of Prince's vocals – while too many of the songs simply repeat themselves without going anywhere, and aren't quite snappy or sharp enough for mass appeal.

For You did nonetheless reach Number 21 on *Billboard*'s R&B chart, while 'Soft & Wet' made it to Number 12 on the R&B chart and Number 92 on the Pop chart. Prince set off on a minor promotional jaunt, appearing at signings in cities where the records were selling well. After being confronted by 3,000 screaming fans on one such occasion in Charlotte, North Carolina, however, Prince was more than a little spooked, and soon began to shy away from personal appearances.

In the summer of 1978 Prince used his Warner Bros advance to move into a new home at 5215 France Avenue in the Edina area of Minnesota. He then set about holding auditions for a band that he could take out on the road with him and chose Del's Tire Mart as a rehearsal space. Bobby Rivkin – the brother of local engineer David Rivkin and an employee of Owen Husney's – came in on drums, while Prince's old school-friend André Anderson (now calling himself André Cymone) played the bass, just as he had done in his mother's basement years earlier. The three of them had played together before, so it made sense to carry on with a well-rehearsed rhythm section.

With a mix of ethnicities already in place (Bobby Rivkin, or Bobby Z as he became known, was white; André Cymone was black), Prince was keen to mix up the band's sexuality as well – just as Sly & The Family Stone had done in the 60s. Prince had his eye on a similar boundary-crossing line-up when he brought Gayle Chapman into the fold, telling her: "You're white, you're blonde, you have blue eyes, and you can play funky keyboards."

Dez Dickerson was next to join. A veteran of the Minneapolis scene with a punkier look than most black guitarists of the time, he was impressed by Prince's professionalism – despite the fact that the singer turned up two-and-a-half hours late for their scheduled rehearsal. "He was very clear that he wanted the band to be an amalgam of rock and R&B," Dickerson later recalled. The only guitarist who opted not to showboat in rehearsals, Dickerson quickly settled into a comfortable, complimentary role in the band. The last member to join was keyboardist Matt Fink, who had been intrigued by Prince ever since Bobby Z played him a demo tape in 1977. He had asked Z to keep him in mind if Prince was ever on the lookout for a keyboard player, and now was the time.

Having assembled the band, Prince spent the rest of the year whipping them into shape while Owen Husney tried to focus his energies on putting together a tour. Since the release of *For You*, however, Prince had begun to see Husney as more of a runner than a manager, perhaps as a result of his frustration that the album hadn't been an instant smash hit.

Prince's demands eventually became too much. After having their equipment stolen from Del's Tire Mart, the band moved into Pepé Willie's basement. "Sometimes the basement was less than balmy," Dez Dickerson recalled. "Prince called Owen and told him to get a space heater and bring it to Pepé's." Husney, however, was waiting on an important call, and didn't think it wise to leave the office. Prince demanded that the job be done there and then. An argument ensued that resulted in Husney quitting on the spot. Prince tried to convince him to return, but the three-page letter he had written detailing what he considered to be a manager's responsibilities didn't jive with what Husney thought the job should entail. Pepé Willie was willing to do the smaller jobs, but that served only to mask a bigger problem: having just released his debut album, and while still trying to get his band tight enough for a tour, Prince lacked a guiding force.

PRINCE HAD HIGH HOPES THAT 1979 WOULD BEGIN WITH A TOUR IN SUPPORT OF *FOR YOU*, BUT HE WOULD FIRST HAVE TO CONVINCE WARNER BROS TO BACK IT FINANCIALLY. IN THE INTERIM PEPÉ WILLIE – STILL DEPUTIZING IN THE ABSENCE OF A REAL MANAGER – ORGANIZED A PAIR OF SHOWS AT MINNEAPOLIS'S CAPRI THEATER.

Prince (JANUARY 1979–APRIL 1980)

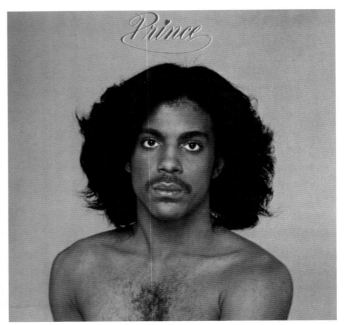

Prince made his live debut as a solo artist on January 5 1979. Given the circumstances, the show was neither here nor there. It wasn't a sell-out, but still drew a crowd of several hundred fans, friends, and family members, all intrigued to see the local-boy-made-good in action. But Prince was still a tentative live performer and often played with his back to the audience. All in all the show – for which each of the bandmembers wore tight spandex, leg-warmers, and high heels – seemed more like a dress rehearsal than a proper concert.

Two nights later a delegation of Warner Bros officials came to watch Prince's second show and decide whether or not he was ready for a full tour. This was unfortunately the night that Dez Dickerson decided to try out a wireless pickup for the first time. It refused to work properly, and as Dickerson later put it: "There were some definite uncomfortable moments … [which] caused a couple of delays." None of this helped Prince, who was already nervous at the prospect of his second ever solo show being his most important to date. The constant breaks to fix Dickerson's equipment disrupted the flow, and when a

"painfully shy" Prince plucked up the courage to address the audience, the guitarist recalled, he "barely spoke above a whisper."

The concert was an unqualified failure. Having put so much effort into proving he could make a record entirely on his own terms, Prince was devastated that he couldn't do the same in a live setting. "I kept trying to speak to him and he wouldn't even talk," recalled his cousin, Charles Smith. "He thought the show was shit." So did the Warner Bros officials, who vetoed any plans for Prince to tour. But this in itself posed another problem: what to do with an artist who had used up virtually all of his three-album budget on one record, wasn't ready to tour, and had just sacked his management?

Warner Bros' main focus was on finding a new management team. The label opted for the Hollywood-based Cavallo & Ruffalo firm, a highly experienced agency run by a pair of Italians, Bob Cavallo and Joe Ruffalo, who had previously worked with Little Feat, Earth, Wind & Fire, and Weather Report. Cavallo & Ruffalo sent runners down to handle Prince's day-to-day requests, and installed

Dez Dickerson's rock sensibilities added another dimension to Prince's early music.

a senior employee, Steve Fargnoli, as his manager. (Fargnoli proved so important to the Prince setup that he was soon invited to become a partner in the company, which was renamed Cavallo, Ruffalo & Fargnoli.)

Prince meanwhile busied himself working on songs for his next album. From late April to late May he recorded at Alpha Studio in Los Angeles with engineer Gray Brandt – Warner Bros having decided, after the Tommy Vicari debacle (which made it clear that Prince wouldn't listen to anybody), that there was little point in insisting on another executive producer. Left to his own devices, Prince recorded the album in 30 days, and needed only a couple more weeks to add overdubs and complete the final mix at Hollywood Sound Recorders – a far cry from the four months spent on *For You*. He even managed to fit in a few sessions with his band – then known as The Rebels – during the same time period.

Prince's self-confidence grew as the sessions progressed, giving him the conviction to trust himself more. One such example came with the recording of first single 'I Wanna Be Your Lover,' which, according to Gary Brandt, "didn't come together until we put the [live] drums on." Prince recorded the drums himself, playing along to what had already been taped. "[Drum machines] are kind of hard to play to," Brandt recalled, "because

they're usually right on the meter." Prince however was "very synchronized," and had no trouble "fit[ting] himself into that track, knowing exactly what would come up."

Prince was released on October 19 1979. It was preceded by the single release of its opening track, 'I

"I knew how to write hits by my second album." PRINCE

Wanna Be Your Lover,' which showed much more commercial promise than anything on *For You*, hitting Number One on *Billboard*'s R&B Chart and Number 11 on the Pop chart. Like much of *For You*, 'Lover' is a simple love song sung in what *Rolling Stone* called "the most thrilling R&B falsetto since Smokey Robinson." It was also a lot tamer than the highly charged 'Soft & Wet,' and as such appealed to a much wider audience.

Taken as a whole, *Prince* sounds like the work of an artist who had learned from the mistakes of his previous album. Where *For You* meandered at times, the follow-up contains a wealth of more varied, interesting grooves. The songwriting is snappier and more hook-laden, as evidenced by 'Why You Wanna Treat Me So Bad?' and 'I Feel For You' (later a hit for Chaka Khan). There are still

Sue Ann Carwell And The Rebels

Ever the workaholic – even at the age of 20 – Prince found it difficult to enjoy his down time. After moving into his new house in Minneapolis during the summer of 1978, Prince met a local singer, Sue Ann Carwell, and was soon working on songs with her both at home and at Sound 80 Studios. But while Prince would later become known for his ability to adapt to a different sound for each project, much of what he recorded with Carwell just sounded like his own material. As such, once Carwell signed to Warner Bros (with the help of Owen Husney), she was assigned to a different producer in order to differentiate her sound from that of the label's other young star.

Prince's interest in masterminding other acts didn't end there, of course. In June 1979, not long after completing work on *Prince*, he told Dez Dickerson of his plan to "record an entire record, with the band, under the nom de plume The Rebels." The band, according to Dickerson's memoir, *My Time With Prince*, "were being asked to come along for the ride and make him look good."

This time around, instead of making something that sounded transparently like his R&B-orientated solo work, Prince decided to build on the rockier elements of

songs such as 'I'm Yours' and 'Bambi.' He also intended for The Rebels to be more of a collaborative effort, even allowing Dickerson and André Cymone to write some of the material. But after working on nine songs at Ears Sound Studio, Colorado, in July 1979, Prince scrapped the project, deciding that the whole thing sounded too generic.

The idea was for The Rebels to be a kind of 'secret' side project, but what Prince learnt from the experience was that, if he

was to successfully mastermind a new act such as this, he should be in control but not necessarily involved on a full-time basis. Similarly, after working with Sue Ann Carwell he realized that there should be some link to his own sound, but not to the point where there was no differentiation between the two. Both experiences proved useful in the long run, however, in that they would inform Prince's plans for the launch of The Time.

hints of Prince's love for MOR rock, notably on 'Bambi.' But while the music is fairly generic, the lyrics – in which Prince tries to convince a lesbian that "it's better with a man" – point toward the sort of taboo subjects that Prince would later mine to great success. The album's ballads, meanwhile, are tighter and more convincing, helped by a more minimal production style, which made them much more club-friendly. Prince himself was very much aware of the difference this made. "I never saw Prince again," Gary Brandt later said, "but I got countless calls from his managers asking me how I recorded various parts of his album."

Prince was still very much an R&B record aimed squarely at female listeners. On the front jacket Prince is pictured topless, with messy hair and thick moustache, against a baby-blue backdrop; on the back he is naked, riding a Pegasus (no explanation necessary). His name is inscribed in purple, with a heart dotting the 'i.' The album

that he could not scandalize the audience by wearing that spandex and no underwear." Prince took Cavallo's instructions literally. "That's all he wore: a pair of bikini briefs!"

In February Prince was invited to join Rick James's Fire It Up tour as the supporting act in what was billed as the Battle Of Funk. Prince's young bucks did to James what The Time would threaten to do to their master a few years later: winning over the crowd with a short, snappy set that had a lot more going for it than the headliner's two hours of overindulgence. As Bobby Z later put it, "We were young and hungry and we started kicking his ass." James found himself struggling to follow Prince's energetic, flamboyant performance, with large chunks of the audience leaving during his set.

The animosity between the two was further fueled by the fact that Prince and his band tended to avoid socializing with James and his party-hard entourage.

> *"I was brought up in a black-and-white world … I want to be judged on the quality of my work, not on what I say, nor on what people claim I am, nor on the color of my skin."* PRINCE

reached Number 22 on the *Billboard* Pop chart – a mere 141-point improvement on *For You* – and even reached Number Three on the R&B chart. Now it was time, once again, to think about touring.

The Prince tour was certainly eventful. To begin with, two months of shows had to be cancelled after the singer caught pneumonia in early December. Then there was the small matter of an appearance on *American Bandstand*, on which Prince and his band were set to perform the album's first two singles, 'I Wanna Be Your Lover' and 'Why You Wanna Treat Me So Bad?' Backstage they met the host, Dick Clark, one of the most respected figures on American television. Everything was going well until Prince came up with a mischevious idea: he and the band should refuse to answer any of Dick Clark's questions. The band was mortified, but the stunt worked. Prince became infamous almost overnight after answering Clark's questions with nothing more than series of hand gestures, such as holding up four fingers when asked how many years he had been playing. Clark later called it the hardest interview he ever conducted.

Another issue to resolve was the group's image. "We were all groping for images of how we wanted to look on stage," Matt Fink recalled. "Prince pretty much left it up to each individual member of the band to figure it out, of course, with his final approval." For Fink this meant everything from prison chic to a doctor's gown and mask (which earned him the nickname Dr Fink). Prince however had an entirely different look in mind: "loud spandex and bright colors," as Dickerson put it. "I overheard Bob [Cavallo] talking to Prince about the fact

James wasn't sure what to do with a group so far from his own sensibilities. "I felt sorry for him," he later recalled. "Here's this little dude wearing high heels, standing there in a trench coat. Then at the end of the set, he'd take off his trench coat and he'd be wearing little girl's bloomers. The guys in the audience would boo him to death."

As the Prince tour wound down in April, further trouble emerged from within Prince's own traveling party. As a member of a religious sect called The Way, keyboardist Gayle Chapman found herself increasingly conflicted about her role in the group. "Prince was tired of the costumes that I was coming up with," she later recalled. "He sent his girlfriend down to the hotel room that I was in, she knocked on the door … dumped this bag of multicolored underwear on my bed, and said, 'Prince says wear this or you're fired.'"

Chapman felt similarly uncomfortable about having to kiss her bandleader rather suggestively during the song 'Head' (which subsequently appeared on *Dirty Mind*). "There had been some tension between her beliefs and what she was being called upon to do in our live show," Dickerson recalled. "There was a developing role that she was given that involved the simulation of some pretty vulgar things on stage."

Things came to a head when Chapman told Prince she planned to go on a trip with her Way group; Prince wanted her to commit to some short-notice rehearsals instead. An argument broke out that resulted in her leaving the group, leaving Prince with another round of personnel issues to deal with. All of this paled in comparison, however, to the kind of shake-up that Prince already had in mind.

After being told that he couldn't wear spandex trousers without underwear, Prince updated his look, wearing underwear but little else.

BARELY PAUSING FOR BREATH AFTER FINISHING HIS FIRST FULL TOUR, PRINCE BARRICADED HIMSELF INSIDE THE MAKESHIFT STUDIO IN THE BASEMENT OF HIS NEW HOUSE ON LAKE MINNETONKA TO START WORK ON HIS NEXT RECORD. *FOR YOU* AND *PRINCE* HAD BUILT HIM A STRONG BLACK FOLLOWING, BUT PRINCE HAD HIS SIGHTS SET ON A WIDER MARKET.

Dirty Mind (MAY 1980–JUNE 1981)

His next move might risk losing an established audience, but would potentially open up a much bigger one. "Nobody knew what was going on," he said, "and I became totally engulfed in it."

For several years a new form of music had been slowly gaining ground in Britain and America. From The Ramones to The Clash, punk had begun to take over the white rock market, which had been dominated for most of the 70s by bands such as Pink Floyd and Led Zeppelin. By the dawn of the 80s bands such as Blondie had begun to add keyboards and a pop sensibility to punk's stripped-down template, creating a sound that was christened 'new wave'.

Prince had noted a similar sea change on the horizon in the disco market, having refused to allow Earth, Wind & Fire's Maurice White to produce his debut on the grounds that it would immediately sound dated. Two years later he hit upon a new sound that shared a number of stylistic similarities with new wave.

Prince had already developed a reputation for being interested in all things carnal thanks to his stage outfits and the brazen sexuality of songs such as 'Soft & Wet.' The new

music he presented to Warner Bros, however, took things a step further. Not only were these stripped-down recordings rough and punky, with an urgent physicality lacking in his earlier work, they were also obscene – and Prince wanted them to stay that way. "It really felt like me for once," he told *Rolling Stone*. "When I brought it to the record company it shocked a lot of people. But they didn't ask me to go back and change anything, and I'm really grateful."

It wasn't quite as easy a sell as Prince might have made it out to be. "The record company, understandably, was very nervous about this sudden change," Dez Dickerson recalled. It wasn't only the lyrical content that bothered Warner Bros, but the blatant shift in musical style. According to Dickerson, the label's attitude was: "We've signed Stevie Wonder and now we've got Ric Ocasek. What happened?" It took quite a lot of smoothing over on the part of Bob Cavallo and Steve Fargnoli before Warner Bros gave the project the green light.

"Mo Ostin did what any 'artist friendly' 80s label head would have done with an artist as gifted as Prince: nurture and support him," Alan Leeds recalled. Prince did agree to give some of the songs a bit more polish in the final mix, but everything else remained as it was when *Dirty Mind* went on sale, four months after Prince had begun working on it, on October 8 1980. Not everybody at Warner Bros was happy, however. "He turned [the company] into disarray," noted the company's vice president, Marylou Badeaux. "The promotions people would call me and say, 'I can't take this to radio! Is he crazy?'"

Just in case the jacket – a stark black-and-white image of Prince, in studded trench coat, neckerchief, stockings, bikini briefs, and a 'Rude Boy' button, standing in front of the bare springs of an upturned bed (in homage to James Brown's *Revolution Of The Mind*) – wasn't enough, the album was sent to DJs with a sticker that implored them to "please audition before airing." The doe-eyed seducer of Prince's previous albums had been replaced with a predatory look – in Prince's own words – of "pure sexuality."

The shockwaves went off far and wide. Songs such as 'Do It All Night' and 'Dirty Mind' say it all in their titles. Here was a man dispensing with the pleasantries and getting straight to business, ditching the sexual revolution of the 60s in favor of the sexual aggression of the 80s. And it got worse. 'Head' tells the story of a sordid meeting with a bride-to-be on the way to her wedding, while 'Sister' – allegedly inspired by Prince's half-sister Sharon – explores the (fictional) concept of losing your virginity in an incestuous tryst. Prince might have expected his father to have something to say about that, but he seemed more concerned with the language than the subject matter. "When I first played *Dirty Mind* for him," the singer told *Rolling Stone* in 1983, "he said, 'You're swearing on the

> *"Dirty Mind was a risky record. Some thought we were losing our minds."* BOB CAVALLO

record. Why do you have to do that?' And I said, 'Because I swear.'"

Dirty Mind is more than just *The Joy Of Sex* set to music. Tracks such as 'Partyup' and 'Uptown' (about a place where "we do whatever we please") show his socially conscious side – something that would continue to surface again and again as his career progressed.

When it came to touring *Dirty Mind*, Prince was able to go back out as the headliner, rather than as somebody else's support act. The addition of Lisa Coleman, the 19-year-old daughter of Hollywood session player Gary Coleman, on keyboards had a significant impact on the group. After a three-hour audition, during which she and

Prince barely spoke, it became clear that Coleman would bring much more to the group than had her predecessor. "Lisa is like my sister," Prince told *Rolling Stone* a few years later. "She'll play what the average person won't. She'll press two notes with one finger, so the chord is a lot larger, things like that. She's more abstract. She's into Joni Mitchell, too."

Prince himself seemed to settle more comfortably into his own skin on the Dirty Mind tour, while the band quickly gelled into a tight musical unit. All manner of hijinks ensued on the tour, from stealing emergency megaphones on airplanes to taking it in turns – rather more dubiously – to be left slumped in wheelchairs, drooling, in airports, pretending to have been left behind.

For all the fun, the tour began on a rather inauspicious note on December 4 in Buffalo, New York, one of several smaller towns and cities that struggled to appreciate this freaky character singing freaky songs in bikini bottoms and stockings. While venues such as the 12,000-seat Cobo Arena in Detroit came close to selling out, Prince found himself playing to half-empty halls in Winston-Salem, Chattanooga, and Nashville. Sales of *Dirty Mind* itself were sluggish as 1980 drew to a close, leading Prince's management to cut the tour short after a show at Chicago's Uptown Theater on December 26 for fear that it would soon start losing money.

While Prince took stock in yet another new house on the outskirts of Minneapolis (which he would soon paint purple), his salvation came in the form of a *Rolling Stone* article headed by the question, 'Will The Little Girls Understand?' Prince's management team had hired publicist Harold Bloom to up their star-in-waiting's media profile. This first piece of serious rock journalism about Prince opened the floodgates for the rest of the music press, including Britain's weekly *New Musical Express* to follow suit. *Dirty Mind* hadn't been selling well – it was performing even more slowly than *Prince* had – but the tipping point, as Dez Dickerson put it, came with "this tidal wave of critical acclaim," notably Ken Tucker's four-and-a-half star *Rolling Stone* review, which called it "the most generous album about sex ever made by a man." The *Minneapolis Tribune* followed suit, heaping praise upon Prince's "own unique instrumental sound, a disco-funk mode that is quite recognizable as his."

The Dirty Mind tour resumed in the wake of this upsurge in critical interest, with Prince booked into smaller clubs this time around to ensure that each date

was a sell-out. The press coverage did its job, and a whole new audience began to check out what all the fuss was about. Minnesota's other boy-done-good, Bob Dylan, came to the hometown opening night at Sam's Club on March 9, while Mick Jagger was part of a sell-out crowd at the New York Ritz on March 22 – the same venue that Prince had struggled even to half-fill three months earlier.

By the time the tour wound up in New Orleans on April 6 Prince had begun to make significant inroads into a new, white market. Buoyed by this success, he started working on another side project, building a completely new band out of Minneapolis group Flyte Time and former Champagne drummer Morris Day. Prince's plan was to make direct, funky music with this new group, which he called The Time, while continuing his assault on the mainstream with his solo work.

The buzz around him had grown by now to the extent that he made his first trip to Europe, playing three club dates in Amsterdam, London, and Paris. While some musicians might have spent their first foreign trip seeing the sights, Prince used it to investigate what was going on in the cities' clubs, seeking out new ideas to bring back home with him.

Despite the success he was now having, Prince still found it difficult to keep his band together. "During the *Dirty Mind* period I would go into fits of depression and get physically ill," he told *Rolling Stone* in 1985. "I couldn't make people in the band understand how great we could be together if we all played our part." More than a decade later, he identified the root of the problem: his bassist. "André's ego always got in the way of his playing. He always played on top of the beat, and I'm convinced that was just because he wanted to be heard. André and I would fight every night, because I was always trying to get him to sound like Larry Graham."

André Cymone, Prince's first ever bandmate, quit the group in April 1981. It didn't come as much of a surprise. As early as 1977 Cymone had turned up at the *For You* sessions with the attitude that it would not be long before he would be doing "my thing." Now he had clearly decided that he had watched from the sidelines for long enough. Even so, he continued to bear a grudge against his old friend, claiming later that Prince stole many of his ideas for The Time, along with the bassline for *Controversy*'s 'Do Me, Baby.'

Once again, as Prince looked toward the next step in the expansion of his empire, he found himself having to replace another disgruntled bandmember.

"Prince refuses to play it safe. If he did, he wouldn't have made this album." *NEW MUSICAL EXPRESS REVIEW*

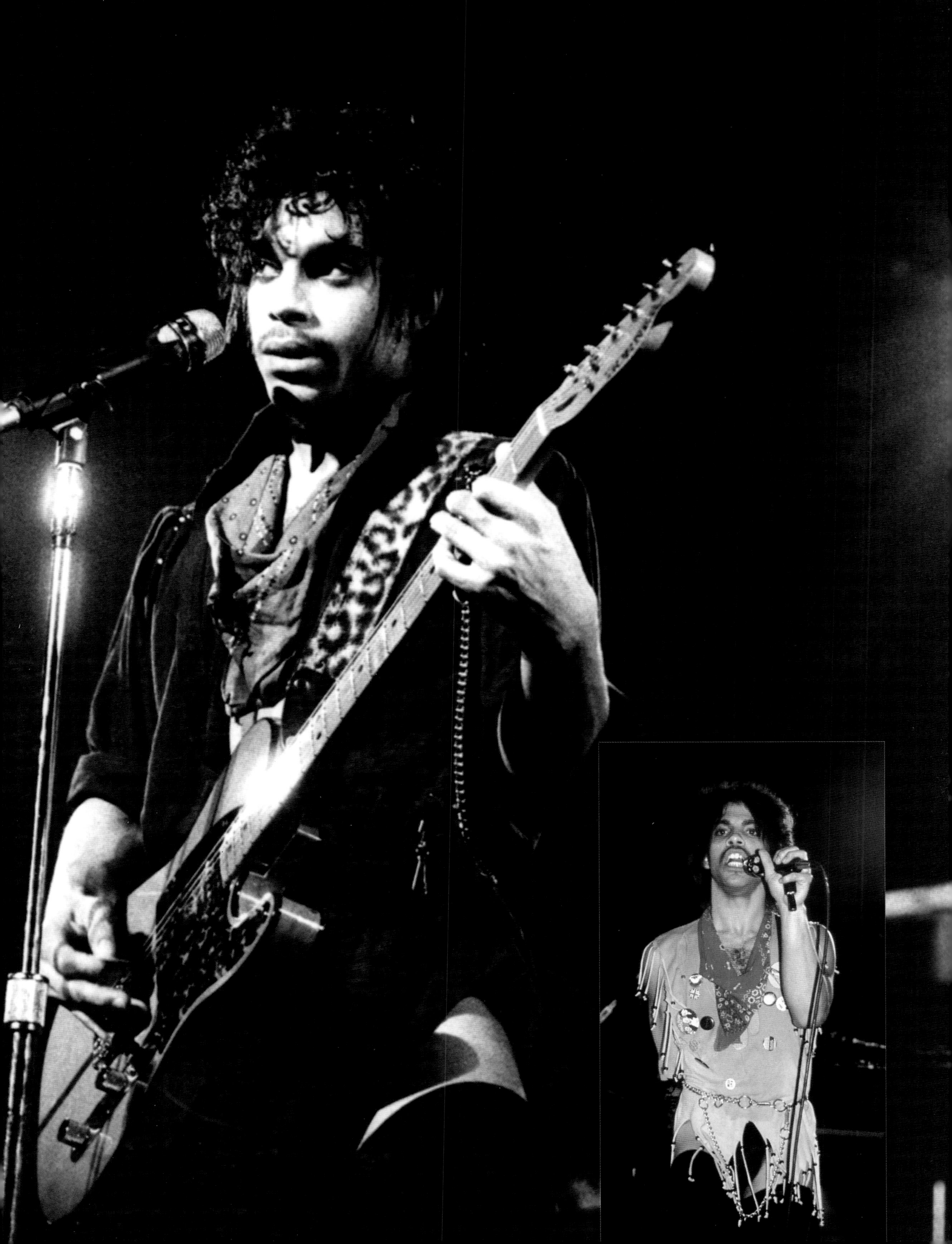

PRINCE STARTED WORK ON THE NEXT PHASE OF HIS CAREER AS SOON AS THE DIRTY MIND CLUB TOUR ENDED ON APRIL 6 1981. OFFICIALLY, THE NEXT ITEM ON HIS AGENDA WAS A THREE-DATE EUROPEAN TOUR IN JUNE, BUT EVEN BEFORE APRIL WAS OUT HE HAD RECORDED AND MIXED AN ENTIRE ALBUM FOR HIS NEW SIDE PROJECT, THE TIME. HE ALLOWED ONLY THE BAND'S LEADER, MORRIS DAY, TO APPEAR – AND EVEN THEN DAY WAS INSTRUCTED TO FOLLOW PRINCE'S GUIDE VOCALS NOTE-FOR-NOTE.

Controversy (JUNE 1981–MARCH 1982)

Prince was overflowing with ideas. "He'd come to our rehearsals for five or six hours, then go to rehearsals for his own band, then [work] all night in the studio," recalled Time keyboardist Jimmy Jam. One happy side-effect of having a new band was that Prince could let the semi-autonomous Time take care of the R&B market and focus his own efforts on his impending crossover into the mainstream. He was also aware that the presence of another successful Minneapolis band would help create a buzz around the city and what Prince himself was doing.

Prince co-credited Morris Day and somebody called Jamie Starr (the supposed engineer of *Dirty Mind*) with production on *The Time*, but rumors quickly spread that Starr was a pseudonym. Prince denied it, which of course served only to increase media interest in the record, which ended up outselling *Dirty Mind*.

After returning from Europe in June, Prince started work on his fourth album, *Controversy*, at home and in Los Angeles. While The Time's songs were funky and played to

the kind of black music stereotypes Prince had seen in his youth, his own material carried on in the *Dirty Mind* vein. It wasn't a mainstream success by any stretch of the imagination, but *Dirty Mind* had attracted a new crowd, and Prince intended to build on that. *Controversy* would end up mixing funk with new wave and seductive ballads, sex with religion and politics, creating a whole that feels as confused as it is confusing. A bewildered review in Britain's *New Musical Express* wondered quite how Prince could be so "temporarily valorous" yet "ultimately conservative." Is that what funk was meant to be?

When he started work on *Controversy*, having already fulfilled his initial three-album deal with Warner Bros, Prince would have been well aware of the fact that he needed to deliver the goods this time. Having been brought in to replace André Cymone on bass, 18-year-old former International House Of Pancakes employee Mark Brown (subsequently renamed Brown Mark) asked his new boss what the plan was. "This album has to make it," Prince told him. "He definitely knew what he was doing,"

Brown noted, "but I don't think he had a clue if it was going to work. I think he was feeling that, if it didn't sell, he'd be dropped."

In Europe, Prince discovered that new wave acts such as Gary Numan were already incorporating the cold, synthesized textures of Kraftwerk and the underground electronica scene of the 70s. On his return, he began to seek out ways of intertwining his synths into his sound more deeply than he had on *Dirty Mind*. He also came across the Linn LM-1 drum machine, the first one capable of sampling real drum sounds, and soon realized that it would help him record entire drum parts cheaply and quickly, without having to play them in real time.

Prince's experiments with overlapping LM-1 rhythms and synthesizer parts reach their peak on 'Private Joy,' a song he wrote for his girlfriend Susan Moonsie. Overall, however, for all of its innovative ideas, *Controversy* feels more like a halfway house between *Dirty Mind* and its fully realized follow-up, *1999*; a taster, of sorts, of a sound that Prince had not yet quite mastered.

Having made a tentative entry into the world of political debate on *Dirty Mind*'s 'Uptown,' Prince stepped wholeheartedly into that arena with *Controversy*. The jacket is almost like a color version of *Dirty Mind*'s, with Prince – wearing slightly more clothes than last time around – standing before a backdrop of newspaper headlines based on the album's sensationalist lyrics (plus one that simply reads "Joni," in honor of Joni Mitchell). On the record, 'Ronnie, Talk To Russia' and 'Annie Christian' demonstrate a desire to say something about the world at large. But the former is decidedly naïve ("Ronnie, talk to Russia before it's too late / Before they blow up the world") and the latter, ostensibly about gun control, is more of an inner-worldview than a political worldview, voiced by a man who "live[s] my life in taxicabs." (Even on 'Ronnie,' "the world" becomes "my world" by the end.)

Perhaps the most interesting aspect of *Controversy* is the level of unrestrained self-obsession on it. 'Private Joy' might have started out as an ode to a girlfriend, but is told from the point of view of Prince himself; what she does for him, and how he likes to keep her entirely for himself, without ever mentioning what *he* brings to the relationship. Likewise, 'Do Me, Baby' plays out a seduction fantasy, almost in real time, during which Prince never once lifts a finger. Only on the final track, 'Jack U Off,' does he offer anything in the way of recompense, offering his services "in the back of a car, restaurant, or cinema." But even then he ends deciding, "as a matter of fact, you can jack me off."

The pinnacle of Prince's self-obsession arrives on the title track, on which he attends to various concerns others might have had about him. Is he black, white, straight, gay? Does he believe in God, or himself? (Both, of course.) He claims not to be able to understand human curiosity,

but seems to have grasped the fact that it might lead to an interest in him. The inclusion of 'The Lord's Prayer' midway through the song only adds to the sense of confusion and contradiction. Here is a man trying to make sense of himself and his place in the world while also trying to make himself appealing to everybody else (and perhaps toning down the explicit image he had thus far embodied).

The confused state of the record was best summed up by *Sweet Potato* magazine, which suggested that there ought to have been "a serious side and a sex side. Which would have made everything nice and cozy if the penis weren't a political tool in Prince's worldview." As far as Warner Bros was concerned, "[*Controversy*] is a musical outrage and a sincere statement of opposing views." That might be stretching the point somewhat. What is important, however, is that each of these songs, from the rockabilly-style 'Jack U Off' to the spoken word 'Annie Christian,' served to unlock the ideas that Prince would develop and in some cases perfect on *1999*.

Controversy sold more strongly than *Dirty Mind* but its chart performance showed that Prince still had some way to go to achieve genuine mainstream appeal. Released as a

> "I was horrible … A lot had to do with me not being quite sure exactly which direction I wanted to go in. Later on, toward the Controversy period, I got a better grip on that." PRINCE

single, the title track stalled at Number 70 on *Billboard*'s Pop chart, despite peaking at Number Three on the R&B listings. It might have helped had Prince deigned to give interviews to explain the ideas behind the album. Instead, hoping that the music would speak for itself, he opted not to walk the promotional treadmill at all.

Prior to setting out on tour in support of the album, Prince played a one-off showcase in Minneapolis and a support slot with The Rolling Stones in Los Angeles. For a boy with his eye on mass appeal, the Stones shows served as a sharp reminder of just how far he was from that goal. The average Rolling Stones fan still rode the coattails of 70s rock'n'roll, about which everything was neatly defined. Men played guitars and slept with women, who were submissive and did what they were told. Prince's songs might often have had a similar message, but his androgynous look – stockings, high heels, bikini bottoms – sent out very different signals, as did the fact of him singing about jacking someone off. That was what women did to men, not the other way around. If Prince was singing about such a thing … well then he must be gay.

Prince's first night supporting the Stones, on October 9, at the open-air Memorial Coliseum, didn't go well. The first out of four acts on the bill, he was booed off stage

"I think he is someone whose talents will not be fully recognized until he goes away ... He's constantly in your face." JIMMY JAM (THE TIME)

Number One Chick

Of all the friends and family members that Prince employed over the years – among them cousin/drummer Charles Smith, stepbrother/bodyguard Duane Nelson, and school friend/bassist André Cymone – none has appeared to mean as much to him as Charles 'Big Chick' Huntsberry.

Huntsberry was a giant of a man, a former professional wrestler who stood six feet eight inches tall and had a gray Santa Claus beard. He joined Prince's entourage in January 1982 midway through the Controversy tour and immediately began to confound expectations – not least those of Dez Dickerson, whose first thought upon catching sight of Huntsberry in a Virginia hotel restaurant was: "Oh Lord, I'm gonna die in Richmond." As it happened, Dickerson later noted, "the guy turned out to be one of the most interesting people I ever met." (Later, having warmed to Huntsberry, Dickerson found himself desperately convincing Prince not to fire his new bodyguard for being too imposing a presence.)

After a brief period during which he was avoided by almost everyone on the tour, Huntsberry – who had once had the job of carrying AC/DC's Angus Young around on his shoulders – found himself getting involved in Prince's stage show. He would pull Dez Dickerson off stage during planned altercations between the guitarist and Prince during 'Let's Work,' and on one occasion was called upon to drag The Time off one by one and replace them with Prince's own band. He also quickly became Prince's closest confidante, and would be seen everywhere with him, even to the extent of leading him to the stage at the 1985 Brit Awards ceremony, where Prince won the award for Best International Artist for *Purple Rain*. (The album's liner notes credit him as 'The Protector.')

The closer Prince and Huntsberry became, however, the more the singer began to use his bodyguard as a barrier against the rest of the world – including his bandmates. Even Alan Leeds, hired as tour manager during the *1999* era, found himself having to speak to Prince via Huntsberry to begin with. Within a few years it was not uncommon for Prince to travel on a separate tour bus to the rest of his band, with only Huntsberry, Leeds, and various girlfriends allowed onboard. *New Musical Express* journalist Barney Hoskyns recalled similar scenes during a post-concert dinner on the

1999 tour: "Only when everybody is settled and ready to order does Prince, engulfed in the shadow of his giant, bearded bodyguard … enter the restaurant, gliding silently past the row of booths and making his way to the other side of the room."

Having already developed a reputation as a reclusive egomaniac, Prince soon found himself having to account for his obsession with protection and privacy. A backlash was inevitable. "Nobody has to walk around their home town with a nine-foot bodyguard," Jesse Johnson, the disgruntled former guitarist of The Time, later recalled, "but Prince has dogged so many people, ripped off so many ideas, that he knows he's gonna get his ass kicked."

The cracks began to show on September 5 1984 when photographers started taking pictures of Prince outside a Sheila E. concert at the Agora in Cleveland. After telling the snappers not to take pictures of Prince, the fearless Huntsberry got physical, and one of the photographers ended up injured. Huntsberry had long since quit the Prince organization by the time the case went to court, on October 4 1988. (With the photographer involved seeking $2.75 million in damages, the judge ruled a mistrial, but not before Prince had been ordered to take the stand to defend his dislike of having his picture taken.)

Huntsberry's decision to quit came in the wake of another similar incident, although this time he wasn't present. During the early hours of January 29 1985, as Prince was leaving a Mexican restaurant on Sunset Boulevard, his bodyguards found themselves having to physically remove several photographers from the singer's limo. Prince was incensed. "I don't have any problem with somebody I *know* trying to get in the car with me and my woman," he told *Rolling Stone* shortly after the incident. "But someone like that? Just to get a picture?"

Unfortunately for Prince, Huntsberry had developed a $1,000-per-week cocaine habit. Needing to fund his addiction after quitting his job, the bodyguard sold his story to the *National Enquirer*, which promptly published a kiss-and-tell expose. 'The Real Prince: He's Trapped In A Bizarre Secret World Of Terror' was based largely on interviews with Huntsberry, who is quoted as describing the singer as "the weirdest guy I've ever met. He feels he's a second Mozart."

Among the 'revelations' were that Prince

lived in an armed fortress with life-size murals of Marilyn Monroe on the walls, which seemed to leave the singer at pains in future interviews to remind people that he lived a normal life. But despite writing a bitter song about the situation entitled 'Old Friends 4 Sale,' which remained unreleased until it was included on *The Vault: Old Friends For Sale* in 1999 – by which time some of the more personal lyrics had been cut – Prince always cared deeply for his former bodyguard. He kept Huntsberry on the payroll and even bought him a house. Just weeks after Huntsberry quit, Prince admitted to *Rolling Stone* that he had "told him that his job was still there and that I was alone … I miss him."

After kicking his drug habit, Huntsberry became a street evangelist. He spent his time preaching in schools and prisons, and set up Big Chick's Ministries. On April 2 1989, after suffering a severe heart trauma, he prayed to God that he be given one more year to live and to preach the gospel. He died exactly one year later, having fallen into a coma after a church service three days earlier, his heart reportedly as big as a basketball.

On April 30 1990 Prince gave his first live performance of the decade at the Minneapolis nightclub Rupert's. It was an intimate show costing $100 a ticket, with the proceeds – $60,000 in total – going to Huntsberry's wife and six children. Prince dedicated 'Purple Rain' to his former bodyguard, who used to play air guitar to the song from the side of the stage.

Chick Huntsberry quickly became one of Prince's closest confidantes, and helped protect the singer from the outside world.

after 15 minutes. "He could only stay on for two or three songs," Bill Wyman later recalled, "because the crowd threw things at him. He made great records, but he couldn't perform on stage." Prince was so shaken by the experience that he flew straight back to Minneapolis and refused to return for the second concert, which was scheduled for October 11. It took an hour-and-a-half on

"Music is like a newspaper to him, and his attitude is: what's the point of reading last week's paper?" ALAN LEEDS

the phone with Dez Dickerson – following pleas from Steve Fargnoli and even Mick Jagger – before Prince would change his mind. Dickerson suggested a few changes to the set that might make the show heavier (and thus more palatable), and appealed to Prince's sense of pride, telling him: "We can't let a few dirtballs run us out of town like this … we got to come back, and show them what we're made of."

Two days later, The Rolling Stones' fans turned up armed and ready for a fight, having heard about what

happened on the first night. Fruit, vegetables, Jack Daniels, and even a bag of rotting chicken came flying through the air at the group. But Prince played on, completing a full set despite the hostile response, and gained a lot of ground with the LA press as a result.

Prince began a tour of his own a month later, on November 20, but even that wasn't without its own set of problems. His longest stint so far as a headliner, it was a huge success in terms of his previous tours. Deciding to make his shows more theatrical, he hired set designer Roy Bennett to build a stage with hydraulics, two tiers of stage, ramps at either side, a fireman's pole, and a set of blinding lights that shone through from the Venetian blinds used as a backdrop.

Prince's stage persona had evolved at a similar rate. He now wore a shirt and trousers beneath his purple trench coat and built long segments of audience participation into the set, in which he more or less acted out the words to 'Do Me, Baby' with the women in the audience. *Dirty Mind*'s 'Head' became the centerpiece of his shows, and found him sitting on top of the speakers, virtually masturbating his guitar to the climax of a ten-minute jam.

With a setlist that largely ignored his first two albums (save for the singles 'I Wanna Be Your Lover' and 'Why You Treat Me So Bad?'), the Controversy tour presented Prince as an ambassador for sexual freedom. For some audience members, however, it was all too cerebral, particularly by comparison to the short, snappy set by The Time that preceded Prince's arrival. Little did Prince realize that his protégés would soon be doing to him what he himself had done to Rick James a year or so earlier.

Tensions increased between the acts, with The Time fighting for more money and more respect. Even though they were bringing *his* music to life night after night, Prince refused to up their pay. Similarly, when he started work on The Time's second album in December, during a break between legs of the tour, he refused to give Morris Day and co any artistic control.

During the final show of the tour, on March 14 1982 at Cincinnati's Riverfront Coliseum, Prince and his entourage threw eggs at The Time while they played. Backstage, Prince's newly hired bodyguard, Chick Huntsberry, tied guitarist Jesse Johnson to a coat hanger so that Prince could throw more food at him. Management ordered that there was to be no interruption to the headliner's set, but as soon as Prince walked off stage a full-scale food-fight ensued, and carried on all the way back to the hotel. As ever, Prince seemed incapable of ending an album-tour cycle without there being some level of dissent within his camp. It was around this time too that Prince decided to scrap an entire film project called *The Second Coming* (named for his entrance music) after an argument with the director, Chuck Statler. Hours of footage shot on tour and at Prince's home went to waste, and Prince instead went back into the studio, where he would cut three more albums in five months.

What Time Is It?

THREE ALBUMS INTO HIS CAREER, PRINCE REALIZED TWO THINGS: FIRST THAT HE NEEDED TO CREATE MORE OF A BUZZ THAN HE COULD SIMPLY BY BEING 'PRINCE,' AND SECOND THAT HE HAD SO MANY IDEAS FOR SONGS AND PERSONAS THAT HE COULDN'T POSSIBLY USE THEM ALL HIMSELF.

Prince's own releases had to follow some of pattern: suddenly making an album of lightweight pop-funk would disrupt a carefully planned chain of events. The way to address this, he decided, was to create a 'ghost band' that would not only give Prince another outlet for his ideas but would also make it seem like he wasn't just out there on his own. The Minneapolis sound, as it came to be known, had its roots in the club circuit that Prince played on with Grand Central and Champagne, but this time he was (theoretically) in control of the whole scene. Each of its bands would be characterized by the same funky rhythms, pop hooks, and new wave elements, and deploy the same instantly recognizable stripped-down production, but none would be better than Prince himself.

After convincing Morris Day to donate his song 'Partyup' to *Dirty Mind*, Prince promised to repay his old friend by making him the frontman of a new band. Unsurprisingly, given that he was still playing in local bands and working as a runner for Prince, Day jumped at the chance. The rest of the band, which was dubbed The Time, also came from Minneapolis. Bassist Terry Lewis, drummer Jellybean Johnson, and keyboardists Jimmy 'Jam' Harris and Monte Moir had all played together in Flyte Tyme, while guitarist Jessse Johnson had played in other local bands. (Before recruiting Day, Prince had courted another local singer, Alexander O'Neal, who later became hugely successful in his own right but wanted more than Prince was willing to pay him to be in The Time.) The crucial final addition to the line-up was dancer/valet Jerome Benton, who became Day's comic foil.

The Time's look was based around the retro-pimp fashions of two generations back: Stacy Adams shoes, bright suits, and long, thin ties. It was perfectly in keeping with the skinny, drainpipe suits of the emerging new wave bands of the era. Morris Day's image – that of a self-obsessed skirt-chaser, as seen in *Purple Rain* – had its origins in a pimp persona Prince used to mess around with, for which he put on an old man's 'hustler' voice. But while Day and his cohorts certainly looked the part, they weren't expecting any great success in their own right.

"We knew we weren't going to make any money," Jimmy Jam recalled. "Prince was very upfront: 'There's not going to be a lot of money in this.'"

Having assembled the band, Prince got to work on both his own *Controversy* and The Time's eponymous debut, while also running his new group through strict rehearsals until he was happy that they could work as a unit. As good as they got, The Time wouldn't be allowed to play a note on their debut album. Prince recorded all the music himself, crediting the production to a pseudonym, Jamie Starr, and to Morris Day (who was at least allowed to sing on the record, but had to follow Prince's guide vocals note-for-note).

The Time's infectious pop-funk was a lot less challenging than *Dirty Mind*, and a lot less weighty than what Prince was cooking up for *Controversy*. Its tightly written, simple songs soon found favor with the record-buying public, many of whom quickly guessed that this

The Time's frontman, Morris Day.

Jamie Starr character – who had also been credited as an engineer on *Dirty Mind* – was actually Prince himself.

Prince took The Time out with him on his Controversy tour in November 1981, but this excursion – as ever – was far from easy. While Prince's own live shows were becoming ever more lofty and conceptual, The Time quickly became a much tighter unit than Prince might have imagined. And like any good students, they made a point of trying to out-do their master on stage. The problem, of course, was that Prince didn't like being shown up.

What made things even more tense was Prince's refusal to acknowledge the fact that, although he was the mastermind behind the music, what brought The Time to life was the band itself, particularly the charisma between Morris Day and Jerome Benton. Well aware of their own worth, The Time began to ask for more money, but Prince wouldn't give it to them. The group began to boil with resentment – particularly Jesse Johnson, who Matt Fink later described as having "a major ego problem."

The bad blood between the two groups boiled over during the final Controversy show in Cincinnati, when during The Time's set Prince and some of his cronies egged their support act from off stage. "I thought it was kind of low," Morris Day later recalled. "I know it was meant in fun, but when you're trying to do your show in front of a bunch of people, throwing eggs is not too cool." Things got even worse after The Time's set. Jesse Johnson found himself handcuffed to a wall-mounted coat rack in Prince's dressing room and subjected to further humiliation after the show. Prince of course demanded that no interruptions be made to his own performance, but as soon as he left the stage a food fight ensued. When the battle continued at the hotel, Prince made Morris Day pay for the damage caused, claiming that he had started the whole affair.

Such was Prince's work rate that, instead of having a cooling-off period after the Controversy tour, he went straight back to work not just on his own *1999* and a record by his other new side-project, Vanity 6, but also a second album for The Time, *What Time Is It?*. The same tensions quickly rose to the surface, as the band was once again given no creative control. The Time became further exasperated when, for the 1999 / Triple Threat tour, it was requested that they play behind a curtain as Vanity 6's backing band before playing an hour-long set of their own, with only a small pay increase to show for it.

Not surprisingly The Time baulked at this offer, so Prince took to bullying them after they finished playing – which naturally served to create further tension between the two parties. To make matters worse, he then decided to drop the group from the line-up when the tour reached major cities such as New York and Los Angeles. As relationships continued to sour, former James Brown tour-manager Alan Leeds was brought in to keep the peace. But the problems didn't end there.

Frustrated at the lack of creative freedom afforded them, Jimmy Jam and Terry Lewis had begun to produce other groups without telling their boss. Midway through the second leg of the Triple Threat tour, the pair missed a show in San Antonio after finding themselves snowed in in Atlanta, where they had been recording The SOS Band. Jerome Benton had to mime playing the bass on stage while Prince played Lewis's parts off stage, and Lisa Coleman stood in for Jimmy Jam.

When the missing members returned, Prince fined them $3,000 each – an extortionate amount for musicians who already felt they were grossly underpaid. When the tour finished in April, he sacked them both, wholly undermining Morris Day's authority as The Time's supposed leader. "That was fucked up," Day recalled. "For me, it was like being the president, but having to answer to the CEO. I had a fair amount of control ... but the bottom line was always his."

By the time shooting began on *Purple Rain*, Monte Moir had also quit the group. Replacements for him, Jam, and Lewis were all found in the shape of bassist Jerry Hubbard and keyboardists Mark Cardenez and Paul Peterson. But The Time didn't have much longer to run, as Morris Day made it clear that, as soon as *Purple Rain* was

The comic performances of Morris Day (left) and Jerome Benton gave The Time's live shows an extra dimension.

finished, so was he. Not only had Prince undermined his power within the band, he had also begun making it more obvious to the public that the Jamie Starr / Starr Company credits were actually pseudonyms.

"When people came to realize how big a role he played in some of these projects," Alan Leeds recalled, "they started to lose a little respect." By the time a third Time album – *Ice Cream Castle*, named for a Joni Mitchell lyric – was released, the group had ceased to exist, despite the fact that, ironically, they had been allowed to play their own instruments this time around. (Undeterred, Prince had already started to assemble a new group out of the wreckage: The Family.)

Jerome Benton stayed in the Prince camp for short while longer, joining an augmented line-up of The Revolution as a dancer. Having had a relatively small part in *Purple Rain*, he was promoted to the role of Prince's comedy foil, Tricky, in *Under The Cherry Moon*. Meanwhile Jesse Johnson struck out as a solo artist, as did Morris Day, who found success both with his 1985 debut, *Color Of Success*, and as an actor. Jimmy Jam and Terry Lewis went on to form Flyte Tyme Productions and create massive chart-busting hits in the Minneapolis sound mould. They won a Grammy for their work on Janet Jackson's 1986 album *Control*, and subsequently worked with a wide range of R&B stars, including Gladys Knight, Luther Vandross, and Mariah Carey.

The original line-up of The Time reconvened for a fourth album, *Pandemonium*, which was recorded and released to tie in with Prince's third movie, *Graffiti Bridge*. The album project was originally called *Corporate World*, and was set to feature only Morris Day and Jerome Benton, but Warner Bros insisted that the original line-up be brought in if Prince wanted the company's backing for the movie. But even then, six years later, The Time still found

themselves forced to stand in their master's shadow. The original idea, according to Jimmy Jam, was that *Graffiti Bridge* would tell the story of The Time in the same way that *Purple Rain* "had told Prince's story ... [but] it turned into a Prince movie with a cameo by The Time."

That could have been it for The Time, but they remain too good a live band to call it quits. A new line-up, billed as Morris Day & The Time, began touring during the mid 90s, and made an appearance in Kevin Smith's 2001 movie *Jay And Silent Bob Strike Back*. The group also performed as part of Prince's 1999 New Years Eve show (actually recorded on December 17) and supported him on a handful of Musicology dates in 2004.

The original line-up reconvened in 2008 for a duet with Rihanna at the Grammy Awards, and followed that with a Prince-like run of shows in Las Vegas. Three years later, on October 18 2011, they released a new album, *Condensate*. However, because their former charge owned the rights to their name, the group's comeback was credited to The Original 7ven. "We are not going to fight him," they asserted. "Friends do not fight over business."

Guitarist Jesse Johnson felt similarly when, just two months later, he quit the band, announcing via his Facebook page that it was time to "walk away while we're still friends." The news was a shock to the rest of the group, who had spent several hours together on a conference call the day before without Jackson's departure ever coming up. "We felt like everyone was committed to this project for the long haul," they said in their own statement, issued a month later, on January 18 2012. Nevertheless, they chose to "respectfully accept" his decision and remained active without him. On June 24 and 25 2016 they performed rapturously received sets at London's Hammersmith Eventim Apollo, appearing on the bill as part of an Autism Rocks charity tribute to Prince.

AFTER COMPLETING HIS CONTROVERSY TOUR, PRINCE GOT STRAIGHT TO WORK ON TWO SIDE PROJECTS: A SECOND ALBUM FOR THE TIME AND A DEBUT FOR VANITY 6. PRODUCTION ON BOTH WAS CREDITED TO JAMIE STARR, THE PSEUDONYM THAT PRINCE SEEMED DESPERATE TO DISTANCE HIMSELF FROM.

1999 (MARCH 1982–MAY 1983)

In his only interview of 1983, conducted with the *Los Angeles Times*, he was keen to get certain facts straight: "One, my real name is Prince. Two, I'm not gay. Three, I'm not Jamie Starr." (Only much later would he admit that he was "just getting tired of seeing my name. If you give away an idea, you still own that idea. In fact, giving it away strengthens it.")

Such was the confusion that, in Britain, *Melody Maker* even went so far as to call The Time and Vanity 6 plagiarists. Mining the same dancefloor-friendly funk and new wave sound as *The Time*, both *What Time Is It?* and *Vanity 6* helped Prince maintain his grip on the black market, while also allowing him to stretch out into ever-more experimental territory on his own next record.

Prince shut himself away like a mad scientist to work on his fifth album. Parts of it were recorded in his own 24-track basement studio (which he called Uptown), with the rest completed at Sunset Sound in Los Angeles with Peggy McCreary, an engineer who had also worked on *Controversy*. Prince seemed more obsessed with this new project than he had been with any before. He often pulled 24-hour stints in the studio, with McCreary forced to stay with him around the clock. With just the two of them in the room, there were regular flare-ups – particularly if there was any sort of hold-up. Prince would pace around waiting for tapes to be rewound for playback or for technical problems to be fixed. (As much as he had embraced new studio technology, it seemed that the machines often weren't fast enough to keep up with him.)

"I remember days when Prince would come into the studio at, like, 9am, kick you out of the room for about twenty minutes, then write a song," recalled Peter Doell, who worked sporadically as an engineer on *1999*, and later with Miles Davis. "Then he'd come back … and you'd better have the drums tuned up and ready, because he's going to play the daylights out of the drums … Then he'd go on and do the bass, keyboards, and by one o'clock you're mixing it, and by four o'clock you run off and have it mastered … He was an unbelievable cottage industry."

As these long and often arduous sessions continued Prince began to push his new ideas further and further, building on his *Controversy* experiments and taking studio

Nasty Girls: Vanity 6

After touring *Controversy* with one 'ghost band' in tow, Prince decided that he needed to create a second group to further increase the hype surrounding the Minneapolis scene – without letting on that it was all the work of one man. It would also give him an outlet for another aspect of his personality that didn't fit with his being Prince.

His initial plan was to create an all-girl group called The Hookers, comprising his girlfriend Susan Moonsie, set designer Roy Bennett's wife Brenda, and Cavallo, Ruffalo & Fargnoli employee Jamie Shoop. The group's image – lacy lingerie, stockings, and heels – was supposed to turn the wholesome 60s girl-group look on its head, presenting instead a group of predatory women out stalking bars and clubs looking for sex.

Things changed in the aftermath of the 1982 American Music Awards, where Prince met Denise Matthews, a lady of Hispanic descent who looked almost like his female counterpart. "Prince sent someone over to

With the line-up of Vanity 6 – named for the number of breasts in the group – complete, Prince started recording a debut album for them, while also working on *What Time Is It?* and *1999*. *Vanity 6* was a moderately successful record full of lightweight pop tunes with titles such as 'Nasty Girl,' 'Wet Dream,' and 'He's So Dull,' and a general mood that veered closer to new wave than funk. The album presented the group as a vampish foil to The Time's gang-of-pimps image, while once again the production was credited to Jamie Starr in an attempt to make it look like another one of this mysterious tycoon's masterpieces.

At the same time as recruiting Matthews for Vanity 6, Prince began a stormy relationship with her. Matthews had left her Niagara Falls home at 15 (following her father's death and her mother's slip into alcoholism and depression) and set her sights on becoming rich and famous. Meeting Prince seven years later was exactly what she wanted. "He told me he was going to make me a star," Matthews recalled, "so I moved out to Minneapolis to live with him."

The relationship was fraught from the start, however. On a professional level, Matthews wasn't keen on Prince's instructions to "get out there, take off all your clothes, and run around naked," but at the same time she craved attention, and enjoyed putting on an aggressive front that hid the scars of abuse suffered at the hands of her father. Then there was the way Prince treated his girlfriends. During the Triple Threat tour, for which Vanity 6 served as the opening act, he continued his relationship with Susan Moonsie and started a third with another potential musical interest, Jill Jones.

the little chap's sheets, actually kips on her own in a separate bus."

In reality Prince – whose preference was for more demure ladyfriends – quickly became weary of Vanity's attitude, particularly after she slipped into a cycle of drink and drug abuse as a way of dealing with the pressure of touring and Prince's refusal to be with her and her alone. ("I did [drugs] on the sly," she recalled, "but nobody tried to stop me.") Nonetheless Prince had her written into the *Purple Rain* script and began to work on a successor to *Vanity 6*. But then in August 1983, during pre-production, Matthews either quit or was sacked (possibly over a pay dispute). She was replaced by Patricia 'Apollonia' Kotero in the newly renamed Apollonia 6.

Matthews retained the name Vanity and recorded two solo albums, *Wild Animal* and *Skin On Skin*. She has also starred in a handful of movies. All the while her drink-and-drugs lifestyle continued to spiral out of control, to the extent that, when she started dating the notorious rock lunatic Nikki Sixx a few years later, his equally wild Mötley Crüe bandmate Tommy Lee was moved to remark: "There's something really crazy about Vanity." Describing their first meeting in his autobiography, Sixx himself recalled: "She opened the door naked with her eyes going around in her head. Somehow I had a feeling we might just hit it off."

By the time she reached her thirties, having smoked crack cocaine for years, Vanity found herself temporarily deaf and blind. She suffered kidney failure (having already lost one kidney), internal bleeding, and a stroke, and spent three days on life-support. After miraculously surviving this ordeal, she renounced her Vanity days and became a born-again Christian, devoting her life to her church in Fremont, California.

Matthews's health took a turn for the worse in late 2015, when she was diagnosed with sclerosis encapsulating peritonitis. She died in hospital in Fremont on February 15 2016, just hours before Prince was due to take to the stage in Melbourne, Australia. "Someone dear to us has passed away," he told the audience, on what was the opening night of his Piano & A Microphone tour. "It's a little heavy on me tonight." He then dedicated several songs to his former lover, adding: "I loved her for the artist she was trying to be … she'd want us to celebrate her life and not mourn her."

"Prince sauntered over to me and said, 'Will you come to the bathroom with me? I want to try on your coat.' It turned out he had nothing on under his own coat." VANITY

talk to me," she recalled. "He took my my number and gave it to Prince, who called me the next day. He came to pick me up that night in a white limo and we went out to dinner." Jamie Shoop was dropped in a flash and replaced by Matthews, who became Vanity (having rejected Prince's original suggestion, which was to call her 'Vagina' – pronounced 'Vageena').

"He juggled the affairs on a day-to-day basis," Alan Leeds recalled. "Some nights Vanity would disappear with Prince, then some nights Jill would appear on the Prince bus, leaving Vanity in the hotel." As Barney Hoskyns, who covered the tour for the *New Musical Express*, recalled: "Nobody seems to remark how peculiar it is that Vanity, supposedly enjoying pride of place between

trickery to the extreme, thereby keeping his peers and his listeners guessing for as long as he could. The Linn LM-1 drum machine became increasingly prominent. It had only featured on one song on *Controversy*, but can be heard all over *1999* in between layer upon layer of synthesizer. The combined effect is that of a cold, hard, mechanized take on Phil Spector's organic, eardrum-crashing Wall Of Sound. What Prince had over Spector, however, was that he could turn out hits for himself as well as for others.

By July Prince had completed a ten-track album, which he took to managers Bob Cavallo and Steve Fargnoli. But as much as they liked what he had done, they felt this new work needed a 'Controversy' or a 'Dirty Mind' – an opening track that could show in no uncertain terms what the rest of the record was about. "He yelled at us," Cavallo recalled, "and then he went back to Minneapolis and kept recording."

Prince recorded the song in question – which would give the new album its title, and end up becoming one of his signature works – in less than a day, between late-night rehearsals with The Time. As Jimmy Jam later recalled, Prince walked in one afternoon at around 2pm and played the assembled musicians his latest creation. "We're going, 'Hey! When did you do this?' 'I did this last night after I left.' Oh, man, it's not fair!"

Prince's defining statement of the era, '1999' touches on a theme that would continue to crop up in his work: that of partying to the end, in the face of a looming apocalypse. The previous album's 'Ronnie, Talk To Russia' voiced similar concerns, but its lyrics were too specific (and too naïve) to appeal to a wider, cross-generational audience. While '1999' has a similarly paranoid, fear-of-the-bomb theme, it isn't rooted in one spot. With one of Prince's catchiest and most danceable tunes beneath it, it remains – like Stevie Wonder's best work – as relevant today as it was in 1982 (and at the turn of the millennium).

"Mommy, why does everybody have a bomb?" Prince asks in a sped-up voice at the end of the song. Never has certain death sounded so inviting. Mimicking the call-and-response vocals of Sly & The Family Stone's 'Dance To The Music,' Prince has keyboardist Lisa Coleman sing the opening phrase, followed by Dez Dickerson, allowing the song to build before coming in himself on the third line. The opening is inspired and disorientating in equal measure, not just because of the switch between voices but also because of the melodic changes it goes through, which came as a result of the fact that Prince, Coleman, and Dickerson recorded their vocal parts together, only for Prince to split them up later on, meaning that some 'lead' parts had been planned as harmonies.

While promoting the wildly eclectic *Emancipation* set in 1997, Prince described *1999* as "nothing but me running the computers myself, which is why [it] isn't as varied." This might well be true, but *1999* remains one of his most successful and enduring works, not least because

of the way that he was able to refine and perfect the cluttered, anything-goes approach of *Controversy*. The lyrics, meanwhile, are deeper but more accessible. 'Little Red Corvette' might sound to begin with like a simple pop song about lost love, but lines about "a pocket full of horses, Trojan" carry a safe-sex message, Trojan being a popular brand of American prophylactic. (The fact that "some of them were used" adding a rather creepy undercurrent.)

Elsewhere, 'Free' is a gospel ballad with an unusually patriotic theme, given that it was written by a man with a reputation for being pop's most morally bankrupt sexual deviant; 'Delirious' is a much stronger take on the rockabilly pastiche of 'Jack U Off'; and 'Automatic' and 'Lady Cab Driver' show off a newfound sadistic streak. ('Lady Cab Driver' features a spoken-word passage in which Prince has sex with the driver in the back of her cab, with each thrust being dedicated to the likes of "the creator of man," "politicians who are bored and believe in war," or the question of "why I wasn't born like my brother, handsome

> 🔲 "The 1999 album was the seismic shift where all of the things that were attempted and all of the things that were pointed towards … came together in this sort of perfect storm." *DEZ DICKERSON*

and tall.") The lyrics are also much more humorous than one might have expected of Prince. He teaches the perennially unfunky to dance on 'D.M.S.R.' – "All the white people, clap your hands on the four" – and whisks a lover away on "Prince International" during 'International Lover''s extended sex-as-flying metaphor.

Perhaps the most remarkable aspect of *1999* is the fact that it never feels overlong or self-indulgent, despite the fact that 'Lady Cab Driver' runs to nine-and-a-half minutes, and that half of the remaining ten tracks clock in at more than six. Taken as a whole, *1999* marks the point at which Prince had learnt to ride a groove for as long as he wanted, endlessly reworking it so as to prevent it from getting stale.

Once Prince had completed work on his most powerful album yet, Steve Fargnoli was given the job of taking it to Warner Bros and trying to convince the label to release it as double album for the price of a standard LP. Once again the Warner executives were being asked to stick their necks out for a relatively underground artist, having already let him produce his own debut and run off into ever-stranger territory on his subsequent releases. Now the label was being asked to release an album that was in serious danger of making a loss.

Fargnoli, however, had become Prince's greatest ally when it came to dealing with Warner Bros, and was able to

convince chief executive Mo Ostin that a double-album was the only way to go. (The label's European arm wasn't so easily convinced. It released *1999* as a seven-track single album to begin with, omitting some of the longer songs, before issuing the full-length version in 1983.)

As it was, Ostin and his cohorts needn't have worried. A few weeks after the album's release, *Rolling Stone* praised the diversity of *1999* and its creator. "[Prince] works like a colorblind technician who's studied Devo and Afrika Bambaataa & The Soulsonic Force," the magazine declared, "keeping the songs constantly kinetic with an inventive series of shocks and surprises." Even Miles Davis, in his autobiography, was moved to call *1999* "the most exciting music I was hearing in 1982" and Prince himself "someone who was doing something different," who he "decided to keep an eye on."

Even so, when the title track stalled at Number 44 on the *Billboard* Pop chart, it seemed like mainstream success might still prove elusive. Not everybody was impressed by Prince's 'Specially priced two record set,' either. The *New Musical Express* thought it was a prime example of the desperate moves a record company makes when "the only people who like you are the people who get their records free." As with *Dirty Mind*, however, there was something of a snowball effect. Prince's live shows were fast becoming unmissable, with newspapers such as the *Philadelphia*

Enquirer going out of their way to "unequivocally recommend [this] wonderful, provocative show."

The 1999 tour built on the Controversy setup. This time Prince presented his full army of talent to the world in the form of a Triple Threat line-up that saw Vanity 6 open and The Time play second on the bill, while his new Roy Bennett-designed stage set included a bed that came up through the floor so that he could reenact the lyrics to 'International Lover' each night. The musical arrangements were similarly ambitious. Bobby Z had his work cut out trying to figure out how to incorporate his own live drumming alongside electronic rhythms triggered by the Linn LM-1. "I felt like an auto-assembly worker looking at a robot for the first time, wondering if I still had a job," he recalled, adding that he got little in the way of guidance from his boss. "Prince said, 'Here it is, figure out what you're going to do with it.' The machine was on the record and I had to augment that and get it to work live."

As with the Controversy tour, the Triple Threat dates were marred by an air of antagonism between Prince and The Time. Feeling overworked and underpaid, the group took their frustrations out on stage, doing their best to outdo Prince each night. As guitarist Jesse Johnson recalled, "Some nights we'd knock on his dressing room door and say, 'We're gonna slaughter you!'"

A new source of frustration came when The Time were ordered to play behind a curtain while Vanity 6 gyrated in their lingerie for 40 minutes while singing the likes of 'Nasty Girl,' 'Drive Me Wild,' and 'Wet Dream.' Vanity wasn't in the best frame of mind either. Her relationship with Prince had begun in a rush of passion, but was slowly fizzling out. She and Prince were no longer 'exclusive,' as he could often be found shacked up with new backing-singer Jill Jones – yet another girl he promised to write an album for – or any other girl who took his fancy. Overwhelmed by sudden stardom and upset by Prince's casual approach to their relationship, she turned to drink and drugs to get through the tour.

Things got so bad for all concerned that midway through the tour Prince had to bring in Alan Leeds, who had previously served as James Brown's tour manager, to keep everything together. Leeds saved the day, despite initially finding himself having to communicate with Prince – like everyone else on the tour – via Chick Huntsberry. In the end Leeds became as close a confidante to Prince as had the bodyguard, but was still never quite sure when to be 'Alan the big brother,' 'Alan the best friend,' or 'Alan the gofer.' The key was knowing what Prince wanted when. "I'd better not confuse the three roles," Leeds recalled, "because if he sends me on a mission and I come into rehearsal empty-handed, and I start laughing and joking like we did in front of the TV last night, I'm not going to last very long."

Despite the internal turmoil within the Prince camp, everything seemed to be going from strength to strength on the outside. Perhaps the most crucial breakthrough came when '1999' began to appear on heavy rotation on MTV in December, just as the Triple Threat tour was taking off. The exposure was invaluable. Not only was Prince now being foisted onto television screens on a regular basis, he was also one of the first black acts to appear on the channel – a few months ahead of Michael Jackson's 'Beat It' – proving to Prince that his music could break down racial barriers.

Fortunately for Prince, this newfound exposure had coincided almost exactly with his decision to take more care over his music videos, which had up to now been rather mundane. The '1999' promo stuck to that same basic formula of filming a live performance of the song, but had enough fast edits – and enough shots of Lisa Coleman and Jill Jones in lingerie – to appeal to the MTV crowd.

Next came 'Little Red Corvette,' for which Prince even performed a brief but elaborate dance routine during Dickerson's guitar solo. The song itself saw Prince finally get to grips with a rock sound that wasn't generic (as his previous stabs at the genre had been). 'Corvette' even had a proper rock guitar-solo, edited together from three different takes played by Dez Dickerson, one of the few musicians to get such a spotlight on a Prince album during this phase of his career. It proved to be just the hit Prince needed, reaching Number Six on *Billboard*'s Pop chart right in time for the launch of the second leg of the tour. (Interestingly, the single stalled at Number 15 on the R&B chart.)

The MTV exposure led to even greater interest in the Prince live experience, which in turn boosted his crossover appeal as a bona fide hitmaker. The *1999* LP soon broke into the US Top Ten and ended up selling three million copies within in a year. By the time the year for which it was named arrived, the album had gone Platinum four times over.

But while the final stages of the 1999 tour should have been one big party, things weren't quite so simple. Prince had irreparably damaged his relationship with The Time, and pushed Vanity into a world of drink, drugs, and depression, making her unreliable and irritating to be around. He was also going to have to find a replacement for Dez Dickerson, who like former bandmate Gayle Chapman had found God and had begun to feel rather conflicted about his role in Prince's band. "I knew I didn't have it in me to continue – spiritually, emotionally, creatively, mentally," he later recalled. Prince let Dickerson go, but continued to support his former sideman. He had Cavallo, Ruffalo & Fargnoli take over Dickerson's affairs, offered to help write and record his solo project, and gave his band, The Modernaires, a showcase spot in *Purple Rain*.

Dickerson had long since wanted to work on his own material, so his departure from the band didn't come as a surprise. Prince had a ready-made replacement to hand in the form of 19-year-old Wendy Melvoin, a friend of Lisa Coleman who had been traveling with her in the tour bus and who would occasionally jam with the band during soundchecks or rehearsals if Dickerson wasn't around. Melvoin was a simple, handy replacement – just the sort of musician Prince needed to capitalize on his newfound commercial appeal. And she had a twin sister, too.

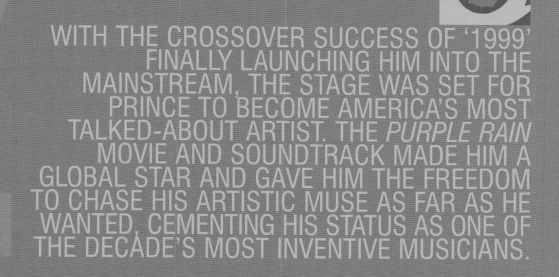

2

WITH THE CROSSOVER SUCCESS OF '1999'
FINALLY LAUNCHING HIM INTO THE
MAINSTREAM, THE STAGE WAS SET FOR
PRINCE TO BECOME AMERICA'S MOST
TALKED-ABOUT ARTIST. THE *PURPLE RAIN*
MOVIE AND SOUNDTRACK MADE HIM A
GLOBAL STAR AND GAVE HIM THE FREEDOM
TO CHASE HIS ARTISTIC MUSE AS FAR AS HE
WANTED, CEMENTING HIS STATUS AS ONE OF
THE DECADE'S MOST INVENTIVE MUSICIANS.

PURPLE REIGN
1983–1989

AT THE START OF 1983, 'LITTLE RED CORVETTE' AND *1999* WERE IN THE PROCESS OF TURNING PRINCE INTO A MINOR CROSSOVER STAR IN AMERICA. THE 'LITTLE RED CORVETTE' VIDEO – ONE OF THE FIRST BY A BLACK ARTIST TO BE SHOWN ON MTV – MADE HIM AN INSTANT SMALL-SCREEN ICON. BUT FEW WOULD HAVE GUESSED THAT, IN JUST OVER A YEAR, PRINCE WOULD BECOME A BIG-SCREEN LEGEND, TOO, NOT TO MENTION A GLOBAL POP PHENOMENON.

Purple Rain (FEBRUARY 1983–APRIL 1985)

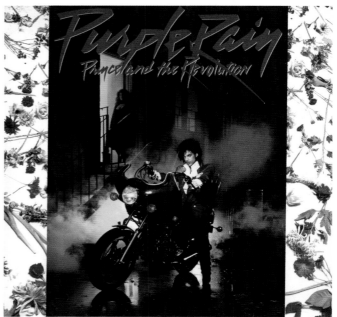

By the end of 1984 Prince had become the first act since The Beatles to simultaneously top the US charts with a single ('When Doves Cry'), album, and movie (both *Purple Rain*). He had also found time to write hit albums for The Time (*Ice Cream Castle*), Apollonia 6 (*Apollonia 6*), and Sheila E. (*The Glamorous Life*), and a hit single for Sheena Easton ('Sugar Walls,' a thinly veiled exploration of her internal anatomy), while Chaka Kahn resurrected his 1979 track 'I Feel For You' and put it back into the charts.

But back in 1983 he was still, as Jimmy Jam put it, "at the point where he wasn't yet a superstar, but was right at the point of doing it." What Jam and everybody else wondered was: "What's your next move gonna be?" As it turned out, Prince's next move was to do what David Bowie did with *Ziggy Stardust*, and write himself into fame.

Prince was (and is) an avid movie fanatic, so it's no surprise that he had long courted the idea of making a motion picture of his own. The man who stamped his dominance over the recording process with the words "Produced, arranged, composed, and performed by Prince"

would naturally have wanted to exert a similar authority over the other main avenue of popular entertainment. He would also have noticed how Sylvester Stallone made himself into a superstar with *Rocky* in 1976. Six years later, when Prince first began to consider making a movie, the *Rocky* franchise was into its third installment.

According to drummer Bobby Z, "Prince was fascinated with the camera," and had already started taping rehearsals and concerts and filming short skits. He had begun to come up with the basic concept for *Purple Rain* as far back as the *Dirty Mind* period. During his Controversy tour of 1982, Prince had started to film his shows for something called *The Second Coming*, which would intersperse concert footage with dramatic elements. In the end the project was scrapped, but much the same concept reappeared for the *Sign "O" The Times* concert movie a few years later.

By the time the second leg of the Triple Threat tour in support of *1999* began in February 1983 Prince had taken to carrying around a purple notebook in which he wrote down ideas for the semi-autobiographical movie that was beginning to form in his mind: *Purple Rain*. He wasn't yet a superstar, but did have some leverage. He had told his managers at Cavallo, Ruffalo & Fargnoli that if they wanted to hold onto him beyond the imminent expiration of his contract they had better get him a movie deal with Warner Bros. "I want to star in the movie," he told Bob Cavallo. "I want my name above the title and I want it to be at a major studio."

Unfortunately for Cavallo, Warner Bros Pictures wasn't particularly keen on the idea of pumping heaps of money into the pipe-dream project of a mid-level singer with only a handful of hits to his name. If he wasn't able to carry on making hit records, the company reasoned, he wouldn't be able to attract the sort of crowds a major motion picture needs to make its money back.

"There was no precedent for this," tour manager Alan Leeds recalled. "Rock'n'roll stars with a couple of hit albums did not make major movies. Let alone somebody from the black community having the gumption to do it in the mainstream." Before it was to agree to such a deal, Warner Bros needed proof that Prince was the star that the movie was supposed to turn him into.

Thankfully Prince still had the full backing of the head of Warner Bros' music division, Mo Ostin. Although no distribution deal had been secured, Ostin put up four million dollars of the label's money to get the ball rolling. Having been given at least something of a green light, Cavallo and his colleagues went out in search of a screenwriter. They soon found 46-year-old William Blinn, who had won an Emmy award for his work on the *Roots* television show and was an executive producer of *Fame*, which had just completed its second series. By the time Blinn was introduced to Prince, the movie concept had formed into something that centered on the incestuous Minneapolis music scene and recalled Prince's early struggle for success in bands such as Champagne.

Blinn found Prince less than willing to communicate at first, making his attempts at writing a treatment (for what was then known as *Dreams*) rather difficult. "Casual conversation is not what he's good at," Blinn later said. "He's an enigma. He wants to communicate but he doesn't want you to get too close." After gathering together "12 to 14 pages" of ideas Blinn flew out to Minneapolis to watch the March 15 Triple Threat show. Later that night he went to Prince's house, where it became clear to Blinn that the singer was on "an honest quest to figure himself out. He saved all the money on shrinks and put it in the movie."

But he very nearly didn't get the chance. After the Triple Threat tour came to an end in May Blinn moved out to Minneapolis to start work on the project, only for Prince to start canceling meetings or walking out of them. Blinn came close to withdrawing from the project altogether when the singer left a meeting at a cinema after 20 minutes. "You've got a rock'n'roll crazy on your hands," Blinn told Steve Fargnoli. "I know he's very gifted, but frankly, life's too short." And with that Blinn got on a plane back to Los Angeles.

Whether or not Prince realized that he was to blame for Blinn's departure or simply didn't want to see his dreams crumble is unclear, but the singer quickly called his screenwriter to apologize for his behavior (which he blamed on stress). Blinn returned to Minneapolis to give the project another chance, at which point Prince played him some of the songs he had already written for the movie on his car stereo. "Behind the strange combination of shyness and creativity," Blinn realized, "he is very, very bright, quite gifted, and quite professional … not always what you find in the rock world." *Dreams* was finally becoming a reality.

While Blinn worked on the script Prince carried on

> "It was about creating a reality that people would respond to." ALBERT MAGNOLI

writing new songs and rehearsing them with a new line-up of The Revolution. Wendy Melvoin came in in place of Dez Dickerson, who had left to pursue his own music career after informing Prince that he was no longer happy with the theatrical direction the music seemed to be heading in.

Another new addition was Alan Leeds. Having joined the Prince entourage as manager of the Triple Threat tour, Leeds was given the job of overseeing the various projects Prince was currently involved in, which now included

much more than just writing and recording music. Prince & The Revolution, The Time, and Vanity 6 were all busy rehearsing in a warehouse in St Louis Park, Minneapolis. They also took acting classes three days per week for three months under the tuition of drama coach Don Amendolins.

Although each musician's movie role would essentially be an extension of his or her own personality, some seemed more cut out for acting than others. Morris Day, Amendolins noted, had "natural abilities" that the others lacked; Vanity was "lazy"; and Prince was "very, very good. He'd flip right out of his persona and be whatever character he had to be." Perhaps surprisingly, he also seemed to take direction better than the rest. An even tougher job fell to choreographer John Command, who had the job of condensing years of dancing training into a few short months.

Everything seemed to be on the up. Prince debuted the now formally named Revolution at Minneapolis's First Avenue, the club that would become the focal point of *Purple Rain*, on August 3 during a benefit concert for the Minneapolis Dance Theater Company, raising $23,000. The show itself was a resounding success, and recordings of it

The Time and Vanity 6, were supposed to be playing his rivals in *Purple Rain*, but as both groups were essentially Prince puppets they were becoming reluctant to cooperate. In April Prince had fired the two main musical talents in The Time, Jimmy Jam and Terry Lewis, after they missed a Triple Threat show because they were stranded in Los Angeles following a recording session with The SOS Band. (Prince was also upset generally that they had begun to produce other artists.) Keyboardist Monte Moir left The Time of his own accord after the sacking, leaving only singer Morris Day – and even he seemed ready to quit as soon as *Purple Rain* was finished.

At least Day was still around to lead a new line-up of the band, for which Prince recruited bassist Jerry Hubbard and keyboardists Paul Peterson and Mark Cardenez. That was more than could be said for Vanity. Depressed about the relationships Prince continued to have with other women, she became addicted to drink and drugs and embarked on affairs of her own. "She was a competitive pistol," according to Alan Leeds, and "wasn't about to let Prince's desire for control sentence her to the confines of her room." Depending on who you believe she was either fired or quit at the end of August, leaving Prince only a few weeks to find somebody else to learn the script and sing to the music he had written for the second Vanity 6 album.

After auditioning close to 1,000 women in Los Angeles and New York, Prince settled on 22-year-old Patricia Kotero. She was practically the mirror image of Vanity, proving that in Prince's world, no one was indispensable. According to Magnoli, she was also "very sweet and tremendously accessible," which to Prince no doubt meant that she was malleable enough to fit the role. She might not have been as talented as Vanity, but certainly had the right look. Prince had little option at this stage but to forge ahead.

Purple Rain began shooting on November 1 1983, which gave the cast a few weeks to try to complete all of the outdoor scenes before the bitter cold of a Minneapolis winter crept in at the end of the month. Not all of them were finished in time, however, so some of the cast and crew were flown out to Los Angeles as indoor shooting continued in Minneapolis. Mo Ostin's four million dollars were beginning to run out, leaving the whole team in desperate need of major financial backing if the project was going to be seen through to the end.

Bob Cavallo and Steve Fargnoli went back to Warner Bros Pictures and this time were able to convince the company of the movie's worth – just as cast and crew were celebrating at the movie's wrap party in Minneapolis at Bloomington's Holiday Inn on December 22. Although a few scenes had to be re-shot in Los Angeles on December 27, post-production on *Purple Rain* could now begin in preparation for the movie's theatrical release.

> "The most interesting thing about Purple Rain *to me was the timeliness of it. It actually captured a musical revolution as it was happening."* JIMMY JAM

made with a mobile truck provided no-fuss backing tracks for 'I Would Die 4 U,' 'Baby I'm A Star,' and 'Purple Rain.' Elsewhere however things had begun to fall apart.

When William Blinn's *Fame* television show was picked up for a third season he decided to quit work on what was now called *Purple Rain*, leaving Minneapolis for good after handing in his first draft on May 23. It took Cavallo, Ruffalo & Fargnoli until September – just two months before shooting was due to commence – before they found a new writer-director. The man in question was Albert Magnoli, who came on the recommendation of director James Foley, but whose previous experience as a director was limited to a 1979 short entitled *Jazz*.

Although Magnoli wasn't interested in rewriting Blinn's script, he had an auspicious first meeting with Prince's management team. "Cavallo asked me what kind of story it would be if I was to make a film with Prince," he recalled. "I just started telling him a story off the top of my head, and in that ten minutes I had outlined the concept of *Purple Rain*." Even more promising was Prince's initial reaction to Magnoli. "We sat down," Magnoli continued, "I pitched him the concept, and the first words out of his mouth were: 'You've only known me for ten minutes, yet you tell me basically my story. How is that possible?'"

Magnoli's arrival might have helped, but the project still refused to run smoothly. Prince's current side-projects,

"*Purple Rain* is the pinnacle of the whole Prince & The Revolution experience." **LISA COLEMAN**

A perfectly orchestrated promotional campaign meant that when *Purple Rain* opened on July 27 1984 it brought in $7.3 million in just three days. It went on to make around $70 million in total, which was reportedly more than ten times the cost of production. According to Albert Magnoli, the movie's excellent opening weekend meant that its distribution needed to be stepped up several gears. Having initially planned to show the film in 200 theaters, Warner Bros now decided to present it on over 900 screens across the USA. Following the word-of-mouth success of the Controversy and Triple Threat tours and the May 1984 single 'When Doves Cry,' the release of the *Purple Rain* soundtrack album raised anticipation for the new movie to fever pitch. The summer of 1984 was set to be Prince's season. Anyone who hadn't yet seen him live clamored to get a look at Prince in action; those who already had were eager to relive the excitement.

In the two decades since its release, the *Purple Rain* movie has become dated on a number of levels. That it helped the define the 80s is without question, but in so perfectly capturing the zeitgeist it also now exemplifies so many of the decade's worst cliches. There's the big hair; the new romantic clothes; the obligatory topless-woman scene, in which the hapless Apollonia is asked if she wants to "purify" herself in Lake Minnetonka; and an awkward scene in which Jerome Benton throws a stereotypically loudmouthed ex-lover of Morris Day's into a dumpster. (When challenged by MTV about the movie's alleged sexism, Prince admitted that "sometimes, for the sake of humor, we may have gone overboard.") Even the editing techniques that once helped tie the visual experience of *Purple Rain* to the fast pace of MTV aren't quite as dazzling as they once were.

As an insight into Prince's psyche, however, *Purple Rain* is indispensable. The Battle Of The Bands trials surrounding rival acts The Revolution, The Time and Apollonia 6 are based on Prince's early days as a struggling musician in Minneapolis, during which time he played in Champagne on the same club circuit as Flyte Time. The scenes work not just as dramatic construct but also as a tribute to Prince's hometown and the people who helped him in his early days.

Most of the characters and musical acts in the film – The Revolution, The Time, Apollonia 6, and even First Avenue club owner Billy Sparks – use their real names, and are essentially extensions of themselves. Prince, however, plays The Kid, a semi-autobiographical construction with an almost magical air. He seems to have the ability to appear and disappear at will, whether on the side streets on his purple motorcycle or in scenes such as the one in which he seems to vanish when Apollonia turns to compliment him on a performance.

In 1996 Prince told Oprah Winfrey that the most autobiographical part of the film was "probably the scene with me looking at my mother, crying." Although Albert Magnoli later suggested that the part where The Kid's father warns him never to get married was based on something Prince once told him, the singer himself seemed adamant, in a 1985 interview with *Rolling Stone*,

that "[the] stuff about my dad was part of Al Magnoli's story. We used parts of my past and present to make the story pop more, but it was a *story*."

Even so, the career of the father in *Purple Rain* – an abusive failed musician named Francis L – seems to echo that of Prince's real father, John L Nelson. Prince has never spoken about exactly what went on behind closed doors in his family. But given that his parents divorced when he was young, and that he then became estranged from his father for lengthy periods (and even made overt references to child abuse on record), it would seem that his was not a particularly happy childhood. That the specter of physical abuse lingers in The Kid's relationship with Apollonia – and that he even envisions his own suicide after his father attempts to take his own life – suggests that Prince was playing out something of an Oedipal nightmare on the big screen.

The *New York Post* review of *Purple Rain* noted that, in The Kid's world, "women are there to be worshipped, beaten, or humiliated." Most other reviews of the movie, however, were content simply to revel in the "affirmation of [Prince's] versatility and substance" (*Miami Herald*); his "taste for androgynous appeal" (*Philadelphia Daily News*); or the fact that the movie "reeks of unadorned sex" (*Detroit Free Press*). Perhaps the lack of armchair psychology in these reviews is a reflection of the two-dimensional nature of the movie, in which Wendy and Lisa are simply the girls of The Revolution; Morris Day – a "full-fledged young comedian" in the eyes of noted critic Pauline Kael – relaxes into a pimp persona; and Apollonia serves as the eye candy.

Albert Magnoli might have tried hard to invest some feeling and motivation into the characters, but what audiences tend to remember about the movie are the performances. *Purple Rain* might not have aged all too well, but the musical segments remain as incredible as they ever were, particularly Prince's, which wring every drop of emotion out of a character that, elsewhere in the movie, seems moody, inarticulate, and self-obsessed.

One interesting aspect of *Purple Rain* is that, although Prince's parents were both black, The Kid's mother is played by Greek actress Olga Kartalos (one of only two professional actors in the movie, the other being Clarence Williams III, who played Francis L). This was in part another example of Prince's efforts to blur the truth of the story, but it might also say something about the light-skinned singer's attempts to appeal to a mixed mass audience. Having tasted mainstream success already with 'Little Red Corvette,' Prince was keen to follow up with something simple and bombastic and cross right right over – just like Bob Seger, whom Prince kept crossing paths with on his 1999 tour. And so Prince wrote 'Purple Rain,' a guitar-led anthem that builds from a simple chordal opening to a huge crescendo with strings, almost five minutes of guitar soloing, and Prince's most impassioned vocal performance to date. The song became an instant lighters-in-the-air classic and helped the accompanying album sell 13 million copies in the USA alone.

The *Purple Rain* soundtrack album still stands as

Some Kinda Lover: Apollonia

With Vanity quitting the *Purple Rain* movie project only a few months before shooting began, Prince and director Albert Magnoli needed to find a replacement as quickly as possible. Hundreds of Vanity clones turned up to the subsequent auditions, but 22-year-old Patricia Kotero stood out from the crowd – partly, as Magnoli recalls, because she turned up in her "baggiest sweats."

"Do you believe in God?" Prince reportedly asked her. "Are you hungry?" Kotero answered "yes" to both and was quickly rechristened Apollonia and given the job of leading Susan Moonsie and Brenda Bennett in the renamed Apollonia 6.

As Prince soon discovered, however, Kotero wasn't the greatest of singers. He soon began to take songs away from the *Apollonia 6* album, either to record himself ('17 Days,' 'Take Me With U'), give to Sheila E. ('The Glamorous Life'), or hold onto until a suitable act came along ('Manic Monday,' which he donated to The Bangles after meeting Susanna Hoffs in 1985).

Kotero found Prince difficult to work with. "There was a side of him that was just a tyrant," she later claimed, noting that he made her keep the fact that she was married secret so that fans might believe they were romantically involved. It was also rumored that Prince demanded she eat and drink only sweets and herbal tea – just like him. "He wanted to make everyone clones of himself," she said. In 2014, Kotero revealed that she almost died during the filing of *Purple Rain*, when, after four takes of the famous scene where she jumps into Lake Minnetonka, she went into hypothermic shock and blacked out.

Prince had lost interest in Apollonia 6 by the time the Purple Rain tour began and so chose to take Sheila E. out as his opening act instead. Apollonia 6 suffered as a result. Released in October 1984, the album only reached Number 62 on the *Billboard* 200, while the first single to be taken from it, 'Sex Shooter,' stalled at number 85. With Apollonia 6 fast fading from memory, Kotero returned to her acting career (she had previously starred in a TV mini-series called *Mystic Warriors*). She released a solo album, *Apollonia*, in 1988.

By the time *Purple Rain*'s 30th anniversary came around, Kotero was one of the few people from that era still in touch with Prince. On July 26 2014, the eve of the album's anniversary, Prince staged an hour-long concert at Paisley Park, and gave her pride of place in the audience, providing her with a chair on stage, right at his side. That year's *Art Official Age* included the song 'This Could Be Us,' inspired by an internet meme that pictured Apollonia riding with Prince on his motorcycle.

Prince's biggest-selling record. After knocking Bruce Springsteen's *Born In The USA* off the top of the *Billboard 200* it remained at Number One for 24 weeks. It served as further evidence, as Bob Cavallo put it, of the fact that Prince was "vitally interested in music, but also in success." Perhaps the most obvious example of Prince's ability to meld creativity with commercially was the leadoff single, the ethereal pop masterpiece 'When Doves Cry.' The opening guitar riff roots the song in rock, but the overlapping vocals, complex drum-machine patterns, and complete lack of bassline came from somewhere else entirely. (It was all too much for Warner Bros, however. According to the vice president of the time, Marylou Badeaux, the label's initial response was: "What kind of fucking record is this, with a bunch of strange sounds?")

"The whole experience was over the top." MATT FINK

The rest of *Purple Rain* served as the best evidence yet of the power of Prince and his arsenal of strange sounds. The opening 'Let's Go Crazy' is perfectly pitched, beginning – as does the movie – with church organ and the words "Dearly beloved, we are gathered here today …" before launching into an uninhibited dance track. Its promises of a mixture of sexual freedom and salvation carry the message that, if you follow Prince, you'll be free to do whatever you chose.

The album also contains one of Prince's most heartbreaking ballads, 'The Beautiful Ones.' Written for Susannah Melvoin, twin sister of guitarist Wendy – whom Prince had met in May 1983, while still in another relationship – it builds around gentle synths and slow drum patterns to the coy question: "If we get married, would that be cool?" Having concluded that you always lose the beautiful ones, Prince lets go for a moment of pure passion, screaming relentlessly to his unrequited love.

The pacing of the album is exemplary, with each of the ballads offset by up-tempo dance tracks. 'The Beautiful Ones' is followed by 'Computer Blue,' a track built out of driving drum loops and dolphin-like squalls of guitar. The emotional intensity builds on 'Darling Nikki,' with its stop-start synths and backwards messages promising that God is coming, and 'When Doves Cry,' before peaking on the final three tracks – 'I Would Die 4 U,' 'Baby I'm A Star,' and 'Purple Rain' – all of which segue into one another, as recorded at the First Avenue benefit show.

While most of *Purple Rain* seemed to replace the crude sexuality of old with a more subtle sensuality, one song in particular landed Prince in hot water. Prince had already written songs about oral sex and incest ('Head' and 'Sister,' both included on *Dirty Mind*), and even declared his intention to "fuck the taste out of your mouth" on *1999*'s 'Let's Pretend We're Married.' But when Tipper Gore (the wife of future US Vice President Al Gore) heard 'Darling Nikki' – in which the "sex fiend" title character "masturbat[es] with a magazine" – playing in her daughter's bedroom she was suitably encouraged to form the Parents' Music Resource Center. Gore's organization led a crusade to clean up popular music, one of the results of which was the introduction of Parental Advisory stickers. It also drew up a list of the 'Filthy Fifteen' – the most offensive records of the time. 'Darling Nikki' headed the list, with the Prince-penned 'Sugar Walls' at Number Two, suggesting that the PMRC had been far too outraged to dig any deeper into Prince's back catalog.

The timing of the record releases leading up to *Purple Rain*'s premiere had been perfectly planned, and so too was the launch of the accompanying tour, which opened two months to the day after the album knocked *Born In The USA* off the top spot on *Billboard*. Those who had seen the movie and bought the album (and, perhaps, some or all of The Time's *Ice Cream Castle*, *Apollonia 6*, and Sheila E.'s *The Glamorous Life*) now had the chance to go to the concert and buy the t-shirt. As New York-based journalist Amy Liden put it, the movie had given mainstream America the chance to "see what this guy was doing on stage." Having done so, many would have been eager to check him out in the flesh.

The Prince live show was now a much bigger production than it had been before. Set designer Roy Bennett took the fireman's pole of the Controversy and Triple Threat shows and added extra balconies, trapdoors, lighting rigs, video screens, and a bathtub that came up from beneath the stage. The tour took in 98 shows in just over six months and meant that Alan Leeds needed to take on an assistant, production coordinator Karen Krattinger (who was ironically the tour manager for The SOS Band, with whom Jimmy Jam and Terry Lewis had been working when they missed their slot on the Triple Threat tour).

Prince himself was also beginning to change in response to his new megastardom. "He just kind of shut himself off," recalled Roy Bennett. "He became a different person at that point. Between Prince and everyone else a wall came up." Alan Leeds's brother Eric joined the tour midway through as a saxophonist and later claimed that the tour was run "like it was the Marines."

Having already begun to use his newfound fame to shut himself off from those around him, Prince also took his biggest tour yet as an opportunity to start to change his image. Maybe he had been stung by Tipper Gore's attacks; maybe he just felt that, with a much bigger fanbase, he should become a more positive arbiter of social mores. Either way, the two-hour shows now incorporated a "conversation with God." But there was still a clear conflict between a Prince who "tried to be good" and an audience that "love it when I'm bad."

For the *Los Angeles Times*, Prince's new "conservative approach sacrificed the challenge and provocation of his earlier performances." But for the most part the Purple Rain shows were Prince's most accomplished yet. After a support from Sheila E., Prince & The Revolution presented two hours of funk-rock, choreographed dance routines, and theatrical set pieces – a show that regularly sold out 20,000-capacity arenas.

The Glamorous Life: Sheila E.

Larry Graham aside, drummer and percussionist Sheila E. is perhaps the only musician Prince worked with who could claim to be better attuned to their instrument than he was. As the daughter of former Santana percussionist Pete Escovedo – and Goddaughter to Tito Puente – it came as little surprise that she followed in her father's footsteps. Having already left school to tour with her dad, she found herself working with bassist Alphonso Johnson in 1976 at the age of 19. Two years later, so the story goes, she met Prince at an Al Jarreau concert. But it wasn't until 1984 that the pair really hit it off.

Prince ran into Escovedo again shortly before the release of *Purple Rain* and immediately began to think of her as a potential replacement for The Time and Apollonia 6 on his upcoming tour. But despite having played over the years with Marvin Gaye, George Duke, and Lionel Richie, Sheila E. wasn't quite ready to front a live band. She did a good enough job, but her performances lacked the pizzazz of The Time. (She did however at least offer rather more depth than Vanity 6.)

Her records were a different story. The first three Sheila E. albums – *The Glamorous Life* (1984), *Romance 1600* (1985), and *Sheila E.* (1987) – seem on the one hand to have been designed to keep Prince prominent in the R&B market, but could often be more rhythmically complex than Prince's other output of the time, and clearly benefited from her exemplary percussion work.

It also soon became clear that Sheila E. would not be just another puppet project. Although her debut album was credited, like all the rest, to the ubiquitous Starr Company, Escovedo claimed that Prince was too busy with *Purple Rain* to have had much to do with it. "He'd call on the phone to see how I was doing," she told Liz Jones, "and on the last day he came to listen to it, but there was no time for him to put any parts on it." This wasn't actually true. Prince's obvious 'guest' vocal on the title track was the first clue to the fact that, as Escovedo's father later revealed to *Rolling Stone*, Prince had actually written and performed every note.

Escovedo was nonetheless an important part of Prince's personal and professional life. She quickly became a rival to Susannah Melvoin for his affections, and would be invited to play percussion at the end of his shows with The Revolution – returning the favor of his frequent guest appearances during her support slots. She also began to ease Bobby Z away from the drum stool in the studio, appearing on such tracks as *Around The World In A Day's* 'Pop Life' and *Parade*'s 'Life Can Be So Nice,' and on some of the *Dream Factory* songs. Prince even let her play on *Lovesexy*, and brought her in for the tours in support of both that album and *Sign "O" The Times*. Even the recently sacked Bobby Z was forced to admit that she was among the world's top-five drummers.

Escovedo left Prince's band in 1990 but carried on making records under her own name. In the years since, she has toured with her father, performed with Ringo's All Starr Band, and played on Beyoncé's 'Work It Out.' She also continued to play with Prince from time to time, notably during his 2006 Brit Awards appearance, and at the three concerts he performed in Minneapolis in July 2007 to publicize the launch of his 3121 fragrance. (Prince returned the favor, playing with Sheila and her family at Harvelles, Redondo Beach, on March 29 2008.) With the E. Family band she has made high-profile television appearances on shows such as *Dancing With The Stars*, while she received an Emmy nomination for her role as musical director of *Fiesta Latina: In*

Performance At The White House. In January 2015, she opened the E Spot Lounge, a live jazz venue in LA.

As well as maintaining her musical career, Escovedo co-founded the Elevate Hope Foundation with former Bride Of Funkenstein Lynn Mabry. On December 13 2003, the foundation put on the Family Jamm in aid of victims of child abuse. Escovedo was joined by numerous Prince alumni, including Carmen Electra, Jill Jones, Eric Leeds, Apollonia, and Matt Fink.

At the time, few would have known just how important the cause was to Sheila. Eleven years later, in her memoir, *The Beat Of My Drum*, she revealed that she had been raped, aged five, by a "distant relative" babysitter. The book sees Escovedo coming to terms with this unfathomably traumatic event, and also contained another revelation: that Prince proposed to her during a concert in the 80s. Though the marriage never took place, they had an unmistakable bond; heartbroken over his death, Sheila immediately started recording a new album, *Girl Meets Boy*, inspired by their time together. She also staged a fitting tribute to Prince at the 2016 BET Awards.

As Prince & The Revolution were fast becoming the biggest band in the world, so Minneapolis was growing into a new role as the epicenter of a cool. The local press had already been writing for some time about a 'Minneapolis sound,' but now the rest of the world was beginning to catch on. Prince reacted to this new level of exposure in his own way. "When the film came out a lot of tourists started coming to First Avenue," he told *Rolling Stone* in 1985. "That was kind of weird, to be in the club and get a lot of, 'Oh! There he is!' I'd be in there thinking, 'Wow, this sure is different than it used to be.'"

The key difference was that, having achieved the fame that he craved, Prince was too big and too famous to enjoy it. In his memoir, *My Time With Prince: Confessions Of A Former Revolutionary*, Dez Dickerson recalls going backstage to see Prince after a show in Washington DC and inviting him on a shopping trip the following day: "At first his eyes got bright, and then, sad, and he answered, 'I can't do stuff like that anymore.' Fame had changed things, and, sometimes, it hurts."

The Revolution

PRINCE FIRST SERVED NOTICE OF THE EXISTENCE OF THIS MOST FAMOUS OF HIS BACKING BANDS ON THE FRONT OF *1999*, ON WHICH THE WORDS "anD thE rEVOLUtioN" ARE PRINTED BACKWARDS WITHIN THE 'I' OF HIS OWN NAME. BUT IT WASN'T UNTIL AUGUST 3 1983 THAT THE GROUP – WHICH WOULD LATER BECOME ALMOST AS FAMOUS AS PRINCE HIMSELF – MADE ITS LIVE DEBUT, AT A BENEFIT FOR THE MINNEAPOLIS DANCE THEATER COMPANY HELD AT THE CITY'S FIRST AVENUE CLUB.

As well as raising $23,000, the show marked the live debut of guitarist Wendy Melvoin alongside longstanding Prince sidemen Bobby Z Rivkin (drums), Matt Fink, and Lisa Coleman (keyboards), and relative newcomer Mark Brown (bass). Such was Prince's faith in this new group, however, that he recorded the entire show, and ended up using three songs from it on *Purple Rain*.

By the time the album came out, The Revolution had become superstars in their own right. They were almost too much of a good thing. Prince had long sought mass appeal, but now that he had achieved it, he found himself criticized for making the white musicians – Melvoin in particular – too much of a focal point, to the detriment of the group's only black player, Mark Brown. He also began to feel threatened by the success of the group, and soon started to cut himself off from them, reminding them that they were *his* band, not part of *the* band. (Conversely, the bandmembers quickly became unhappy with the size of their paychecks, which seemed to bear no relation to the huge sums Prince himself was now earning.)

As much as he might have hated to admit it, Prince needed The Revolution – particularly Melvoin and Coleman. "The more famous he got, the more he relied on us to speak," Melvoin recalled. The group had also coalesced into a potent musical force. Midway through the Purple Rain tour, Prince invited saxophonist Eric Leeds (brother of tour manager Alan) to jam with the band during the encores – the first time that he had allowed brass instruments on stage with him.

Leeds also began to educate Prince about jazz, with which he quickly became enamored. Melvoin and Coleman, meanwhile, had started to introduce him to white pop and rock'n'roll from the 60s and 70s, as well as other more recent music that the singer had missed while locked away in the studio for the past half-decade. Prince's inner circle started to resemble a kind of university clique, trading ideas and inspirations back and forth. He was, Melvoin recalled, "hungry for influences to take him further, so he relied heavily on me and Lisa to guide him in the directions he couldn't think of himself."

The spirit of collaboration continued in the studio. Melvoin and Coleman would hole up with Prince and help him on his way to new musical discoveries on *Around The World In A Day* and *Parade*. "It's true that I record very fast," he told MTV in 1985. "It goes even quicker now that the girls help me."

Live performance, however, was another matter entirely. During the Purple Rain tour, Prince added saxophonist Eric Leeds, drummer Sheila E., and various dancers and backing singers to the Revolution line-up. By the time of the 1986 Ht & Run tour, he had turned the band into what Eric called the "counter-Revolution" bringing in trumpeter Matt 'Atlanta Bliss' Blistan, bodyguards-turned-dancers Wally Salford and Greg Brooks, and ex-Time dancer Jerome Benton, as well as finding a role for his girlfriend, Susannah Melvoin (twin sister of guitarist Wendy).

Few among the original line-up were happy about this turn of events, but for Prince, it all made perfect sense. Having been criticized for courting the white market, he wanted to return to his roots with a larger-scale soul/funk revue in the same vein as George Clinton's P-Funk groups. He was also keen, as always, to make his shows more theatrical. This was simply the live equivalent of his sometime habit of sacrificing subtlety on his later records in favor of building up layer upon layer of overdubs.

Prince made some concessions to The Revolution, such as giving Melvoin a lead vocal on *Parade*'s 'I Wonder U' and even worked with them on a group effort entitled *Dream Factory*, but the tensions continued to rise. "Prince is an entertainer," Wendy Melvoin later recalled. "He wanted more entertainment, and Lisa and I wanted less." In July 1986 Melvoin, Coleman, and Mark Brown all threatened to quit before the Hit & Run tour kicked off, but all three were convinced to ride it out.

By the end of the tour, however, Prince himself had had enough. He had started to argue with Melvoin and Coleman regularly during the *Dream Factory* sessions, partly because of the fact that his relationship with Susannah Melvoin was in disarray. On the final night of the tour – September 6 1986 at Yokohama Stadium, Japan – Prince smashed up all of his guitars after a final encore of 'Sometimes It Snows In April.'

Prince had never done anything like it before. Perhaps unsurprisingly, it marked the end of his association with The Revolution. In early October, he invited Melvoin and

Prince with The Revolution's Wendy Melvoin in Purple Rain.

Coleman to dinner at his rented Beverly Hills home and fired them both. He then called Bobby Z to tell him that he was going to be replaced by Sheila E., with whom Prince had been working in the studio for several years already. Matt Fink opted to stay on, but Mark Brown quit, partly out of loyalty to the others but also because he was unhappy at Prince's decision to return to making funk-based music.

As far as Prince was concerned, they all "needed to play a wide range of music with different types of people" so that they could "come back eight times as strong." Others around him were less than convinced. Having hit what looked like a creative peak with The Revolution during the *Dream Factory* sessions, he now seemed to want to go back to where he had been several years ago – that is, recording everything on his own.

Melvoin and Coleman were left further embittered by what they saw as a lack of credit on *Sign "O" The Times*, which features re-recorded versions of tracks from the *Dream Factory* sessions. The pair did nonetheless go on to establish themselves as session players, and as a duo in their own right (as Wendy & Lisa). They have also composed a number of movie soundtracks together, including *Dangerous Minds* and *Toys*.

Prince made intermittent contact with the duo during the 90s, but neither of the collaborative projects that he suggested came to fruition. Having initially invited them both to play on a song entitled 'In This Bed Eye Scream,' he eventually decided it would be better just to dedicate it to them. He then toyed with the idea of making a new Revolution album based at least in part around older

recordings, to be called *Roundhouse Garden*, but that never made it beyond the planning stage either. Asked why not, Prince told fans at a Q&A session to "ask Wendy and Lisa," fuelling rumors that, having recently become a Jehovah's Witness, he would not work with them unless they publicly renounced their homosexuality.

It took until the early 21st century for the trio to patch things up. Prince and Wendy Melvoin played together as a duo on the *Tavis Smiley Show* in February 2004 in support of *Musicology*. Then, on February 15 2006, both Melvoin and Coleman joined Prince for his show-stopping appearance at the Brit Awards. The duo also appear on two tracks on his 2007 *Planet Earth* LP, 'The One U Wanna C' and 'Lion Of Judah.'

In 2011, drummer Bobby Z. suffered a heart attack. The following February, The Revolution reunited to perform a concert at First Avenue, raising money for the American Heart Association. Prince did not join them, but for guitarist Dez Dickerson the event was "an opportunity [for fans] to have a moment with us sans the icon." In the days following Prince's death, the group announced that they were reuniting once more.

Though Prince himself consistently refused to get the band back together ("for what?" he asked in 2015), during the Piano & A Microphone Gala Event at Paisley Park, on January 21 2016, he took time out to show his "love and appreciation" for Wendy and Lisa, recalling that the latter had written the distinctive harpsichord motif that became 'Raspberry Beret.' With clear admiration, he told the audience, "That's the whole song, right?"

AS THE PURPLE RAIN TOUR DREW TO A CLOSE, EVERYONE EXCEPT PRINCE SEEMED CONFUSED AS TO WHAT WOULD HAPPEN NEXT. SOME MEMBERS OF THE REVOLUTION WERE SURPRISED THAT HE HADN'T OPTED TO MILK THE ALBUM AND MOVIE FOR ALL THEY WERE WORTH, BUT PRINCE HAD BEEN UNWILLING TO SIGN UP FOR ANYTHING BEYOND A SIX-MONTH TOUR OF THE USA, WHICH MEANT THAT NO ONE ELSE GOT TO EXPERIENCE THE PHENOMENAL LIVE SHOW UNTIL THE VHS RELEASE OF *PRINCE & THE REVOLUTION: LIVE*.

Around The World In A Day

(FEBRUARY 1984–APRIL 1985)

Worse news was to follow on April 2 1985 when Prince's manager, Steve Fargnoli, announced the singer's plan to retire from live performance completely following the completion of the tour. "I'm going to look for the ladder," Prince had reportedly told Fargnoli by way of explanation. "Sometimes it snows in April." A decade later, Prince gave a less cryptic explanation to *Icon* magazine: "I was doing the 75th Purple Rain show, doing the same thing over and over – for the same kids who [now] go to Spice Girls shows. And I just lost it. They put the guitar on me and it hit me in the eye and cut me and blood started going down my shirt, and I said, 'I have to go on stage.'"

There were suggestions from outside the Prince camp that the singer's personality had been adversely affected by the success of *Purple Rain*. The Time's guitarist Jesse Johnson would later claim that Prince was "such an asshole" that he "had to change my phone number to stop him calling me. He'd just say, 'Jesse, your album sucks,' and hang up." (A year later, having heard that Johnson's second solo album, *Shockadelica*, didn't actually contain a song by that name, Prince recorded one himself in an effort to 'prove' his idea that every great album title needed a great song to back it up. He then had his own 'Shockadelica' pressed up for club play in advance of the release of Johnson's album, which subsequently made it look like Johnson had stolen the idea from him, rather than the other way around.)

To others however it seemed that Prince was finally starting to get on better with people. During the Purple Rain tour he had begun to take influence from the jazz records played to him by new Revolution saxophonist Eric Leeds, and also the 60s and 70s acts Wendy Melvoin and Lisa Coleman grew up with. As Alan Leeds put it, the three of them "made it their own project [to turn] Prince onto different kinds of music. He had a very genuine interest in expanding his musical curiosity."

Their influence fed into a newly collaborative way of working as Prince started to invite members of The Revolution – particularly Melvoin and Coleman – into the studio with him as he recorded the follow-up to *Purple Rain*. The catalyst for this was in fact a song that that

We Are The World

Since releasing his debut album in 1979, Prince seemed barely to have put a foot wrong as far as music critics were concerned. Each record he made was another bold step in an artistic career trajectory, with *Purple Rain* marking his artistic and commercial peak. But having made six albums in seven years under his own name (and plenty more for The Time, Vanity 6, Apollonia 6, and Sheila E.), it was inevitable that there would be some kind of backlash – and that Prince would play a large part in engendering it himself.

On January 28 1985 Prince performed 'Purple Rain' and won in three categories at the American Music Awards – Favorite Album in both the Black and Pop fields, and Favorite Single for 'When Doves Cry.' If the assembled audience of contemporary stars and living legends didn't already think him slightly strange, more than a few eyebrows would have been raised by the fact that he was accompanied by bodyguard Chick Huntsberry each time he went up to get an award.

After the show 45 of America's most prominent musical acts of the time had been asked to go and take part in the recording of 'We Are The World,' a song written by Michael Jackson and Lionel Richie and scored and arranged by Quincy Jones in aid of USA For Africa, a charity set up to raise money for famine relief in Ethiopia. Prince was among the artists invited to the session, along with Bob Dylan, Bruce Springsteen, Huey Lewis, Stevie Wonder, Diana Ross, Tina Turner – the kind of mix of rock and soul that Prince himself had helped bring together a few years earlier.

But while the tape rolled, Prince was having dinner at a Mexican Restaurant on Sunset Boulevard. A piece of paper with his name on it might have been taped to the floor next to Michael Jackson's, but he never turned up to sing. Prince felt he had a perfectly good explanation for this. "We had talked to the people that were doing [it]," he told *Rolling Stone* a few months later, "and they said it was cool that I gave them a song for the album." This, he said, was the best thing for all concerned: "I'm strongest in a situation where I'm surrounded by people I know … [but] I probably would have just clammed up with so many great people in the room."

That might well have been true. Bob Dylan later recalled that he felt so uncomfortable that he had to be guided through the recording by Stevie Wonder. But Dylan still turned up. Prince's 'explanation' served only to fuel rumors that he was selfish egoist. It didn't help that, after leaving the Mexican restaurant at 2am, Prince had a paparazzi photographer forcefully ejected from his limo by a bodyguard. All of a sudden, he had gone from being the hero of the Awards night to the villain of the piece – the man who cared nothing for charity, and would be prepared to let his bodyguards loose on anyone who dared try to get close to him.

In his defense, Prince had indeed agreed to donate a song of his own to the USA For Africa album. He spent February 2 recording it with Wendy Melvoin and Lisa Coleman at New Orleans's Superdome during a break in the Purple Rain tour. But as much as the resulting '4 The Tears In Your Eyes' might have been a beautiful ballad about striving to maintain hope and faith in a dire situation, it was too little too late. Whatever good Prince might have done, it was overshadowed by his no-show, and his apparently mean-spirited behavior.

Prince gave his side of the story in 'Hello,' the B-side – rather aptly – to his 'Pop Life' single, which addresses the (mostly negative) effects of fame. Bemoaning the press's treatment of him, he sought also to remind his critics of his past charitable work: "We're against hungry children / Our records stands tall / There's just as much hunger here at home." Or, as he told *Rolling Stone*, paraphrasing 'Hello''s lyrics: "We'll do everything we can, but y'all got to understand that a flower that has water will grow, and the man misunderstood will go."

Coleman's brother David had recorded in a three-day session at Sunset Sound in June 1984 that Prince paid for as a birthday present – an act of kindness that seems to be rather at odds with Jesse Johnson's opinion of him. (In a similar moment of benevolence, Prince reportedly gave his father a co-writing credit on his forthcoming album's 'The Ladder' just so that he could earn some money from the royalties.) David Coleman used those three days to record a demo tape with Wendy Melvoin's brother, Jonathan, which they promptly gave to their sisters. "There was song on it called 'Around The World In A Day,'" Lisa Coleman recalled. "Wendy and I flipped, and played it to Prince. There were a lot of different types of instruments on it, interesting sounds – Arabic music, the oud, cello, finger cymbals, darbuka."

Inspired by this wide sonic palette, Prince re-recorded the song, with David Coleman's input and blessing, as the title track for his new album. He was so enthusiastic about it, in fact, that he started work on the new project straightaway, despite the fact that he was midway through recording a second solo album for Sheila E. Whenever he had a break from touring he would stop off at any available studio to work on the record – or, failing that, use a mobile recording unit. By the early hours of Christmas Day 1984, Prince had recorded and mixed the entire album, having put down vocals for the closing track, 'Temptation,' with engineer Susan Rogers during the final session.

On February 21 1985, with the end of the Purple Rain tour still two months away, Prince played *Around The World In A Day* to executives in Warner Bros' Los Angeles office. The quick turnaround was a shock to the label, which hadn't expected a follow-up to *Purple Rain* so soon. According to a report in *Rolling Stone* magazine in April, the label received a phone call late that afternoon to say

The Beautiful One: Susannah Melvoin

When Prince hired Wendy Melvoin to replace Dez Dickerson in 1983, he had no idea it would lead to one of the most intense relationships of his life, but that's exactly what happened. Shortly after hiring Melvoin in May 1983 he met her sister, Susannah. The pair were instantly attracted to each other, and it wasn't long before she had split up with her boyfriend of the time and moved from California to Minneapolis to be near Prince. She quickly took pride of place among Prince's girlfriends of the time, driving Vanity away and pushing Jill Jones into the background.

Coming from the same stock as her sister Wendy, it's no surprise that Susannah had an affinity for music. She quickly began to introduce Prince to new influences in literature, art, and music, and would soon be working in the studio with him as one of two singers in The Family – a band some felt Prince had formed just so that he could keep her near. She also added backing vocals to *Parade*, joined the ever-expanding line-up of The Revolution for a time, designed the *Dream Factory* jacket, and – unlike the rest of The Revolution – even

received a credit on *Sign "O" The Times*. Such was Prince's devotion to Susannah that he even planned to give her the lead female role in *Under The Cherry Moon*. There were even suggestions that he had proposed to her shortly before they flew out to Paris together in August 1985 to begin pre-production. When it became clear that she couldn't act, however, Prince sent her home, replacing her with Kristin Scott-Thomas (with whom he then allegedly had an affair).

Despite behaving, on the one hand, like a committed monogamist, Prince continued to flaunt his affairs. This made life difficult not just for Susannah but also for her sister and Lisa Coleman. Whenever Prince upset her, she would confide in Wendy, who in turn would talk to Coleman – which made it almost impossible for them all to work together. "It was hard," Coleman told Prince biographer Liz Jones. "We couldn't take sides. Prince was trying to draw the lines all the time." Such is Prince's hold over his girlfriends that Susannah stuck it out until December 1986, and even then moved only to a nearby apartment.

Prince, it seems, just didn't know how lucky he was at the time. Susannah inspired some of his greatest ballads, including 'The

Beautiful Ones' and 'Nothing Compares 2 U,' and had a profound impact on *Sign "O" The Times*. His obsession with her is writ large on a song once slated for *Dream Factory*, 'Big Tall Wall,' on which he declares his intention to build said wall around his lover "so U can't get out," and confirmed by the dark themes of much of the material he wrote during and immediately after the break-up of their relationship.

That Prince never fully let go of her became clear in a 1997 web-chat with AOL. Despite usually being so deft at avoiding anything approaching a personal revelation, he gave a simple, honest response to the question of who had inspired 'Forever In My Life' (despite being married to Mayte at the time): "Susannah. She knows." It seems fitting, then, that the song most directly inspired by her has never been heard by anyone other than Prince and his engineer, Susan Rogers.

Shortly after Susannah finally left him for good, Prince recorded a song called 'Wally,' in which he reportedly confided his deepest thoughts about her to his bodyguard and dancer, Wally Safford. Prince erased the song once, before recording it again for posterity but never releasing it.

that its biggest star would be there in 45 minutes. Prince arrived in a limo, dressed in a purple kimono, holding a single rose, flanked by his father, bodyguards, management, and Wendy Melvoin. He led around 150 executives to a fourth-floor conference room, played them the album – barely speaking, except in a low whisper to Mo Ostin – and then left as suddenly as he had arrived. One employee present subsequently told *Rolling Stone*: "Everyone sort of stood up and applauded after the record was over, and then he wasn't there anymore."

The record blindsided Warner Bros just as it would the public when it was released on April 22, a mere two weeks

videos, and not even any adverts in magazines. Prince seemed adamant that only 'real fans' find out about the album, which should be seen as the work of a creative artist and not just another commercial product.

"I had a sort of F-you attitude," Prince told The Electrifying Mojo, a Detroit-based DJ, on June 6 (the day before he turned 27). "I was making something for myself and my fans, and the people who supported me through the years." For some in the Prince camp, this seemed like a serious misstep, but the singer himself was anxious not to be pidgeonholed. "I saw kids coming to concerts who screamed just because that's where the audience screamed in the movie," he explained to *Entertainment Weekly* in 1999. "I wanted to totally change that."

This might well have been the case, but most critics were left unconvinced by the album's surface-level psychedelic sheen, particularly when it came to the Eastern-sounding title track or the Beatles-esque escapism of 'Paisley Park.' These criticisms weren't entirely

> 🎵 *"I think the smartest thing I ever did was record Around The World In A Day right after I finished Purple Rain."* PRINCE

after the completion of the Purple Rain tour. The label wanted *Purple Rain 2*, but what Prince gave them seemed to sound more like a late-60s psychedelic album. If that wasn't enough, *Around The World In A Day* came with an insistence that there would be no singles, no promotional

accurate – Prince certainly hadn't abandoned his old sound quite as dramatically as some reviewers suggested – but then nor was the singer's claim in an interview with MTV around the time of the album's release that "*Around The World In A Day* is a funky album."

"I felt it was a mistake, timing-wise, to put something else out so soon after Purple Rain." MATT FINK

There are however hints of almost everything that came before it on *Around The World In A Day*. The utopian themes of 'Uptown' resurface on 'Paisley Park,' which Prince told *Rolling Stone* was his attempt "to say something about looking inside oneself to find perfection." Elsewhere, there are the usual extended sexual metaphors ('Raspberry Beret' and 'Tambourine,' a barely disguised tribute to masturbation); heart-wrenching ballads ('Condition Of The Heart'); strident, rock-based patriotism ('America'); plus the usual battle between religious fulfillment (the gospel ballad 'The Ladder') and sexual obsession ('Temptation,' a close relative of 'Darling Nikki,' complete this time with a conversation with God).

All in all, it was pretty much standard Prince fare – or as close as you might get to such a thing. But coming so soon after *Purple Rain*, it was also something of an eye-opener. If the previous album's 'Darling Nikki' was, as Prince later suggested, "the coldest song ever written," then 'Paisley Park' is about as warm an invitation as you might reasonably expect to come in, sit down, and relax.

"If there was a theme to *Around The World In A Day*," Alan Leeds recalled, "[it] was that it was the anti-*Purple Rain* record." This, it seems, was the only thing critics could settle on. Whether it was any good or not was a

different matter. The *New York Times* was impressed, having decided that Prince was "asking, perhaps demanding, to be taken seriously." For the *New Musical Express*, however, it was one creative leap too far. "Prince's position is presently unassailable," it claimed, "[but] contrary to his own high self-regard, this does not make him infallible."

> *"I think he really had fears of being typecast as Mr Purple Rain. He was so sick of that music and that whole concept."* ALAN LEEDS

The only other thing reviewers could agree on was the album's somewhat superficial debt to psychedelia, notably The Beatles. For *The New York Times*, the album "might more accurately have been titled *Around Great 60s Rock In A Day*", while the *Detroit Press* noted that "The Beatles, and John Lennon in particular, bear heavily on 'Paisley Park' ('Penny Lane') and 'The Ladder' (an 'Instant Karma' for the 80s)." For *Newsweek*, the album seemed like "an eerie attempt to recapture the utopian whimsy that characterized The Beatles' *Sgt Pepper*."

Prince of course disputed this. "The influence wasn't The Beatles," he told *Rolling Stone*. "They were great for what they did, but I don't know how that would hang today." He made a point too of defending his decision not to make *Purple Rain 2*: "You know how easy it would have been to open *Around The World In A Day* with the guitar solo that's on the end of 'Let's Go Crazy,' just put it in a different key? That would have shut everybody up who said that album wasn't half as powerful. I don't *want* to make an album like the earlier ones. Wouldn't it be cool to put your albums back-to-back and not get bored?"

To his credit, much of the album's power came from subtle textures rather than rock-star posturing. But criticism seemed unavoidable this time around, even when it came to the artwork, which many took to be a rather too obvious reference to The Beatles' *Yellow Submarine*. "The cover art came about because I thought people were tired of looking at me," he explained to *Rolling Stone*. What he was going for this time, he said, was something "a little more happening than just another picture ... some way I could materialize in people's cribs when they play the record." Rather tellingly, however, the gatefold jacket includes a drawing of Prince, holding his 'cloud guitar' and dressed in the cloud-covered suit he wore in the 'Raspberry Beret' promo video. The cartoon Prince looks considerably older than his real-life counterpart did at the time, as if to suggest that his recent ascent to superstardom had had quite the aging effect.

Despite the muted critical response and deliberate lack of promotion, *Around The World In A Day* still peaked at Number One on *Billboard*, ironically knocking the *We Are The World* album off the top spot. But while *Purple Rain* had clung onto the top spot for 24 weeks, its successor only hung on for three, by which time its creator's confidence seemed to be faltering. Relaxing his earlier standpoint, he rush-released 'Raspberry Beret' as a single,

shot a promo video for it, and gave his first interview for two years to *Rolling Stone*.

For the most part, however, Prince seemed too busy to let the response to *Around The World In A Day* bother him, noting that it had been bought by "the same three million" people who bought *1999*. "It's important to me that those people believe in what we're trying to say," he said, "as opposed to just digging it because it's a hit."

Even before the album was released, Prince was well on the way to making the follow-up, *Parade*. He might not have ended 1985 as the most bankable pop-star of the year, but was still the most creative, and still had enough credit in the bank that his carte blanche would not yet be revoked. If nothing else, *Around The World In A Day* put him on the path toward what he considered to be the ultimate artistic expression. Although some of his critics didn't like what he was doing, he retained a level of respect as he forged on, bucking ever more against the conventional wisdom about what a commercially successful musician should do.

Keeping It In The Family

After The Time disintegrated is 1984, Prince was left for a short time without a full-band side-project to work with. But while Morris Day and Jesse Johnson embarked on their solo careers, Prince pulled the remains of The Time back together to form The Family. Keyboardist Paul Peterson was given the task of fronting the new group, with Prince's girlfriend of the time, Susannah Melvoin, taking the role of co-vocalist. Jerome Benton carried on as dancer/comic foil, with Jellybean Johnson on drums. They were joined by Miko Weaver, who also played guitar with Sheila E., but here seemed to be more of a nominal presence than a fully-fledged group member.

Prince began work on *The Family* during the summer of 1984 in much the same way as he had The Time's albums: writing all of the songs, playing all of the instruments (except for saxophone and strings), and laying down guide vocals for Peterson – now known as St Paul – to follow. Unlike Morris Day, however, Peterson was clearly a sideman, not a frontman, and struggled to keep up with the recordings. As Susannah recalled three decades later, Prince wrote the songs "literally within days" before they were recorded: it was all coming out of him "in such an immediate way."

Leaving aside the quality of the material, *The Family* just didn't have the drive of The Time – and nor did it have Prince's total commitment. It was released on his Paisley Park label in August 1985 while the singer himself was busy shooting *Under The Cherry*

Moon. He had little interest in promoting the album, so simply left it to Warner Bros. Peterson then left the group after just one concert at First Avenue, citing a lack of creative input; the remaining members of The Family found their way into the ever-evolving line-up of The Revolution.

Ultimately it seems that forming The Family was just Prince's way of keeping Susannah Melvoin by his side for as long as possible. The album artwork makes plain his infatuation with her. She dominates the main jacket artwork (by *Vogue* photographer Horst P Horst), and features in several interior snaps taken by Prince himself.

Just as importantly, however, The Family gave him an outlet for his first tentative experiments with both live saxophone (played by Eric Leeds) and string arrangements by Clare Fischer. Both of these elements would be more fully developed on *Parade*, but for now just meant that *The Family* was jazzier and less accessible than anything The Time had done.

The Family also released a single, 'The Screams Of Passion,' but the group's most lasting legacy came with their recording of the original version of 'Nothing Compares 2 U,' as famously covered by Irish singer Sinead O'Connor. Prince had nothing to do with O'Connor's rendition, however, and in fact – if she is to be believed – later had a fiery meeting with her. "Prince started to give out to me for swearing in interviews," O'Connor told *The Mirror* newspaper in 2007. "When I told him to go fuck himself he got very upset and became quite threatening ... A few

blows were exchanged. All I could do was spit. I spat on him quite a bit."

O'Connor's comments (to which Prince never responded) coincided not only with Prince's 21 Nights In London residency but also The Family's announcement that they were to return to music. They released a new album, *Gaslight*, in 2011, though they were forced to rename themselves fDeluxe after their former boss refused to let them use their original name. Peterson saw it as a blessing in disguise: "It's a brand new band that we feel made us move forward." Susannah Melvoin agreed: "We are a live band that can blow everybody off the stage. Thirty years ago, we were a pop band."

The reunion proved fruitful. Not only has fDeluxe become a successful live draw, they have released more music than they did during their initial incarnation, including, on May 4 2016, at 5:07pm Central Time – seven hours and thirteen days since Prince was pronounced dead – a brand new version of 'Nothing Compares 2 U.'

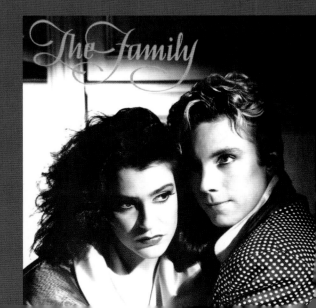

WITH *PURPLE RAIN*, PRINCE HAD SHOWN HIMSELF TO BE JUST AS CAPABLE OF MAKING HIT MOVIES AS HIT RECORDS. FOR THE FOLLOW-UP, HOWEVER, HE WAS KEEN TO PRODUCE A MORE SERIOUS, ARTISTIC AFFAIR – SOMETHING THAT PROVED HIM TO BE MORE THAN JUST A FLASH-IN-THE-PAN POP STAR WHO HAD MADE A LUCKY BREAK ONTO THE BIG SCREEN.

Parade (APRIL 1985–SEPTEMBER 1986)

"I'm hoping that everyone understands where I was trying to go with it," Prince told Detroit DJ The Electrifying Mojo in 1985. "There's a message behind it all and I hope people think about it when they leave. That's the main thing."

Given the huge success of *Purple Rain*, Warner Bros seemed happy to stump up ten million dollars to produce the follow-up. Prince and Steve Fargnoli hired screenwriter Becky Johnson to come up with a draft script, which was based on an idea the singer had had about playing a bar-room pianist-cum-gigolo who falls in love with an heiress in the Côte d'Azur (a concept he planted the seeds for on *Around The World In A Day*'s 'Condition Of The Heart').

Setting it in the South of France was important to Prince, who had developed a taste for travel after years of never leaving North America. In June 1985 he and Steve Fargnoli went looking for shooting locations, following much the same MO as had The Beatles for *Help!*: find a place you've not visited before and make a movie there.

Having settled on Nice – hardly the cheapest place to make a movie – Prince and Fargnoli returned to Minneapolis to work out the details of the shoot. By then Prince had decided that he wanted to shoot the movie in black-and-white – a risky business, since most popular movies of the time were bright and brash. (Black-and-white movies wouldn't become commercially viable until Steven Spielberg made *Schindler's List* in 1993.)

Prince should have been making a bright, poppy movie held together by a string of live musical performances. Instead, *Under The Cherry Moon* was inspired by black-and-white comedies from the 20s, 30s, and 40s, and included just two musical sequences – one of them over the end credits. Prince was keen to show his serious side, but since much of the praise for *Purple Rain* had been for the musical segments, this didn't seem like the greatest of ideas. Both label and management team started to object. "We had a whole different plan, a whole different screenplay," manager Bob Cavallo later recalled. "We had secret writers writing on it and all that, but he wouldn't [do it]."

Warner Bros did at least manage to convince Prince to shoot in color first, and convert to black-and-white later – presumably in the hope that he would change his mind in

due course and stick with color. In an effort, once again, to give *Under The Cherry Moon* some artistic weight, Prince asked the French photographer Jean Baptise Mondino to direct it, but Mondino was too busy. (He would later photograph Prince for *Lovesexy*, and direct his 'I Wish U Heaven' promo.) Instead he brought in a German cinematographer, Michael Ballhaus, as lighting and photography director, and gave the job of directing to Mary Lambert. Like *Purple Rain* director Albert Magnoli, Lambert had no major experience of moviemaking, but had recently shot stylish promo videos for Madonna's 'Like A Virgin' and 'Material Girl,' which suggested that she might be able to make a movie for the MTV generation.

Casting wasn't particularly straightforward either. Since this was no rock'n'roll movie, Prince was keen to avoid using The Revolution, but wanted his girlfriend of the time, Susannah Melvoin, to play Mary Sharon, the heiress with whom Prince's Christopher Tracy falls in love. But Melvoin was far too inexperienced – particularly given that the cast already included another novice actress, Emmanuelle Sallet – so the part went instead to Kristin Scott-Thomas, who had initially only read for a much smaller role. Jerome Benton, Morris Day's old sidekick in The Time, was given the role of Tracy's friend Tricky in an attempt to re-create *Purple Rain*'s much praised comedy-duo element.

After a quick rewrite of the script, shooting began on September 16 in Victorine Studios, Nice, and on the

French Riviera itself. "The preparation and filming of *Under The Cherry Moon* was an exciting time in the Prince camp," Alan Leeds recalled. "That we spent three months in the South of France didn't hurt." That might well have been true, but the project quickly ran into trouble. Prince had moved out to France with Susannah Melvoin in August, having reportedly proposed to her, but soon decided that a movie set was no time for monogamy, so quickly sent her home again.

Mary Lambert was the next to go, having already been demoted to an 'advisory' role just four days into shooting. Having previously spoken positively of working with someone who "knows what he wants," Lambert issued a statement to confirm that she was leaving "under totally amicable circumstances," noting that "Prince has such a

"I don't regret anything about Under The Cherry Moon. I learned that I can't direct what I didn't write." PRINCE

strong vision of what this movie should be ... that it makes no sense for me to stand between him and the film anymore." Lambert was followed by the actor Terence Stamp, who had been due to play Kristin Scott-Thomas's father, but left because of 'timetable clashes.' He was replaced by Steven Berkoff.

Prince as Christopher Tracy in *Under The Cherry Moon*, with Kristin Scott Thomas (inset) as Mary Sharon

What's Mine Ain't Yours

When Prince was at his songwriting peak, he seemed able to write for anybody. Even if he hadn't masterminded a group's sound and image, he could still provide them with hits. Perhaps the finest example of this is 'Manic Monday,' a track left over from the Apollonia 6 album that subsequently became The Bangles' biggest hit. But while all of this was certainly impressive, Prince's cavalier attitude almost ended up causing him to miss out on one of the biggest hits of his career.

During a break from touring with The Revolution, bassist Mark Brown started playing with another group on the Minneapolis club scene, Mazarati. Not wanting to end up the same way as Jimmy Jam and Terry Lewis, he wore a mask on stage and called himself The Shadow. After a while however Brown knew that he would

have to come clean to Prince or face serious consequences. But when he did, Prince surprised him by deciding to take Mazarati under his wing.

Prince was too busy to produce the group himself, but by the time Mark Brown and David Rivkin started work on the group's eponymous debut in LA's Sunset Sound – where Prince was recording *Parade* – he had already donated one song to the project, '100 MPH.' As the sessions continued, Prince offered them another unused track, a bluesy, acoustic tune called 'Kiss.'

Rivkin and Brown sat up all night wondering what to do with the song before opting to give it a strident funk backing. When Prince returned to Sunset Sound the following day and heard it, he quickly changed his mind about the song's worth. "It's too good for you guys," he told them, "I'm taking it back." Prince had originally

suggested that he would reward Rivkin for his efforts by giving him a co-production credit, but eventually listed him only as the song's arranger – even though the main elements of the song originiated from Rivkin and Brown's version of it.

Before long Prince had completed the minimal final version of 'Kiss,' stripping away a lot of the detail Rivkin and Brown had added to it, and chose it to be the first single from his forthcoming LP, *Parade*. Warner Bros felt that it sounded like a demo, but Prince was determined to release it without any changes.

And he was right to: 'Kiss' would become his first transatlantic Number One hit since 'Let's Go Crazy.' The other song he had written for Mazarati, meanwhile, fared rather less well. '100 MPH' stalled at Number 19 on the R&B chart, and didn't even register on the Hot 100.

Prince soon found himself stuck directing the movie and working with a European crew that spoke limited English. He shot the movie quickly, often happy to go with the first take. The whole thing was done by November 21, two months after the shoot began. A day later Prince shot the promo video for 'Girls & Boys' with The Revolution, before returning to Minneapolis. A few extra scenes were shot in April 1986, by which time he had almost completed editing the rest. As far as Prince was concerned, he had taken to moviemaking as easily as he had to recordmaking. "There's no difference [between the two]," he told The Electrifying Mojo. "People have tried to tell me [that] a movie is a little bit more complex, but to me it's just a larger version of an album."

Under The Cherry Moon received its world premiere on July 1 1986 in the less-than-glamorous location of Sheridan, Wyoming as a result of an MTV competition in which the 10,000th caller to a special hotline had the event staged in his or her hometown. The winner was a 22-year-old hotel chambermaid, Lisa Barber, who had also won the right to be escorted to the screening (at the Centennial Theater) by the leading man, who sat with her throughout. After the movie Prince & The Revolution performed at the local Holiday Inn – the only local venue big enough to stage a concert.

The fact that a publicity stunt such as this was employed spoke volumes about how the movie was expected to perform. Had this been another *Purple Rain* it would almost certainly have opened in Los Angeles to hordes of screaming fans. Instead it was shown in a town best known, according to

one local resident, for its fishing lures. "We don't care about no boy who wears tight pants and struts around like a woman," he told *People Weekly*.

The media's response to *Under The Cherry Moon* was similarly harsh. "Don't even turn up on the same continent where this is playing," *USA Today* warned, while Glenn Lovell of the *San Jose Mercury News* described Prince's performance as the most "outrageous, unmitigated display of narcissism" since Barbra Streisand in *A Star Is Born*. The movie's storyline – gigolo falls in love, gives up his lifestyle for the woman he loves, but ends up getting assassinated by her father – just wasn't very appealing. It didn't help that Prince gave himself one of the most self-indulgent death scenes ever – perhaps fittingly, given that the *New York Times* would call his character "a self-caressing twerp of dubious provenance."

Prince fans still had plenty to latch onto, however, as they watched him act coy, funny, and cute for the camera. "That film went through many drafts," he said in an AOL web chat in 1997, admitting that "much was lost in the

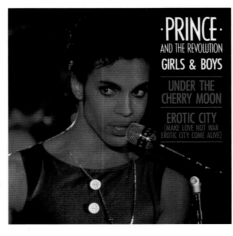

shuffle," but claiming that there are still "some very funny scenes." But while some moments, such as when Prince's Christopher Tracy mocks Scott-Thomas's Mary Sharon for being unable to pronounce the word 'wreckastow' (a slangy pronunciation of 'record store'), are still fondly remembered by fans, there's little for anyone else to savor. Warner Bros had reportedly wanted a greater sense of conflict in the script, but Prince himself mistakenly felt that the 'atmosphere and music' would be enough to keep audiences entertained.

The *Philadelphia Daily News* summed the movie up perfectly: *"Purple Rain is a psychological/autobiographical glorified rock video starring Prince & The Revolution, while this new one … is a movie starring Prince." Under The Cherry Moon* ended up winning eight Golden Raspberry Awards, losing out only in the category of Worst Actress – won by Madonna for her role in *Shanghai Surprise*.

Thankfully, this first major artistic misstep of Prince's

career could be overlooked to some extent in favor of its soundtrack album. *Parade* is another relatively collaborative album in the *Around The World In A Day* mold. This time, however, Prince shifted the focus from 60s rock'n'roll to jazz, as introduced to him by saxophonist Eric Leeds. *Parade* is also notable for being the album on which Prince returned to live drums in favor of the programmed patterns of the Linn LM-1, and finally assented to using real horns in place of synthesized ones. It is also the first Prince album to feature string arrangements by Clare Fischer, who would go on to add color and character to some of his greatest works.

Fischer had previously worked with Rufus, the group that launched Chaka Khan. He was subsequently brought in by David Rivkin to add strings to Prince's latest side project, The Family. After hearing his contribution to tracks such as 'Christopher Tracy's Parade,' the superstitious Prince decided they were so perfect that he never wanted to meet Fischer face-to-face for fear of breaking the magic on future recordings. (They have still never met.)

The collaboration with Fischer established the method by which Prince now preferred to work: "sending tapes back and forth, and just being interested enough hearing what he would do left to his own devices," as Alan Leeds put it. Between April and December 1985, Prince worked on most of the basic tracks for *Parade* on his own, but

Prince attends the world premier of *Under The Cherry Moon* with MTV competition winner Lisa Barber.
Morris Day's old sidekick Jerome Benton as Tricky in *Under The Cherry Moon*.

would send them to Lisa Coleman and Wendy Melvoin for augmentation. He found this to be the most comfortable method of collaborating, and would stick to it throughout his career – even when it came to working with Miles Davis.

Prince took over the three studios at Sunset Sound while working on the album. He used one for *Parade*, another for The Family, and a third for an album by Mazarati, which was being produced by David Rivkin and Revolution bassist Mark Brown. Legend has it that he had cut the first four songs for *Parade* on the spot, in sequence: that he sat down behind the drums, asked Susan Rogers to roll the tape, and played through all of the drum tracks, using only his handwritten lyrics as guidance, then added the bass, keyboards, guitars, and vocals to each of the songs, one after another.

All that was left was for Susannah Melvoin to provide vocal overdubs, Clare Fischer to add his string arrangements, and Wendy Melvoin to perform a lead vocal for 'I Wonder U.' As Alan Leeds recalled, "He would get an idea and just couldn't rest to the degree of burning out engineers … he was an engineer's nightmare, because he had no patience with the technology – just waiting for them to rewind tape was tedious for him, to the point where he would yell, 'Can't you make that move a little faster?'"

The only truly collaborative track on *Parade* is 'Mountains,' which was recorded with the newly expanded line-up of The Revolution. (Revolution drummer Bobby Z had been usurped in favor of Sheila E. when it came to adding cowbells to 'Life Can Be So

Nice.') This put The Revolution in the odd position of being asked to contribute to a project that they were generally being kept at arms' length from.

Released on March 31 1986, *Parade* met with a critical fervor that *Under The Cherry Moon* had failed to attract and was hailed as a total artistic comeback by those critics who had disliked *Around The World In A Day*. "Stunning in its scope" was how the *Sunday Times* chose to describe it, while the *Detroit Free Press* hailed it as "a confirmation of Prince's place as a superior melodist, arranger, and player, as well as a celebration of his creativity."

The album is so concise and tightly written that it seems a lot shorter than its 40-minute run time, and, with its off-kilter rhythms, weird ebbs and flows, and instrumental subtleties, doesn't sound like anything else in the Prince canon. From a musical perspective it's one of Prince's densest records, but the production is closer to the stripped-down sound of *1999*.

Jazz is the main influence on piano-led tracks such as 'Under The Cherry Moon' and the instrumental 'Venus De Milo,' but even the 'rock' tracks – including 'Anotherloverholenyohead' – don't sound like anything Prince had recorded before. The funky 'Girls & Boys,' the celebratory 'Mountains,' and the piano-ballad 'Sometimes It Snows In April' – one of Prince's most affecting songs – are all augmented with such unusual instrumentation and unexpected twists that they still manage to surprise even after they seem to have settled into a recognizable structure.

'Kiss,' a song originally given to Mazarati but reclaimed a day later, was most listeners' highlight: a taut, sparse blend of funk and R&B sung in a falsetto Curtis Mayfield would have envied. The promo video features just Prince, Wendy Melvoin, and an unidentified female, showing just how valuable Melvoin was to Prince at the time.

Part of the album's genius is the way that it runs through all sorts of tried-and-tested Prince tricks while still sounding like nothing that came before it; part of its charm is the way that it sounds like Prince is stretching himself beyond his comfort zone to incorporate influences he hasn't fully mastered. It marks one of the few occasions where he has sounded out on a limb. Ironically, it would be kept of the top of the US charts by Janet Jackson's *Control* – an album produced by sacked Time members Jimmy Jam and Terry Lewis.

Given that Warner Bros had put up ten million dollars to make *Under The Cherry Moon* but only recouped three million, it was decided that the best way to turn both projects into full-blown commercial successes would be for Prince to go out on tour. As ever, however, the singer was still of a mind to do things the hard way. His US 'tour' consisted of ten Hit & Run dates, for which the city and venue of each performance would only be announced hours before showtime. This created enough fervor that each night was sold out, but still came as a disappointment to Warner Bros, who had high hopes for a blockbuster tour. Prince did perform a further 15 shows in Europe and four more in Japan, but that was as far as the promotional jaunt for *Parade* went.

The tour itself was bittersweet. Tensions between Prince and The Revolution had grown, largely because the show was now essentially a funk revue, the props of previous tours replaced by horn players, bodyguards-turned-dancers, Sheila E. on percussion, Miko Weaver on rhythm guitar, and various remembers of the now-defunct Family. "I was behind the piano, next to Bobby Z," Mark Brown recalled, "and behind three guys that used to be bodyguards. I started feeling a little underappreciated."

The tour did introduce a new, iconic part of Prince folklore: the aftershow gig, which would see the band take to the stage of a smaller venue in the early hours of the morning and play a much looser, jam-based set. "The aftershows were a natural outgrowth of an artist who was intrigued [by] the idea of performing often and in a variety of venues," Alan Leeds explained. "Prince enjoyed the intimacy and immediacy that small clubs provided."

After several years of playing together, Prince & The Revolution seemed to have reached their musical high-water mark. But it was not to last. The final night of the tour, at Japan's Yokohama Stadium on September 9, marked the end of an era in Prince's career. At the end of the show Prince smashed his guitars and walked off. It would be the last time he played with The Revolution,

closing the curtain on the most collaborative phase of his career and dismantling one of his most celebrated backing bands – with whom he had recently cut another (unreleased) album, *Dream Factory*.

Wendy Melvoin and Lisa Coleman were fired a month later, Bobby Z was replaced by Sheila E., and Mark Brown left of his own accord, leaving only Matt Fink from the

"I remember the first time that I heard the song 'Kiss,' really feeling that he had managed to re-capture some of that raw R&B emotion from some of his earlier music." DEZ DICKERSON (GUITARIST, 1978–83)

original line-up. Prince would subsequently put together a new backing band from the musicians he had left, but things would not continue as they were. With the *Parade* era over, Prince decided that he wanted to reclaim everything for himself again.

Prince Vs The King Of Pop

PRINCE AND MICHAEL JACKSON WERE BOTH INSTRUMENTAL IN BRIDGING THE GAP BETWEEN BLACK AND WHITE MUSIC IN THE EARLY 80S, AND BOTH COULD CLAIM TO HAVE BEEN THE DECADE'S MOST IMPORTANT MUSICAL FIGURE.

But while Jackson certainly sold more records – including *Thriller*, the biggest-selling album of all time – Prince produced a much wider and more powerful array of music. Comparing the two men in his autobiography, Miles Davis wrote, "I like Prince a little better as an all-round musical force. Plus he plays his ass off as well as sings and writes."

There were more similarities between the two men than might be immediately apparent – not least the fact that casual observers tend to think that both lost their minds somewhere along the line. More specifically, both became megastars at a young age and used their newfound wealth to build their own playgrounds: Jackson's Neverland Ranch, and Prince's Paisley Park. Both made headlines over their alleged sexual preferences and what can be interpreted as somewhat ambivalent attitudes toward race. They're also both fantastic dancers.

The main 'rivalry' between the two men began when 'Little Red Corvette' came out in February 1983, one month before Jackson's 'Beat It.' Both records stormed into the white mainstream market and made unprecedented strides on MTV. They also both featured rock guitar solos, leading Bobby Womack to complain that the two men had "groomed their music for the white audience." Although with *Thriller* Jackson surged ahead of Prince in terms of sales, it took him until 1987 to issue a follow up, *Bad*, which received much less ecstatic reviews. During the same timeframe, Prince had written and recorded ten albums for himself and others, all the while becoming more and more critically fêted.

Prince was always keen to play down any rivalry between the two. "I could talk to you about Michael Jackson," he told the *New Musical Express* in 1995, "but I would just be doing the job that a journalist does so there's no point." According to Robin Power, star of *Graffiti Bridge*, Prince was offered a lucrative licensing deal with Coke shortly after Jackson signed up with Pepsi, but turned it down. "He didn't want to be compared to Jackson," Power told Prince biographer Liz Jones. "He felt he should be compared with Miles [Davis] or [John] Coltrane," Power added, which perhaps gives another reason why he didn't want to appear on 'We Are The World,' which Jackson co-wrote.

Despite what Prince told the press, there clearly was some enmity between the two men. In December 1985, while working on *Under The Cherry Moon* in San Francisco, Prince was visited by Jackson, whom he challenged to a game of table tennis. Prince's competitive streak reportedly got the better of him, leading him to hit the ball across the table at Jackson as hard as he could. While paying a return visit a month later, Prince shared a pizza with Jackson's pet monkey, Bubbles, leading to reports in the *National Enquirer* that Prince had used mind-control tricks to send Bubbles mad. (The two men had also been in a studio together briefly in 1978, when Prince asked to sit in while Jackson worked on *Off The Wall*, though they never spoke.)

The *Bad* sessions threw up another interesting tale. Jackson had his producer, Quincy Jones, speak to Prince about the possibility of a duet on the album's title track. The plan was for Jackson's management to plant false

> *"You don't understand – if I'm not there to receive these ideas, God might give them to Prince."* JACKSON TO MUSICAL DIRECTOR KENNY ORTEGA

news stories in the press about a bitter rivalry between the two men leading up to the release of the single – which would serve as a supposed final battle. Problems arose, however, when Prince began to look in detail at the song's lyrics – and the first line, "Your butt is mine," in particular. "Who's singing that to whom?" Prince asked, "'cause you sure ain't singing that to me." Instead he offered up a reworking of his 1976 song 'Wouldn't You Love To Love Me?,' but Jackson rejected it.

Personal and financial problems largely drove Jackson into exile throughout the 00s, but the old rivalry was rekindled in 2007. Prince's 21 Nights In London residency at the O₂ Arena gave rise to rumors of Jackson's plans to perform a 25 or 30-night run at the same venue. Similarly,

after Prince's universally praised halftime show at Super Bowl XLI on February 4 2007, it was rumored that Jackson would give an even greater performance at the 2008 event, but in the end the role fell to a distinctly less showy Tom Petty.

Jackson never did get the chance to prove himself. During preparations for a planned run of 50 concerts that were also to take place at the O$_2$ Arena – an attempt to best Prince by no fewer than 29 shows – he died in depressingly similar circumstances to the way Prince would almost a decade later. After Prince's own death, Pitchfork declared that the pair were still competing on the charts, in an article that compared their posthumous album sales.

"U must become a prince before U're king, anyway," Prince sniped in 1992, but in the weeks after Prince's death, Stevie Wonder made it clear exactly who wore the crown: "If Michael was the King Of Pop, Prince should be the Emperor."

IN MARCH 1986, THE CASUAL OBSERVER MIGHT HAVE EXPECTED PRINCE'S FOCUS STILL TO BE ON *UNDER THE CHERRY MOON*, WHICH WAS STILL IN NEED OF A FEW EXTRA SCENES, AND *PARADE*, WHICH WAS DUE TO GO ONSALE IN A COUPLE OF WEEKS' TIME.

Dream Factory (MARCH 1986–JULY 1986)

Continually discarding old ideas in favor of new ones, Prince had already started work on yet another new project under the glow of a stained-glass window in his new home studio in Chanhassen, Minnesota, which would serve as Prince's main base of operations while he waited for Paisley Park to be built. That project was *Dream Factory*, the culmination of his recent embrace of the spirit of collaboration.

Having traded tapes regularly with Wendy Melvoin, Lisa Coleman, and Clare Fischer while making *Parade*, Prince took things a step further at the tail end of 1985, forming The Flesh with Sheila E. on drums, Levi Seacer Jr on bass, and Eric Leeds on saxophone. The group made a series of impromptu, jazz-based recordings at Sunset Sound studios around the turn of the year. Prince had

Although Sign "O" The Times is widely considered to be among Prince's finest works, Dream Factory could have been even better.

them pressed up as *The Flesh* but never released it, although 'Junk Music' found its way into *Under The Cherry Moon* and 'U Got 2 Shake Something' turned up as 'Shake!' by The Time on *Graffiti Bridge*.

The Flesh might never have materialized, but it was clear that Prince had grown more interested in the idea of working with a group in the studio. So it was that he invited The Revolution to work on what is now one of his most famous unreleased albums, *Dream Factory*. Although Prince recorded most of 'The Ballad Of Dorothy Parker' and 'Starfish & Coffee' on his own, the remaining seven songs all prominently feature The Revolution – notably 'Visions,' a solo instrumental piano piece by Lisa Coleman, who also sings the lead vocal on 'A Place In Heaven.'

The sessions seemed to gratify the band, particularly Melvoin and Coleman, with whom Prince worked most

closely. Having expanded the live line-up of The Revolution to a point where some felt the chemistry had been ruined, Prince seemed to be using these sessions to assuage tensions within the group. But as they continued it became clear that he wanted to reclaim the album for himself.

By May 1986 the Hit & Run shows had begun to take off, and the original members of The Revolution once again found themselves sidelined by new members. Arguments between Prince, Melvoin, and Coleman were exacerbated by the fact that Prince's relationship with Melvoin's twin sister, Susannah, was falling apart, leaving Wendy stuck between her boss and her sister.

Keen to avoid any further conflict, Prince worked on in the studio alone. By the end of June he had assembled enough material to expand *Dream Factory* to a 19-track double album featuring lengthy solo tracks such as 'Crystal Ball' and 'Movie Star.' At one point he even reportedly considered turning the project into a Broadway musical about the trappings of fame.

On July 18 Prince had a final master of *Dream Factory* pressed. The artwork, which was designed by Susannah Melvoin and included a space for each member of The Revolution to draw something to represent him or herself, seemed to suggest that this was very much a group record, but many of the truly collaborative songs – including 'Sexual Suicide,' 'Big Tall Wall,' and 'Teacher, Teacher' – had been removed and replaced by solo recordings (some of which would later resurface on *Sign "O" The Times*).

The Revolution felt foxed again. Midway through the Parade tour it became clear that these would be their last shows together. But by then Prince was already thinking about shelving *Dream Factory* and moving on to something new.

Although the album that rose from its ashes, *Sign "O" The Times*, is widely considered to be among Prince's finest works, *Dream Factory* could have been even better. It would

Wendy Melvoin was one of Prince's closest collaborators during the *Dream Factory* sessions.

certainly have been his most eclectic record. The tentative sessions during 1984–85 from which Prince picked up rock, pop, and jazz influences from his bandmates here reached their natural conclusion, with the band hitting new creative peaks all the time. Perhaps their greatest moment together came with the recording of 'Power Fantastic' at Prince's home studio. As Alan Leeds writes in the liner notes to *The Hits/The B-Sides*, "Lisa Coleman found herself playing the grand piano in the upstairs living room while the rest of the band huddled in the basement studio. Connected only by mics and earphones, The Revolution still managed to pull off the exquisite song in a single take – even the jazzy intro that Prince suggested just as tape was ready to roll."

There weren't too many other moments like this on the final version of *Dream Factory*, but Prince was still wise enough to hold onto the group recordings of things he couldn't do alone. Lisa Coleman's solo-piano piece, 'Visions,' is about as low key an opener as one might find on a Prince record, but contrasts well with what follows: the squelchy funk of the title track, on which Prince – in his sped-up 'Camille' voice – renames Hollywood "Holly Rock" and describes fame as a dream factory, designed to keep you unaware of reality. Elsewhere, 'Strange Relationship' has an Eastern psychedelic feel that's missing on the *Sign "O" The Times* version, and 'All My Dreams' takes the carnivalesque sound of *Parade*'s opening tracks to its logical conclusion.

Despite being a sprawling double-album, *Dream Factory* is brighter and more cohesive than *Sign "O" The Times*. The material set for inclusion on it spanned the length and breadth of Prince's abilities, from 'Movie Star,' a hilarious spoken-word piece about a Morris Day-like character trying to woo clubbers with his looks, to 'Crystal Ball,' a nine-minute run through jazz, funk, and reggae that sounds more like a mini-album than a single song. Written in the wake of Prince's sudden return from France following America's air raid on Libya in April 1986, 'Crystal Ball' reprises the '1999' theme of partying in the face of death – or, in this case, staying close with an expert lover who draws "pictures of sex" on the walls.

Much of the solo *Dream Factory* material later appeared in altered form on either *Sign "O" The Times* or the three-disc outtakes collection *Crystal Ball*. But the fact that nobody got to hear it as it was originally intended – alongside the last gasps of The Revolution – is a travesty. *Dream Factory* proved exactly how important the group were to Prince's artistic growth, and could well have had an even greater impact than *Sign "O" The Times*. Not one to look backward, however, Prince let the *Dream* fade away, and turned instead his attention to a new, semi-collaborative project, Madhouse, and the eventual follow-up to *Parade*.

AFTER SACKING THE REVOLUTION IN OCTOBER 1986, PRINCE FOUND HIMSELF ALONE, MUSICALLY SPEAKING, FOR THE FIRST TIME SINCE 1978. WITH *DREAM FACTORY* ON THE SHELF AND HIS NEW PAISLEY PARK STUDIO COMPLEX STILL NOT COMPLETE, HE WENT BACK DOWN TO HIS BASEMENT STUDIO TO START UP A NEW PROJECT WITH ONLY SUSAN ROGERS FOR COMPANY.

Sign "O" The Times

(OCTOBER 1986–SEPTEMBER 1987)

The recordings Prince made after that would prove to be a lot darker than the *Dream Factory* songs, suggesting that he had been deeply affected by the loss of The Revolution and arguments with Susannah Melvoin – and also perhaps the fact that sales of his albums continued to slip, despite the ever-increasing critical fervor with which they were greeted.

Prince's response to all of this, of course, was to retreat into the studio and let his anger manifest itself on tape. Within ten days he had completed work on an album called *Camille*, which had its roots in 'Erotic City,' the B-side to his 1984 single 'Let's Go Crazy.' Prince had figured out a way of recording high-pitched vocal tracks by slowing the tape down, singing in real time, and speeding it back up. The result made it sound like he had recently ingested a large quantity of helium.

Prince used the effect again on 'Dream Factory' to ask the question: "Got any dreams you ain't using?" The voice fascinated him to the extent that he decided to give it the name Camille. Although he has never quite admitted it, it seems likely that Prince took it from the nickname of the 19th-century French hermaphrodite Herculine Barbin. (When an interviewer for Yahoo! put it to him that his brother believed this to be the case in 1997, Prince replied simply: "Your brother is very wise.") Prince's plans for Camille even extended at one point to a movie, for which he planned to play both himself and his high-pitched alter ego.

While messing around with Camille in the studio in late October, Prince recorded a new song that set James Brown-style horn and guitar riffs against murky, hollow-sounding drums. 'Housequake' would become an important signifier of his continuing musical evolution. "It came at a time when there were other changes in his life," Susan Rogers recalled. "'Housequake' represented a new [style of] dance music for him."

With 'Housequake' in the bag, Prince quickly cut a whole album's worth of Camille material. By November 5 a self-titled album (to be credited to Camille, not Prince) was ready for mastering. A 'Housequake'/'Shockadelica' test pressing went out to clubs soon after that – partly so that Prince could get 'Shockadelica' out there before Jesse

Johnson's album of the same name was released – but the album ended up being shelved almost as quickly as it had been made, despite it already having a catalog number and artwork (a stick drawing of a man with crosses for eyes).

"Concepts for albums were coming to him almost as quickly as the songs were." ALAN LEEDS

His work on the project wasn't entirely in vain, however. 'Rebirth Of The Flesh' aside, all of the *Camille* songs resurfaced in some form or other, either on *Sign "O" The Times*, as B-sides, or on the soundtrack to *Bright Lights, Big City.*

Prince's reasons for scrapping *Camille* aren't clear, but it's likely that he had concerns about the commercial viability of the project. With sales of his recent albums dropping incrementally, he knew that he needed to come up with a sure-fire hit this time around – particularly with The Revolution gone, and all eyes on him alone. He

needed to show that he had grown as a musician, and that he hadn't needed The Revolution to get where he was. Picking up the pieces of *Dream Factory* and *Camille*, Prince decided that his next release would be his defining statement: a three-LP set called *Crystal Ball*, with the song of the same name as its centerpiece.

Continuing at the same frantic pace that had yielded *Camille*, Prince had completed the 22-track triple album by November 30 and promptly sent Steve Fargnoli to play it to Warner Bros. "He knew that just having the balls to do three records would create a big bang," Alan Leeds noted. It did, of course, but the 'bang' was more destructive than creative. Having made concession after concession for Prince up until now, the label baulked at the idea of putting out a triple album.

Prince's attitude, as Alan Leeds recalled, was: "Don't mess with me, this is it!" But this time Warner Bros flatly refused. Prince might have been the label's most creative artist, but that wasn't enough to justify the expense of putting out a three-record set. It would be too costly to produce, and too expensive for the casual fan to want to buy. Already concerned by the rate at which Prince put out new albums – which confused casual buyers and made it virtually impossible to maximize their commercial potential – Warner Bros refused to agree to release an album that seemed to be aimed only at critics and die-hard fans. Chief executive Mo Ostin insisted that the album be no longer than a double, forcing Prince to cut down his carefully constructed masterpiece.

This was the first real feud between label and star, but is indicative of problems that would emerge down the line. As far as Prince was concerned, Warner Bros had no business telling him what to do with his art. Despite losing interest in what *Crystal Ball* ended up being almost as soon as it was completed, he retained a bitterness about the overall situation for much longer. "I delivered three CDs for *Sign 'O' The Times*," he said in 1996. "Because people at Warner were tired, they came up with reasons why I should be tired too. I don't know if it's their place to talk me in or out of things."

As 1986 came to a close, Prince had lost his biggest Battle to date with Warner Bros, watched Susannah Melvoin walk out of his door for the last time, and been forced to trim his masterpiece by 30 per cent. Stripping away the lengthy 'Crystal Ball' along with several *Camille* songs and others dating back to *Dream Factory*, Prince pushed 'Sign "O" The Times' up to the front and made it this new, slimmer album's title track. (The songs featuring sped-up vocals are, of course, still credited to Camille.)

The only new addition was the second disc's hard-rock opener, 'U Got The Look,' which Prince recorded in December, and which went on to become one of his most successful singles. But had it not been for Sheena Easton, who happened to visit Prince while he was working on it, the song might never have been completed. Prince had been struggling to get the song right until Easton turned

PRINCE
SIGN "☮" THE TIMES

IF YOU GO TO ONLY
ONE CONCERT!
THIS YEAR, THE
PRINCE MOVIE
IS THE ONE!

" 'Sign O' The Times' is a first-rate concert film that captures Prince and a crack ten-piece band at the top of their form . . . visually riveting."
—Anthony DeCurtis, *Rolling Stone*
". . . better than 'Purple Rain.' "
—Nelson George, *Billboard*

PRINCE SIGN "☮" THE TIMES
A CAVALLO, RUFFALO & FARGNOLI PRODUCTION
STARRING PRINCE DIRECTOR OF PHOTOGRAPHY PETER SINCLAIR
ORIGINAL SONGS COMPOSED AND PRODUCED BY PRINCE CO-PRODUCED BY SIMON FIELDS
PRODUCED BY ROBERT CAVALLO, JOSEPH RUFFALO, STEVEN FARGNOLI
DIRECTED BY PRINCE

PRINCE SIGN "☮" THE TIMES ALBUM AVAILABLE ON PAISLEY PARK RECORDS, CASSETTES & COMPACT DISCS MANUFACTURED AND DISTRIBUTED BY WARNER BROS. RECORDS, INC.   A CINEPLEX ODEON FILMS RELEASE

up and added her vocals. (Her presence on the record – and in the video, which was shot during a day off in Paris in June 1987 – led to speculation that she had become yet another one of Prince's girlfriends.)

Sign "O" The Times was finished by the middle of January 1987, and released on March 30 to some of the strongest reviews Prince has ever received. Unaware that it had once extended across an even wider musical terrain, critics fell over themselves to praise the album's diversity, scope, and musicianship. "Prince's virtuoso eclecticism has seldom been so abundantly displayed," exclaimed *Rolling Stone*. For the *New York Times*, "Prince isn't just rearranging ordinary songs; he's started to warp the songs themselves."

The *New Musical Express* was slightly more cautious. Noting that some of the tracks on side one sounded like demos, the paper nonetheless concluded that, while this might signal the end for any other artist, for Prince it could "only enhance" a career that has "so far been brilliantly stage-managed." There were still a few criticisms from elsewhere: some reviewers simply found the whole thing too eclectic for its own good, suggesting perhaps that trimming down *Crystal Ball* hadn't been quite so bad an idea after all.

The *Sign "O" The Times* jacket shows a more mature-looking Prince on the set of a local production of *Guys & Dolls*. He has his musical equipment set up in front of fading city lights screaming about Drugs, Arcades, and Girls Girls Girls, suggesting that he had decided to put music before the rock'n'roll lifestyle. In contrast with the backdrop, Prince himself is out of focus, staring out into space, leaving his sex-obsessed past behind him. One rather pointed addition, however, is the glowing, purple crystal ball sitting on top of the drum riser – a clear sign that he had not yet forgiven or forgotten Warner Bros' decision to veto the original triple-album concept.

Such personal messages would of course have been lost on the casual buyer, who would have had no choice but to marvel at this two-disc magnum opus. As he had with *1999*, Prince chose to open the record with a note of social commentary, but 'Sign "O" The Times" is no call to hedonistic arms. Over a sparse drum pattern, Prince makes reference to AIDS, gang violence, and drug addiction. "Some say a man ain't happy," he concludes, "unless a man truly dies."

'Sign "O" The Times' was the most mature statement Prince had yet made, but it also served to wrong-foot his audience. It's not until 'The Cross' – two thirds of the way through the

second disc – that he returns to the world outside of his usual themes of sex, love, and partying. The way he treats these themes, however, marks *Sign "O" The Times* out as a much more mature work than anything that came before it. Alongside typical tales of lust – 'Hot Thing,' 'It,' 'U Got The Look' – Prince deals with the breakup of his relationship with Susannah Melvoin in a much more honest, conflicted manner than might have been expected. Having closed disc one with 'Forever In My Life''s declaration that "I wanna keep U 4 the rest of my life," he then goes on, in 'If I Was Your Girlfriend,' to express his jealousy at the close bond between the Melvoin sisters, asking, "Would U run 2 me if somebody hurt U / Even if that somebody was me?" Then, on the aptly named 'Strange Relationship,' he admits he "can't stand 2 see U happy," but also "hate[s] 2 see U sad."

Sign "O" The Times does more than just play out the demise of a relationship: it gave Prince the chance to show

"I hate the word 'experiment.' It sounds like something you didn't finish." PRINCE

the world exactly what he was capable of musically. At its best, the album can be seen as the culmination of everything Prince had done – and been exposed to – previously, without ever betraying his musical roots. As *Q* magazine put it, the album's funk edge "slices straight through the white gut of pop."

'Housequake' and 'It's Gonna Be A Beautiful Night' (the latter recorded live in Paris with The Revolution in 1986) are the album's funkiest moments, while the likes of 'Play In The Sunshine' and 'I Could Never Take The Place Of Your Man' offer up perfect pop-rock for the mainstream. For all its brilliance, *Parade* betrays Prince's struggle to harness new sounds and styles that he wasn't yet familiar with. On *Sign "O" The Times* he seemed to have mastered

them effortlessly, shifting with ease from rock to psychedelia to funk to jazz, all the while maintaining his role as the world's leading loverman. (The closing 'Adore' is one of his greatest ballads and a vocal tour de force with overlapping harmonies that are among Prince's most complex.)

Sign "O" The Times is a perfect blend of Prince's own formative influences and the new musical worlds he had been introduced to by The Revolution. In many ways it is his equivalent of Sly & The Family Stone's *There's A Riot Goin' On*: a masterpiece

All That Jazz

The emergence of Madhouse marked a change in the way Prince approached his side projects, which he had previously used as a means of maintaining his standing in the R&B world while his own work veered off in ever more experimental directions. This time however his intention was to explore new ideas that didn't fit on his solo records.

By the mid 80s Prince was becoming increasingly interested in jazz, as evidenced by his shortlived experiments with The Flesh and his collaboration with Miles Davis. Having scrapped plans for a fully collaborative jazz record, he spent four days at the end of September 1986 recording a jazz-funk album by the name of *8*, with contributions from Eric Leeds (saxophone and flute) and Matt Fink (a few synthesizer solos).

The album was released on January 17 1987 and credited to Madhouse, with no other names anywhere on the jacket. While in the past Prince had left clues to his involvement in records by The Time, Vanity 6, and others, he was keen this time to distance himself from the project completely, either out of a genuine wish to let the music speak for itself, or because he feared a backlash from 'serious' jazz critics.

He was right to be wary: *8* demonstrates only a superficial understanding of how jazz works, and is far too regimented – because Prince played most of the instruments himself – to sound truly improvised. By comparison to Miles Davis's late-60s and early-70s fusion work on albums such as *Bitches Brew* and *On The Corner*, *8* is incredibly tame.

Nonetheless, it didn't take fans long to recognize the Prince sound and buy enough copies to push *8* – a completely instrumental oddity – to Number 25 on *Billboard*'s R&B chart, and Number 107 on

the Pop chart. One of its eight numbered tracks, 'Six,' then reached Number Five on the R&B singles chart.

Prince took his new side project out on the road with him as the featured support act on his European Sign "O" The Times tour. Keen to mask their identities as much as possible, Madhouse performed in sunglasses and hooded black robes. (Prince would even step out to play drums with them from time to time.)

For the second Madhouse album, *16*, Prince brought in drummer John Lewis as well as Eric Leeds, Levi Seacer Jr, and Matt Fink from his live band. Released on November 18 1987, *16* had more of a harder-edged group dynamic than its predecessor, but failed to make as much impact. The single 'Ten' stalled at Number 66 on the R&B chart, while the album itself didn't chart at all.

Since then Madhouse has been stuck in a kind of limbo, with Prince recording several prospective *24*s over the years. A ten-day session with Eric Leeds in December 1988 yielded eight more tracks, each with subtitles such as '17 (Penetration)' and '18 (R U Legal Yet?),' but none were released. ('21' to '24' were grouped under the name 'The Dopamine Rush Suite.')

In July 1993 he made another attempt, bringing in Eric Leeds and various members of the New Power Generation – Michael Bland on drums, Levi Seacer Jr on guitar, and Sonny Thompson on bass. The only numerically titled track, '17,' later appeared on the compilation album *1-800-NEW-FUNK*, but Warner Bros had no interest in putting out the likes of 'Asswoop' and '(Got 2) Give It Up.'

A few years later, Prince reportedly reworked some of his *Kamasutra* album (as included alongside 1997's *Crystal Ball*) as a

third Madhouse record. Though a couple of tracks from the project surfaced in 1998 and 2001, a full third Madhouse album has never appeared. However, tapping into the original idea behind the group, in 2013 Eric Leeds and Paul Peterson began the bebop-funk crossover project LP *Music*.

The two surviving Madhouse albums are not masterpieces in any sense, but are interesting because of their dissimilarity to anything else in Prince's 80s output. But if this is the best jazz-fusion that Prince could offer, it's clear that he had only just begun to scratch the surface of what Eric and Alan Leeds had been introducing him to. Listening to *8* and *16*, it becomes clearer why Prince might not have wanted to collaborate directly with Miles Davis (as opposed to trading tapes): he was simply no match for a real master of the genre.

built on a foundation of subdued, murky funk, and the culmination of a creative surge that would never again be repeated.

Part of the album's unusual feel stems from Prince's acceptance of happy accidents. A snowstorm caused a power shortage during the recording of 'The Ballad Of Dorothy Parker' (a song Prince claimed to have written in a dream, but which seems to reflect his arguments with Susannah Melvoin). When the power came back, Prince carried on recording, but the sound desk wasn't yet back to full power. "Half the new console wasn't working," Susan Rogers recalled, "[and] there was no high end at all." But rather than try to rework or remix the song, Prince stuck with the supposed imperfections of the recording,

willing perhaps to accept it as a sign of good fortune from a higher power.

The same was true of the recording of 'If I Was Your Girlfriend.' The distortion on Prince's voice wasn't planned, but came from a mistake Rogers made while setting up the equipment – the kind of thing Prince would never have stood for in the past. Having "inadvertently switched something the wrong way," Rogers was relieved to find that Prince "never said a word. He had this attitude, 'Well, maybe that was meant to be.'"

Despite the acclaim with which it had been received by the critics, *Sign "O" The Times* peaked at Number Six on the *Billboard* chart, two spots lower than where *Parade* had ended up. The title track reached Number Three on the

Paisley Park: The Label

After hitting his commercial peak with *Purple Rain* – and establishing himself as a successful hitmaker with The Time and Vanity 6 – Prince was able to convince Warner Bros chief executive Mo Ostin to put up two million dollars so that the singer could start his own Paisley Park Records label. "Paisley Park is an alternative," he told *Rolling Stone* in 1985. "I'm not saying it's greater or better. It's just something else. It's multicolored and it's very fun." In reality, however, it was little more than a name.

Although Warner Bros made a significant investment to get it off the ground, Paisley Park was essentially a vanity label, created to keep the singer under the impression that he had more control than he really did, much like the Stones' Rolling Stones Records. The Paisley Park logo would subsequently be seen alongside the Warner Bros logo on Prince's own records, those of his side projects, and any other acts Prince chose to work with (or that his management signed to keep the label afloat as a commercial entity).

As it turned out, the multi-colored novelty would soon wear off. Paisley Park was an alternative, but not in the way Prince had anticipated. Instead it became a shining example of how not to run a record label. While Warner Bros continued to reap success with each new Prince record, the singer didn't seem to be pulling his weight when it came to the other Paisley releases. By the end of the 80s he seemed to be coming to the end of his run of great records, leaving him with little to spread around elsewhere.

He also adopted a rather passive approach to the business of running a label. Instead of signing new artists to try to build a formidable roster, he only seemed to be interested in working with members of his existing tight-knit group – Sheila E., The Family, Jill Jones, and his own Madhouse project. According to Alan Leeds, who resigned from his post as president of Paisley Park Records in 1992, "Prince wasn't taking the responsibility to produce competitive records and turn the label around." In the rare instances that he did branch out, Prince ended up working with the likes of George Clinton, who was well past his best by the early 90s. His attempts to refashion Mavis Staples as a modern R&B star were similarly unwise.

Therein lay the problem: Prince knew how to make records, but he was not a 'producer.' Rather than let an artist's personality shine through, he forced his own ideas onto them, resulting in a series of records that each sounded too similar to the last. As Alan Leeds recalled, Prince rarely had much enthusiasm for the outside groups Cavallo, Ruffalo & Fargnoli brought in, and "failed to disguise his lack of interest."

Paisley Park quickly became home to half-baked ideas that came and went in a flash. Prince's interest could seemingly only be roused by album projects that involved girlfriends: Jill Jones, Taja Sevelle, Ingrid Chavez, and The Family (fronted by Susannah Melvoin). Asked in 1990 why nothing from a reported session with Bonnie Raitt ever saw release, Prince told *Rolling Stone*: "I was just working on a lot of things at the same time, and I didn't give myself enough time to work with her … I used to do that a lot – start five different projects and only get a couple done."

"I ended up spending several very frustrating years trying to get Warners and the industry to take Paisley Park Records seriously when [it] simply didn't want to be taken seriously," Alan Leeds recalled. In 1992, the year that Leeds resigned from the company, Prince renegotiated his contract with Warner Bros. Among his demands were that the label continue to fund Paisley Park Records as a joint venture – despite the fact that it had quite obviously become a monumental waste of money.

Desperate to keep Prince happy, Warner Bros agreed, and even gave him his own office suite and 12 members of staff in the West LA commercial district of Century City.

But there was no improvement in the quality of Paisley Park's output. Eyebrows were raised in 1993 when the planned release of a Rosie Gaines album – a rare project with genuine promise – was postponed so Prince could focus on his latest discovery: Carmen Electra. Gaines's album disappeared entirely to make way for an awful rap record by an identikit Prince-girl that sank without a trace.

This might well have been the final straw. In February 1994, just as Prince was beginning to wage war against Warner Bros, the company pulled the plug on Paisley Park Records, refusing to throw more money away on vanity projects that brought nothing in return. Prince took the label's master-tapes with him, but has never reissued any of its albums. In a further demonstration of his lack of interest in the label, it later transpired that he had never set foot in his Century City office suite during the two years he owned it.

Prince of course blamed Warner Bros for the failure of Paisley Park Records. "I was under the assumption that it was a joint effort," he told the *LA Times* in 1996. "All we do as artists is make the music. I didn't think I'd have to be marketing the records, or taking them to the radio station. If Michael Jordan had to rely on someone to help him dunk, then there would be trouble." According to Alan Leeds, however, Warner Bros took the view that "a succession of 'girlfriend' records and Prince's generosity towards legacy artists past their prime weren't representative of a real label."

Prince's response to this setback was to set up NPG Records entirely on his own. Following further arguments with Warner Bros, he released 'The Most Beautiful Girl In The World' on it. Much to Warner Bros' dismay, it became his biggest hit for several years, and his first UK Number One.

On the face of it, NPG Records became much more successful than its predecessor. Prince might not have attempted to assemble a roster as big as Paisley Park's, but released one-off albums by artists such as Chaka Khan and Larry Graham as well as the occasional NPG band release. He once claimed that, in some cases, he made up to 90 per cent profit from NPG releases over the years because there are fewer overheads and no parent label to pay. Despite selling to a more limited fanbase, he could boast of having made more money from NPG than he ever did with Paisley Park.

P-Funk legend George Clinton, who signed to Paisley Park Records in the early 90s.

Hot 100, but any momentum was broken by Prince's surprising choice to follow it with 'If I Was Your Girlfriend,' which staggered in at Number 67. Undoubtedly a brave release as far as singles went, its gender-twisting lyrics and unflinching honesty were too

"According to the press, he bought me an apartment, which then became a mansion … and our affair ended telepathically, so I think that speaks for itself." SHEENA EASTON

much for the charts. According to Alan Leeds, "'Girlfriend' stopped radio in its tracks. Homophobes misinterpreted the lyrics and its charming eccentricity didn't fit a format." Everybody else had expected 'Housequake' to be the next single, but for Prince, Leeds recalled, that was just "*too* obvious."

The album's initial commercial impact was slowed further by Prince's decision to begin the accompanying tour in Europe rather than America – and, indeed, to take his jazz-funk side project Madhouse with him as the support act. Why he did this is unclear, but it could have well been that, like other groundbreaking American artists, including jazz legends such as Miles Davis and Charlie Parker, he found his European fans to be more open to new ideas. (It might also have had something to do with his irritation at the way his record sales in America continued to decline.)

The Sign "O" The Times tour began in Sweden on May 8 1987. Rehearsals had begun four months earlier with an almost entirely new band. While Matt Fink remained from The Revolution, and Eric Leeds and Atlanta Bliss stayed on to play live horns, the nucleus of the group came from Sheila E.'s band: Sheila herself on drums, Levi Seacer Jr on bass, Miko Weaver on guitar, and Boni Boyer on keyboards and backing vocals. Jerome Benton, Wally Safford, and Greg Brooks reprised their dancing roles, but were often sidelined to make way for Prince's new onstage foil, Cat Glover. A longtime fan, Glover choreographed the shows and brought a charged sexuality to the performances, which saw Prince slide through her legs, tear off her skirt, and emerge with it in his mouth during 'Hot Thing.'

The European tour took in 34 concerts during May and June (surprisingly missing out Britain), and focused largely on the *Sign "O" The Times* material. "The music was first rate, the band was on fire, and the show was wonderfully imaginative, without the over-the-top largesse of the [next year's] Lovesexy tour," Alan Leeds recalled. Impressed by his new group's proficiency, Prince designed the set to showcase their talents on songs such as a cover of Charlie Parker's 'Now's The Time' and his own 'It's Gonna Be A Beautiful Night.' The show as a whole was his most

exciting yet, all performed on a stage designed to mirror the album artwork.

The *Sign "O" The Times* songs seemed to change every night as the band grew in confidence. But any progress that was being made came to an abrupt halt in June when Prince opted not to tour the USA. Despite the success of 'U Got The Look'/'Housequake,' which hit Number Two on the Hot 100, he had no desire to perform an album he had little interest in for an audience he was unhappy with. Instead he opted to film the final four European dates, deciding that any market he hadn't yet visited could make do with seeing the Sign "O" The Times tour on the silver screen.

This failure to maintain the momentum of the Sign "O" The Times tour was, in a lot of people's eyes, one of the biggest mistakes Prince ever made. To make matters worse, when he returned to Minneapolis he found that most of the concert footage he had was too grainy to be useable. He did what he could by shooting new performance scenes and short dramatic segments at Paisley Park, but this in turn served only to interfere with the energy of the live show.

Paisley Park: The Studio

Along with the symbol to which he changed his name in the mid 90s, Paisley Park Studio is synonymous with Prince and his music. A 65,000-square foot complex in the Chanhassen district of Minnesota, on the outskirts of Minneapolis, it was to Prince what the Neverland Ranch was to Michael Jackson.

Prince had long dreamt of owning his own studio, finding that he was much more comfortable recording at home than anywhere else. Flush from the success of *Purple Rain*, he was able to make this a reality in May 1985, buying a 200-acre plot of land just ten minutes away from his home in Edina. Keen never to have to risk losing the property, Prince paid in cash. ("He had no mortgages on anything," recalled his manager of the time, Bob Cavallo.)

Asked why he wanted to withdraw into his own castle, Prince told *Details* in 1998 that he had "heard 'Prince is crazy' so much that it had an effect on me. So one day, I said, 'Let me just check out.'" Paisley Park gave him the "solitude" and the "controlled environment" that he craved. But he was keen to point out that this large concrete block wasn't just seen as a retreat from the real world. "I don't live in a prison," he told *Rolling Stone* in response to revelations in the *National Enquirer*. "I am not afraid of anything. I haven't built walls around myself."

Since officially opening the doors to Paisley Park on September 11 1987, Prince used it to record all of his albums from *Lovesexy* onward. The complex boasts four studios, an editing suite, a games room, a 12,000-foot soundstage, a nightclub, dressing rooms, a hair salon, production offices, conference room, and an art department – all of which needed to be manned. Every single room was allegedly wired for sound so that Prince could record whatever he liked, wherever he liked – and perhaps so that he could hear what was going on when he was not in the room. In the early 21st century he held his Celebration weeks on site, and he shot many of his promo videos – as well as the features *Graffiti Bridge* and *The Undertaker* – on the soundstage. He also staged benefit gigs, playbacks, and even fan question-and-answer sessions in the building.

"Man, Prince has got a hell of a complex out there," Miles Davis wrote in his autobiography. "[There's] record and movie equipment, plus he had an apartment for me to stay in. The whole thing seems like it's about half a block." The vast scale meant that, having ploughed ten million dollars into building the complex, Prince soon found he had stretched his finances to the limit. The obvious solution might have been to rent the facilities out to others, but for a long time Prince refused to let any outside groups in.

"It became evident to all of us that he had enough projects in mind that he could fill up every studio and soundstage in the building," Alan Leeds recalled. This might have been a good thing from a creative perspective, but also meant that it soon became "an enormous [financial] drain" – as did the fact that Prince had the studios manned 24 hours a day, just in case he decided to drop in on a whim.

Even after he did start letting in other acts, Prince just didn't have the skills required to run it as a business. When his financial situation threatened to spiral out of control in 1994, he gave his stepbrother and head of security, the late Duane Nelson, the job of arbitrarily firing staff. After that, Paisley Park was run on more of a skeleton crew, though in 2004 Prince told *Ebony* magazine of his plan to "have interns in here working and learning every aspect of the music business."

It took almost ten years, but in 2013 Prince welcomed the public back into his home. Initially the internet provided a buffer, as he broadcasted band rehearsals via Livestream, at one point considering offering the streams to fans on a pay-per-view basis. In time, however, he would start staging events – from album launch parties to charity drives, press announcements, and tour previews – at the Park, often under the Paisley Park After Dark banner. He also gave other acts showcase spots, including rapper Kendrick Lamar and British electronica star FKA Twigs, and, of course, his own protégés. (In 2014, Minneapolis radio station The Current noted that while Paisley Park was no longer "the center of the pop universe," it had "re-emerged as a sort of petri dish for some of the most intriguing soul-infused pop artists of the future.")

Most famously, Paisley Park is home to The Vault, a storeroom for countless songs, albums, and even full-scale promotional videos that Prince has made but never released. Estimates vary, but the number of unreleased songs in The Vault has been rumored to run into the thousands. Following Prince's death, fans were anxious to learn the fate of this material: would it ever get released? And, more importantly, by whom?

It soon emerged that Bremer Trust, a special executor temporarily brought in to handle Prince's estate, had been forced to drill into The Vault in order to properly account for his assets, sparking new concern over the way Prince's legacy would be handled. And while it now seems almost inevitable that some of the material will see the light of day, there will always be the question of how Prince would have wanted it presented – if he ever wanted it made public at all.

So protective was Prince of Paisley Park that when the Spanish newspaper *El País* asked what he would do if the complex was destroyed by a fire, he angrily replied: "This will never happen. If you leave a piece of bread on a table, someday it will become moss, and this will become medicine. In the same way, Paisley Park will never be destroyed, it will just become something else."

In the years leading up to his death, Prince had begun working on turning it into a Graceland-like museum. "He's been gathering memorabilia and stuff from the tours," Sheila E. told ET Online shortly after his death, noting that though Prince didn't care too much for them, "he displayed it for the fans." She described a mural that depicted Prince holding his hands out: "On one side is all the people he was influenced by and the other side is all of us who have played with him. ... It's beautiful."

The *Sign "O" The Times* movie concept was similar to what Prince had envisioned for *The Second Coming* and ended up receiving rave reviews from critics who were no doubt pleased not to have to sit through another *Under The Cherry Moon*. *Rolling Stone* called it "a first-rate concert film" that captures Prince and co "at the top of their form," while the *Philadelphia Daily News* saw it as a reaffirmation of Prince's status as "the most provocative, all-things-to-all-people sex symbol to hit the pop arena since Elvis Presley."

Once again, however, critical acclaim was no guarantee of commercial success as the movie struggled to compete with a rush of seasonal hits aimed squarely at the Christmas market. "A number of us told him that the release date was a mistake," recalled Warner Bros Vice President Marylou Badeaux, "but in his mind we were just trying to undermine him."

Its impact was dented even more by the fact that concert movies tend as a rule not to hang around for too long anyway. Unsurprisingly, then, it failed to make the kind of money that Prince would have earned from touring the USA. Many of the people who would surely have gone to see him play just weren't interested in seeking out a limited-run concert movie. (Because of Warner Bros' unwillingness to back another potential turkey, *Sign "O" The Times* was independently distributed, and opened in only 30 US cities.)

Apart from a New Year's Eve benefit for the Minnesota Coalition For The Homeless, for which Prince charged $200 per ticket for a performance inside Paisley Park, that was pretty much it for *Sign "O" The Times*. Warner Bros might have wanted more time to work with the record and maximize its commercial potential, but as far as Prince was concerned it was done with.

Despite seeing the New Year in by jamming with his idol Miles Davis, Prince seemed to be heading into 1988 lonelier than ever. He had a great new band, but would never allow himself to become as close to them as he had to The Revolution, having decided that he had already learnt everything he needed to know. In a few short years he had pushed away almost everybody close to him, from Dez Dickerson and Chick Huntsberry to Lisa Coleman, Wendy Melvoin, and, most devastatingly, Susannah Melvoin. He continued to date Sheila E., but his closest confidante was probably Alan Leeds.

Prince had begun 1987 alone, but had at least felt that he was on an artistic high. Now, a year later, reality seemed to be seeping through. He was still alone, and now had to follow what most people felt to be his crowning artistic achievement – with or without Camille.

Princes Of Darkness

PERHAPS THE MOST TANTALIZING COLLABORATION OF PRINCE'S CAREER TO DATE WAS WITH THE LEGENDARY JAZZ TRUMPETER MILES DAVIS.

Having been opened up to the possibilities of jazz by saxophonist Eric Leeds on the Purple Rain tour, Prince began to idolize Davis, and with good reason: by the mid 80s, Davis had changed the face of jazz at least five times in as many decades. He had also become known for his no-nonsense attitude to other people. This might have been seen by most as a sign of arrogance, but was actually symbolic of the survival instincts of a man who had been through everything from heroin addiction to racist beatings at the hands of the New York City police force.

"Young black guys were attracted to Miles because of his politics – he was an icon," Alan Leeds later noted. "I think as Prince learnt more about [him], he started to see some of himself in Miles." This certainly seems plausible. It's not hard to imagine Prince being in awe of one of the few musicians who had been even more prolific than he had himself.

Prince himself has not spoken often about Davis, but his recollections of a visit by the self-styled Prince Of Darkness to his home are telling. "As he was passing by my piano," Prince told *Musician* in 1997, "he stopped and put his hands down on the keys and played these eight chords, one after the other. It was so beautiful ... I couldn't decide whether it was him or an angel putting his hands on the keys."

Davis had a similarly high opinion of Prince. "[He can be] the new Duke Ellington of our time if he just keeps at it," he wrote. "I learn things from Prince. [His] music is pointing towards the future." Davis did however find some elements of Prince's career amusing: "If I said 'Fuck

After that initial meeting, Prince proposed a more relaxed get-together, suggesting that Davis spend some time with him and Sheila E. By December 26 the collaboration seemed to be taking shape. Prince sent Davis a track called 'Can I Play With U?' and suggested that he record whatever he wanted over the top and include it on his forthcoming album, *Tutu*. But when Prince received a tape of the finished song in March he didn't seem to like what Davis (as well as his keyboardist and bassist) had done to it. "When we sent him the tape and he heard what was on there he didn't think his tune [worked with the rest of *Tutu*]," Davis recalled. "Prince has high musical standards, like me." The song was pulled from the album, but with the hope that something could be done with it at a later date.

Davis continued to hold out for a proper in-studio collaboration, but Prince shied away from the idea. He preferred instead to send tapes back and forth to see if the recordings could fit together, giving himself time and space to work at his own pace. Working with Davis in real time posed all sorts of problems. As Alan Leeds put it, "If Miles is a control freak, multiply that by five when you come to Prince." Davis had surrounded himself with younger musicians throughout his career, but Prince didn't want to put himself in the position of having to tell his idol what to do. According to Leeds, "The idea of being in a studio with Miles and trying to direct him was foreign to him and he just couldn't even conceive of that scenario."

Davis wasn't prone to giving up easily, however, and would leave messages at Paisley Park telling "that little purple motherfucker to contact me." But while they met several times following the failure of 'Can I Play With U?,' it was never in a

🔲 *"When Prince makes love he hears drums instead of Ravel"* MILES DAVIS

you' to somebody they would be ready to call the police. But if Prince says it in that girl-like voice that he uses, then everyone says it's cute."

Despite the obvious respect the two men had for each other, their attempts at collaboration were not particularly successful. They first met at an airport in early December 1985, shortly after Davis moved from Columbia to Warner Bros. Davis later claimed that Warner Bros had first proposed the idea of a collaboration; it's certainly not hard to imagine that the label would have been keen to have two of its highest-profile stars work together.

recording studio. Davis had dinner at Prince's home in 1987, and sat in and watched Prince rehearse at Paisley Park later the same year, but didn't have his trumpet with him. He did bring it along to Prince's New Years Eve benefit show on December 31 1987, and took to the stage at the end of the 80-minute set for a rendition of Madhouse's 'Six.' Prince however seemed so shy that he barely looked at Davis, let alone tried to interact with him, save for a bit of scatting in response to Davis's trumpet playing.

The Prince-Davis partnership largely fizzled out after that, but the two men continued to show their respect for

each other. Davis took to playing the *Dream Factory* outtake 'Movie Star' during his 1991 concerts, and worked on a few tracks from the aborted third Madhouse album for himself. But when Davis played at Prince's Glam Slam club, Prince declined several requests to jam with his idol on stage.

The opportunity for these two musical giants to work together in the studio disappeared when Miles Davis died on September 28 1991. Two days later, Prince recorded his 'Letter 4 Miles' at Paisley Park. Like many of the songs closest to his heart, however, it has never been released to the public – nor has the "indescribable music" Prince once told *Guitar World* he had made with Davis before he died. (Since there is no documentary evidence to support this, however, it seems doubtful that such recordings actually exist.)

WITH THE SIGN "O" THE TIMES TOUR BEHIND
HIM, PRINCE DECIDED IT WAS TIME TO FACE UP
TO WHAT SOME FELT TO BE A MARKED
'WHITENING' OF HIS SOUND IN RECENT YEARS.

Lovesexy (OCTOBER 1987–NOVEMBER 1988)

During October and November 1987 he spent time in the studio revisiting a selection of funk songs recorded the previous year, to which he added one new composition, 'When 2 R In Love,' to create one of the most contentious albums of his career: *The Black Album*.

Some have since suggested that *The Black Album* was never intended for general release. According to Susan Rogers, "The tracks were odds and ends, things we would do on a day off … sometimes he wanted to break away and do something [different] just to get it out of his system." That this was the case is given further credence by the fact that Prince sat on them for so long, since he tended usually to release new material as soon as he completed it.

'Le Grind,' 'Bob George,' and '2 Nigs United 4 West Compton' had all appeared on an acetate pressed up for Sheila E.'s birthday on December 11 1986, but none were deemed suitable for *Sign "O" The Times*. Having been stung, once again, by suggestions that he had left his roots behind, Prince perhaps felt the need to prove to his critics

that he still had it in him to be funky. At any rate, having called in Eric Leeds and trumpeter Matt Blistan to play on the songs, and Cat Glover to sing on them, an album began to take shape, and found itself scheduled for release on December 8 – less than a month after the opening of the *Sign "O" The Times* concert movie.

The trouble was that, after ten years in the business, Prince wasn't having as many bright ideas as he used to – and without anyone to bounce them off, they weren't as varied, either. Prince's prolific workrate seemed to be getting the better of him. "For every great song [he wrote]," Warner Bros Vice President Marylou Badeaux recalled, "there were ten kind-of-okay songs."

Originally set to be called *The Funk Bible*, *The Black Album* certainly constituted a return to Prince's roots. It's a dark, uninviting record that harks back, with its lyrics about masturbation and uncharacteristically aggressive attitude to sex, to the controversial themes of *Dirty Mind*. But it served also to highlight Prince's struggle to fit into the musical climate of the late 80s – particularly when it

"I was very angry a lot of the time back then, and that was reflected on that album." *PRINCE*

came to hip-hop, which was well on its way by then to becoming one of popular music's most commercially successful strands.

As far as Prince was concerned, hip-hop was distinctly unmusical. His feelings are summed up by 'Dead On It,' on which he laments switching on the radio to hear a "silly rapper talking silly shit." The largely instrumental '2 Nigs 4 West Compton,' meanwhile, was intended as a musical swipe at the likes of NWA, whose *Straight Outta Compton* was just around the corner, and whose glorification of gang violence and misogyny Prince detested. (Changing his tune somewhat, Prince would later take the misguided decision to add rapper Tony M to his backing group, and tell Spike Lee in 1997 that he "did" gangsta rap years ago, citing his "half-sung" vocals on tracks such the 1982 B-side 'Irresistible Bitch.')

All in all, *The Black Album* seemed symbolic of Prince's concerns about his place in the contemporary music scene. (On one track, 'Bob George,' he slows his voice down to an approximation of an overbearing pimp and calls himself "that skinny motherfucker with the high voice.") It's a fun, funky album, but hardly anything groundbreaking. Prince might have felt that he had more musical talent than any of the hip-hop acts out there, but his sales were slipping. Going back to the sexually explicit material of the past might not have been the best way to boost his profile – particularly when the album in question is just seven funk tracks and a ballad ('When 2 R In Love') stitched together without the care and consideration of past glories such as *Dirty Mind* and *1999*.

When Prince presented the new album to Warner Bros, the label was once again concerned about the lack of space between his previous album and this prospective follow-up. It was also alarmed by Prince's design concept for the record: no credits, no image, just a plain black jacket with a catalog number (in peach) on the spine. With sales falling, Prince needed to make his latest releases easier to find, not harder.

This coupled with its less impressive musical content meant that *The Black Album* was something of a thorn in the company's side. Even so, Warner Bros still agreed to release the album. This time it was Prince who got cold feet, calling Mo Ostin and begging him not to release it. Several differing reasons have since been given for this volte-face. Some have suggested that, just before the album's release, Prince took ecstasy for the first time and had a 'bad trip' that resulted in him thinking *The Black*

Album was the work of the devil. But these claims are at odds with the fact that hardly anyone has ever even claimed to see Prince drink alcohol, let alone take drugs. (When pressed on the subject by the *New Musical Express* in 1995, Prince would admit only that he is "interested in all experiences.")

Prince himself has claimed that he saw the word 'God' floating above him in a field and was convinced from then on that *The Black Album* was an 'evil' recording. Others have put this down more tangibly to the influence of the spiritual poet Ingrid Chavez, with whom Prince had recently begun to work. The furthest Prince has gone toward explaining his decision came in the Lovesexy tour program, in which he describes how his alter-ego, Camille, had "set out to silence his critics" and found a new color, "black: the strongest hue of them all" – perhaps suggesting that he truly felt that *The Black Album* might revive his commercial fortunes – but subsequently realized that he had allowed "the dark side of him to create something evil." Leaving aside any religious or drug-related epiphanies, however, it seems most likely that, having, in his own words, "[cut] off people in my life and disappear[ed] without a glance back," Prince decided that he ought to be making something more spiritually uplifting instead of returning to morally bankrupt funk.

The Black Album was recalled from warehouses a week before its release. While this did at least leave Warner Bros with a longer gap between Prince albums, the company still had to shoulder the cost of pressing (and then destroying) the first run of around 500,000 copies. What happened next, of course, was that *The Black Album* became the biggest-selling bootleg since the first, Bob Dylan's *Great White Wonder*. The album became so notorious, in fact, that it was even reviewed in some of the more trendy music magazines. Alan Leeds remains of the opinion that *The Black Album* would have represented "a turning point, for better or worse, at a time when he needed one" – and would have had a much bigger impact that *Parade*, *Sign "O" The Times*, or *Lovesexy*.

Having fought off his dark urges, Prince immediately set about recording another new album. *Lovesexy* would become his defining spiritual statement, leaving no doubt as to where his heart and soul really lay – while also making amends for its 'evil' predecessor. He recorded the whole thing in seven weeks, taping the songs in more or less the order in which they appear on the album, and performing everything himself except for a spoken word

introduction by Ingrid Chavez (billed as Spirit Child), a rap by Cat Glover, and some of the more complex drum tracks (played by Sheila E.). So strong was his belief in this new work that he had begun rehearsing his band for a Lovesexy tour before Warner Bros had heard a note.

When it came to presenting the album to the label in March, Prince once again arrived with a series of awkward demands. This time around, instead of wanting to have a plain black jacket, he enlisted Jean Baptiste Mondino (his original choice of director for *Under The Cherry Moon*) to photograph him sitting naked on a large flower. There he sat, staring out as though in a trance, his genitalia covered only by a raised thigh. Warner Bros was concerned that

> **"I don't think Prince ever directly explained Lovesexy. But casual conversations with some of us revealed a lot."** ALAN LEEDS

some stores would refuse to stock the album, which did prove to be the case, even though the imagery is rather more passive than the covers of *Dirty Mind* and in many ways even *Purple Rain*. For Prince, however, there was nothing to be concerned about. "All that album cover was, was a picture," Prince told *Rolling Stone* in 1990. "If you looked at that picture and some ill came out of your mouth, than that's what you are – it's looking right back at you in the mirror."

Further headaches ensued when Prince announced that the nine-track CD should be presented as a single 45-minute piece, without track breaks. To him, of course, this was just another way of ensuring that the listener appreciated his art as a single entity, not as a collection of songs. To Warner Bros, however, it was another way of alienating the casual fan. (Prince got his way, although later pressings of the album are split into individual tracks.)

Prince had also decided that, as with *Around The World In A Day*, the album should be taken on its own artistic merits, and thus released without the accompaniment of promo videos or anything else that might diminish the air of mystery around it. It was fast becoming clear that, while still a bona fide musical genius, Prince had begun to lose his business savvy. Thankfully, he eventually relented and made a promo video for 'Alphabet St' – but only at the 11th hour, resulting in Alan Leeds having to scrabble around to find a director at short notice on a Sunday morning. The result was a quickly dated, blue-screened affair that sees Prince dancing and driving his "white rad ride" through a dense fog of letters which, at one point, spell out the phrase, "Don't buy *The Black Album*, I'm sorry." (Somewhat ironically, given Prince's recent attitudes toward hip-hop, 'Alphabet St' features a rap by Cat Glover.)

As far as Prince was concerned, *Lovesexy* was his most

intensely personal album yet. Most critics agreed, but were unsure exactly what conclusions to draw from the battle between sex and religion expressed in the songs. Even those closest to Prince weren't entirely sure what to make of it. The *St Paul Pioneer Press* described it as "a hasty note from a troubled soul," while *Rolling Stone* saw fit to exclaim that "the hardest questions may not lend themselves to easy answers, but make for much better music." Others were more cagey, with the *Detroit Free Press* suggesting that it "may take some time for listeners to get a handle on."

Most of the strengths and weaknesses of *Lovesexy* stem from the fact that it came from such an honest splurge of this-is-what-I-am-thinking recording. As Alan Leeds later noted, Prince responded to "an unpleasant reality" in the same way he always did: by "construct[ing] a reality of his own." In this case, having reached a low ebb and apparently unnerved himself with the darkness of *The Black Album*, he had found religion. Luckily for Prince, this particular religion was one that allowed him to reconcile his sexual and spiritual feelings with ease; one that allowed him to sing about "drippin' all over the floor" ('Lovesexy') and bodies jerking "like a horny pony" (Alphabet St) while also exclaiming, "Love is God, God is love" ('Anne Stesia').

Elsewhere on the album, the likes of 'Dance On' and 'Positivity' mark a return to socio-political concerns, notably gang warfare, while 'Anna Stesia' can be read as a direct acknowledgment of Prince's loneliness and need for salvation. The opening 'Eye No,' meanwhile, welcomes listeners to "the New Power Generation," which marks his first use of the term.

Musically, however, there was nothing particularly new about *Lovesexy*. The beats might have been harder and more complex than before – evidence of the fact Prince had become a semi-regular fixture on the Paris and London club scenes – but by now it was hardly surprising to hear a blend of different musical styles on a Prince record. The main talking point here concerned whether or not Prince had forgotten how to write tight, structured, melodic songs, or whether he had deliberately wanted to try to create one long movement. His insistence on a 'one track' CD suggests the latter, as does his later declaration that the album was intended to be "a mind trip, like a psychedelic movie." There are some neat production tricks throughout, too, not least the way Prince and either Glover or Sheila E.'s vocals mutate into Prince's own voice on the title track.

Prince himself was clearly happy with how *Lovesexy* turned out, but it sold only 750,000 copies, making it his least successful album since his debut, *For You*. It remains a firm fan favorite, although there is still some debate as to whether it marks a final creative peak or the start of a slow, steady decline into mediocrity. Its failure to sell irked Prince, who clearly felt that his most honest work to date should have been received with unparalleled enthusiasm.

It's unlikely that releasing *The Black Album* would have

made a difference to Prince's overall career path. But it might have helped reassert his dwindling credentials in the R&B world, and held a slightly broader appeal, but still showed no real progression or departure from what came before. Both albums were simply consolidations of old tricks – it just depended which tricks listeners preferred.

Even after *Lovesexy* struggled in at Number 11, Prince refused to believe that his most personal concept to date could fail, and had begun to plan the most extravagant tour of his career. Until now he had worked with neat, economical stage sets. The Controversy and Triple Threat tours made much of a simple set of ramps, lights, and a fireman's pole, while the Sign "O" The Times stage set was essentially a large-scale reproduction of the album art.

The Lovesexy set, however, took in swings, a miniature basketball court, and a set of hydraulics that would lift its star up toward the roof during the 'spiritual rebirth' part of 'Anna Stesia.' It cost two million dollars even before the costumes were made and a 90-person team brought in to run the show. Then there was the wireless technology required for the band to be able to get around the massive stage, not to mention the three-quarter-scale '67 Thunderbird Prince had built – at a cost of $250,000 – to take him to and from the stage. One final extravagance was nixed in the planning stage. "There was also supposed to be a fountain that poured hundreds and hundreds of gallons of water down into the center of the stage," recalled set designer Roy Bennett. "That would have been a very short show."

As well as generating the vast expense of building, storing, and transporting the stage set, Prince put his band on the payroll for six months of rehearsals before the tour had even started. He then took the crucial decision to switch the tour around right before it was due to kick off, scrapping the American leg in favor of taking the show to Europe, where *Lovesexy* was performing much more strongly. As with the Sign "O" The Times tour, however, it would surely have been more prudent to try to boost the album's performance at home first rather than allow it to sink even further down the charts. Switching territories at the last minute incurred all manner of costs, suggesting once again that Prince had lost his business sense.

From a musical perspective, however, the Lovesexy tour was as astounding as it was ambitious. Played in the round, it was set up to tell the good-versus-evil story of Prince's spiritual awakening. After running through a greatest hits set of earlier, sex-obsessed songs – 'Erotic City,' 'Jack U Off,' 'Dirty Mind,' and so on – Prince (as Bob George) would be shot down by a fleet of policemen. Then, after an extended reading of 'Anna Stesia,' during which Prince would literally be taken higher and higher into the arena, bathed in golden light, the show turned into a celebration of *Lovesexy*, with a smattering of old favorites such as 'When Doves Cry' and 'Purple Rain.' (When the accompanying tour movies, *Livesexy 1* and *Livesexy 2*, were released on VHS, the sets were reversed, giving the *Lovesexy* songs prominence.)

By the time the Lovesexy tour made it to the USA in September, Prince fans seemed to be losing interest in *Lovesexy* and the man himself – somewhat surprisingly, given that he had not been out on a full-scale tour of the country since 1985. It all ended up being reminiscent of the Dirty Mind tour, with sell-out crowds in Prince strongholds such as New York and Detroit, followed by a struggle to half-fill arenas elsewhere.

The US leg of the tour ended in November 1988. More than ever before, Prince was in need of a hit. As he sat at home in the months before an eight-date Japanese tour schedule for February 1989, he found his focus returning to an idea he had drafted more than a year earlier. After years of trying to escape it, he was beginning to come around to the idea of making a *Purple Rain Mk II*. But before that project got off the ground, another sure-fire commercial hit landed in his lap, attached to another movie project which, tellingly, wasn't one of his own.

FRUSTRATED BY THE RESPONSE TO *LOVESEXY*, PRINCE TURNED HIS ATTENTION AT THE END OF 1988 TO HIS ATTEMPTS TO RESURRECT A PLAN FOR *GRAFFITI BRIDGE*, A BIG-SCREEN FOLLOW-UP TO *PURPLE RAIN*, BUT ONCE AGAIN PROGRESS WAS FAR FROM SMOOTH. FOLLOWING DISAGREEMENTS ABOUT HOW TO PROCEED WITH THE PROJECT, HE SACKED HIS LONG-STANDING MANAGEMENT TEAM OF CAVALLO, RUFFALO & FARGNOLI AND BROUGHT IN ALBERT MAGNOLI, THE DIRECTOR OF *PURPLE RAIN*, TO HANDLE HIS AFFAIRS INSTEAD.

Batman (JANUARY 1989–JUNE 1989)

Magnoli knew he had a difficult job on his hands. Prince was desperate to re-establish himself as a creative force within the movie industry and repeat the commercial success that had eluded him since *Purple Rain* – and thus halt an alarming financial freefall, exacerbated recently by the losses made on the Lovesexy tour and the hefty severance packages paid to Cavallo, Ruffalo & Fargnoli. Fortunately for all concerned, Magnoli's first move was a masterstroke (or at least a slice of extremely good luck).

In October 1988 Warner Bros Pictures had started shooting the first serious big-screen adaptation of *Batman* with goth-lite director Tim Burton at the helm. While putting together rough edits of some early footage, Burton had used '1999' and 'Baby, I'm A Star' to backdrop specific scenes. Prince's songs worked so well that Burton got in touch with Magnoli to see if the singer would be interested in contributing to the soundtrack. (His original scheme was for Michael Jackson to soundtrack the 'light' side of the movie, with Prince providing the 'dark' songs, but that didn't last for long.)

Prince wasn't sure about the idea at first, but flew out to London in January 1989 to meet Burton on the Gotham City set at Pinewood Studios. Suitably impressed by a 20-minute showreel – and, some have suggested, a meeting with Kim Basinger – Prince decided to put his own movie plans on hold and work on the *Batman* soundtrack instead. The fact that one of the first songs he learnt to play on his father's piano was the original 60s *Batman* theme would have helped – as indeed would the reported commissioning fee of one million dollars. So enthusiastic was Prince about the project, in fact, that he tried to cancel the Japanese leg of the Lovesexy tour in order to get straight on with it, but was convinced otherwise.

On his return, Prince spent six weeks in February and March working on songs for the soundtrack. Despite having originally been asked only to 'contribute,' he presented Burton and Warner Bros with a full eleven-track album. Deciding that the *Batman* brand had enough commercial clout to warrant both a Prince soundtrack and an instrumental score by Danny Elfman, the company gave him the green light. Burton, however, rejected two of

The Batman songs 'Electric Chair' and 'Trust' were intended to represent The Joker, played in the movie by Jack Nicholson.

the songs Prince had recorded, '200 Balloons' and 'Rave Unto The Joy Fantastic.' Prince subsequently released '200 Balloons' as the B-side of 'Batdance,' but ended up hanging on to 'Rave' until 1999's *Rave Un2 The Joy Fantastic* LP.

The final nine-track *Batman* album went on sale on June 20 1989, three days before the movie opened in the USA. Those who bought it after having seen the movie might have been slightly confused by its contents, however: only 'Partyman' and 'Trust' appear prominently in the movie, while 'Scandalous' (co-written by Prince's

not written specifically for the movie, since 'The Future,' 'Electric Chair,' and 'Vicki Waiting' all came from 1988 recording sessions. The song that Prince seemed to put the most effort in on is 'Batdance,' a dance-orientated collision of samples of movie dialogue and other songs from the soundtrack put together so meticulously – in the manner, somewhat ironically, of hip-hop acts such as Public Enemy – as to suggest that Prince had spent more time on it than anything else on the record.

Nonetheless, the success of the movie helped push the genuinely catchy singles 'Partyman' and 'Batdance' up the charts – the latter beat the *Ghostbusters II* soundtrack single 'On Our Own' by Bobby Brown to Number One – and resulted in the album selling more than four million copies, making it Prince's most commercially successful offering since *Purple Rain*. It also added him to a very select group of artists to have released two *Billboard* Number One soundtrack albums. The only downside, it seemed, was that Prince had had to agree to sign the publishing rights to the songs used in the movie over to Warner Bros, which

"The one-man band from Minneapolis knew from the get-go that Batman ... was going to be the biggest tie-in this side of shoelaces." ROLLING STONE

father, John L Nelson) plays over the second half of the end credits. Nothing more than snippets of the other tracks were used, suggesting that Prince's over-enthusiasm might have gotten the better of him.

Batman is hardly a great piece of work and, while some reviews praised its commercial appeal, others were quick to note a distinct lack of major artistic progression. The stripped-down funk sound is closer to *The Black Album* than *Lovesexy*, but despite Prince's efforts to interject the psychological quirks of Batman/Bruce Wayne and The Joker into most of the songs, there are no great stretches of the imagination (except perhaps for Kim Basinger's moans of pleasure on 'Scandalous').

Rolling Stone was correct to assume that some of the songs had simply been "sitting around Paisley Park" and

means that only the single B-sides '200 Balloons,' 'Feel U Up,' and 'I Love U In Me' appear on the comprehensive compilation *The Hits/The B-Sides*.

For Prince himself, however, the commercial success of *Batman* was a mixed blessing. On the one hand, it must have irked him to some extent that something so commercially minded, throwaway, and unrepresentative of his true artistic vision had become such a big hit when albums much closer to his heart (particularly *Lovesexy*) were widely ignored. What he couldn't argue with, however, was the fact that *Batman* had re-established him as a commercial force in both the music and movie worlds after years of diminishing financial returns, giving him much greater clout when it came to convincing Warner Bros to back his *Graffiti Bridge* project.

Lemon Crush: Prince And Kim Basinger

Prince has tended, over the years, to avoid having relationships with other public figures – except, of course, those involved in his various side-projects. What this tells us about him is open to interpretation, but it's interesting to note what happened when he tried to pull another star with a profile as high as his own into his orbit.

Prince met Kim Basinger in January 1989 at London's Pinewood Studios on the set of *Batman*, in which she plays the part of Vicki Vale. He fell so hard for her that some have suggested that her involvement in the movie is what really made him want to record the soundtrack. (It's not hard to imagine him relishing her seductive admission to The Joker: "I just *love* purple.")

Basinger had previously played the female lead in *9½ Weeks*, a steamy look at the dark side of relationships that was, perhaps unsurprisingly, one of Prince's

favorite movies of recent times. When it came time for her to join Prince in the studio to add her vocals to what is essentially a tribute to her, 'Scandalous,' the pair reportedly staged their own homage to *9½ Weeks*' sex-and-food shenanigans, leaving the Paisley Park engineers to clean honey off the mixing desk the following morning. (Basinger's contributions to the main edit of 'Scandalous' are limited to a few groans of pleasure, but the 'Sex Suite' mix includes a series of suggestive exchanges between her and Prince.)

The pair's relationship was strange and shadowy from the start. It was once rumored that Prince offered up as much as five million pounds to speed up Basinger's immediate divorce from make-up artist husband Ron Britton, while others have suggested that Prince had an almost hypnotic hold over her. She even sacked her manager and installed Albert Magnoli in his place. She also worked with Prince on a third draft of *Graffiti Bridge* and agreed to play the female lead – with Prince offering to record an album for her in return.

Then, almost as suddenly as the relationship started, it was over. Basinger left Paisley Park in January 1990, throwing another spanner into the *Graffiti Bridge* works. It's not entirely clear what happened between them, since almost every word spoken about the relationship is based on rumor and allegation. Perhaps the weirdest tale told is the one that claims that Basinger's family had become so concerned about her infatuation with Prince that they essentially had to kidnap her from Paisley Park. Whether this is true or not, Basinger did leave in such a hurry that she left her car in Prince's driveway. (He eventually had it towed.)

Neither party has said a lot about the affair since. In 1990, Prince told *Rolling Stone*, "I really don't know her that well." But he seems to have harbored feelings for her since, and even allegedly offered to help with the eight million dollar lawsuit she faced after pulling out of the movie *Boxing Helena* in 1993. (That year he also released 'Peach,' which is based around her distinctive moans and groans.)

"Holy hit singles, Batman! Prince has done it again!"

DETROIT FREE PRESS (JUNE 19 1989)

3

DESPITE STARTING THE DECADE WITH HIS SECOND BIG-SCREEN FLOP, *GRAFFITI BRIDGE*, PRINCE QUICKLY HIT ANOTHER PURPLE PATCH WITH *DIAMONDS AND PEARLS* AND THE SIGNING OF WHAT HE CLAIMED WAS A '$100 MILLION' DEAL WITH WARNER BROS. AS THE DECADE CONTINUED, HOWEVER, HIS STAR BEGAN TO FALL. HE BECAME EMBROILED IN A BITTER WAR WITH WARNER BROS AND ENDED UP CHANGING HIS NAME TO AN UNPRONOUNCEABLE SYMBOL IN AN EFFORT TO REDEFINE HIMSELF.

WHAT'S MY NAME?
1989—1995

AFTER THE WIDESPREAD FAILURE OF *UNDER THE CHERRY MOON*, IT TOOK PRINCE A LONG TIME TO GET THE FOLLOW-UP OFF THE GROUND. HE HAD BEEN CARRYING AROUND A TREATMENT FOR *GRAFFITI BRIDGE* – NAMED FOR A REAL MINNEAPOLIS LANDMARK – SINCE SEPTEMBER 1987.

Graffiti Bridge (JULY 1989–NOVEMBER 1990)

Back then the plan was for Madonna to play Ruthie Washington opposite Prince's Camille Blue. But when Madonna came to Paisley Park to look at the script she told Prince that it was terrible and that she wanted nothing to do with the project. (The pair did nonetheless collaborate on her 'Love Song,' later featured on her 1989 LP *Like A Prayer*.)

Similarly, Bob Cavallo assumed that the 20-page treatment Prince gave him in advance of a meeting with Warner Bros in December was a draft, and suggested hiring a professional writer to turn it into a screenplay. Prince of course felt that the 'draft' was all he needed, but for Cavallo it looked like a disaster waiting to happen. "He didn't really wanna work with us anymore," Cavallo later claimed, "but if I could have gotten that film made, I think he would have." As things stood, however, Cavallo didn't feel particularly inclined toward raising funds for a project that already seemed doomed to failure.

Prince's response to this, on December 31 1988, was to fire his entire management team, along with his lawyer and financial advisor. This would prove to be a big

mistake. Cavallo, Ruffalo & Fargnoli – and Steve Fargnoli in particular – had played a crucial role in keeping Prince's career on track over the years. They had done all the fighting with Warner Bros on his behalf, and had managed to get him almost everything he wanted. Without them, Prince would find himself in a much weaker position at the negotiating table. Sacking his lawyers and financial advisors at the same time only exacerbated the problem, and left him in the position of having to install a new team at a time when his financial situation was less than buoyant.

Fortunately, Prince had recently been back in touch with *Purple Rain* director Albert Magnoli, who had shot some of the Lovesexy shows for a planned documentary, and whose movie-industry contacts would certainly be useful when it came to trying to get *Graffiti Bridge* made. (Unlike Cavallo, Magnoli seemed unconditionally supportive of the project – at least to begin with.) But while his loyalty was so far uncontested, Magnoli had yet to prove himself able to turn around Prince's deteriorating financial situation and do battle with Warner Bros.

Magnoli's first move as Prince's manager – getting him

"It was one of the purest, most spiritual things I've ever done. Maybe it will take people 30 years to get it. They trashed The Wizard Of Oz at first, too." *PRINCE*

the *Batman* soundtrack – was hugely successful. It turned around a run of seemingly poor decisions – withdrawing *The Black Album*, replacing it with the poor-selling *Lovesexy*, and then going off on a loss-making tour – that had left Warner Bros feeling decidedly unsure about the idea of investing in another risky, big-budget project. But once Prince had proven he was still capable of multi-million sales, the company became more open to the *Graffiti Bridge* project – particularly now that it was being billed as a follow-up of sorts to *Purple Rain*.

Prince came away from *Batman* with a newfound commercial clout and Kim Basinger – whom he now planned to cast as *Graffiti Bridge*'s female lead – on his arm. But while Albert Magnoli was already talking about setting up a movie production company in partnership with Prince to "do projects that are diversified and take the entire gamut of entertainment," the singer was in fact still struggling to raise enough money for the first one. As 1989

"Graffiti Bridge should be bronzed immediately and delivered to Hollywood's Hall Of Shamelessness, where it might draw bigger crowds than it's likely to at movie theaters."

WASHINGTON POST

drew to a close, Magnoli started to feel the same way as Bob Cavallo had a year earlier.

"My idea for the film was for a higher-budget, more elaborate concept," he recalled. "But Prince wanted a lower-budget approach and to get the film out within a year. So I just said, 'Why don't you do that, 'cause I'm shooting for the moon here.'" And so it was that Prince found himself looking for his third management team in the space of a year.

This time he hired Arnold Stiefel and Randy Phillips, who had promised to secure the financial backing needed to make *Graffiti Bridge*. In what can be seen as an important shift in priorities, Prince now seemed to be hiring people who would tell him what he wanted to hear, not what he needed to hear. "He was beginning," recalled Warner Bros Vice President Marylou Badeaux, "to not listen to anyone who was not a 'yes' man."

In fairness to Stiefel & Phillips, they did make good their promise to secure seven million dollars of Warner Bros Pictures' money – exactly the same amount that Mo Ostin had put up in order to get *Purple Rain* off the ground. Warner Bros had been sold on the fact that the movie was set to reprise the feud between Morris Day and The Kid, and agreed to finance it on the condition that the original line-up of The Time would appear.

This didn't seem like it would be a problem. Prince had already started working with Morris Day and Jerome Benton on a new album called *Corporate World*, so could easily use those recordings as a springboard to The Time's *Pandemonium*. He was also able to convince Jimmy Jam, Terry Lewis, and Jesse Johnson to return on the basis that *Graffiti Bridge* would tell The Time's side of the story.

Unsurprisingly, however, the plot emphasis began to shift almost as soon as the movie entered production, and as seemed to be the case whenever Prince tried to make a movie, this one step forward was followed by another step back. Having split up with Kim Basinger in January 1990, he was left looking for a new female lead – just as had been the case when Vanity quit on the eve of shooting *Purple Rain*. Since his other on-off girlfriend of the past few years, Anna Garcia, had already packed her bags and flown back to Britain, Prince approached Ingrid Chavez, whom he had met

For the Nude tour Prince brought in a new hip-hop element in the form of The Game Boyz.
RIGHT Jerome Benton (left) and Maurice Day returned to reprise their *Purple Rain* roles in *Graffiti Bridge*.

around the time of *The Black Album*. (Chavez has been credited with kick-starting Prince's spiritual rebirth – she appears as 'Spirit Child' on *Lovesexy* – so seemed like an obvious candidate for *Graffiti Bridge*, which has a strong spiritual grounding.)

Having already completed work on the accompanying soundtrack album, Prince and his cast of bandmates and friends – including Mavis Staples and George Clinton, both of whom were signed to Paisley Park Records at the time – shot the movie in six weeks during February and March 1990. Most of the scenes were shot on the Paisley Park soundstage on sets that Prince admitted were cheap before musing, in a *Rolling Stone* interview, "Man, what I'd do with a $25 million budget. I'll need a big success to get that, but I'll get it. I *will* get it."

Elsewhere in the interview, which runs the gamut between cheeriness and defensive uncertainty, Prince refuted the idea that he had taken a gamble in making *Graffiti Bridge*. "What gamble?" he asks. "I made a seven million dollar movie with somebody else's money, and I'm sitting here finishing it."

Graffiti Bridge might not have seemed like a gamble to Prince, but it certainly was for Warner Bros, whose money the singer was cheerfully spending. When test audiences reacted poorly to the movie in April, the company demanded that Steve Rivkin – brother of Prince alumni David and Bobby – be brought in to oversee further edits and try to salvage the project. Prince postponed a planned European tour by six weeks in order to work on a new edit, but still hadn't completed it by the time he stepped onto the stage at the Stadion Feijenoord in Rotterdam, Holland, on June 2.

For the three-month Nude tour of Europe and Japan Prince assembled a line-up of old hands – Matt Fink, Miko Weaver, and Levi Seacer Jr – and new members, among them keyboardist Rosie Gaines, drummer Michael Bland,

and three hip-hop dancers, Tony Mosley, Damon Dickerson, and Kirk Johnson, whom he christened The Game Boyz. The Nude tour marked another change of approach for Prince. Whereas in recent years he had played on extravagant stage sets and focused on new material, he now seemed content to run through the hits against a less showy backdrop of ramps and poles – the sort of stripped-down stage set he had utilized on earlier tours. There was some suggestion that the move was financially motivated – a claim given further credence by the fact that the singer had recently started construction of a Minneapolis nightclub, Grand Slam, which put a further strain on his resources. But as far as Prince was concerned, "kids save a lot of money for a long time to buy tickets, and I like to give them what they want." To that end, having seemingly conceded defeat in his war on hip-hop, he even let Tony Mosley rap during *Batman*'s 'The Future.'

The Nude tour might have been slicker and less experimental than previous Prince shows, but it was a resounding success. The promise of back-to-back hits provoked a huge response from concertgoers, notably in London, where Prince played a record-breaking 16-night run at Wembley Arena. (Dire Straits had held the previous record of nine nights.)

Even so, Prince was still left to sort out the mess of *Graffiti Bridge*, which he was now attempting to edit on VHS machines in hotel rooms. He then had to shoot additional scenes in Hollywood in September after completing the Japanese leg of the tour. The movie had been due for release during the summer, but was delayed until November 2, whereupon it received even more scathing reviews than had *Under The Cherry Moon* and took only $4.2 million at the box office.

"I didn't want to make *Die Hard 4*," Prince told *Rolling Stone* in an attempt to defend *Graffiti Bridge*. "But I'm also

not looking to be Francis Ford Coppola. I see this more like those 50s rock'n'roll movies." For *Entertainment Weekly*, however, the movie could "barely muster the energy to get from one shot to the next." The *St Paul Pioneer Press* did its best to take a positive perspective, noting that there are "so many good musical numbers … that the plot barely has time to exist." The *Washington Post*, by contrast, simply begged Warner Bros to "stop him before he films again!"

Graffiti Bridge is essentially a visual version of *Lovesexy*: a confusing splurge of Prince's innermost thoughts. His close-cropped beard says it all: this will be my defining, most mature artistic statement. But while *Purple Rain* had an element of psychodrama, *Graffiti Bridge* merely proves that Prince believed that the movie (like its predecessor, *Under The Cherry Moon*) could succeed on the strength of its music and the barest of good-versus-evil plotlines. He would later claim that the aim of the movie was to be "non-violent, positive, and [have] no blatant sex scenes," having apparently forgotten that the scene that test audiences had most objected to was the one of him masturbating to the song 'Tick, Tick, Bang.'

It's difficult to think of *Graffiti Bridge* as anything other than an abject failure, from the weak plot to the terrible acting and unconvincing rivalry between Morris Day and The Kid (who do battle over the ownership of a fictional nightclub). Unsurprisingly, it marked the last time Prince ever received financial backing for a big-screen feature.

Fortunately, however – and just as had been the case with *Under The Cherry Moon* – the accompanying soundtrack album was much stronger, and gave critics something to rally around. *Rolling Stone* gave it a four-and-a-half star review that praised the work of an artist "reasserting his originality … with the ease of a conqueror." *Time* called the album a "groovable feast," while *Q* felt it "practically impossible to choose anything that doesn't deserve to be there. How long is it since that can honestly be said about a Prince album?"

For the *New York Times*, *Graffiti Bridge* was the work of a "far less conventional" Prince now able to "take chances that didn't exist for him with *Purple Rain*." The singer himself seemed to be in total agreement. "'Thieves In The Temple' and 'Tick, Tick, Bang' don't sound like *nothing* I've ever done before," he told *Rolling Stone*. The level of praise heaped upon the record seemed to be based mostly on the fact that *Graffiti Bridge* is much more song-based than *Lovesexy*, and also a lot more varied. It also makes good use of songs by other artists featured in the movie, including Mavis Staples, George Clinton, the child R&B star Tevin Campbell, and The Time.

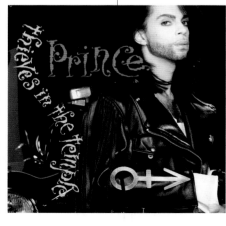

The fact that many of the songs had been around for quite some time probably helped, too. 'Tick, Tick, Bang,' the most explicit track on the album, dates back as far as 1981, while the masterful 'Joy In Repetition' was originally slated to appear on *Crystal Ball*. The funk-gospel 'Elephants & Flowers' had been reworked from a 1988 recording session, while fan-favorite ballad 'The Question Of U' was written in 1985.

Of the three songs recorded with *Graffiti Bridge* in mind, only lead-off single 'Thieves In The Temple' hits the heights of the older material, while the 'joy of repetition' seems a little more dubious on the opening 'Can't Stop The Feeling I Got,' which does nothing that earlier rockabilly-style tunes such as 'Jack U Off' and 'Delirious' hadn't done better before.

All in all *Graffiti Bridge* seemed like the perfect album for those fans who had been turned off by the high concepts but wanted something a bit meatier than *Batman*. It proved that, even if the best tracks came from The Vault, Prince could still put together an album of proper songs. But for all its strengths, and all the praise heaped upon it, the album sold less than a million copies, putting it on a par with *Lovesexy* in terms of commercial success (or failure).

Looking back now, it seems that the project most indicative of Prince's future direction in 1990 was not *Graffiti Bridge* but the Nude tour. Not only did it get Prince to focus on his past hits – and thus start thinking about writing some new ones – its incorporation of hip-hop elements suggested that Prince was ready to reconnect with the black audience many felt he had left behind in the 80s.

"We were his first black band," Rosie Gaines recalled of the group that would soon become known as the New Power Generation, "and our thing was to help him get his audience back." In the past few years Prince's singles had seemed to perform better on *Billboard*'s R&B chart than the Hot 100, and it now seemed that he was returning to the idea of recording songs for songs' sake, and not to serve grand, overlying concepts. At the end of the year he would bring in Tony Mosley (now calling himself to Tony M) to work on a record that would bring him back to his black roots like nothing since the shelved *Black Album*.

IN DECEMBER 1990, SHORTLY AFTER COMPLETING WORK ON THE FOLLOW-UP TO *GRAFFITI BRIDGE*, PRINCE DECIDED ONCE AGAIN TO SHAKE UP HIS MANAGERIAL INFRASTRUCTURE. ONE MIGHT HAVE EXPECTED HIM TO RE-HIRE ARNOLD STIEFEL AND RANDY PHILLIPS, WHO HAD DONE A REASONABLE JOB FOR THE DURATION OF THEIR INITIAL 12-MONTH CONTRACT, BUT PRINCE SAW THINGS DIFFERENTLY.

Diamonds And Pearls

(DECEMBER 1990–JULY 1992)

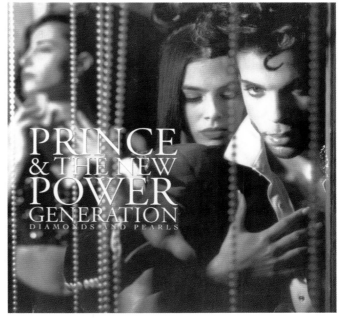

As far as he was concerned they had done what he wanted of them – securing financial backing for *Graffiti Bridge* – and could now be shown the door. When it came to replacing Stiefel and Phillips, Prince opted not to seek out professional businesspeople but to promote from within his already close-knit circle. And so it was that Gilbert Davison stepped up from head of security (a role he had inherited in 1985 from Chick Huntsberry) to manager and President of Paisley Park Enterprises, while press officer Jill Willis, formerly of the New York PR company Rogers & Cowan, was installed as Vice President.

Prince's touring band – now known officially as The New Power Generation – was given a similar overhaul. When Matt Fink told the singer that he wasn't available for two appearances at the Rock In Rio festival in January 1991, he found himself replaced by Tommy Elm, whom Prince rechristened Tommy Barbarella after the cult Jane Fonda movie. (The move was similar to the sacking of Jimmy Jam and Terry Lewis from The Time in 1983 in that Fink had been busy producing another band at the time.) Meanwhile, Levi Seacer Jr switched from bass to guitar, following the departure of Miko Weaver at the end of the Nude tour, and Sonny Thompson was brought in on bass.

Prince had planned to spend the early months of 1991 trying to drum up interest in his forthcoming *Diamonds*

> 🎵 *"Prince's music in the 90s suffered because, for the first time, he allowed outside trends to influence his work."* ALAN LEEDS

And Pearls, but instead found himself distracted by other matters. On February 1 he was sued by his former managers, Cavallo, Ruffalo & Fargnoli, who claimed $600,000 in severance pay and damages for breach of contract, fraud, and denial of contract in bad faith. Prince was also charged with ignoring his managers' advice since 1985 and continuing to flood the market with competing product (a claim that would perhaps have hurt the singer more than the others). He retaliated by suing his former lawyers, arguing that they had negotiated an unfavorable settlement with Cavallo, Ruffalo & Fargnoli.

The whole mess was eventually settled out of court, but meant that it wasn't until March that Prince could really concentrate on the business of convincing Warner Bros to release his new album. The company had been keen instead to release a greatest hits set in an effort to break a run of increasingly low-selling albums. What the label executives hadn't anticipated, however, was that, on *Diamonds And Pearls*, Prince had stopped chasing his artistic muse and decided, for the first time ever, to concentrate specifically on writing hits.

In fact, Prince was so determined to make a success of *Diamonds And Pearls* that he went out on the promotional circuit well before the album's release, performing at industry showcases, making one-off television appearances, and playing 'Gett Off' in his 'assless' pants at the MTV Video Music Awards. He even hired a pair of dancers, Lori Elle and Robia La Morte, to play the roles of 'Diamond' and 'Pearl.' These were the very sorts of promotional activities that Prince would have baulked at a few years earlier, but now they were helping to push his media profile up to its highest point since *Purple Rain*.

Another change could be seen in relation to the singer's attitude toward promo videos. In the past he had sometimes refused to make them at all, insisting that his art be judged on its own merits, but this time he went into overdrive, issuing a video EP with promos not just for the album's first single, 'Gett Off,' but also for its B-sides. According to the director, Rob Borm, Prince worked like a man possessed on the main 'Gett Off' promo, even going so far as to make executive decisions on the edit from the back of his limo. "He would call me up," Borm recalled, "and say, 'Rob, you know that third shot in [the] sequence? Trim two frames off the tails.'" The high-concept piece, which Prince wanted to look like the 1979 movie *Caligula*, ended up costing five times more than its original $200,000 budget.

The well-oiled promotional machine had certainly done its job by the time *Diamonds And Pearls* went on sale in October 1991. Prince might almost have driven himself and his band – who had had to get used to nine-hour rehearsals and three hours' sleep – into the ground, but it all paid off in the end. The album ended up selling more than six million copies worldwide and found its way into the upper reaches of both the British and American album charts.

It's not hard to see why. *Diamonds And Pearls* has a neat, polished, early-90s sound and contains little that might challenge the casual listener. "You know when you buy someone's record and there's always an element missing?" Prince asked *Details* magazine. "The voice is wrong or the drums are lame or something? On mine there's nothing missing."

In reality, however, that's part of the problem. Denser

"Black awareness is really taking an upturn today, and he really wants to be a part of that." TONY M (RAPPER, 1991-93)

even than *Lovesexy*, the album almost sinks under the weight of its over-production. Tracks such as 'Thunder' and 'Cream' – two of six singles to be drawn from the album – are undeniably catchy, but are so slick that they could easily pass as standard pop-radio fodder. So too could the fan-favorite title track, which shows Prince at his most bombastic. The falsetto-sung 'Insatiable' is more subtle, but is essentially a re-write of 1989's 'Scandalous.' And while Prince's heart is in the right place on 'Money Don't Matter 2 Night' and 'Live 4 Love' (which focuses on the Gulf War), neither song quite manages to drive its message home.

Prince recorded much of *Diamonds And Pearls* live in the studio with The New Power Generation – something of a bone of contention among the bandmembers, who later felt that he had failed to credit them properly for their input. As talented a bunch as these musicians were, however, they lacked The Revolution's capacity for risk and experimentation, resulting in a series of arrangements largely devoid of the quirks and twists that made otherwise simple songs such as 'Mountains' work so well. (While *Sign "O" The Times* had been recorded on a six-track machine, *Diamonds And Pearls* makes use of as many as 48 tracks.)

The album is hampered further by a smooth R&B sheen designed to win back the favor of the black audience many critics felt Prince had left behind. Even those involved with the record weren't entirely convinced by this particular change. "I was dismayed that Prince wanted to emulate the sound of current black music," recalled engineer Michael Koppelman. "It was frustrating to see what I consider to be a very talented musician fucking around with a lot of trendy crap."

The most glaring change to the Prince sound is the singer's wholesale embrace of hip-hop – something he had spoken out against several years earlier. During the previous year's Nude tour Prince had brought in three male backing dancers, The Game Boyz, and quickly discovered that one of them, Tony Mosley, could rap. After giving him a few solo spots on the tour, Prince invited Mosley to rap on a number of tracks on *Diamonds And Pearls*, even basing an entire song, 'Jughead,' around his less than engrossing delivery about managers being "parasites" and "money minders."

'Jughead' certainly had an impact, but not in the sense that Prince might have anticipated. After hearing it, Steve Fargnoli served him with a five-million-dollar lawsuit, claiming defamation and breach of contract (Prince and Cavallo, Ruffalo & Fargnoli were forbidden from talking publicly about each other as part of their previous settlement).

Prince's attempts to ingratiate himself with the hip-hop world didn't end there. In case anyone had missed the point, he took to singing into a gun-shaped microphone on stage, but it didn't seem to have the desired effect. As Alan Leeds later recalled: "The 'keep it real' hip-hop community wasn't buying Tony M or a gun-shaped microphone from a guy Prince's age [33] who had grown up in a relatively middle-class Midwestern environment." Even his most supportive critics failed to rally round Prince this time. The general feeling was that Prince needed a rest; or, as *Entertainment Weekly* put it, that "too many years churning out records by himself in his Paisley Park complex have taken their toll." As far as the *New Musical Express* was concerned, it all served as proof that Prince was no longer a "vital force acting on pop music's zeitgeist."

Prince's use of a gun-shaped microphone was all part of a concerted effort to reassert his 'masculine' qualities. He seemed determined to keep that going offstage, too. As keyboardist Rosie Gaines recalled, "when he was with the boys I was just another woman to him. He was kind of a male chauvinist at that point." While Prince tended to travel with Diamond, Pearl, and his latest discovery, Mayte Garcia – a 19-year-old dancer whose mother had sent the singer a video of her dancing to 'Thieves In The Temple' a year earlier – Gaines found herself stuck for long stretches on a tour bus with the rest of the male membership of the group, by whom she was often bullied. Unsurprisingly, she left at the end of the tour. (She was replaced, for the next album, by Morris Hayes.)

Like the album itself, the Diamonds And Pearls tour was Prince's most conventional to date. The stage set, which included various statues and a 'love symbol'-shaped spaceship, was certainly extravagant, but the musical arrangements left little room for improvisation and felt more like a revue, while the newly hired brass section – which brought total membership of The New Power Generation up to 17 – played much more of a straightforward R&B role than the jazzy duo of Eric Leeds and Matt Blistan had in years past.

The tour was a resounding success, but the cost of the stage show, huge entourage, and regular bonuses for bandmembers who played at aftershows cut right into any potential profits. "The amount of money spent on the road was just ridiculous," recalled Prince's UK publicist of the time, Chris Poole. "His accountants told me later that it didn't make any money. That he spent it all, basically."

This didn't seem to matter to Prince, who still seemed not to have grasped how precarious his financial situation had become. Perhaps he simply felt that, having re-

> "I was brought up in a black-and-white world ... I always said that one day I would play all kinds of music and not be judged for the color of my skin but the quality of my work." PRINCE

established himself as a commercial success, he didn't need to worry anymore. He had almost completed his next album even before the Diamonds And Pearls tour finished, and was so confident in the material that he took to playing tracks from it over the public address system before taking the stage during his eight-night run at London's Earl's Court Arena. His intention was to release these new songs on an album with an unpronounceable title as quickly as possible. But as is so often the case with Prince, things didn't work out quite as he had planned.

THE SUCCESS OF *DIAMONDS AND PEARLS*, HIS BEST-SELLING RECORD IN YEARS, PUT PRINCE IN A MUCH BETTER POSITION WHEN IT CAME TO RENEGOTIATING HIS CONTRACT WITH WARNER BROS IN AUGUST 1992. FROM THE LABEL'S PERSPECTIVE, THE NEW DEAL WAS GEARED TOWARD ENCOURAGING PRINCE TO CARRY ON MAKING HIT RECORDS.

Love Symbol (AUGUST 1992–SEPTEMBER 1993)

It reportedly gave him a 20 per cent royalty rate and a huge advance of ten million dollars per album – on the condition that the previous album managed to sell more than five million copies.

Prince's view on this was that his new '$100 million' deal put him on an ever higher pay-scale than Madonna and Michael Jackson, who had both recently negotiated $60 million contracts with Warner Bros and Epic respectively. More conservative estimates suggested that he stood to make around $30 million. As far as the public was concerned, the new deal made Prince pop's most bankable act. But for Warner Bros, the litmus test would be his 14th studio album, given the title of an unpronounceable symbol, and later dubbed *Love Symbol*, which the singer had once again recorded with, and co-credited to, The New Power Generation.

Warner Bros had high hopes that, despite its unpronounceable title, the new album would repeat the success of *Diamonds And Pearls* when it was released on October 13 1992, almost exactly one year after its predecessor. In the event, however, it barely managed to sell a million copies. So much for the ten-million-dollar advance on the next one.

Part of the problem lay in the choice of singles used to promote the album. Prince decided to follow 'Sexy MF,' which was unplayable on radio because of its course lyrics and limped in at Number 66 on *Billboard*, with the unrepresentative 'My Name Is Prince,' a hip-hop track unlikely to attract any new listeners. Warner Bros had wanted to release the majestic, Eastern-tinged '7' instead, and would be vindicated when they eventually did, as '7' fittingly reached Number Seven on the Hot 100 (a marked improvement on 'My Name Is Prince''s Number 36).

By then, however, the *Love Symbol* LP's fate had been sealed. The critics found the album to be as confusing as any Prince release to date. Some reviewers even confused themselves, with *Spin* arguing on the one hand that the record broke no new ground, and on the other that it served as further evidence of Prince's "silly and crafty genius." The *Minneapolis Star-Tribune* was firmer in its findings, declaring the album to be "a royal disappointment."

The confusion was Prince's own fault. In the press

release that accompanied the album, he described it as a "rock soap opera" designed to play out across the record's 75-minute runtime. The plan – at least to begin with – was for it to tell the story of how he met and wooed the Crown Princess Of Cairo, played by his latest love interest, Mayte Garcia, while being hounded in a series of spoken-word segues by a news reporter (played by Kirstie Alley). But then, right at the last minute, he decided to add a new song, 'Eye Wanna Melt With U,' and had to cut some of the segues to make room for it.

This left only his battles with Alley – which seem only to confirm the singer's obsession with avoiding interviews and frustrating journalists – and made it virtually impossible to understand what was going on in narrative tracks such as '3 Chains O' Gold.' The *3 Chains O' Gold*

VHS, which strung together several promo videos, helped clarify matters a little – until you get to the '7' clip, which serves only to muddy the waters further as Prince suddenly finds himself having to kill off seven of his past selves.

Love Symbol is much more impressive without the 'rock soap opera' tag. In terms of scope, it's not quite up there with *Sign "O" The Times*, but certainly trumps *Graffiti Bridge*. One major improvement on *Diamonds And Pearls* is the performance of The New Power Generation, who appear on around half of the songs. After tightening up on the road and growing more accustomed to working in the studio, the musicians sound willing and able to go wherever their leader wants to take them. (On *Diamonds And Pearls*, by contrast, Prince seemed at times to be pandering to his cohorts' limitations.)

Welcome 2 The New Power Generation

Along with his 'love symbol,' the very phrase 'New Power Generation' came to represent much more to Prince than just a name. To the man himself, it had evolved into more of a concept. On 'Eye No,' recorded in 1987 and included on 1988's *Lovesexy*, he welcomes listeners to his new power generation, explaining that his "voice is so clear" because "there's no smack in my brain."

Right from the outset the NPG seemed to symbolize self-improvement and the quest for a better, healthier lifestyle. That the idea first emerged on Prince's most spiritual album to date was no accident. He took the concept even further a year later on *Graffiti Bridge*, naming the album's second track 'The New Power Generation' and declaring: "We want 2 change the world." Even before he started referring to his band by the same name, he seemed to have decided that the NPG should lead the way when it came to advocating a better life.

It's somewhat ironic then that the band which eventually took the name, and which was deemed important enough to be credited alongside him on albums such as *Diamonds And Pearls*, initially seemed like nothing more than a tight, proficient group of session musicians. As far as Prince was concerned, this was just what he needed. He could, he told *Rolling Stone*, "keep switching gears on them and something else funky will happen." But while The New Power Generation certainly had the hard R&B chops required to keep up with current trends in the black music market, they would never be anywhere near as innovative or influential a band as The Revolution.

For a while, Prince seemed to hide behind his new group in an effort to push forward a more masculine – and more black – image. After that the group became a useful tool to hide behind when it came to recording and releasing music. Warner Bros didn't want Prince to keep releasing so many albums, and wouldn't let him license his recordings to any other labels. So when *Goldnigga* and *Exodus* were released, in 1993 and 1995, respectively, they were credited to the New Power Generation, despite being helmed by Prince himself.

No one was fooled, of course, but Prince continued to use the name as an outlet for ideas that didn't quite fit the 'Prince' formula. Since the mid 90s the concept has expanded. The 'band' released its third album, *Newpower Soul*, in 1998, while the NPG brand came to include a record label (replacing Paisley Park Records), the NPG Orchestra, and NPGMusicClub.com, Prince's successful early 21st-century website, fan club, and download store.

The New Power Generation mirrored George Clinton's P-Funk crew in its revolving-door membership policy. There were 34 official members over the years (not including dancers and guest players), among them Rosie Gaines, Maceo Parker, and esteemed musicians such as Rhonda Smith, John Blackwell, and Renato Neto. On and off, Prince continued to credit the group on his albums, including *3121* (2006) and *Planet Earth* (2007). Whatever the line-up, Prince's goal seemed to be to surround himself with the best musicians he could at any given time. "I love this band," he told *Vibe* magazine in 1994, before noting in an interview with AOL that a later line-up "stomp much booty."

Letting the group evolve over time

seems to be particularly important to him. "I have been blessed with having these people come to me," he told Spike Lee in 1997. Seven years later, he seemed keen to explain that using new musicians is "one of the ways we keep it fresh ... I like to find new young kids that have something that they can bring to the sound."

Noting that the crowds they played to were "more diverse than ever" in 2011, Prince said of The New Power Generation, "The name actually refers to the audience now." A couple of years later, he put the group on hold while he explored a new sound with 3rdEyeGirl. For large festival shows, however, he favored merging the two, at times performing with over 20 musicians on stage. And while various configurations of the NPG – sometimes the full band, at other times just the horn section – were routinely sent out to support protégés such as Andy Allo and Liv Warfield, it's perhaps fitting that The New Power Generation were back to receive co-credit on Prince's final album, *HITnRUN Phase Two*.

Prince and guitarist Levi Seacer Jr on the Act II tour.

The album isn't without flaws – the reggae-lite touches on 'Blue Light,' Tony M's raps on both 'My Name Is Prince' and 'Sexy MF' (a catchy riff in search of a song), the throwaway ballad 'Sweet Baby' – but they are more than outweighed by its strengths. The straightforward R&B tracks on *Diamonds And Pearls* seemed to get lost under the weight of over-production, but here Prince manages to pull his songs back from the brink of bloated excess. The Eastern-tinged '7' remains one of his finest moments on record, its interlocking vocal parts as accomplished as anything else he has recorded. 'Eye Wanna Melt With U' might not push many boundaries, but its hard club beats sit perfectly between the softer 'Blue Light' and 'Sweet Baby.' All in all, the competing elements of rock, hip-hop, funk, reggae, jazz, and dance music might sometimes be baffling, but they're always intriguing. When he does fail, you can at least tell that Prince is doing his best to reassert himself as pop's greatest risk-taker.

In March 1993 Prince began his first full American tour

II in Europe at the end of July. Not only had he disposed of The Game Boyz, he had also changed his name to the unpronounceable album symbol that gave his most recent album its title. Taking to the stage each night as O{+> with gold chains hanging down over his face, he would begin by explaining his dissatisfaction with Warner Bros – which had started to object more strongly to the rate at which he wanted to release his music – to the audience. Then, having scrapped the high-concept theatrics of Act I, he would play a straightforward, career-spanning greatest hits set. This would be, he claimed, the last opportunity to her these songs live, since they now belonged to Warner Bros and 'Prince' – somebody that O{+> was no longer willing to be.

"No one works more quickly … if something's missing in his arrangements, he just does it himself and moves on." HANS-MARTIN BUFF (ENGINEER)

for five years, Act I. He might have ditched Diamond and Pearl, but the show was very much the 'rock soap opera' than *Love Symbol* had set out to be. The first half of the set saw him act out the album's attempted storyline in a manner that made a lot more sense on stage than on record. Having plucked his Arabian princess, Mayte, out of the audience, he would find himself on the run from assassins desperate to reclaim the Three Chains Of Turin from her. After an interval, the second half of the set comprised a more straightforward run through the hits.

A lot had changed by the time Prince commenced Act

For a while it seemed that, despite the name change, Prince would carry on working exactly as he had done before. He had already recorded his next project – *I'll Do Anything*, a movie soundtrack that would ultimately be scrapped when the director opted to cut the movie's musical element – and would continue to put out low-selling albums by other artists on Paisley Park Records while gearing up for the release of his next solo album. Warner Bros, however, was beginning to show signs of a serious case of Prince fatigue, and when the label finally opted to release its long-awaited greatest-hits album, it sent the singer off in a completely different direction.

"*His name is Prince and he is funky – funkier, in fact, than he's been in ages.*" **ROLLING STONE**

WARNER BROS HAD BEEN KEEN TO TAKE A BREAK FROM SATURATING THE MARKET WITH NEW PRINCE MATERIAL EVER SINCE THE SINGER CAME ALONG WITH *DIAMONDS AND PEARLS* – HIS 13TH ALBUM IN AS MANY YEARS – IN MARCH 1991. A GREATEST HITS SET, THE LABEL REASONED, WOULD GIVE CONSUMERS A BREAK FROM THE ENDLESS STREAM OF NEW PRINCE PRODUCT THAT SEEMED INCREASINGLY TO BE COMPETING WITH ITSELF, WHILE ALSO CONSOLIDATING AND CELEBRATING A REMARKABLE BODY OF WORK ACCRUED AT SUCH A FRANTIC PACE SINCE THE LATE 70S.

The Hits/The B-Sides

(SEPTEMBER 1993)

As far as Prince was concerned, putting out greatest hits albums was something you did once you had passed your prime. Fortunately, *Diamonds And Pearls* proved to be his most commercially minded work in years. There were no convoluted concepts, the overall sound was aimed squarely at the contemporary R&B market, and it ended up selling more strongly than any Prince record since *Purple Rain*. But the idea of a greatest hits set didn't go away completely.

By July 1993, Prince was trying to push yet another new project onto Warner Bros, having already followed *Diamonds And Pearls* with the *Love Symbol* album the previous October. *Goldnigga* was billed as the full-length debut by his backing band, The New Power Generation, but Warner Bros flatly refused to release it, and instead decided to finally unveil the greatest hits collection it had been sitting on for the past two years.

The Hits/The B-Sides gave Warner Bros a chance to recoup some of the money it had lost when *Love Symbol* failed to generate even a fifth of the revenue of *Diamonds*

And Pearls. The first two *Hits* discs (also made available to buy as separate albums to begin with) are largely focused, as one would expect, on Prince's single releases, and provide a remarkable non-chronological document of one of the greatest artistic trajectories of any musician in the history of pop. For anybody wondering where Prince might be going in the 90s, it served as a reminder that he had done more than enough in the 80s. The likes of 'When Does Cry' sounded no less innovative in 1993 than they had when originally released nine years ago.

The *B-Sides* disc, available only as part of the three-disc set, would have been revelatory to listeners who had not bought the original singles. It contains some of Prince's greatest material, from the electro-funk 'Erotic City' and the pop-rock 'She's Always In My Hair,' to the live favorite 'How Come U Don't Call Me Anymore' and two genuinely moving ballads, 'Another Lovely Christmas' and 'I Love U In Me' (another track in the gender-shifting mould of 'If I Was Your Girlfriend').

The package also includes a handful of rarities aimed

squarely at the Prince completist: 'Power Fantastic,' from the *Dream Factory* sessions; an alternate version of '4 The Tears In Your Eyes' originally broadcast during Live Aid; two recent recordings, 'Peach' (a rock track built around a Kim Basinger sample) and 'Pope' (another less-than-essential excursion into hip-hop); 'Pink Cashmere,' a ballad written for ex-girlfriend Anna Garcia; and a flawless live duet of 'Nothing Compares 2 U,' sung with Rosie Gaines on the Diamonds And Pearls tour. The only thing missing, because of contractual complications, was anything from *Batman*, but nobody seemed to mind.

By the time *The Hits/The B-Sides* was released, Prince had publicly declared that he would now only offer Warner Bros archival material from The Vault and not new songs, but *Rolling Stone* didn't seem too concerned. "If 'She's Always In My Hair' and 'Another Lonely Christmas' are any indication of the reported 500 songs Prince has in his vaults," the magazine supposed, "his label might just get its money's worth," before concluding that *The Hits* stood among the "essential documents of past decade."

Rolling Stone's opinions were amplified elsewhere. According to Q magazine, "Most truly essential compilations contain a few stars from pop's astrological map; these three [discs] contain a whole galaxy." *Entertainment Weekly* described *The Hits* as a "vital affirmation that, at one time, Prince's very strangeness and eccentricities had a point; he was never weird simply for weirdness' sake."

Running to 56 tracks and more than three hours of music, complete with illuminating linernotes by Alan Leeds, *The Hits/The B-Sides* remains the best one-stop for Prince's Warner Bros years, covering as it does pretty much everything except *The Gold Experience*. Subsequent Warner Bros compilations pale in comparison. *The Very Best Of Prince* (2001) and *Ultimate Prince* (2006, complete with a second disc of relatively obscure 12-inch mixes) are just slimmed-down versions of what came before.

It's interesting to note that Warner Bros released all three compilations – at least in part – with the intention of knocking the wind out of the sales of whatever else Prince was doing at the time. *The Hits/The B-Sides* came out right when Prince had begun to publicly criticize the label in the media, somewhat undermining

his attempts at waging war with the company. In July 2001, *The Very Best Of* was released a few months before the singer's return to using the name 'Prince' with the rather more challenging *The Rainbow Children*, while

Running to 56 tracks and more than three hours of music, complete with illuminating linernotes by Alan Leeds, The Hits/The B-Sides remains the best one-stop for Prince's Warner Bros years.

Ultimate Prince was initially intended to coincide with his much trumpeted major-label return, *3121*, before Prince and Universal managed to convince his old sparring partners to delay its release until August 2006. Even a decade after Prince and Warner Bros officially ended their relationship, it appears that at least one party can't help but return to the battlefield from time to time.

The Battle With Warner Bros

PRINCE HAD BEEN GIVING HIS EMPLOYERS CAUSE FOR CONCERN EVER SINCE THE RELEASE OF HIS THIRD ALBUM. THE COMPANY WAS SHOCKED BY THE LYRICAL CONTENT AND OVERALL IMAGE PRESENTED ON *DIRTY MIND*, BUT HAD BEEN CONVINCED BY CAVALLO, RUFFALO & FARGNOLI TO RELEASE IT AS IT WAS.

The album wasn't a huge commercial success, but it paved the way for Prince to become one of the most progressive and innovative musicians of his age. Further risk-taking strategies followed, such as selling the double-disc *1999* at the prince of a single album, and releasing the bass-less 'When Doves Cry' as a single. These gambles paid off. But as the hits began to dry up, and Prince's ideas grew increasingly introspective, Warner Bros began to lose confidence in his decisions. *Batman* and *Diamonds And Pearls* aside, each of his releases since the mid 80s seemed to sell less than the last.

Prince insisted on putting out an album a year, tossing each record aside almost as soon as it came out in order to make way for the next one. His work rate meant that his albums were directly competing with each other for space on record-store shelves, and made it almost impossible for Warner Bros to make its money's worth out of each one. The singer also seemed increasingly unwilling to compromise on any decisions relating to his recorded output. Generally speaking, an artist would bring his or her new record to the label and, as Warner Bros Vice President Jeff Gold later recalled, "decide mutually" about what tracks stood out as singles, how best to promote the record, and so on. Prince, however, "would show up … and kind of railroad you. All you could do was present your best case, appeal to the management."

The final straw – for Prince at least – came when Warner Bros refused to release the decidedly uncommercial New Power Generation album *Goldnigga*. It wasn't the first time the label had turned down one of his albums: in 1987 the singer had agreed to cut down the three-disc *Crystal Ball* to a more manageable, two-record *Sign "O" The Times*. This time, however, he took matters into his own hands, pressing *Goldnigga* up himself and selling it at concerts and through the NPG music store. He then began telling audiences on the Act II tour exactly what he thought of Warner Bros and its attempts to hold him back and stifle his creativity. The singer's views quickly spilled over into the press, kickstarting a battle that would ultimately become a source of embarrassment for all concerned.

A further threat to Prince's reputation – at least in the eyes of the wider public – came on June 7 1993 (his 35th birthday) with the announcement that he had legally changed his name to an unpronounceable symbol and that he would no longer be providing Warner Bros with new songs, but instead planned to fulfill his contract by giving the company previously unreleased material from his vast archive, The Vault. (Two months earlier, he had issued a press release announcing his retirement from the music

> *"Our dispute was not the content but the quantity. He had artistic control. We didn't want to stifle his creative spirit."* BOB MERLIS (WARNER BROS SENIOR VICE PRESIDENT)

industry to "pursue alternative media projects, including live theater, interactive media, nightclubs, and motion pictures.") Even the singer's UK publicist, Chris Poole, was stunned by this latest development. "My immediate reaction was pretty much the same as everybody else's," he later recalled. "He's finally gone mad."

"Everybody at Paisley Park was on a short leash and couldn't say 'Prince' after this press release had gone out," Jeff Gold recalled. "We'd have fun with it, because you'd call Paisley Park to talk to somebody in his management [and] try to get them to say 'Prince,' which they would never do." Warner Bros continued its gentle mockery of the name change with an advertisement in *Billboard* for the singer's forthcoming retrospective set *The Hits/The B-Sides*. "We here at Warner Bros treat our artists with a lot of heart," the ad – made up from a mixture of words and symbols – began, before requesting: "Don't call him Prince, call him O{+>, OK?"

A week later, Prince retaliated with a similar advertisement, which read, "We here at NPG treat our artists with respect. It makes us sad when they are sad. If they have new music they want to give to their fans, that's cool." What should have been a private battle was fast becoming very, very public.

Prince's decision to change his name is sometimes said to stem from a spiritual awakening the singer claimed to have had in Puerto Rico in December 1992. But while there might be some truth in this, it seems also to have been borne out of naivety.

Despite what his press release said, the change was simply not legal: it's impossible to change your name to a soundless glyph, even if you hope "one day [to] hear a sound that will give me a feeling of what my name will sound like." (In the meantime, he seemed quite happy for people to call him "Sir.") It seems quite likely, however, that the singer believed that changing his name would release him from his contractual obligations, since Warner Bros had signed 'Prince,' not 'O{+>.' His plan now was to

came up with their own nicknames. New York shock jock Howard Stern began to refer to the singer as The Artist People Formerly Cared About, while *Minneapolis Star-Tribune* columnist and Prince-watcher Cheryl Johnson took to calling him Symbolina.

Prince later wrote the bitter 'Billy Jack Bitch' in response to some of Johnson's comments, but took most of the criticisms in his stride. "I hear they're calling Diana 'The Artist Formerly Known As Princess' now," he joked on *The Oprah Winfrey Show*, before revealing, "Recent analysis has proved that there's probably two people inside of me." (The "other person," he added, appeared to be "someone I created when I was five years old.")

All jokes and wild claims aside, Prince was lucky not to be sued by Warner Bros, given that he was doing his best to destroy one of the company's most bankable brands *and* refusing to hand over any new material. "We have a new album finished," he brazenly told *Vibe* magazine in 1994 (referring to *The Gold Experience*), "but Warner Bros doesn't know it. From now on Warner Bros only gets old songs out of The Vault."

> "He has good points in his arguments and tons of sympathy from other artists, young and not so young, but for a while it seemed like he spent more energy in promoting his views and marketing concepts than creating the music itself." ALAN LEEDS

The label's position was made all the more difficult by the fact that Prince's management team was shifting at such an alarming rate that nobody ever really knew who to talk to. Similar changes were taking place at Warner Bros, too. The two most artistically sympathetic chairmen at the company, Mo Ostin and Lenny Waronker, both left in 1994, after several years of restructuring following its takeover by Time Inc in 1990, and the subsequent adoption of a more corporate mindset as Time Warner.

These changes left little room for long-term artistic development of the kind that Ostin and Waronker had

release as much new music as he wanted under his new name while killing off the old one with old music from The Vault. "I was a little ashamed of what Prince had become," he told Spike Lee in 1997. "I really felt like a product."

Having already used a number of pseudonyms in the past, Prince appeared to have no qualms about taking things a step further, and seemed adamant that this O{+> character represented an entirely new persona. "Prince never used to do interviews," he told *Time Out* in 1995. "You'd have to ask Prince why ... but you're not talking to Prince now. You're talking to me."

The press response to all of this was a mixture of skepticism and ridicule. Some thought it was a mere publicity stunt; others thought the singer had lost his mind. Warner Bros had sent out floppy discs with the glyph on, requesting that it be used in print instead of the word 'Prince,' but the most common response was to call him The Artist Formerly Known As Prince or TAFKAP.

Prince's PR team shortened the new name, somewhat pretentiously, to The Artist. Still, media commentators

championed. When Danny Goldberg replaced former Warner Music Group Chairman Robert Morgado, he took on the job of trying to repair the company's relationship with Prince. As far as the singer was concerned, there were two major sticking points: his own next album, *The Gold Experience*, and *Exodus* by The New Power Generation. He had wanted to release *The Gold Experience* (by O{+>) simultaneously with *Come* (by Prince), but the label refused to put out two records in direct competition with each other, so released *Come* on its own.

A verbal agreement was reportedly made in September 1994 to release *The Gold Experience* before the year's end, but nothing came of it. Prince ended up withdrawing the album, allegedly because Warner Bros had told him that it would not count toward the four that he still owed the company. He then took the surprising decision to release *The Black Album* instead, seven years after recalling it at the last minute (and only three months after putting out *Come*).

Part of the problem was that Prince was now dealing with Warner Bros directly, rather than leaving the job of

Goldnigga (The New Power Generation)

Around the same time that he was working on the *Love Symbol* album, Prince started another project with his band, The New Power Generation, that put particular emphasis on rapper Tony M, one of the Game Boyz. M might not have featured as prominently on *Love Symbol* as he does on *Diamonds And Pearls*, but Prince was still keen to prove that he could corner the hip-hop market as easily as he had the worlds of rock, pop, and funk.

Prince seemed to have more faith in *Goldnigga* than in any of his other early 90s projects, but the album ended up having more significance as an artifact than as a piece of music. When he presented it to Warner Bros in 1993, the label decided that now might be a good time to take a break from new Prince product. The singer's recent collaborations with Tony M on his own material ('Sexy MF,' 'My Name Is Prince') had hardly set the charts alight, so basing an entire album around the rapper hardly made good business sense.

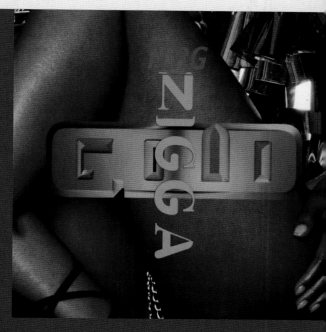

The most important aspect of *Goldnigga* is that it was the first self-released Prince album. He had copies of it pressed up and ready to sell at NPG stores and concerts, and thus took in all of the profits himself. This seemed to fit well with the album's main lyrical themes: a 'goldnigga' is defined on the record as a black man who earns money through "knowledge and creative efforts," and who, working without a label, "can feel good because there's no blood on his hands."

Prince had already made clear his feeling that record labels and managements did nothing but steal profits from their artists' work on 'Jughead' (another showcase for Tony M, as featured on *Diamonds And Pearls*). He used *Goldnigga* to drive the point home, even going so far as to include a skit in which the title character squares up to record label executives. It was almost as if Prince knew what Warner Bros' reaction to the record would be, and was using Tony M to air his views about the company, without having to say them himself.

Goldnigga was credited to The New Power Generation, but nobody was fooled as to whose work it really was. Despite not taking any direct action, Warner Bros was less than happy that one of its artists had made an album outside of the terms of his recording contract. Prince himself features prominently on several of the album's funky jams, while several more are focused on his usual preoccupations (sex and race). But while *Goldnigga* might sound like a Prince record, Warner Bros was certainly right to pass on it. Only the truly devoted would

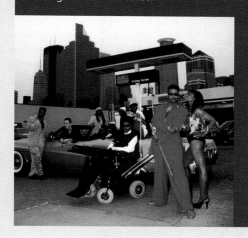

have been able to stomach 47 minutes of Tony M rapping over the most turgid, jam-based funk Prince had yet recorded. The whole thing was aimed squarely and transparently at black audiences, with song titles such as 'Black MF In The House,' and artwork full of fast cars, scantily clad women, and gaudy jewelry.

Goldnigga was only given a limited release, and as such has become rather collectable among Prince completists. The first CD pressing – featuring an extra song, 'Guess Who's Knockin',' that had to be removed from later editions as it lifted the chorus from Paul McCartney's 'Let 'Em In' – is particularly sought-after. But in the grand scheme of things, the album is mediocre at best, and important only in that it helped accelerate the breakup of Prince's relationship with Warner Bros.

negotiating with the company to the likes of Cavallo, Ruffalo & Fargnoli. This led only to further frustrations between the two parties, as Prince would go in shouting in the label executives' faces. Now he was demanding not just that he be allowed to release what he wanted, when he wanted, but that he be given full ownership of his entire back catalog. As Warners' Jeff Gold later noted, it's not unheard of for established artists to request such a deal, "but there's always some compensation for it. They'll take a lesser royalty, or they'll re-sign for less money than they ordinarily would." Prince, on the other hand, "wanted to have his cake and eat it, too."

Things took a sharp turn for the worse when Prince started coming to meetings – and making public appearances – with 'SLAVE' written on his face in eyeliner. This served only to detract from whatever considered, salient points he might have been making

about artists' rights and the inherent unfairness of recording contracts. More than anything, he was setting himself up for ridicule by the media, particularly when he decided to compare his adoption of O{+> to the decisions of Cassius Clay to become Muhammad Ali and Malcolm Little to rename himself Malcolm X (thereby erasing the slave names given to their respective families). Why should I call myself Prince Nelson, he asked himself, if I don't know who 'Nell' was?

For many in the media (and elsewhere), this was a step too far. For the man who had reportedly signed a $100-million contract a few years earlier to compare his plight to that of African-Americans being forced to work as slaves was nothing less than an outrage. Prince might have been making a point, during the early 90s, of trying to identify more closely with his black roots, but this was something else.

At first, Prince tried to justify his stance. "People say I'm a crazy fool for writing 'SLAVE' on my face," he told *Rolling Stone* in 1996, "but if I can't do what I want to do, what am I? When you stop a man from dreaming, he becomes a slave … If you don't own your [master tapes], your master owns you." But it wasn't long before he realized that he was losing support in his crusade against Warner Bros, and started to backtrack. Within a few months he would claim to only have written on his face to remind Warner Bros "that I know what time it is," and that he "never meant to be compared to any slave in the past, or any slave in the future." He went even further in a subsequent interview with the *St Paul Pioneer Press*, explaining, "I did it because I had become a slave to myself … I felt like I was in a box spiritually, not creatively."

Prince seemed to have done enough to retain the support of the black market he had gone to such lengths to chase during the early 90s. "Black people still call me Prince," he told Spike Lee in 1997. "Sometimes I ask them [why], and they say, 'Because you are a prince to us.'" In other quarters, however, he seemed to be walking on thin ice. The name change, the public outbursts, and the 'SLAVE' incidents were simply too much for Warner Bros.

Twenty years earlier, a young Warner Bros employee, Russ Thyret, had sat on the floor talking about music with Prince and his manager of the time, Owen Husney, eager to convince the other two men that Warner Bros was the right label for this bright young star in the making. By 1996 that same man had become the chairman of the Warner Bros music division, but even he had had enough, and decided that the best thing for all concerned would be

"If I knew then what I know now, I wouldn't be in the music industry." PRINCE

to officially end the two parties' 18-year union – a relationship that had generated an estimated $300 million.

"We've come to a point where we feel that if he's happier somewhere else, we don't have any beef with him," Warner Bros Vice President Bob Merlis told the *Los Angeles Times*. Noting that the company had been puzzled by – rather than angry about – the singer's behavior, Merlis confirmed the reasons behind the split: "He wanted to release more albums than his contract called for; he wanted a different contract, which ran contrary to good business practices. Eventually, we agreed that his vision and ours didn't coincide."

On April 26 1996, Prince successfully amended his 1992 Warner Bros contract with the help of a new lawyer, L. Londell McMillan (a replacement for Gary Stiffleman, who had helped broker the original '$100 million' contract). After *The Gold Experience* was released in September 1995 (on NPG Records/Warner Bros), he was

still required to deliver three more albums, but this was cut down to two sets of unreleased material – *Chaos And Disorder* and *The Vault … Old Friends 4 Sale* – in return for a reduced royalty rate and an agreement not to publicly slander his former employers.

"I have decided to part company with Warners," Prince told *The Times* on July 6, "but surprisingly we're now on the most amicable terms we've been on for a long time." His final appearance with 'SLAVE' written on his face came two days later during a performance of 'Dinner With Delores' on *The David Letterman Show*. "I was bitter before," he explained a week later, "but now I've washed my face. I can just move on. I'm free." (He did however continue to use the name O{+> until his publishing contract with Warner Chappell Music expired at the end of 1999.)

Shortly after helping Prince terminate his contract with Warner Bros, L. Londell McMillan asked *Forbes* magazine: "Is this artist the kind of mercurial crazy some people say, or is he the wise one who understands where he fits at the start of a new century?" Once the dust settled, it became clearer to see what Prince had actually been fighting for. He had never had a problem with anyone in particular at the label, he said, just the system they were governed by. "They don't even realize what they're saying," he explained in an interview with *USA Today*. "It's all habit now."

What Prince wanted was a new system in which artists owned their work and were free to distribute it themselves. "In Mozart's time, word of mouth built an audience. People found him and heard him play. Then someone came along and said, 'We can sell this experience.' Right there, you got trouble."

"I want to find out who the first person was who saw fit to sell music," he told the *St Paul Pioneer Press* in 1996. Continuing on the same theme a year later, he told the Spanish newspaper *El País* that it would be "fantastic" if one day artists could achieve independence from their record labels. "But that is a very delicate question," he said, "because many artists are too weak and frightened to just go outside."

Despite the ridicule at the time, it's now clear that Prince provoked a major rethink of the music industry. It took many people to catch up but, in 2007, Radiohead released *In Rainbows* online without any input from a major label, allowing fans to pay whatever they saw fit. Throughout the following decade, many artists set up their own boutique labels – or, in the case of Jay Z, his own digital streaming service, Tidal; unsurprisingly, Prince soon transferred the rights to stream his music from Warner Bros to the artist-owned venture.

"[In] situations where we finally get into a position to run things – we should all help," Prince told told *Ebony* in 2015. "To stay afloat, it's gonna need the Kanye Wests and the Kendrick [Lamar]s … and they're going to dictate what the deal is gonna look like."

Don't Play Me

During the 80s Prince pursued his side projects with as much enthusiasm as he did his own releases. Albums by acts such as The Time, Vanity 6, Apollonia 6, and Sheila E. might not have sold as strongly as Prince's own records, but they were still commercially viable enough for Warner Bros to be content with the way the singer was handling his Paisley Park Records output.

In the 90s, however, the quality of Prince's extra-curricular output seemed to decline at the same rate as that of his own work. It might have been that he just didn't have enough songs to go around, but he seemed to lose interest in Paisley Park. He threw a few musical bones to the likes of T.C. Ellis, whose 1991 album *True Confessions* includes three Prince co-writes, but for the most part he had lost his enthusiasm and let the projects govern themselves.

In 1989 Paisley Park took on two veteran artists who would make cameo appearances in *Graffiti Bridge*, George Clinton and Mavis Staples. Clinton – as big an influence on Prince as Jimi Hendrix, Joni Mitchell, James Brown, or Sly Stone – offered up a half-baked, dated album called *The Cinderella Theory* that hardly anyone bought. Prince became more involved in the making of Staples's *Time Waits For No One*, but his modern production techniques served only to make her sound like a fish out of water. (He tried again in 1993 with Clinton's *Hey Man … Smell My Finger* and Staples's *The Voice*, but neither reached a wide audience.)

In these two cases, Prince was at least trying to give something back to the musicians who had influenced him so much during his formative years. When it came to newer artists in greater need of a leg-up, however, he hardly seemed to care. Ingrid Chavez had been something of a spiritual guide for Prince while he made *Lovesexy*,

but he kept putting off work on her debut album. Sessions began in 1987, but the album wasn't released until September 1991, and even then it relied as much on the work of guitarist Levi Seacer Jr and engineer Michael Koppleman as it did on Prince himself.

Prince's long-term sax player Eric Leeds was another member of his inner circle to receive the gift of a Paisley Park album release. Unfortunately for Leeds, however, the album was based around scrapped sessions for a third Madhouse record. By 1991, hardly anyone was interested in Prince-related jazz excursions – least of all Prince himself, who was busy chasing current trends in R&B and hip-hop. The album was simply stamped with the Paisley Park logo and sent off into the wilderness.

The artist most damaged by Prince's lack of interest was Rosie Gaines. "Rosie is like a tornado," he told *Details* after the Nude tour. "There's never enough hours in the day for her voice. There's never enough tape for her voice." As usual, Prince promised to make her a solo album, with the working title *Concrete Jungle*.

Shortly after the sessions began in the summer of 1990, however, Prince met 18-year-old Tara Leigh Patrick in a Los Angeles nightclub. True to form, he lost interest in Gaines's record almost immediately and started work on a rap album with Patrick instead. Patrick became Carmen Electra, and was given a support slot on the Diamonds And Pearls tour (on which Gaines served as a keyboardist and backing vocalist). Her set revolved around her struggle to rap terrible, half-baked material such as 'Go Go Dancer' and 'Step To The Mic' in front of an audience that wasn't even particularly keen on Prince's own hip-hop excursions, let along those of a low-level Vanity. Prince did his best to blame the hostile critical response on anything but Electra – her backing band, which he sacked and replaced with his own; the venues – before finally dropping her from the bill in June.

Warner Bros was similarly unconvinced by the music on *Carmen Electra*, which ended up being delayed until February 1993. Even then it sank without a trace, but not before the entire project – which included several promo videos shot in Egypt – had cost a couple of million dollars. Later the same year Prince had Electra play both Penelope and Calypso in his *Glam Slam*

Ulysses stage production, a loose adaptation of Homer's *Odyssey* for which he wrote all the music. The show closed down after two weeks and a critical mauling. (Plans to give the production a full US tour were quietly dropped.)

Throughout the Carmen Electra debacle the Rosie Gaines recordings – perhaps the most commercially and artistically viable of all of Prince's early-90s side projects – were left stagnating in The Vault. Anyone who had witnessed her performances on the Nude and Diamonds And Pearls tours could see how talented she was.

Prince failed to take full advantage of that talent, but didn't want anybody else to, either. When Gaines quit Prince's group following the Diamonds And Pearls tour, he refused to let her out of her contract with him. It's possible that he genuinely wanted to return to the recordings, which Gaines continued to work on without him; and it's quite feasible too that he was scared that, if he allowed her to take them to Motown (as she wanted to), they would become a hit without him.

Either way, *Concrete Jungle* sat on the shelf until it was formally scrapped in 1994, at which point Gaines was finally allowed to sign to Motown. Her debut album was eventually released in June 1995 as *Closer Than Close*, featuring two songs co-written by Prince, 'I Want U (Purple Version)' and 'My Tender Heart.' But although the title track was a modest chart success, the album as a whole suffered from years of being sat on and soon disappeared from the charts.

Despite all that she had been through over the years, Gaines returned to Prince's side to add her vocals to *Emancipation*'s 'Jam Of The Year' and *1999: The New Master*. She has since claimed that she was never paid for either appearance.

The chances of Rosie Gaines (above) having a successful solo career dropped significantly when he turned his attention instead to the dancer Tara Leigh Patrick, whom he renamed Carmen Electra (right).

AFTER WARNER BROS OPTED TO RELEASE *THE HITS/THE B-SIDES* INSTEAD OF *GOLDNIGGA*, PRINCE BECAME EVEN MORE DETERMINED TO RELEASE HIS MUSIC ON HIS OWN TERMS – AS MUCH OF IT, AND AS OFTEN, AS HE LIKED.

'The Most Beautiful Girl In The World'/ 1-800-NEW-FUNK

(DECEMBER 1993–AUGUST 1994)

I n February 1994, having already harangued his employers into letting him release 'The Most Beautiful Girl In The World' independently, he responded to Warner Bros shutting down Paisley Park Records by immediately forming another label, NPG Records, with which to put out the single. Warner Bros reluctantly agreed to this scheme with the proviso that Prince put up all of the money to promote and release the single himself. He duly spent two million dollars manufacturing and marketing 'The Most Beautiful Girl,' enlisting the help of Bellmark, an independent label run by Al Bell, a former Vice President of Stax, to distribute it.

Prince saw this as his one chance to prove he should be left alone to do things his way, and devised an ingenious promotional scheme guaranteed to draw attention for what was perhaps his most important release since *Purple Rain*. In December 1993 he booked advertising space in European and American magazines as an "eligible bachelor seek[ing] the most beautiful girl in the world to spend the holidays with," requesting that photo and video responses be sent to Paisley Park. Seven of the 50,000 applicants were chosen to appear in the promotional video for the single, while photographs of a further 30 of them were used in the artwork.

The campaign was an unqualified success. Released, fittingly, on Valentine's Day 1994, 'The Most Beautiful Girl In The World' sold 700,000 copies, rising to Number Three on the *Billboard* Hot 100 (and Number Two on the R&B chart), and becoming Prince's first ever Number One hit in Britain. But there was a lot more to the single than just clever marketing. A love song to Mayte, it was nothing short of a masterpiece from an artist whose best days had seemed to many to be far behind him. Prince's vocal delivery is one of his most convincingly impassioned, while the multiple layers of vocal harmonies and instrumental overdubs prove that he was capable of piling up the production without sapping a song of its energy and emotional power. The song's euphoric peak and climax are almost as grand as 'Purple Rain.'

'The Most Beautiful Girl In The World' was a much-needed artistic and commercial success, suggesting that O{+> could be just as vital as the singer's former incarnation. For Warner Bros, however, the whole affair was particularly galling, the label having only agreed to the release in an attempt to get Prince off its back, not expecting the song to become his most successful single since 1989's 'Batdance.'

For Prince, all of this was proof that Warner Bros didn't know what it was doing, and by extension that he should be allowed to release what he wanted when he wanted. The single's success made him even more determined to break free from the label and encouraged him to drum up further support by publicly declaring that the album from which the song was taken, *The Gold Experience*, would never see the light of day because Warner Bros refused to release it.

He was however able to convince the label to let him put out a second record through NPG a few months later, a full-length compilation album named for the free-phone

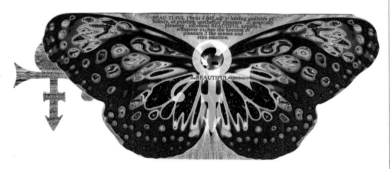

telephone number he had set up to take orders for Prince and O{+>-related merchandise. Distributed once again by Bellmark, *1-800-NEWFUNK* was unable to repeat the success of 'The Most Beautiful Girl.' It barely sold at all, in fact, and only reached Number 45 on the *Billboard* R&B chart.

The only song on the album credited to O{+> is 'Love Sign,' a duet with Nona Gaye, the daughter of Motown legend Marvin Gaye. Prince wanted to release it as a single but Warner Bros refused to grant him permission, perhaps fearing a reprise of 'The Most Beautiful Girl''s storming success. Undeterred, Prince pressed up promo copies for R&B radio stations, performed the song live on several television shows, shot a video for it, and placed adverts in *Billboard* magazine. But the single never materialized.

The rest of *1-800-NEWFUNK* mixes previously released material, such as George Clinton's 'Hollywood,' with new

work, including '17' by Madhouse, 'Minneapolis' by the NPG offshoot MPLS, and Mayte's remarkably successful version of 'If Eye Love U 2Night,' a Prince-penned song

> *'The Most Beautiful Girl In The World' was a much-needed artistic and commercial success, suggesting that the singer could be just as vital as O{+> as he had been as Prince.*

previously recorded by Mica Paris. Despite its poor commercial performance, the 11-track album remains a worthy addition to the Prince canon, its mixture of upbeat funk and ballads yielding a number of fine examples of Prince's 90s update of the Minneapolis sound. It might not have sold very well, but to Prince it served as further proof that he could carry on alone, without Warner Bros' backing.

Prince and "the most beautiful girl in the world," Mayte Garcia, celebrate the opening of his NPG store in London, England.

HAVING HAD TO SIT THROUGH 1993 WITHOUT A MAJOR RELEASE, PRINCE MADE CLEAR HIS INTENTION TO MAKE UP FOR LOST TIME WHEN HE PRESENTED WARNER BROS WITH TWO NEW ALBUMS DURING THE FIRST HALF OF 1994. FIRST CAME *COME*, WHICH CONSISTED MOSTLY OF OLD MATERIAL RECORDED BEFORE HIS NAME CHANGE, AND THEN *THE GOLD EXPERIENCE*, MADE UP LARGELY OF NEW SONGS.

Come/The Black Album

(MARCH–NOVEMBER 1994)

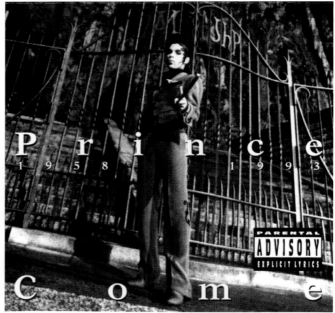

Prince's plan was for *Come* to be credited to 'Prince,' with *The Gold Experience* to be credited to O{+> – and for both to be released on his 36th birthday (one year to the day after his name change). His exact reasoning is unclear, but it seems that he wanted to pit his two 'brands' against each other and see which one the public responded to best.

This kind of deliberate sabotage went against all good business sense and Warner Bros refused point blank. One new Prince album would be more than enough – particularly at a time when record-store shelves were already swamped with his recent output. The label found little to get excited about when Prince first delivered *Come* in March and requested he rework it – and add 'The Most Beautiful Girl In The World' to the tracklisting.

Prince returned in May with a new, much darker-sounding pressing of the album that still didn't feature his recent smash-hit and now omitted upbeat tracks such as 'Endorphinmachine' and 'Interactive,' which he had since decided were O{+> songs, not Prince songs. At the same time he also delivered *The Gold Experience*, which did

include 'The Most Beautiful Girl' (and 'Endorphinmachine') but was credited to O{+>.

Of the two, Warner Bros eventually opted to release *Come*, largely because it was the one credited to the still-bankable Prince moniker. But this ultimately meant that on August 16 the label put out a dated album by a man who had no interest in promoting it, and whose audience had probably already grown tired of the soap opera surrounding his name-change and public battles with his label. *Come*'s jacket shows Prince staring out gravely in front of a cathedral, with his birth and 'death' dates, 1958–93, emblazoned across the front. (As if to hammer home the point there are photographs inside of a live-and-well Prince dated 1958 and a 'dead' Prince dated 1993.)

Sick of the name-calling and name-changing, *Rolling Stone* headed its review 'Oh, whoever,' before imploring its readers to "appreciate these moves as part of what has become the most spectacular slow-motion career derailment in the history of popular music." The *Detroit Free Press* voiced its disappointment by calling *Come* a "toss-off that doesn't merit the excitement usually accorded Prince albums."

The album does have its moments. The *St Paul Pioneer Press* drew attention to its inclusion of a few songs that sound like "an old friend exposing something of himself, risking something real." Perhaps the strongest of these is 'Papa,' a brutal, spoken-word retread of the child-abuse story hinted at on *Love Symbol*'s 'Sacrifice Of Victor.' Over a sparse musical backdrop, Prince declares: "Don't abuse children, or else they turn out like me." The song eventually rises to a more upbeat, cathartic conclusion, with Prince singing of how "there's always a rainbow at the end of every rain." 'Solo,' meanwhile, is a largely a-cappella meditation on loneliness on which Prince's voice seems to echo out from the biggest, emptiest mansion in Minneapolis.

It's moments like these that mark *Come* out as one the singer's most interesting (and downright weird) albums, particularly when compared to the Prince-by-numbers themes that dominate the rest of the songs. The opening title track is an 11-minute paean to oral sex, 'Race' yet another so-so socially conscious collision of hip-hop and funk, 'Space' a largely unsuccessful attempt at trip-hop, and 'Loose!' and 'Pheromone' aimless retreads of early-90s dance music (the latter a blatant re-write of *Love Symbol*'s 'Continental').

While *Come* sold only 345,000 copies on its release in the USA, some fans now think of it as something of a 90s classic. But while it might sound good by comparison to the likes of *Chaos And Disorder* and *Newpower Soul*, it certainly doesn't come close to his best work of the 80s.

Comparing old and new Prince became a legitimate exercise in November when Prince opted finally – and somewhat puzzlingly – to allow Warner Bros to release *The Black Album*. Although it didn't get him any closer to fulfilling his contractual obligations to the label, Prince did pick up a reported one-million-dollar fee for *The Black Album* as part of a three-album deal (from which he later withdrew) that also included *The Gold Experience* and an unnamed movie soundtrack.

Warner Bros might have been glad to finally release *The Black Album*, But it didn't fare well with fans or critics. Seven years late, it was now, as the *Detroit Free Press* put it, "little more than an interesting period piece." *Time* magazine seemed to hit the mark when noting that, while listeners in 1987 "probably wouldn't have known what to make of [the album's] bitter outlook, today it [sounds] almost conventional."

Most of the fans who might have bought *The Black Album* had it been released in 1987 had moved on by 1994, or would have been content with their bootlegs of the original. The hardcore supporters that remained

> The Detroit Free Press voiced its disappointment by calling Come a "toss-off that doesn't merit the excitement usually accorded Prince albums."

weren't enough to send the record hurtling to the top of the charts. As another year rumbled to a close, Prince was left feeling even more despondent about his situation. His newest work, about which he felt most enthusiastic, remained in limbo; the older material that did make it out onto the shelves had failed to set the world alight. All he wanted to do now was make more records, but even that would prove difficult.

Money Don't Matter 2 Night

AFTER *PURPLE RAIN* MADE HIM AN OVERNIGHT MILLIONAIRE, PRINCE WAS SUDDENLY THRUST INTO A WORLD WHERE MONEY WAS NO LONGER A CONCERN. ACCORDING TO BOB CAVALLO, HIS MANAGER THROUGHOUT THE 80S, PRINCE PAID FOR PAISLEY PARK IN CASH AND, BY THE TIME HE WAS 27, HAD $27 MILLION IN THE BANK.

One might justifiably assume that this would have made him financially secure for life. But just a few years later, Prince faced severe fiscal difficulties following the loss-making Lovesexy tour and a string of albums that, while critically successful, had failed to reap the financial returns their reviews warranted.

In attempting to scrap the Japanese leg of the Lovesexy tour in favor of getting on with the *Batman* project, Prince was also beginning to demonstrate a tendency toward making questionable business decisions. Had manager Steve Fargnoli not been able to convince him otherwise, Prince could have been sued for as much as $20 million for pulling out of the concerts.

Prince seemed unwilling to listen to sound financial advice, opting instead to do what he wanted, when he

"I'm not scared of poverty. I grew up being poor." *PRINCE*

wanted. "We had a big graph," Bob Cavallo later recalled. "I put it on an easel showing the decline in revenue and increase in spending. He just walked [up] and turned it over."

Fortunately, *Batman* was Prince's biggest commercial success since *Purple Rain*, and was followed in 1991 by another hit, *Diamonds And Pearls*, which helped put him back in the black following the failure of the previous year's *Graffiti Bridge* movie. Within a few years, however, Prince's finances would begin to fall apart again. By January 1995 the situation had become so bad that the *St Paul Pioneer Press* was reporting, "Paisley Park Enterprises, the company that oversees most of Prince's business interests, is not paying its bills on time or at all."

Prince's extravagant spending appeared to have finally caught up with him. Since opening Paisley Park he had kept the studios fully manned for 24 hours a day on the off chance that he might want to record. Meanwhile, in Los Angeles, he spent around $500,000 per year on having a studio manned and ready at the Record Plant, in case he decided to drop in on a whim.

Studio costs were just the start of it. Paisley Park's in-house catering team and ten-strong tailoring department,

employed to make bespoke clothes for Prince, his band, and his girlfriends, were all employed full-time, as were his band and road crew – even if they weren't recording or touring. By the mid 90s, Prince was also filming expensive promotional videos on the Paisley Park soundstage for songs that would never get released, even though the space was supposed to be hired out for movie productions. Having agreed to allow for *Grumpy Old Men* to be shot there, Prince only let filming start when Warner Bros executives got involved.

Prince might have claimed to have signed a $100 million contract with Warner Bros in 1992, but the reality was that his albums were not selling enough for him to be earning anywhere near that. Even so, he had no problem with wasting two million dollars on his Glam Slam Minneapolis nightclub, or another two million dollars on recording and promoting the hopeless Carmen Electra album. He made numerous other decisions without giving any consideration to cost or practicality, such as opening further Glam Slam clubs in Miami and Los Angeles, setting up a series of NPG music stores, building extravagant stage and movie sets, and even buying multiple copies of the same bespoke canes from a local company during a period in the 90s when the cane became his fashion accessory of choice.

Prince's decisions weren't just costly to the singer himself. Having previously worked on the 'Gett Off' promo video (which went five times over its $200,000 budget in less than a week), director Rob Born found himself working on '7.' "Before we even shot film," he later recalled, "we had probably spent $90,000." Then, with a set almost complete at Paisley Park, Prince decided he had had a better idea and moved the entire project to Los Angeles.

This was all very well except that, by 1993, Born was due $450,000 for his work. When he tried to get it, Paisley Park could only afford to pay him 70 cents on each dollar owed. By the time he did get paid Born had already fallen into debt himself, and ended up giving all $315,000 to his creditors before declaring bankruptcy.

Born might even have been one of the lucky ones. Plenty of others found themselves unable to collect debts owed by Paisley Park. Cane-makers Suzy and Gary Zahradka were forced to threaten legal action before receiving a

Exodus (March 1995)

In 1994, having already turned down The New Power Generation's Goldnigga a year earlier, Warner Bros passed on the follow-up, Exodus. Prince had started work on the album in May, shortly after being sent back to the studio to make Come more commercially appealing.

Fully ignoring his contractual obligations to the label, he wrote and recorded all of the material on the album and released it on his own NPG Records on March 27 1995. (He also appears prominently throughout as both musician and singer, but used the pseudonym Tora Tora in the linernotes and covered his head with a scarf when making promotional appearances with the band in order to mask his identity.)

If *Goldnigga* was Prince voicing his dissatisfaction with Warner Bros, *Exodus* is a long, meandering expression of his complete and utter distain. For once it's the full-band performances that stand out; Prince's solo pieces, by contrast, are conspicuously colder and less engaging. The album's most forward-thinking concept comes during the spoken word intro, in which it is announced that NPG Records is looking for new talent – with the proviso that any prospective musicians be "free" because, "when it comes to downloading your work into your fans' computers, you can't have any contractual obligations."

What follows is, for the most part, a densely produced mess. While it might have been paper-thin, *Goldnigga* did at least gave a plotline. *Exodus* is just a series of jam-based funk ramblings and dull ballads held together by a series of loose, uninteresting segues, most of them featuring bassist Sonny T, who takes the place of Tony M in pushing the stereotypical black angle.

Everything that happens within these 12 dramatic segments – including various seductions and childhood reminiscences, and the drinking of some spiked soup – turns out to have been a dream, although few listeners are likely to have cared either way by the time they got to the last of the album's 21 tracks.

Exodus does contain a couple of moments worth hearing. 'Get Wild' is a dense, funky number that stands as a triumph of Prince's busy, mid-90s production style, while his attempt at an Italian accent during the 'mashed potatoes' segue provides a genuinely (if unintentionally) funny moment. The rest is eminently forgettable. The album is dedicated to 'His Royal Badness' in memory of 'Prince,' but it probably would have been more appropriate to dedicate it to his dearly departed sense of quality control.

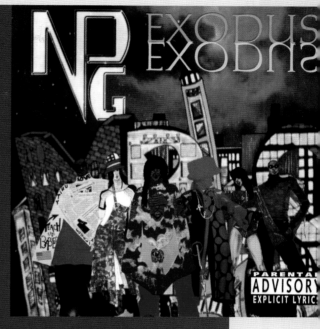

belated check in return for their $4,500 invoices, while the Record Plant ended up withholding a master tape Prince had accidentally left on the premises in order to ensure that a $150,000 bill got paid. Others simply met with confusion when they tried to get in touch with Paisley Park.

Part of the problem stemmed from Prince's revolving-door employment policy, and his decision to put people with little or no experience in charge of various key divisions of Paisley Park Enterprises. When, in late 1990, the management team of Arnold Stiefel and Randy Phillips reached the end of their initial 12-month contract with Prince, the singer opted not to renew it and instead named former bodyguard Gilbert Davison as the company's new president, promoting his PR, Jill Willis, to the position of vice president.

In October 1994, with Paisley Park's finances spiraling out of control, Davison resigned. Prince brought in his half-brother and former head of security, the late Duane Nelson, as Davison's replacement, with Julie Knapp-Winge and Therese Stoulil flanking him. Nelson was then left in charge of what have since been called arbitrary firings at the company. Rather than cut back on his spending, Prince was keen to cut back on his staff. All wardrobe director Heidi Presnail was told was that she was "being fired on a cutback, and they were eliminating my position."

Within two years, Nelson, Stoulil, and Knapp-Winge were also gone, which meant that there had been more changes in the company during the past five years than there had been throughout the entire 80s. Even Levi Seacer Jr, the bassist who took over as head of Paisley Park Records after Alan Leeds resigned in 1992, had upped and left in November 1994 – along with his girlfriend, publicist Karen Lee – while Prince was safely out of the country at the European MTV Awards.

By 1996, what remained was a company without a head, and with no one for Prince himself to answer to. Less and less information came out of Paisley Park in the years that followed, making it difficult to determine with accuracy the state of Prince's financial situation at any given time. For a while, however, self-releasing albums to a dedicated fanbase allowed him to sell fewer copies but make more from each one. He took a much larger cut of the profits from *Emancipation* than he would have done under his Warner Bros contract. When it came to the follow-up endeavor, the multidisc *Crystal Ball* set, he even waited until he had received enough pre-orders to make the project commercially viable before manufacturing it, thereby ensuring that he would break even at the very least. He would go on to cut several deals with major labels, but only when it suited him; on other occasions, he went directly to distributors as varied as Target in the US, and newspaper publishers in the UK and Europe, for up-front payment and the ability to place his albums directly into stores.

Prince's refusal to license his music for use in film and TV, or to allow Warner Bros to reissue his old albums, doubtless denied him an additional source of income. And then there are the countless unreleased projects that he recorded but never released. Director Kevin Smith was involved in one such venture in 2001 and recalled speaking to a senior Paisley Park employee who told him, "I've produced 50 music videos. You've never seen them, 'cause they're for songs you've never heard. He puts them in The Vault. Fifty fully produced music videos with costumes and sets. Everything. That's just the way Prince is."

However, following his 'comeback' in 2004, Prince's live shows provided a greater income stream than his record sales. Lengthy residencies such as 3121 Jazz Cuisine and 21 Nights In London ensured that, by staying in one place for an extended period, he didn't have to face the expensive transport costs that usually came with touring. He also took to playing one-off events, including private parties, for vast sums. In December 2007, Prince reportedly earned $2 million for performing at the 40th birthday of Turnberry real-estate heir Jeffrey Soffer, while he stood to make more than double that for an appearance at the 2008 Coachella festival. In 2014, he topped Business Insider's list of most expensive gig bookings; his asking fee of $1.5–2 million surpassed the cost of hiring the likes of Jay Z, Aerosmith, and Adele by up to $1 million. (Two years later, claiming that Prince once turned down an $85 million offer to stage

a large-scale world tour, organizer Kim Worsøe recalled him saying, "I don't do tours, I do events.")

Though much has been made of his profligacy, in the days following Prince's death, many people were at pains to bring his philanthropy to light. Speaking to CNN, a tearful Van Jones, founder of the Rebuild The Dream, asserted that his Welcome 2 America shows "were a cover for him to be able to go into cities and help organizations." While the *Chaska Herald* claimed in March 2011 that Prince risked losing property in Chanhassen after failing to pay $368,382 on a $605,000 mortgage he'd taken out in 1994 (a situation that was resolved by the end of April), he had, in the previous month, donated almost five times as much as that to New York organizations alone. Following four shows at Madison Square Garden, held across December 2010 and February 2011, he donated $1.5 million to groups such as Harlem Children's Zone and American Ballet Theatre And Uptown Dance Academy.

Citing Prince's religious beliefs as a reason why so much of his humanitarian work was kept under wraps, Jones told CNN anchorman Don Lemon, "I guarantee you, anybody struggling, anywhere in the world, he was sending cheques, he was making phone calls." Jones was not the only one to unburden themselves of the secret – and he was right that America was not the only country to benefit from Prince's humanitarianism. In May 2016, it emerged that, at around the same time that Prince was touring Welcome 2 America, he gave $15,000 to Physiotherapy And Rehabilitative Support For Afghanistan, and thereafter continued to make annual donations of $6,000. He'd become aware of PARSA via his work with Helping And Loving Orphans, a non-profit organization run by the 'Angel Of Saigon,' Betty Tisdale, who died, aged 92, in 2015. Marnie Gustavson, executive director for PARSA, recalled that, in return for his support, Tisdale had a strict non-disclosure agreement with Prince: "She could call him up and say, 'I need money for this, three thousand for this, five thousand for this,' and he'd give it to her."

When a will failed to materialize in the months following his death, Prince's wishes for his estate were open to speculation. However, while the County Carver District Court was trying to ascertain who Prince's legal heirs were, and with the estate facing a huge tax bill in 2017, Bremer Trust, the special administrator temporarily brought in to manage his affairs, was granted the authority to start monetizing Prince's estate.

Accounting for both his body of music and the amount of property that he owned, the media valued Prince's assets at somewhere between $100 to $300 million, with some reports speculating that, as posthumous income came in, the figure would increase over time. Looking far into to the future, one report even declared that The Vault contained enough music to release an album a year for a century. Speaking to Esquire.com, entertainment attorney Donald David said that as long as his estate is well managed, and the heirs aren't tempted to "go for a quick hit by doing something like selling his publishing rights," Prince's music could produce income for several generations "without any problems."

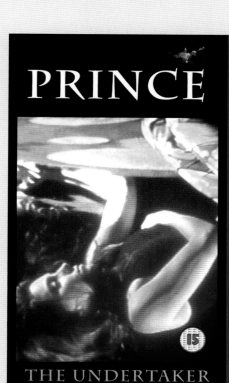

The Undertaker/The Sacrifice Of Victor

A few weeks after announcing his intention to concentrate solely on "alternative media projects," Prince holed himself up on the Paisley Park soundstage for most of June and July 1993 to film *The Undertaker*. The original plan was to make a feature-length movie starring Nona Gaye and the television actress Vanessa Marcil, but that ended up being scrapped in favor of a wholly musical project.

Most of what became *The Undertaker* was drawn from a 30-minute live set recorded by Prince and NPG bassist Sonny T and drummer Michael Bland in mid June. Some of the footage featuring Vanessa Marcil was later inserted in between the seven songs, reducing the 'feature-length movie' concept to a slick, three-man jam interspersed with barely related dramatic moments – a half-baked mess attractive only to die-hard Prince fans hungry for long, blues-based jams. (None of the scenes shot with Nona Gaye were used.)

The movie begins in black-and-white with Marcil's character entering Paisley Park needing to use the phone. She is told where to find one, but ordered not to go past "the sign," because there's a rehearsal going on. After the man she calls, Victor, refuses to believe that she's "changed," the girl becomes distraught and takes an overdose of pills before wandering into the rehearsal

room. From here the viewer is treated to stripped-down versions of 'The Ride,' 'Poorgoo,' 'Honky Tonk Women,' 'Bambi' (from *Prince*), a snippet of 'Zannalee,' 'The Undertaker,' and 'Dolphin,' a studio version of which would subsequently appear on *The Gold Experience*.

As the band plays, Marcil's character dances, becomes ill, and then seems to die while Prince is singing the title track (another warning about the dangers of gang warfare and drug addiction). During 'Dolphin,' however, the girl comes to, throws her pills away, and leaves Paisley Park. A line from the title song – "Don't let the Devil make U dance with the undertaker" – flashes up on the screen as the credits roll, but the film's overall message is lost in a mess of muddled editing and overuse of primitive visual effects such as negative coloring and image warping.

All in all, it's hard to ascertain the point of the project beyond Prince's need to keep recording music. *The Undertaker* was given a limited VHS release through the NPG music store at the end of the year, and then distributed more widely by Warner Music Vision in March 1995, but seems mostly to have been an exercise in wasting money at a time when Prince really should have been more frugal. (He also reportedly pressed up CDs of the soundstage recording and planned to give them away free with *Musician* magazine in early 1994, but was blocked by Warner Bros.)

Prince had slightly more success with the March 1995 release of *The Sacrifice Of Victor*, a 45-minute edit of a live performance shot at Bagley's Warehouse in London during the early hours of September 8 1993. He had ended his Act II tour a few hours earlier at Wembley Arena

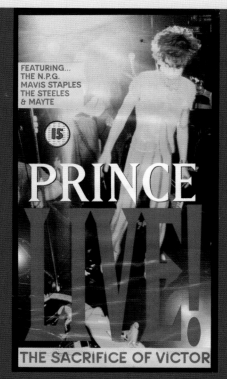

Experience. Mavis Staples popped up at one point to sing 'The Undertaker' and 'House In Order' (from her Paisley Park Records LP *The Voice*), while The Steeles and the NPG (fronted by Tony M) also played brief sets.

The Sacrifice Of Victor is certainly more enjoyable than *The Undertaker*, but is still not one for the casual fan, with 'Peach' the only well-known song on the setlist. It is probably most interesting as an indicator of Prince's mindset during the latter part of 1993. The opening footage is taken from the September 7 Wembley Arena show, and shows him taking to the stage in a black-and-white suit that could easily be mistaken for a skeleton costume and announcing: "London, my name is not Prince, and my name damn sure ain't Victor" (in response, it seems, to suggestions that 'The Sacrifice Of Victor,'

> *The Sacrifice Of Victor is certainly more enjoyable than The Undertaker, but is still not one for the casual fan, with 'Peach' the only well-known song on the setlist.*

and hired the Warehouse for an all-night end-of-tour party. Taking the stage at 3am, he performed a full set with The New Power Generation that included a number of tracks from *The Undertaker* and previews of material from *Come* and *The Gold*

which references child abuse, is autobiographical). After this announcement he is wrapped up in a black shroud and carried off stage as if in a funeral procession, having seemingly done everything he could to make it clear that 'Prince' is dead.

ALREADY UNHAPPY WITH THE WAY WARNER BROS WAS HANDLING HIS WORK, PRINCE BECAME INCENSED WHEN THE COMPANY REFUSED TO RELEASE *THE GOLD EXPERIENCE* AT THE SAME TIME AS *COME*. HE RESPONDED BY STEPPING UP HIS PUBLIC BATTLE WITH THE LABEL, APPEARING ON STAGE WITH 'SLAVE' WRITTEN ACROSS HIS FACE AND TELLING ANYONE WILLING TO LISTEN THAT HIS EMPLOYERS WERE HOLDING BACK HIS 'BEST ALBUM YET.'

The Gold Experience

(MAY 1994–JANUARY 1996)

He spent much of the rest of 1994 ignoring *Come*, which he completely refused to promote. When he did make a public appearance – either at Paisley Park or at his Glam Slam clubs – he would use it to showcase the unreleased *Gold Experience* material, or would give copies of its songs to DJs to play over the PA system. Tentative moves to release the album were made in September and October, but nothing came of them. Prince withdrew from the first set of talks, while the second was scuppered by a shift in personnel at Warner Bros.

As 1995 began the battle showed no sign of slowing down. On February 20 Prince was named Best International Male at the Brit Awards. "Prince? Best?" he began in a speech that left many thinking he had totally lost the plot. "*Gold Experience* better. In concert, perfectly free. On record, slave. Get Wild. Come! Peace, thank you."

Things became a little clearer a month later when he launched the Ultimate Live Experience tour, on which he intended to play mostly new material, going back no further than 'I Love U In Me' and '7.' The 20-date tour stopped at various European cities during March 1995, but was not the success Prince had envisioned. "This tour is crucial for him," UK promoter Chris Poole pointed out at the time. "He has a small cash-flow problem. He's not broke, but he's been spending his money on his music."

Unfortunately for Prince, where he had previously played a record-breaking 18-night stint at London's Wembley Arena, he was now struggling to sell tickets for four shows at the same venue. It got worse elsewhere: the Sheffield Arena was reportedly less than half full on the two evenings he played there. With touring being the main way for a musician to make money, this was not a good sign. (In a desperate attempt to raise more funds, fliers were handed out at each concert advertising that night's official aftershow event in the hope that fans would be willing to pay for another live experience immediately after the first.)

Prince made no secret of the fact that he was planning to play a lot of new, previously unheard material from *The Gold Experience*. He even implored fans to bring their tape recorders – somewhat ironically, given his subsequent aggressive stance toward those who trade in live

"It was through Prince that I think I gained my own sense of what people say. Forget what the record company says you must do to be successful. Do what the voice in your head tells you to do." *TERENCE TRENT D'ARBY*

recordings – telling them that this would be their only chance to hear the music. Such a scenario was no doubt off-putting to those casual fans who had come to see Prince on his record-breaking Nude tour in 1990, and who have continued to turn out to hear him run through the hits "for the last time" in the years since.

The poor turnout affected the show itself, as Prince found himself having to cut back the production costs for fear of ending up seriously out of pocket. When the Ultimate Live Experience opened at Wembley Arena, Prince emerged from the Endorphinmachine – an extravagant structure flanked by representations of male and female genitalia, which took its name from one of the *Gold Experience* songs – and traveled to the front of the

stage on a conveyor belt. Because of the expense of transporting the hugely cumbersome set Prince ended up leaving most of it, save the womb-like center, in London.

Even then the show was beset by technical problems that made the tour his most shambolic in a long time. After hiring and firing several sound engineers along the way, Prince had taken, by the end of the 20-date tour, to mixing the sound himself from within the womb. If this was the only chance his fans would get to hear the *Gold Experience* songs, he wasn't exactly presenting them in their best light.

The tour continued sporadically back in America, with several shows at Paisley Park after it was opened up to the public on August 1. Then, after much wrangling with

Warner Bros, *The Gold Experience* was finally released on September 26 1995. Despite the fact that much of it was already two years old, the album was well worth the wait, and sounded fresher than anything Prince had recorded in years. Finally, for the first time since *Sign "O" The Times*, he seemed able to put together an album full of commercial hooks and a sense of adventure that wasn't bogged down by weighty concepts.

Aside from references to Prince being "muerto" and further suggestions of a growing interest in internet technology and interactive media, *The Gold Experience* is, more than anything else, a collection of mostly great songs. It covers little new thematic ground, but that barely matters when the songs are as good as 'P Control,' 'Endorphinmachine,' and of course 'The Most Beautiful Girl In The World.' Even when he tries out Shuggie Otis-like sunshine funk on 'Shy,' or lets fly with his anger toward *Minneapolis Star-Tribune* columnist Cheryl Johnson (who took to calling him Symbolina after his name change) on 'Billy Jack Bitch,' the effect is much more powerful – and in the latter case, much funnier – than *Come*'s lumpen funk and dreary diatribes against Warner Bros. All in all, Prince seemed to have rediscovered his muse, notably on 'Dolphin,' one of his most lyrical and inventive power ballads, and the anthemic closer 'Gold,' a kind of 'Purple Rain' for the 90s.

Commercially, however, *The Gold Experience* was a disappointment. After two decades in the music business Prince seemed to have reached a point whereby hardcore fans would continue to buy whatever he released, but younger listeners were more interested in a new generation of stars. The album only just managed to sell 500,000 copies in America – partly, perhaps, because Prince had done most of his promotional work in support of it long before it was actually available to buy, and partly because everything he did seemed to be overshadowed by his battle with Warner Bros – but did at least allow O{+> to beat Prince in the charts. (*The Gold Experience* reached Number Six, compared to *Come*'s Number 15.)

> *"A lot of the guys [at Warner Bros] who caused me problems have gone now, but I'm still waiting to see if things change. I still believe that The Gold Experience will never be released. They wouldn't even let me release a ballet I had written."* PRINCE

To those critics who had rolled their eyes at the Prince/O{+> shenanigans, *The Gold Experience* was evidence that all was not lost. According to the *St Paul Pioneer Press*, it "fully redeems O{+> as the ruler of his wildly imaginative, funky, sexy kingdom," while *Vibe* called it a "Prince experience par excellence" and "his best effort since the 90s almost happened without him."

While it's true that *The Gold Experience* is Prince's best album of the 90s by some distance, it's also something of a backhanded compliment to focus on it purely in those terms. The album proved, after a string of disappointments, that Prince still had some spark left. The question was: how much? After touring Japan in January 1996 with what was essentially a continuation of the Ultimate Live Experience, Prince sacked The New Power Generation, many of whom had been playing with him since 1991. Having officially announced his intention of terminating his contract with Warner Bros in December 1995 it seemed that, just as had been the case when he let go of The Revolution almost a decade earlier, Prince now wanted to take back his music for himself in 1996.

4

HAVING LEFT WARNER BROS, THE ARTIST NOW KNOWN AS O{+> WAS FREE TO RECORD AND RELEASE AS MUCH MUSIC AS HE WANTED. SETTING UP HIS OWN NEW POWER GENERATION LABEL TO DO JUST THAT, HE BECAME THE FIRST ARTIST TO SERIOUSLY HARNESS THE POWER OF THE INTERNET. IN HIS EFFORTS TO REMOLD THE MUSIC BUSINESS, HOWEVER, HE STRUGGLED TO MAKE THE KIND OF MUSIC THAT WOULD SEND HIM BACK TO THE TOP OF THE CHARTS.

EMANCIPATION
1996–2003

Girl 6 (MARCH 1996)

A nyone interested in Prince in 1996 would be forgiven for thinking that his first release of the year was simply another consolidation of former glories. *Girl 6* is another compilation album, but there is very little overlap with *The Hits/The B-Sides*, released three years earlier. Only 'Erotic City,' 'How Come U Don't Call Me Anymore,' and 'Pink Cashmere' appear on both. The rest of *Girl 6* is made up of recordings by Vanity 6, The New Power Generation, and The Family, alongside 'Girls & Boys,' three from *Sign "O" The Times*, and three previously unreleased Prince recordings.

The album was compiled as a soundtrack to Spike Lee's movie of the same name, which tells the story of a phone-sex operator – all of which seemed surprising, given how protective Prince tends to be of his music. Similarly surprising was how pleased the singer was with how the project turned out. "The scene where you used 'How Come U Don't Call Me Anymore,' he told the director in 1997, "is my favorite scene. In fact it forced me to put that song back into our set … I used to think I couldn't do it better than I did with my band, The Revolution, but your film gave me a newfound respect for the music."

While the old songs on *Girl 6* are pretty flawless, the three previously unreleased recordings don't exactly set the world alight. 'She Spoke 2 Me' and 'Don't Talk 2 Strangers' were recorded in the early 90s. The former passes by in a light, jazzy way, while the latter is a more moving piano ballad, sung in falsetto and originally intended for a mother to sing to her daughter in the movie *I'll Do Anything*. The third new song, 'Girl 6,' is credited to The New Power Generation, presumably because of its hip-hop influence, but Prince himself features prominently. It samples various old songs of his as well as snatches of dialogue from the movie, but contains no real hooks.

Those that did bother to review *Girl 6* were fairly positive about its mix of old and new. But despite the album being plastered with the words 'SONGS BY PRINCE,' it still only reached Number 45 on *Billboard* and ultimately sold less than 100,000 copies.

Prince and Spike Lee watch the NBA All-Star game at Madison Square Garden, New York, in February 1998.

Chaos And Disorder

(JULY 1996)

Three months after settling a deal with Warner Bros to part ways after two more albums, Prince delivered the first of them, *Chaos And Disorder*. It was, he said, recorded in little over a week, with input from The New Power Generation and Rosie Gaines, and certainly sounds like it. The liner notes seem at pains to point out that the material was originally intended "4 private use only," and that it serves as "the last original material recorded by O{+> 4 Warner Bros." The artwork – a footprint over a smashed record on the front – carried much the same message: this relationship is over.

Chaos And Disorder's 11 tracks tend toward the most boring, straightforward rock Prince had yet recorded, his conflict with Warner Bros seemingly having consumed him to the point where even his biggest fans might struggle. While he might have taken a certain perverse satisfaction from the fact that it sold less than 500,000 copies worldwide (thus generating very little in the way of profit for Warner Bros), he was also putting the loyalty of his fanbase at risk by releasing something so lackluster. The lyrics to the closing track, 'Had U,' say it all. Having opened his debut album, *For You*, by stating that "all of this and more is for U," he now sang of how he had "hurt U," "disappoint[ed] U," and "fuck[ed] U."

As far as Prince was concerned, everything else paled in comparison to the battle he had won. But this in turn made it impossible to find any real excitement anywhere on *Chaos And Disorder*. 'Dig U Better Dead' might offer a fairly interesting take on the singer's label troubles (including such notes-to-self as "One minute you're hot /

Tell the truth and you're not" and a paraphrasing of record label advice not to "dress 2 freaky and make their daughters stare") but it's spoilt by the music. Confirming the absence of fresh ideas was 'I Will,' its squealing, echo-laden finale sounding just like the end of *Sign "O" The Times'* 'I Could Never Take The Place Of Your Man.'

The only single to be drawn from the album was 'Dinner With Delores,' a dull, by-numbers tale of an encounter with a sexually forthright woman. Although Prince made a less-than-engaging promo video for the song and performed it, under duress, on *The Late Show With*

"Someone told me Van Halen did their first record in a week. That's what we were going for: spontaneity." PRINCE

David Letterman, the single was not released commercially in America, and stalled at Number 36 in the UK.

Incredibly, *Chaos And Disorder* was hailed by some reviewers as "a welcome return to basics" (*Billboard*) and even "Prince's best effort since *Purple Rain*" (*Chicago Sun-Times*). The *New Musical Express*, on the other hand, seemed to offer a more accurate appraisal, noting the thick layer of irony in 'I Rock Therefore I Am''s claim that "I sing the song / The best I can" before concluding that the album is "the sound of a man with too much time and too many names pouring his talent straight the plughole." It's hard to argue with that.

THE PRESSURE WAS MOUNTING FOR PRINCE DURING THE SPRING OF 1996. HE AND HIS NEW WIFE, MAYTE GARCIA, WERE EXPECTING THEIR FIRST CHILD IN THE FALL, AND IMPENDING FATHERHOOD THREATENED TO CHANGE HIS LIFE IRREVERSIBLY.

Emancipation (APRIL 1996–JANUARY 1998)

His terrible financial situation added to the strain, with the threat of bankruptcy looming large, while his battle with Warner Bros was due shortly to reach its conclusion.

These stresses and strains came to a head on April 21. Prince had been suffering heart palpitations for the past few months, and had been taking painkillers in an effort to combat them. He had also recently become a strict vegetarian, and was perhaps lacking in nutrients when, that evening, he polished off a bottle of wine and suffered bouts of nausea before being rushed to Minneapolis's Fairview Southside Hospital.

Prince had become notorious over the years both for not sleeping much and for drinking even less. Now it seemed his body had almost collapsed under the strain of a sudden combination of painkillers, alcohol, and a radical change in diet.

Three days after the scare, Prince finally came to an agreement to terminate his contract with Warner Bros. He spent much of the next few months out of the public eye, his focus presumably on looking after himself and spending time with Mayte. (He also started rehearsals with a new line-up of The New Power Generation, retaining only Morris Hayes on keyboards from his previous line-up, and hiring bassist Rhonda Smith, guitarists Kat Dyson and Mike Scott, and drummer Kirk Johnson.)

In July Warner Bros released the first of its two final Prince albums, as agreed in April, *Chaos And Disorder*. Prince did nothing to promote it except for performing 'Dinner With Delores' on television. His attention was focused on his forthcoming *Emancipation* album, his first since negotiating the split with Warner Bros, and the one with which he aimed to show the world that he could do it all on his own.

"All the stakes are higher," he told the *New York Times*, "but I'm in a situation where I can do anything I want." And that's exactly what he did. With a nod perhaps to Warner Bros' refusal to release the similarly sprawling *Crystal Ball* ten years earlier, he unveiled a three-disc set of 36 songs that ran to 180 minutes.

"The album is probably the most joyous one I've made. It's by far the most romantic because I've never been this much in love."

PRINCE ON OPRAH (1996)

Just as he was about to plow his efforts into promoting the album, however, another tragedy struck. On October 16 Mayte gave birth to a son with Pfeiffer syndrome, a rare genetic defect; a week later, after several unsuccessful operations, she and Prince took the heartbreaking decision to switch off the baby's life-support machine.

It's impossible to know exactly what effect the tragedy had on Prince, but he seems to have responded to it by doing what he always does: throwing himself into his work. He had signed a pressing and distribution deal with EMI-Capitol for *Emancipation* a week before the baby's birth and now, three days after his death, was playing a warm-up show with the NPG at Paisley Park. He then went on a quick promotional trip to Japan before he and Mayte filmed a perplexing promo video for the album's first single, a cover of The Stylistics' 'Betcha By Golly Wow!,' in which the couple act out a happy childbirth.

The video's theme was certainly puzzling, but then it did come at a time during which Prince felt he had been through something of a spiritual rebirth. He certainly felt like a different person now that the Warner Bros cloud no longer hung over his head. A year later he made a telling remark while describing a newly written song, 'Comeback,' to Spike Lee. "If you ever lose someone dear to you," he told Lee, explaining the song's message, "never say the words, 'They're gone,' and they'll come back." Perhaps it was all as simple as that: avoid the pain, don't wallow in it.

Avoiding the pain was made more difficult, however, by the fact that his new album was essentially a love song to Mayte and impending fatherhood. (The beat of one song, 'Sex In The Summer,' came from a recording of an Ultrasound scan of his unborn child's heartbeat.) With Prince at his most open and talkative in years, interviewers were inevitably going to take this opportunity to dig into his private life. This put Prince in the position whereby he had to talk about where the music came from, but didn't want to tell anybody about what he had just been through.

The result was a muddying of the waters. Prince would describe *Emancipation* as coming from a period of reflection on his life. "Having a child helps you do that," he told *Rolling Stone*, seemingly suggesting that his son was still alive. "It's all good, never mind what you hear," he told Oprah Winfrey on November 4, further confusing the issue. Then, in an interview with *USA Today*, he appeared to deny outright the suggestion that his son had died. "My skin is so thick now," he said. "I care much more about my child than what anyone says or writes."

With *Emancipation* set for release on November 19, Prince showed no sign of stepping off the promotional machine. As well as having the weight of his own private tragedy to deal with, he had also forced himself into a position where he had to prove, beyond any doubt, that releasing an album on his own was the right move, and that he was blazing a trail for future artists. "This is my

debut," he told *USA Today*. "My name represents this body of work, not what came before."

Such declarations were tempered by a hint of fear. "I ain't scared of nobody," he told *Rolling Stone*, but seemed to be trying to convince himself as much as anyone else. "Tell me how many singles you hear," he continued. "I wanna read that." Speaking to the *New York Times* around the same time, he seemed keen to preempt any suggestion that the album might be too sprawling. "I play a lot of styles," he explained. "This is not arrogance; this is the truth … Sometimes I just stand in awe of what I do myself. I feel like a regular person, but I listen to this and wonder, where did it come from?"

Fortunately, the majority of reviewers seemed to agree with him. The press response to *Emancipation* set out the stall for the way most of Prince's subsequent high-profile

> "I worked for a year and I must admit I'm amazed by the results. I think Emancipation is, without a doubt, the best album of my whole career." PRINCE TO HELLO MAGAZINE (1996)

albums of solid yet safe music would be received. *USA Today* gave the album four out of four and called it "outstanding"; the *Detroit Free Press* declared it to be his best effort since *Sign "O" The Times*. "By reviving a flair for songwriting long gone in modern R&B," the *New York Daily News* concluded, "while rendering his vocals more sober and his lyrics more thoughtful, one of pop's most maddening figures rewards our patience at last."

At the heart of most of the reviews, it seemed, was a sense of relief that Prince had returned to making music to a formula that was relatively easy to understand, rather than putting together concept albums about things that were only fully defined in the singer's mind. By comparison to his previous album, *Chaos And Disorder*, it's hard not to see *Emancipation* as a bit of a masterpiece. It's also not inconceivable that the press genuinely wanted to see Prince do well now that he'd ended his long, drawn-out battle with Warner Bros and stepped out on his own.

Ultimately, *Emancipation* can be viewed in much the same way as most of Prince's more popular, post-*Lovesexy* output. The songs are well written and the production is immaculate, but the overall package was never likely to set the world alight. In the context of mid-90s R&B it was certainly a success, but then R&B at the time was in a decidedly unhealthy state. That Prince wanted to make the album palatable to the mainstream listener is made clear by his inclusion, for the first time, of covers of other artists' songs alongside his own, including a version of Joan Osborne's 'One Of Us.'

The album is however full of wonderfully inventive touches, particularly the way that Prince harmonizes with himself throughout. Thematically, it's also much clearer than a lot of his other work of the time. It's hard to listen to the run of songs at the end of the second disc – 'The Holy River,' 'Let's Have A baby,' 'Savior,' 'The Plan,' and 'Friend, Lover, Sister, Mother/Wife' – without being overwhelmed both by Prince's apparent joy while recording them and a knowledge of what soon followed. Elsewhere, there are enough unusual moments to keep the listener engaged right through to the end, from 'Emale''s tale of sexual blackmail by email to 'In This Bed Eye Scream,' which is something of an apology to Wendy Melvoin and Lisa Coleman. (Prince contacted the pair at one point to ask them to work on the song with him, but ended up finishing it off on his own and dedicating it to them instead.)

Overall, *Emancipation* might be a little too polished, but it's certainly got more grit than the likes of *Diamonds And Pearls*. It didn't sell quite as well as Prince had hoped, but the pressing and distribution deal he had struck with EMI-Capitol made it a resounding success in business terms. The deal provided the model on which Prince would base all of his future arrangements, whenever he felt like working temporarily with a label that had more clout than his own NPG Records. He retains the copyright and master tapes, and receives a much larger royalty rate than he would under a normal contract. In return, Prince assumes all recording and promotional costs, while the label pays for manufacturing and distribution in return for a fee for each copy sold. Or as Prince later put it, labels are like "a florist – they just deliver the flowers."

Under the terms of his old Warner Bros deal, Prince would have had to have sold 500,000 copies of *Emancipation* just to break even. Now however it was being reported that, having sold 450,000 copies, he was already five million dollars in profit. If these figures are even close to the truth, the move away from Warner Bros had proved to be very successful indeed, even if it was hampered somewhat by the shutting down of EMI-Capitol in April 1997.

After pushing *Emancipation* so strongly in the press,

idea was scrapped following EMI-Capitol's demise. Instead Prince simply took a month off before starting again with a longer run of shows dubbed Jam Of The Year. The 65 US dates amounted to his longest American tour since the Purple Rain shows a decade earlier.

Just as *Emancipation* had inaugurated a new way of releasing and distributing albums, the Jam Of The Year shows provided a template for future tours. The Prince team would book 15,000-seater venues just a few weeks in advance and then handle ticket sales and promotion itself. Once again, cutting out the middleman – and performing on a much less extravagant stage set – yielded greater financial benefits. It has since been estimated that Prince earned $30 million from the Jam Of The Year tour alone, and had completely turned his financial situation around by the time it came to a close in January 1998.

For a man close to bankruptcy just a few years ago, Prince certainly seemed to have something to celebrate. As the new year dawned, however, he found himself stuck once again, this time in a struggle to produce a worthy follow-up to his recent critical and financial success. He might have taken control of his business situation, but he was also on the verge of slipping slowly but surely from musical prominence.

"The record is important for me because it's the first time that I've recorded an album in a state of complete freedom." PRINCE ON OPRAH (1996)

Prince's next job was to take it out on the road. On January 7 1997 he embarked on the 21-date Love 4 One Another Charities tour – his first full-scale US tour in four years, for which he gave some of the profits to good causes. Perhaps surprisingly, his set was made up largely of old 'Prince' songs, with only a handful of *Emancipation* tracks thrown in, suggesting that the singer had already put the album – and its difficult themes – behind him.

The tour was originally intended to be a small-scale warm-up for a full-scale trek around the world but that

The Most Beautiful Girl

AT THE AGE OF 32, ROCK'S MOST ELIGIBLE BACHELOR DID THE UNTHINKABLE: HE FELL IN LOVE. HE'D BEEN THERE BEFORE, OF COURSE, BUT THIS TIME HIS FEELINGS WERE SO ALL-CONSUMING THAT THEY LED TO HIM GETTING MARRIED FOR THE FIRST TIME.

The girl he fell in love with, Mayte Jannell Garcia, was born in 1973 and grew up in Germany and the USA, moving around a lot as a result of her father's job in the military. At the age of eight she became the youngest professional bellydancer to appear on television when she performed on *That's Incredible!*

On July 25 1990 her mother took her to see Prince's Nude show in Barcelona, Spain. Although Mayte wasn't much of a Prince fan before the show, her mother sensed that there might be opportunity for her to dance professionally for the singer, and so encouraged her to send him a videotape of her dancing.

The tape Mayte sent to Prince, via Kirk Johnson of The Game Boyz, is said to have contained footage of her dancing to 'Thieves In The Temple.' (The song was chosen by her mother, who had enthused about its Middle Eastern overtones.) Mayte was quickly invited to bring another tape to Prince, which she did two weeks later after a show in Germany. When she met him, Mayte's first thought was, "Wow, he's really small!" but Prince would later claim to have fallen in love the moment he saw her.

This isn't so surprising given that Mayte shared many of the best elements of his past girlfriends. She had the exotic looks of Vanity (her parents are both of Puerto Rican ancestry) and the enrapturing charm of Susannah

Melvoin and Kim Basinger. When Mayte left the backstage area, having performed her party trick of flipping coins on her belly, Rosie Gaines reportedly told Prince that he had just met the girl he would marry.

Mayte was still only 16, so she and Prince began a long-distance courtship designed to bring her closer into the Prince fold in time for her 18th birthday. "Prince was very protective of me," she later recalled, "and my father was happy to place me in his care … It was all quite innocent, but quite intense." With her father's blessing, she and Prince wrote to each other regularly, while Prince sent her tapes of new songs, which she filmed herself dancing to. By the time of the Diamonds And Pearls tour she was living in Minneapolis and working as part of the backing group as a supplementary dancer to Diamond and Pearl.

As the *Love Symbol* album began to take shape – with Mayte as the Crown Princess of Cairo – she also became the center of attention on stage, just like Cat Glover before her. Prince even wrote a solo album, 1994's *Child Of The Sun*, for her, but as with Susannah Melvoin's record with The Family it seemed to have been designed mostly as a means of keeping her close by in the studio.

Mayte became more and more of a rock for Prince to cling to as his personal troubles grew during the early 90s. In 1995 Prince gave an interview to the UK TV show *The*

Sunday Show, whispering his answers to Mayte, who in turn relayed them to the host. He began telling the press that she made it easier for him to talk to God, among other things, and wrote a series of love ballads for her, the most notable being 'The Most Beautiful Girl In The World.' "Mayte grounds me," he told *Harper's Bazaar* in 1997. "She doesn't try to change me, but she makes me aware of certain things."

Prince and Mayte were married on Valentine's Day 1996 in a small ceremony at Minneapolis's Park Avenue Methodist Church. Only Mayte's parents and sister attended from her side, while Prince invited his mother, stepfather, and Bernadette Anderson, but not his father. By then the couple were virtually inseparable, with Mayte pointing to a O{+> symbol hanging around her neck rather than speaking her husband's name to the priest. It wasn't long before they were expecting a baby.

Prince has always been reticent about discussing personal matters, but seemed to change his tune when it came to Mayte. He took great pleasure in pointing out the similarities between the two of them, such as that Mayte's mother's name was Nell, and that his surname was Nelson – or Nell's son. This, he decided, was proof that they were "made to be together," and that "all the ingredients were there to unite us." He would even claim, in an interview with Oprah Winfrey, that it "felt like she was either my sister or we were the same person or something in another life. There's a closeness [that] you know is right and you don't argue with."

Mayte's influence clearly changed Prince for the better. With his wife by his side, he began to see the world in a different light. "When I opened Paisley Park, I was so excited to have my own studio that I just started recording and didn't come out for 20 years," he told MSN Music Central in 1996. "After I got married I finally looked at the place." (Mayte, he later told *Guitar World* magazine, had put him on "studio rehab.") He seemed to surprise even himself with the revelation, "I haven't had a nightmare since I decided to get married. That's extraordinary!"

Prince made clear his dedication to Mayte on 1996's *Emancipation*, a triple-album love-song to his wife and their unborn child. (Her pregnant stomach is pictured in the liner notes.) Shortly after the album's release he claimed, "You can now hear that my soul has been in love with Mayte for thousands of years."

Prince and Mayte's relationship might have looked like textbook married bliss to the outside world, but it wasn't quite as traditional as it seemed – perhaps unsurprisingly, given the age difference, and how easily the elder Prince would have been able to influence the younger Mayte. "I wasn't allowed to call him, ever," she later revealed. "Even when we were married; I had to wait for him to call me. I've no idea why, he never actually said."

Tragedy struck as the couple prepared for parenthood. In mid September Mayte was rushed to hospital with sharp

abdominal pains. She was seven months pregnant at the time, and feared that she was about to give birth prematurely. Although this wasn't the case, it was subsequently revealed by doctors that the couple's baby was likely to be born with physical abnormalities. The child was born on October 16 with Pfeiffer syndrome, a rare genetic defect that causes an unborn baby's cranial bones to fuse together prematurely, resulting in severe physical deformities. After a week of unsuccessful operations, Prince and Mayte decided to take their son off life support and let him pass away as peacefully as possible.

Although the fate of the child identified only as 'Boy Gregory' on his death certificate would soon become public, Prince began making cryptic comments about the baby's health in the media. "It's all good, never mind what

> *Mayte's influence clearly changed Prince for the better. With his wife by his side, he began to see the world in a different light.*

you hear," he told Oprah Winfrey a few weeks after the baby had died. A year later, he explained to Spike Lee in *Interview* magazine, "I'm a firm believer in reincarnation for people who either have more work to do or have so much debt to pay back that they have to be here … my work was finding Mayte and having a child, which we will continue on until there are several here." Prince's denials drew a number of criticisms, but according to Mayte, "We believed he was going to come back, that souls come back. We didn't want to acknowledge he was gone. It was our way of grieving."

The situation was made even more difficult by Prince's decision to carry on promoting *Emancipation* in the

months after his son's death. At a time when many would have argued that he should have stayed at home with his wife, he was out on the road instead, seemingly throwing himself into his work as a way of dealing with what had happened.

To make matters worse, two former Paisley Park employees then decided to make Prince and Mayte's personal heartbreak public by selling their story to the press – and in doing so turned an unavoidable tragedy into a homicide case. Erlene and Arlene Mojica were twins from Puerto Rico who had been employed as Mayte's nanny and bodyguard respectively. They were fired in December 1996, reportedly because of suggestions that they were planning to speak to the press about life behind the closed doors of the Prince estate. (Prince later claimed that they had signed confidentiality agreements, but the Mojicas have said that their signatures were forged.)

Shortly thereafter, and apparently in retaliation to their having been sacked, the sisters contacted a local Minneapolis journalist, Tom Gasparoli, and gave their side of the story. Among their claims was the groundless insinuation that Prince had not given the baby enough of a chance to live before taking him off life support. Having heard the sisters' testimony, Gasparoli told them to go public with their claims. "I don't know if it's a crime," he told the Minneapolis radio station KSTP, "but it sure didn't sound right to me."

On March 9 1997 Britain's *News Of The World* ran a story entitled 'Bizarre Truth Behind Death Of Star's Baby.' The article was based on a number of the Mojicas' claims, including that Prince refused to allow Mayte to eat any meat during her pregnancy (and that the sisters had to sneak her out to a nearby TGI Friday's so that she could); that he wouldn't let her have an Ultrasound scan during her first trimester; and that he prevented doctors from giving her magnesium in order to avoid a miscarriage when she first started having contractions.

Thanks to Gasparoli, who shared the Mojicas' claims with any media outlet that would listen, the noise became so loud that local homicide detectives in Minneapolis were forced to get involved. Thankfully, it didn't take long for them to decide that it was "a natural death. We don't plan to investigate. There's no case here." The verdict was made official in June and the Mojicas were taken to court. They haven't spoken publicly about the affair since, but their 'revelations' clearly put further strain on Prince and Mayte's relationship.

"Some couples are brought together after the loss of a child," Mayte later noted. "Others are driven apart. In our case the latter happened." Their split was complicated and drawn out, but appears not to have been bitter. With Prince on tour for so much of 1996–97, it's entirely possible that he and Mayte simply grew apart at a time when they should have been working on making their relationship stronger.

The situation was further complicated by reports that Mayte had become involved with the Spanish dancer Joaquín Cortés, shortly after Prince bought her a mansion in Marbella. (The lyrics to *Rave Un2 The Joy Fantastic*'s 'I Love U But I Don't Trust U Anymore' appear to support these theories.) Meanwhile, Prince himself is alleged to have been dating his future second wife, Manuela Testolini, as early as 1998.

A further strain was placed on the marriage when Prince became a Jehovah's Witness. He had been introduced to the faith, while at a rather low ebb, by Larry Graham, the former Sly & The Family Stone bassist, at the after-show party following the Nashville date of the Jam Of The Year tour during the early hours of August 22 1997.

Prince's new religious beliefs seemed to replace Mayte as the guiding force in his life. In 1999 he told *Paper* magazine that marriage contracts originated from Pontius Pilate's consensus to crucify Jesus, before explaining to the *New York Times* that he and Mayte had renounced their marriage vows after "read[ing] them over" and deciding that "there were a lot of things in there we didn't like."

A little while later he told the *Minneapolis Star-Tribune* that he and Mayte had "decided to do this whole thing together" for the benefit of their "spiritual wellbeing." He subsequently sent the newspaper a follow-up letter spelling out his distaste for "CONtracts" and reasserting various views that he felt had not been given adequate space in the original article. "These days Mayte and O{+> refer to each other as 'mate' or 'counterpart,' not husband and wife," he wrote, before explaining that the couple planned to renew their marriage with new vows that better suited them. (This never happened.)

Several years after splitting up with Prince, Mayte made a number of illuminating comments about him in an interview with the online magazine *Fiya*. "Now I know other men," she said, "I can see how in tune [Prince] is with women. It's the way he notices every detail about you … and when he looks at you he makes you feel like you're the center of the universe. That's very beguiling." Lamenting the fact that their marriage was allowed simply to fade away, she conceded, "I hate the fact I'm divorced. I'm now very wary of ever getting married again, because I believe marriage should be for life."

In 2012, Mayte took on a role in VH1's *Hollywood Exes*, a reality TV show that purported to follow five women "on their journey without their famous husbands and ex-lovers … [who] want to establish themselves as independent, successful women." Several years later, in June 2015, it was reported that she was writing a book about her life with Prince, with a view to a Christmas 2015 release. No such book materialised, but in March 2016, she sought to auction much of her Prince memorabilia through the Nate D. Sanders auction house. Among the 95 pieces that went up for sale, Mayte offered a number of Prince's old stage costumes, along with her own wedding dress (starting price $25,000), her 2.2-karat diamond engagement ring and proposal letter ($100,000), and, from their wedding day, china place settings decorated with a mix of Prince's love symbol and Matye's first initial.

"I loved him then, I love him now, and will love him eternally," she said in a statement following Prince's death. Then, referencing Boy Gregory, she added, "He's with our son now."

AFTER FREEING HIMSELF FROM HIS WARNER BROS
CONTRACT, MOST OBSERVERS EXPECTED PRINCE TO START
RELEASING AS MUCH MUSIC AS HE POSSIBLY COULD.
HAVING SPENT THE MAJORITY OF 1997 OUT ON THE ROAD,
HOWEVER, HE DIDN'T GET AROUND TO RELEASING A
FOLLOW-UP TO *EMANCIPATION* UNTIL JANUARY 1998 –
AND EVEN THEN, IT WAS A COLLECTION OF OLD MATERIAL.

Crystal Ball (MAY 1997–JANUARY 1998)

Prince's recent albums might not have pushed the musical envelope in the same way as had his 80s output, but he was still plugging away at reinventing the music business. With *Crystal Ball*, he would become the first artist to sell an entire album online. In May 1997, he had started taking pre-orders for the multi-disc set via his new website, Love4OneAnother.com, and his 1-800-NEW-FUNK hotline. *Crystal Ball* was set to include three discs of archival material and a fourth disc of new songs, *The Truth*.

Prince was footing the bill for the production of the set himself, so decided not to start manufacturing it until he received a certain number of pre-orders (somewhere between 50,000 and 100,000). Whatever the figure, it didn't take long to reach it. With the promise of unreleased material cherry-picked from The Vault, demand among hardcore fans was high.

Crystal Ball was originally due to be sent out in June, but that proved to be a somewhat optimistic goal. Lacking the kind of manufacturing and distribution setup available

to proper record labels, Prince's organization was overwhelmed from the start and couldn't keep up with demand. The first copies of the set were not sent out until January 29 1998, and even then there were problems with the mail order system, resulting in some fans receiving more than one copy while others didn't get theirs for months. As if to add insult to injury, *Crystal Ball* was then made available through conventional channels in March – and with a full-color booklet that wasn't included with pre-ordered copies. (Prince encouraged his fans to download the artwork from his website instead, as he would continue to do with the release of *Planet Earth* in 2007.)

The disastrous distribution served only to fuel fans' loss of faith in Prince as the 90s progressed, but that wasn't the only disappointment. *Crystal Ball* was supposed to come in a spherical, clear-plastic case, but when it finally saw the light of day it arrived in a flat, circular dish. The musical content, meanwhile, seemed hardly to represent the promised explosion of choice recordings from The Vault. Most of the unreleased songs from *Dream Factory* are present, but had been overdubbed since the original 1986 sessions. The oldest track on the collection, 1983's 'Cloreen Baconskin,' might have offered the tantalizing prospect of a vintage collaboration with Morris Day, but is actually just an aimless 15-minute jam. And for every enjoyable mid-90s rarity, such as 'She Gave Her Angels' or the *Gold Experience* outtake 'Interactive,' there are dire remixes of *Come* and *Love Symbol* material. "As usual the music is funky and fun," wrote the *Minneapolis Star-Tribune*, "but most of it is for fanatics only."

The best part of the set was *The Truth*, an album of new material, most of it solo, acoustic, and embellished with only the lightest of overdubs. The performances are more intimate than anything Prince had recorded in years, while the songs pick up where *Emancipation* left off, continuing to trace the singer's life as a mature artist. The

blues-based 'Don't Play Me' alone makes the whole set worth owning for the way it demonstrates Prince's ability to assert himself without resorting to the bluster of *Chaos And Disorder*.

The *New Musical Express* described *The Truth* as a "minor revelation [that] sounds like nothing Prince, Squiggle, or The Artist has ever recorded." It's a shame then that pre-ordered copies of *Crystal Ball* followed it with a fifth disc tacked on in an attempt to appease those fans who felt they had wasted time and money on it. Prince wrote *Kamasutra* for his wedding to Mayte, and credits it here to The NPG Orchestra. The overall effect however is something that would better suit a new-age mail-order TV channel than a marriage ceremony, and suggests that Prince had little idea about the workings of classical music.

When Prince Met Larry (And Chaka)

As a member of Sly & The Family Stone during the late 60s and early 70s, Larry Graham pioneered the 'slap bass' technique, and is widely considered to be one of the best bassists of the rock era. He met Prince at an after-show party at the Music City Mix Factory in Nashville, Tennessee, in August 1997, and the two quickly became inseparable. It wasn't long before Graham had become Prince's foremost spiritual guide, or before Prince had offered to produce an album for his new mentor in much the same way as he had for romantic muses such as Susannah Melvoin and Mayte.

Prince started work on the album shortly thereafter, while also recording his own *Newpower Soul* release. *GCS 2000* would be Graham's first album since 1985 – and the first to be released under the name Graham Central Station since 1979 – and was scheduled for release in early 1999. By then Prince would also have recorded and released *Come 2 My House*, an album by Chaka Khan, famed for her role in the late 70s disco band Rufus and her 1984 cover of Prince's 'I Feel For You.'

The making of these two albums recalled the position Prince found himself in at the start of the decade, when he had tried to resuscitate the careers of Mavis Staples and George Clinton. Instead of letting Graham and Khan shape their own musical identities, Prince tried to remold them in his image, giving *GSC 2000* and *Come 2 My House* the same sound as his own *Newpower Soul*. He had also thrown his weight behind two artists well past their prime – just as had been the case with

Staples and Clinton. While there might have been some interest in seeing Graham or Khan live, younger audiences were unlikely to want to listen to new records given an artificial contemporary sheen.

Prince took Graham and Khan out with him for the press tour in support of *Newpower Soul*, but did little to promote either act's new album beyond having them sit beside him while he praised their work. He seemed more interested in pushing the NPG label and its ethos. "I have no contract with Larry," he told *Good Morning America*. "We have a joke, you know, he says to me, 'Contract? Let's see, what would we put on it?' The prefix on contract is 'con.' I'm not trying to con him. I trust him and he trusts me."

The situation was much the same, it seemed, with Khan. "Chaka is another artist who was temporarily choked by restrictions, contracts, and bad business deals," Prince told *Guitar World* around the same time. "She's free now ... One of the pleasures of my life is being able to work with some of my musical heroes, and in doing so pay back some dues and have a great time."

It wasn't long before Prince realized that he didn't have the resources to run a label in the way he had previously, when Warner Bros bankrolled his Paisley Park imprint. His comments in the media began to take the form of pleas to bigger fish in the music industry to pick up Khan and Graham's albums for distribution.

"I don't want to see [Khan] get lost," he told Tavis Smiley on *BET Tonight*. "I challenge the radio stations, I challenge the record stores to take care of her." After praising Best Buy, Blockbuster, and HMV for being "really cool with us" for stocking the record, he

noted how so many contemporary artists – "the Lauryn Hills and the Erykah Badus" – have "much love for her." Larry Graham, he continued, "is Michael Jordan on the bass. Open and shut book. Now how do you not stock that if you love music?"

What the poor uptake of *Come 2 My House* and *GSC 2000* proved, however, was that retailers also loved money, and tended to avoid stocking records that were unlikely to generate a profit. At a time when Prince's own albums weren't selling too well, his side projects were even less successful. Khan and Graham's comeback LPs weren't the last non-Prince albums to be released on NPG Records, but more than a decade would pass before he tried again to get a new artist into stores off his own back.

Former Sly & The Family Stone bassist Larry Graham on stage in 1998.

PRINCE'S SECOND NEW ALBUM OF 1998 WAS THE FIRST SINCE 1995'S *EXODUS* TO BE CREDITED TO THE NEW POWER GENERATION. HIS REASON FOR RETURNING TO THE NAME IS UNCLEAR, SINCE HE NO LONGER HAD TO HIDE BEHIND IT TO AVOID THE WRATH OF WARNER BROS.

Newpower Soul

(APRIL–DECEMBER 1998)

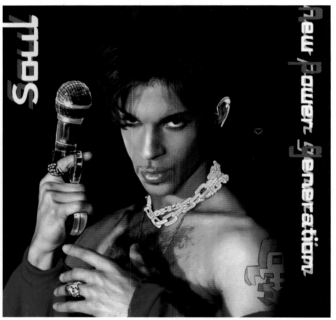

Perhaps he had finally come around to the idea that flooding the market with too many Prince/O{+> albums might be unwise; perhaps he realized that the album wasn't very good, and didn't want to highlight it as a bona fide solo record. If the latter is true, it doesn't really fit with the fact that *Newpower Soul* is the NPG album on which Prince features most prominently – he even put himself on the sleeve. If he thought he was revealing a great secret in doing so, however, he was mistaken.

Released on June 30, *Newpower Soul* performed more strongly than *Chaos And Disorder*, suggesting that Prince fans were more willing to indulge his funk missteps than his rock follies, despite the fact that it's one of the worst and least interesting albums of his career. Prince spends most of it plundering George Clinton, until he gets to 'Push It Up,' which cannibalizes his own 'Jam Of The Year.' The UK single 'Come On' is the best of a bad bunch of aimless funk songs; only 'Mad Sex' and the hidden track (number 49) 'Wasted Kisses' – a particularly dark tale sung from the perspective of a man who has just killed his lover – offer anything different. The rest of the album is made up of the sort of lukewarm funk everybody knew Prince was capable of making, but hardly anybody wanted to hear.

Prince put a fair amount of effort into promoting *Newpower Soul* live and on television, but most of the interviews he gave focused not on the music but on his assertion that he had made the right decision to go out on his own. "I think I'm better suited to market my own music," he told Tavis Smiley on *BET Tonight*. "I am in a position now with New Power Generation Records that I can take the music and repackage it … I was never allowed this before. You're talking about a lucrative sum of money, and I've made a lot of money since I left Time-Warner."

More interesting than *Newpower Soul* itself was the series of short tours Prince undertook in support of the album in the USA and Europe, giving fans another chance to see stripped-down performances of the hits, this time without second guitarist Kat Dyson but with the addition of backing singer Marva King. The shows were made all the more interesting by regular guest appearances from Larry Graham and Chaka Khan, funk veterans who both had NPG Records albums of their own to promote. In a decade full of low points, however, *Newpower Soul* stands as Prince's lowest.

Prince & The Muppets

The second season of *Muppets Tonight*, a spin-off from the long-running *Muppet Show* series, opened with a bang on September 13 1997 when it featured Prince (still calling himself O{+>) as a guest star. The culmination of a series of Prince-as-everyman television appearances, which had begun a year earlier with an incredibly open interview on *Oprah*, it was taped during a break from the Jam Of The Year tour, with the singer still ostensibly promoting *Emancipation*, almost a year after its release.

He also seemed keen still to score points against Warner Bros, a year after his departure from the label. At one point a ventriloquist's doll asks the singer if he would consider working with dummies, to which Prince replies: "I already have, but in my business they're called executives."

For the most part he was there to have fun, however, and appeared to be a lot more relaxed with The Muppets than he tended to be when fulfilling press and media obligations with human beings. Cue gentle mockery of his new name (a security guard tells Prince he is "the bear currently known as unamused"); a group of Muppets dressed as Prince from different eras, singing 'Delirious'; the singer himself dressed as a country bumpkin, with an alligator disguised as a pet dog; and a re-recorded version of 'Starfish & Coffee' filmed as a black-and-white flashback to the school days of the Muppets' take on a young Prince.

The show closes with 'She Gave Her Angels,' one of the many Prince songs of the time written for and inspired by Mayte. All in all, *Muppets Tonight* was one of the most bizarre television appearances Prince has ever made. It's also one of the few times in his career that he has seemed to let his guard down.

1999: The New Master

(DECEMBER 1998–FEBRUARY 1999)

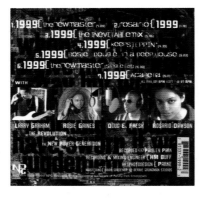

With the new millennium fast approaching, it came as no surprise that '1999' began to play on the minds of Prince, his fans, and even casual listeners who had heard the singer's breakthrough hit at some point since its release in 1983. The Warner Bros executives would have been only too aware of the commercial potential of so timely a song, but when they decided to reissue it as a single in December 1998, Prince was enraged.

As far as Prince was concerned, the dissolution of his contract with Warner Bros meant that only he should be able to make money off new releases bearing his name. But since Warner Bros owned the '1999' master tapes, the label could release the song whenever it wanted (and would do so again the following December). In retaliation Prince decided to re-record and overdub the original '1999' for a new release on his own NPG label, the *1999: The New Master* EP.

"Once Warner Bros refused to sell me my masters, I was faced with a problem." PRINCE

"Once Warner Bros refused to sell me my masters, I was faced with a problem," he told *USA Today* shortly after the EP's release. "But 'pro' is the prefix of 'problem,' so I decided to do something about it."

What he seemed to have decided to do, however, was destroy the legacy of the original, replacing a lean blast of future-funk with an overproduced mess that made misguided concessions to dance and hip-hop. Ironically, the new additions – DJ scratches, sampled Rosie Gaines vocals, a rap

by Doug E Fresh, and a Latin breakdown that probably would have worked much better live than on record – made the 'new master' sound more dated than the original.

The remaining six tracks on the EP comprise a series of tired variations on the same theme, including an 'Inevitable Mix' that replaces Lisa Coleman and Dez Dickerson's original vocals with the less fitting voices of Larry Graham and Rosie Gaines. The EP's most interesting moment is a poem read by actress Rosario Dawson over the instrumental intro of 'Little Red Corvette,' an anti-Christmas rant drawing on the Jehovah scriptures that says more about Prince's mindset at the time than a torrid remake designed to strike back at his former employers.

Perhaps the most notable aspect of the release was the fact that singer broke his 'Prince' boycott and credited it, somewhat cynically, to Prince & The Revolution. But not even that was enough to encourage his fans to buy it. *The New Master* EP only reached Number 150 on the *Billboard* pop albums chart, and Number 58 on the R&B albums chart. By contrast, Warner Bros's 1998 and 1999 reissues of the original single made it to Number 40 and Number 56 on the Hot 100 respectively.

For a while Prince threatened to tackle the rest of his back catalog in the same way, telling *Paper* magazine that, since Warner Bros wouldn't give him back the original masters, "I'm going to re-record them. All of them." This, he claimed, would result in "two catalogs with pretty much the same music – except mine will be better – and you can either give your money to WB, the big company, or to NPG. You choose." On the evidence of *1999: The New Master*, it's just as well he didn't bother. There would have been plenty of disappointment on both sides.

The Vault... Old Friends 4 Sale

(AUGUST 1999)

Since the 1996 release of *Chaos And Disorder*, Warner Bros had been sitting on the one last Prince album it was owed as part of the deal to terminate the singer's contract. Rather cannily, the label waited until Prince announced his return to another major label before putting out *The Vault … Old Friends 4 Sale* in an effort to steal some of the thunder from *Rave Un2 The Joy Fantastic*, which was scheduled for release through Arista in November 1999. That Warner Bros opted to credit *The Vault* to Prince – rather than O{+> – only heightened the snub.

Like *Chaos And Disorder*, *The Vault* came with a number of reminders that it was not necessarily something that Prince wanted released, from the "originally intended 4 private use only" disclaimer to the lack of detailed information in the liner notes (particularly by comparison to NPG Records' *Crystal Ball*). The prospect of more unreleased material from The Vault was enough to send the album to Number 85 in the USA and Number 47 in the UK, but most of those fans that bought it were left disappointed. As far as the *New Musical Express* was concerned, *The Vault* had been "cobbled together to cash in on a dwindling hardcore rump of completist fans."

Perhaps the biggest fault to be found with *The Vault* is the fact that it contains material that had previously been available on bootlegs and that might now have been of superior sound quality but was far less impressive from a musical standpoint. 'Old Friends 4 Sale,' for example, was written in the immediate aftermath of Chick Huntsberry's story about the singer appearing in the *National Enquirer*, and could potentially have resulted in one of Prince's most brutally honest recordings. The *Vault* version was recorded in the early 90s, however, and any meaning to be found in the lyrics is crushed under the weight of schmaltzy over-production.

The Vault might be marginally more enjoyable to listen to than *Chaos And Disorder*, but many of the songs included on it are either unfinished or simply aimless. Three tracks come from the aborted soundtrack to *I'll Do Anything*, of which 'There Is Lonely' is an interesting ballad without a conclusion and 'My Little Pill' is an odd spoken-word piece that doesn't make much sense outside of its original context. Much of the rest of the material is jazz-orientated, but it's often so vague and bland that it passes by unnoticed.

> *The album's musical value is summed up by 'Extraordinary,' which is anything but.*

The album's musical value is summed up by 'Extraordinary,' which is anything but. It sounds instead as if Prince entered the title into a songwriting machine, pressed the 'falsetto ballad' button, and put the results onto disc without even listening to them.

One or two tracks do make for pleasant listening, among them 'Old Friends 4 Sale' and '5 Women+.' But if *The Vault … Old Friends 4 Sale* was designed to offer tantalizing evidence of the vast collection of unreleased excellence that Prince has everyone believe exists, it failed miserably. Many fans would have been thinking the same as *The Guardian* newspaper when it asked, in its review of the album, "What became of the talent formerly known as Prince?"

AFTER PROVING THAT HE COULD SUCCEED ON HIS OWN TERMS WITH *EMANCIPATION* IN 1996, PRINCE BEGAN TO LOOK INTO ALTERNATIVE METHODS OF DISTRIBUTION, INCLUDING WORKING IN CONJUNCTION WITH INDEPENDENT LABELS AND SELF-RELEASING AN ENTIRE PACKAGE ONLINE (SOMETHING NOBODY ELSE HAD EVER DONE).

Rave Un2 The Joy Fantastic

(APRIL–DECEMBER 1998)

But with *Newpower Soul* failing to set the charts alight, and the same fate befalling NPG Records releases by Chaka Khan and Larry Graham, he must have started wonder whether he would ever have any major commercial clout again. The year that gave the title to one of his major breakthrough hits was fast approaching, and the song itself looked likely to overshadow almost everything he had done during the 90s.

"If the sky has blood in it," Prince to told *BET Tonight* host Tavis Smiley, in response to a question about the ominous approach of the year 1999, "blue and red make purple." He gave a slightly less cryptic response during a similar discussion with *Details* magazine. "I have nothing against the music industry," he said, "I just wanted to be free of it to explore all options for releasing my music. And I'll tell you this – I'll work with the music industry again, probably to release my next album."

Prince had been fairly quiet during the early months of the year, releasing nothing except his torrid 'new master' of '1999' in an act of defiance against his old record company. His only other act of note had been to lash out with lawsuits against fan magazines and websites that he claimed were cashing in on his copyrights. Then in April 1999 he began making tentative contact with various major labels with the help of L. Londell McMillan, the lawyer who had negotiated the deal to extract the singer from his Warner Bros contract.

Most of the meetings went badly. Prince found himself making the same complaints as before: that the labels wanted him to record identikit 'Prince' music, and stood to make much more out of it than he would himself. He seemed to have stepped right back into his mid-90s mindset in an interview with *Paper*, in which he compared the modern music industry to the movie *The Matrix*. "All the levels keep dissolving until you can't see what's behind anything," he said. "I'm not against the record industry. Their system is perfect. It benefits the people who it was designed to benefit: the owners."

Fortunately for Prince, one of the men he met with was Clive Davis at Arista. Davis was and is a legend in the music business, having signed Janis Joplin, Billy Joel, and Bruce Springsteen while at Columbia during 1967–72 before founding his own label, Arista, and putting together one of the most varied rosters in the business. By 1999 the label had been purchased by the Bertelsmann Music Group; Davis himself was gearing up for the release of Carlos Santana's *Supernatural*, a star-studded collaborative album that would eventually sell more than 25 million copies. Davis was the man with the midas touch, and was ready to put his powers to work on lifting another fallen star out of the doldrums and back onto primetime radio.

A deal was struck in May shortly after Davis listened to what Prince had recorded so far. In return for agreeing to work with a major label for the first time three years,

Prince was given an $11 million advance and a one-album deal that allowed him to keep his master tapes. All he had to do now was complete the album, which Arista would then use its own resources to promote and distribute, leaving Prince free to go his own way if he wasn't happy with the results.

"It's like going back to school and knowing that you don't have to stay," Prince told *USA Today*. There was nonetheless some surprise in the media that the man who had declared himself a slave to the industry three years earlier could even consider returning to a major label. Prince justified his decision by praising Davis, making it

Joy In Repetition

With the 90s "almost happen[ing] without him," as one reviewer put it, Prince's artistic and commercial success fell into a sharp decline. But the rate at which he changed his mind and scrapped one project in favor of another remained the same. Given the quality of the material that *did* make it out into the world, it's unlikely that any of these unreleased works would have bothered the charts. But the lack of information about projects such as *The Dawn* (1997), *Madrid 2 Chicago* (2001), *High* (2001), and *Last December* (2002) serves only to increase speculation about them.

Little is known about any of these albums except for their titles and the fact that they were all 'announced' at some point or other. (One or two tracks earmarked for each may perhaps have ended up being released officially elsewhere.) There were also plans for several box sets: a seven-disc set of Prince samples for DJs with a suggested retail price of $700; a second volume of *Crystal Ball*, with the tracklisting set to be chosen by the fans; and another seven-disc set, *The Chocolate Invasion*, comprising all of the material that had been made available through the NPG Music Club until 2003. There were even rumors of a *3121* movie to accompany the album of the same name.

The most tantalizing of all the unreleased albums of the period was *Roundhouse Garden*, which Prince announced in 1998 as being a Revolution reunion album based on recordings from the mid 80s. Whether it would have entailed a full-scale reunion is unclear, but he did meet with his former bandmates at some point to discuss working together again. Problems arose when he allegedly demanded that Wendy Melvoin and Lisa Coleman renounce their homosexuality

before he could work with them, leading Bobby Z to withdraw from the project. (Prince later blamed Melvoin and Coleman for the fact that the album never saw the light of day, suggesting that people ought to ask *them* why it was never released.)

If *Roundhouse Garden* was the dream collaboration that never was, the weirdest unreleased project Prince began around the turn of the millennium was a planned *Rainbow Children* movie directed by Kevin Smith. While shooting his fifth movie, *Jay & Silent Bob Strike Back*, Smith got in touch with Prince to ask whether he could use 'The Most Beautiful Girl In The World' on the soundtrack. Prince declined, but offered Smith The Time's 'Jungle Love' instead, while also proposing an idea of his own.

It transpired that Prince was an avid fan of Smith's fourth movie, *Dogma*, a satire of Catholicism that led to death threats being sent to the director. As Smith later recalled in *An Evening With Kevin Smith*, Prince seemed to have got the wrong end of the stick. "Sitting there, listening to him talk about it," Smith said, "it's starting not to sound like the movie I made."

Prince nonetheless felt that Smith was the man to direct his next movie project, and invited him to Paisley Park to film the second annual fan event in June 2001. Part of Smith's job was to film a series of Q&A sessions, as well as fan responses to playbacks of *The Rainbow Children*. According to Smith, Prince wanted to make something that was "kind of like a concert film," but which included "bold things" like putting the words 'Jesus Christ is the son of God' on a screen and letting the crowd "deal with it."

Despite finding it impossible to connect with the project, Smith spent a week at Paisley Park and shot hours of footage. Along the way he picked up a lot of curious

information about the laws of 'Prince World,' including that, according to a producer by the name of Stephanie, the singer would often make outlandish requests, such as asking for a camel to be brought to him at 3am.

Perhaps unsurprisingly, the *Rainbow Children* movie never materialized. Smith was later asked to return to Paisley Park to edit the footage, which had already been through the hands of a number of other film technicians, after Prince decided to try to turn it into a recruitment video for Jehovah's Witnesses. Smith felt that he had "already [done] my recruitment film for Catholicism," so passed on the project. "If you're ever approached by a bunch of Jehovah's Witnesses and they say we'd like you to watch this video," he joked at the taping of *An Evening With Kevin Smith 2: Evening Harder*, "that's my latest film."

Dogma director Kevin Smith, who was hired to film fan reactions to *The Rainbow Children* at Paisley Park.

clear that he felt a bond with the man, not the company.

"When I was at Warner Bros I always heard from a third party," Prince claimed, perhaps forgetting the personal support he'd received in the early days. "Record companies want to own [our] creations, but no one owns the creations but the creator … Clive agrees you should own your masters. He also told me, 'I have free will, too.'"

Davis for his part went around telling journalists what a genius Prince was, and making it clear that this was a comeback of the highest order. (The singer himself challenged journalists who used the 'c' word, asking, "Comeback from what?") Undeterred by Warner Bros's release of *The Vault … Old Friends 4 Sale*, Prince pushed his new album, *Rave Un2 The Joy Fantastic*, as hard as any since *Emancipation*.

With *Rave* featuring guest appearances by the legendary saxophonist and former James Brown sideman Maceo Parker, Public Enemy's Chuck D, Ani DiFranco, and Gwen Stefani, comparisons to Santana's *Supernatural* were obvious, and all eyes were on Davis's power to mastermind another smash-hit. Prince of course tried to play down the comparison.

"I knew nothing about [Davis]," he told the *New York Times*, somewhat dubiously, "but he knows me. We agreed that this album is full of hits. It was just a question of whether or not we could agree on how it should be put out." As with *Emancipation*, Prince seemed rather too eager to prove his continuing relevance. "Tell me that's not a hit," he almost begged Anthony DeCurtis of the *New York Times* after playing him the album's first single, 'The Greatest Romance Ever Sold.'

Interest in the album rose when it was announced that, for the first time ever, a guest producer would be brought in on *Rave*, only for the excitement to die down when the man in question was revealed to be 'Prince' (the album itself is credited to O{+>). Despite 'O{+>''s assertion that 'Prince' had always been his best editor, many observers began to suspect that they would be getting another lackluster album in the *Newpower Soul* vein.

The disappointing identity of the 'guest' producer wasn't the only link back to Prince's heyday. The title came from a project he had shelved in 1988 because the title track, now resurrected, "sounded so much like 'Kiss'

that I wanted to put it in The Vault and let it marinade for a while." He also returned to using the Linn LM-1 drum machine for the first time in years. But none of this would be enough to make *Rave* a hit. Prince had been on the promotional trail for almost a month when 'The Greatest Romance Ever Sold' was released on October 5, but the single still failed to make a major impression. Part of the problem was that, after the success of 'The Most Beautiful Girl In The World,' he believed ballads were his best route into the charts. While Santana's Latin rock had lain dormant for long enough that it felt almost like a 'new' sound, 'The Greatest Romance' was just another Prince ballad.

When *Rave* itself was released on November 9, the most reviewers could agree on was that it was the sound of Prince at his most unashamedly commercial, which is true: it's undoubtedly his most chart-orientated album since *Diamonds And Pearls*. But while *Diamonds* did its best to capture the zeitgeist of early-90s R&B, *Rave* seemed to lag far behind the sound of contemporary producers such as The Neptunes and Timbaland.

According to the *New Musical Express*, *Rave* suggested that Prince had been "killed at the turn of the decade, and his record company have kept the incident a secret, releasing off-cuts from his previous sessions as new albums." *Entertainment Weekly* was kinder, noting that "when he's on, almost anything – even that nasty messiah complex – seems 4giveable," but still describing his cover of Sheryl Crow's 'Every Day Is A Winding Road' as a "borderline travesty."

Rave has its moments – notably 'Eye Love U But Eye Don't Trust U Anymore' – but for the most part it sounds like a tired, cynical attempt to get back into the charts, with the likes of 'Baby Knows' coming off like a tenth-generation retread of 'U Got The Look.' Of the guest collaborators, meanwhile, only Gwen Stefani was truly contemporary enough to attract a younger audience.

Taken as a whole, the album suffers from the same complaint as Prince's debut, *For You*: in trying to prove his ability to make hit records, he made everything much too clinical. There's none of the fun, spontaneity, or trust in happy accidents that so benefited the likes of *Sign "O" The Times*. "Once again I don't follow trends, they just follow me," he sings on the hip-hop-edged 'Undisputed,' but the album's musical content does nothing to back up the claim.

Ironically, with Prince keen for once to focus his efforts on pushing a major release in the USA, Arista's German-based parent company forced him to start in Europe, making television appearances and giving a handful of live performances in major cities such as Madrid, London, Paris, and Cologne. Given that the album only reached Number 145 in the UK, for example, it seemed like a wasted effort – particularly when it had hit Number 18 on *Billboard*. Some might have been happy enough with that

"This is a poet, a renaissance man, an iconoclast. This is someone who is bringing the state of music further along. I don't want to get involved in whether this is hype or not – this man is at the top of his form." CLIVE DAVIS (PRESIDENT OF ARISTA)

– it was, after all, Prince's best US chart placing since the release of *Emancipation* – but the man himself felt that Arista had botched the promotional campaign, and that Clive Davis had failed to deliver on his promise of hits.

Prince made a final stab at promoting the album in December, appearing on TV and even filming a pay-per-view New Year's Eve celebration, *Rave Un2 The Year 2000*, at Paisley Park. But as the millennium drew closer, he felt once again that he had been let down by a major label, and started posting messages on his website suggesting that Arista lacked commitment (while also pulling the plug on his own promotional efforts).

Prince also demanded that Arista release a second single from the album, but Davis refused to spend more money on an artist who had lost all interest in working the record himself. A stalemate ensued, resulting in Davis pulling the plug on *Rave* and leaving it to slide back down the charts.

Mirroring the release of *1999: The New Master* a year earlier, Prince released a remixed version of the album entitled *Rave In2 The Joy Fantastic* to members of his NPG Music Club in April 2000. He left some tracks the same, remixed some of the others, and replaced 'Every Day Is A Winding Road' with 'Beautiful Strange,' a murky soundscape reminiscent of some of the weirder moments on *Come*.

All in all, the new *Rave* was another case of preaching to the converted, and as such was unlikely to find its way onto casual fans' stereos, even if it is marginally more interesting than its predecessor. As the new millennium dawned, Prince seemed like nothing more than an independent artist with a firm yet modestly sized fan-base.

Rainbow Child

PRINCE'S EARLY GROUNDING IN RELIGION CAME FROM THE BIBLE CLASSES HE ATTENDED AS A CHILD AT MINNEAPOLIS'S SEVENTH DAY ADVENTIST CHURCH. LIKE MOST ADOLESCENTS, HE GREW INTERESTED IN SEX, LEADING TO ALL MANNER OF RUMORS ABOUT WHAT HE GOT UP TO IN HIS BASEMENT HOME BENEATH BANDMATE ANDRÉ ANDERSON'S HOUSE. MUCH OF HIS SUBSEQUENT RECORDING CAREER CAN BE SEEN AS AN ATTEMPT TO RECONCILE HIS SPIRITUALITY WITH HIS SEXUALITY.

In the early days, on songs such as 'Let's Pretend We're Married,' Prince appeared to have no qualms about setting "I'm in love with God, he's the only way" against his desire to "fuck the taste out of your mouth." But by the mid 80s he seemed to have realized that, in his new role as a musical superstar, he ought to be a little more measured in his opinions, and took to addressing on stage his divided loyalties to a God who wants him to be a good, and an audience who "love it when I'm bad."

"I believe in God," he told *MTV* in 1985. "There is only

one God. And I believe in an afterworld." Acknowledging the fact that he has been accused of "a lot of things contrary to this," he added, "I'm sincere in my beliefs. I pray every night and I don't ask for much. I just say 'thank you' all the time."

By 1988 Prince's beliefs had strengthened to the point where he seemed to be erasing part of his past self entirely. The overall message of *Lovesexy* was muddled, but at its heart was a wish to fuse his sexual desires with a deeper faith. It might have been lost on many, but as far as Prince was concerned he was gradually getting closer to God – hence his symbolic killing-off of one of his old personae on stage each night on the accompanying tour.

Prince's spiritual struggles continued right through the 90s. "The only time you can get tranquil is when you are at one," he told the *New Musical Express* in 1995. "The only time that happens is when you are with God. He tells me to carry on doing what I'm doing, which is my music." With the music in question still gravitating toward the carnal, it's no wonder he was conflicted.

When Prince changed his name to O{+> in 1993, he claimed he had been told to do so by his 'spirit.' In subsequent interviews it did genuinely seem as though a huge burden had been lifted, and that he had become a better man in the process. But as the 90s progressed he seemed to be struck by one tragedy after another. At his lowest ebb following the death of his infant son in October 1996, he once again went looking for spiritual guidance. His search would lead him to reconnect with God in a much deeper way than ever before.

Toward the end of 1997's Jam Of The Year tour – arranged in support of *Emancipation*, an album written in 1996 in celebration of marriage and impending fatherhood – Prince met Larry Graham, who had become a Jehovah's Witness in 1975 after the hectic fallout from Sly & The Family Stone and quickly began to open up to Prince about the faith, which takes a literal approach to *The New World Transcription Of The Holy Scriptures*, a revised edition of The Bible published in 1950.

Prince took to the religion almost immediately, and before long Graham had replaced Mayte as the singer's spiritual and emotional confidante and moved his family

Prince during the Lovesexy tour in 1988, and shrouding himself for an appearance at the 2005 People's Choice Awards.

to Chanhassen, Minnesota. "Larry's a special individual", Prince told *Guitar World* in 1998. "Not only has he shown me so much spiritually about The Truth, he's given me a lot of bass licks I can steal."

He went on to explain how his newfound faith had changed his perspective. "['The One'] went from a love song to a song about respect for the Creator," he said, adding that the meaning of the lyrics changed significantly for him after he read the *New World* Bible. "It has to be the *New World* translation because that's the original one," he added. "Later translations have been tampered with in order to protect the guilty."

Prince's religious conversion provoked a mixed response from fans when the singer started changing the lyrics to some songs and refusing to play others on

Prince took to the Jehovah's Witness faith almost immediately, and before long Graham had replaced Mayte as the singer's spiritual and emotional confidante and moved his family to Chanhassen, Minnesota.

account of their lyrical content. *Controversy*'s 'Sexuality' became 'Spirituality,' with a new cry of "Spirituality is all we ever need"; 'The Cross' became 'The Christ,' reflecting the Jehovah's Witnesses' rejection of Christian symbolism.

Many fans were upset by this. The man who once made it his business to break down as many barriers as possible was now advocating a conservative worldview and following a straight doctrine that ordered the world in a precise hierarchy: God, Man, Woman, Child, Animal. The more Prince became engrossed in his new faith, the less accessible he became to fans. "I don't believe in idol worship," he told *Entertainment Weekly* in 2004. "When I get asked for my autograph, I say no and tell them why, because I'm giving them something to think about."

Prince had spent much of his life changing on an almost yearly basis, but seemed to settle into a more established routine after converting to the Jehovah's Witness faith. Speaking to *Giant* magazine in 2006, he praised The Bible as "the guidebook to help men and women with their sins," noting that, if he needed relationship advice, there was nobody better to consult than Solomon, "the guy who had a thousand women!"

After polarizing opinion in 2001 with the overt religious content of *The Rainbow Children*, Prince reportedly began a more direct method of recruitment two years later – at least according to Cheryl Johnson, the *Minneapolis Star-Tribune* columnist with whom the singer had become embroiled in a public feud during the 90s. In 2003 Johnson reported that Prince and Graham had turned up in a "big black truck," knocked on a door, and started preaching the good word to a woman by the name

(in the article at least) of Rochelle. Not only was this a Jewish household, but the two men had picked the evening of Yom Kippur to try to convert a Jewish woman to the Jehovah's Witnesses.

For Prince, spreading the word fulfilled his mission from God. As his former private chef Margaret Wetlzer recalled, he "kept a floor-to-ceiling stack" of Bibles at Paisley Park, and "gave one to every guest" he entertained. Yet his religious zeal sometimes made him appear disappointingly ignorant of other beliefs. In a 2008 interview with the *New Yorker*'s Claire Hoffman, Prince, when "asked about his perspective on social issues – gay marriage, abortion," tapped his Bible and said: "God came to the earth and saw people sticking it wherever and doing whatever, and he just cleared it all out. He was, like, 'Enough.'"

The piece hit the newsstands on November 17, just days after the controversial California Marriage Protection Act, known as Proposition 8, was voted into effect. It subsequently took five years to repeal the legal declaration that "Only marriage between a man and a woman is valid or recognised in California"; Prince, though he hadn't openly denounced gay marriage, hadn't shown his support for it, either. His gay fans felt abandoned by the man whose sexual liberation in the 80s was as important as Bowie's had been the previous decade.

Inevitably, the damage limitation began – but still without a direct clarification from the artist himself. Prince told the *LA Times*' Ann Powers that he had gay friends, and that they "study The Bible together," while blogger Dr Funkenberry was quick to claim that the unimpeachably diligent *New Yorker* had run an article "chock full of misquotes," especially "the parts about religion." Surprisingly, despite Prince's uneasy relationship with the press, his most sympathetic supporter seemed to be Claire Hoffman herself. "For what it's worth, the way he said it wasn't hateful so much as sad and resigned," she told the *New Yorker*'s website. "Prince is a true believer, and I think that's important to keep in mind in hearing his viewpoint."

Three years later, his viewpoint seemed woefully naïve. Speaking to the *Guardian*'s Dorian Lynskey, Prince, who had performed in the United Arab Emirates the previous winter, declared: "It's fun being in Islamic countries, to know there's only one religion ... You wear a burqa. There's no choice. People are happy with that." When Lynskey asked about those unhappy with having no choice, Prince brushed the question off: "There are people who are unhappy with everything. There's a dark side to everything."

Once again, Dr Funkenberry came to the rescue. The interview, it transpired, had been conducted alongside a

French journalist from *Le Parisien*, and Funkenberry drew fans' attention to the "similar but slightly different" report in which Prince was quoted as saying, "I really like the Muslim culture. I don't understand what people have against veiled women/women in burqas. How can you stop people dressing how/the way they want to?" The *Guardian*, however, defended its journalistic integrity, pointing out that the interview had been conducted in English, which had then been translated into French for publication in *Le Parisien*, before being translated back into English for Funkenberry's blog. Fans were left to decide where the misquote might have crept in.

Prince subsequently trod carefully when talking about religion. When *V* magazine asked him how he reconciled his religious impulse with his sexual one, Prince embarked on an answer that started off asking what wars were "about" before noting that God created humans as "sensual beings" and that religion should be thought of as an electro-magnetic life-force. "I don't want to talk about this," he then demurred, adding that words were "tricky" and that only if the interviewer were a student and Prince was teaching could they "get into that."

Like anyone, Prince had a highly personal relationship

When he wasn't on tour, on many Sunday mornings he attended services at the Kingdom Hall Of Jehovah's Witnesses in Minnetonka, where he was known as 'Brother Nelson.'

with religion. In conversation with *Rolling Stone* in 2014, he declared that anything he had believed in at the time of his conversion he believed in "more now – it's just expanded." The magazine noted that, while still "deeply Christian," Prince spent time studying "what appears to be an Afro-centric interpretation of history, along with the physics of sound, some Eastern philosophy (chakras are 'science,' he says) and a selection of unabashed conspiracy theories," among them thoughts on the JFK assassination, AIDS, and chemtrails, a subject that had occupied him as early as 2008.

Through it all, Prince's commitment to the Jehovah's Witnesses was unshakable. When he wasn't on tour, on many Sunday mornings he attended services at the Kingdom Hall Of Jehovah's Witnesses in Minnetonka, where he was known as 'Brother Nelson.'

"Religion, when used properly, actually is like a health regimen," he told *Ebony* in December 2015, before claiming that "people who have faith live longer … it says so in the book." Yet following his death, many observed that Prince's secret use of painkillers might have been avoided had the Jehovah's Witnesses allowed him to receive the blood transfusion necessary for a hip replacement. (The results of the post-mortem examination carried out on Prince's body recorded a scar on his left hip, however, suggesting that Prince did receive some sort of hip surgery.)

In an interview with the *Minneapolis Star-Tribune*, Larry Graham, the man who introduced Prince to the Witnesses in 1997, denied any knowledge of Prince's use of opiates. Defending the faith, he asserted that medical science offered alternatives. "We recognize that life is a gift from God," he said. "Any medical treatment that will make us well again, we seek that."

Though Prince did not appear to have left a will, he did make it clear to his family that, in the event of his death, he wanted a quiet service with little fuss. In keeping with his wishes, and in accordance with his faith, Prince was cremated in a small ceremony within a week of his death, on Saturday, April 23 2016.

AFTER FAILING TO RE-ESTABLISH HIMSELF AS A MAJOR ARTIST AGAIN WITH *RAVE UN2 THE JOY FANTASTIC*, PRINCE SPENT MOST OF 2000 OUT OF VIEW, SEEMINGLY STUNG BY THE DISAPPOINTMENT. HIS ONLY PUBLIC APPEARANCES BEFORE NOVEMBER WERE AT PAISLEY PARK, TAKING THE FORM OF A SERIES OF EARLY-HOURS PARTIES AND THE FIRST ANNUAL PRINCE: A CELEBRATION FAN EVENT, WHICH RAN FROM JUNE 7–13.

The Rainbow Children

(SEPTEMBER 2000–NOVEMBER 2002)

Then, on November 7, he embarked on the first leg of his Hit N Run tour of the USA, giving fans yet another chance to see him perform the hits with another revamped NPG. The line-up this time included a second keyboard player, Kip Blackshire, brought in to bolster Morris Hayes's sound; Jerome Najee Rasheed on saxophone; Geneva, Prince's first official dancer since Mayte; and John Blackwell, perhaps the most powerful Prince drummer since Michael Bland. A second leg followed in April 2001 prior to a six-date mini-tour in June dubbed A Celebration.

To the wider world Prince appeared to have lost his way, with nothing left to offer but the same old greatest-hits sets. Anyone paying closer attention however would have noticed the release of a new single, 'The Work Pt. 1,' via Napster, the controversial, pioneering file-sharing site, in April 2001. But while the method of distribution was certainly innovative, the song itself was little more than a James Brown-style pastiche reminiscent of *Rave Un2 The Joy Fantastic*'s 'Prettyman.'

Two months later, Prince opened Paisley Park up for a second weeklong fan event, which this time took its name from the title of his forthcoming new album, *The Rainbow Children*. Prince had been quietly working on the record since the fall of 2000, and gave it its first airing at listening sessions during the event. Fan opinion was polarized, just

> ◪ The Rainbow Children marked the return of Prince the artist, as opposed to Prince the hit-maker.

as the critical response would be when the album went on sale in November (having been available to NPG Music Club subscribers as a download since mid October).

One of the most striking aspects of *The Rainbow Children* is the fact that, after letting his publishing deal with Warner/Chappell expire, Prince decided to return to using his original name for the first time since *Come*. Anyone expecting this to herald a return to pop-orientated material would have been disappointed, however, as *The Rainbow Children* instead marked the return of Prince the artist, as opposed to Prince the hit-maker. But while the move away from turgid funk delighted some fans, others just couldn't get past the subject matter.

Having been introduced to the Jehovah's Witness faith by Larry Graham in 1998, Prince used *The Rainbow Children* to make his feelings about the religion public. In the past, on albums such as *Lovesexy*, he had attempted to reconcile his sexual desires with his religious beliefs. On *The Rainbow Children* his focus is entirely spiritual. A fully fledged concept album, it tells the story of how The Rainbow Children and their leader, The Wise One, have been penned in by a Digital Garden built by a group of evildoers known as The Banished Ones, and now have to go knocking door-to-door to find people willing to do The Work and help deconstruct the Garden.

So far, so thinly veiled, but some fans were at least glad that Prince seemed to be returning to more mature themes than the sex'n'dancing of old. More troubling however was that he seemed now to subscribe to a theocratic order than put women below men, and also seemed to have instilled in him some distinctly questionable views on race. "Holocaust aside, many lived and died," he sings on 'Muse 2 The Pharaoh,' before seemingly suggesting that it is better to be "B dead" than to be sold into slavery. He makes a similarly unwise claim on 'Family Name,' reminding listeners that, when all is said and done, the Jews were at least allowed to retain their original surnames, unlike those slaves whose names were taken by their white masters.

Coming from a man who once made it his business to break down racial and sexual barriers, all of this was nothing short of a travesty – not lease because there is much to enjoy elsewhere on the album. Many found it to be Prince's most daring and experimental release since the

80s – at least once they got past the distracting, slowed-down voice he used to narrate it (a deliberate contrast, perhaps, to his high-pitched evil twin, Camille). The album's organic, live-sounding production is certainly preferable to the over-egged R&B sound of much of his 90s output. Not all of its jazz-funk excursions are successful, but there is more flair to the arrangements than anything since *Lovesexy* – or even *Sign "O" The Times*.

The likes of 'Last December' and the title track make a good stab at stretching out and taking the listener on their own microcosmic journeys, and sound positively revelatory by comparison to Prince's other recent output. Some do however fall into Madhouse-lite territory, while the standout dance-track '1+1+1=3' bears more than a passing resemblance to the 1984 B-side 'Erotic City.' This time, instead of promising a night of unbridled passion, Prince explains to his future wife that him, plus her, plus God, equals three, and that there "ain't no room 4 disagree".

The critical response to the album was about as polarized as could be expected. On the one hand, *USA Today* called it "one of Prince's most challenging and fascinating works to date, whatever your take on the

Diamonds And Pearls. Named after a stripped-down album sent out to members of the NPG Music Club in May 2002, the One Nite Alone ... tour took in 64 dates in the USA, Canada, Europe, and Japan, plus a one-off show recorded for a DVD released the following year.

Whereas recent tours in support of albums such as *Emancipation* and *Newpower Soul* had often seen Prince play to the strengths of his back catalog, One Nite Alone ... put the focus on his band, marginally revamped since the Hit N Run shows. The rhythm section of Rhonda Smith and John Blackwell remained, while keyboard virtuoso Renato Neto replaced both Kip Blackshire and Morris Hayes.

Prince also hired a full brass section for the first time in a while, with Maceo Parker taking over most of the saxophone duties alongside Candy Dulfer, who joined midway through the American leg, with new trombonist Greg Boyer coming on board from the start. When the hits eventually arrived they were given radical new arrangements designed to show off the band's versatility. Prince threw a few more obscure songs into the set, such as *The Vault*'s 'Extraordinary,' *Parade*'s 'Venus De Milo,' and the instrumental 'Xenophobia.' He also played a fair number of songs from *The Rainbow Children* tracks, using the likes of 'Family Name' to proselytize the audience.

During the shows he would challenge fans in the front rows as to whether it was better to give or to receive. If they opted to 'give,' he would ask them to swap seats with someone at the back of the hall. "For those of you expecting to get your 'Purple Rain' on, you're in the wrong house," he told the assembled throngs. "We're not interested in what you know, but what you are willing to learn."

"I wanna put up the words 'Jesus Christ is the son of God' on the screen and let them deal with it ... I want to talk about religion and lead that into race and lead it into the music biz and radio, and basically at the end of the week I wanna change the world."

FILMMAKER KEVIN SMITH RECALLS PRINCE'S PLANS FOR HIS SECOND ANNUAL A CELEBRATION EVENT

enigmatic valentines to God." The *Boston Globe* seemed in broad agreement, noting that, while not a "classic," *The Rainbow Children* "may be the most consistently satisfying Prince album since 1987's *Sign 'O' The Times*." *Rolling Stone* however took a rather different tone, bemoaning "a long trudge across the desert ... with freak-in-the-pulpit leading the way, waving his synthesizer of holy justice."

For all its flaws, *The Rainbow Children* was at least a valiant attempt at creating something interesting. That Prince himself thought highly of the album is clear from the effort he put into promoting it, touring it determinedly like nothing since *Love Symbol* or even

These heavy-handed, didactic moments aside, the One Nite Alone ... tour was one of Prince's most successful live engagements in recent memory. He ended the tour in November as content as he had been in some time. *The Rainbow Children* might have been the first major Prince album since his debut to fail to reach the *Billboard* Top 100, but he seemed happy to enter 2003 as a niche musician more interested in creating pure art than chasing chart placings. Through the NPG Music Club, he could now show his most devoted fans that he didn't have to try to make hits anymore, but instead serve up new music that charted his artistic maturation.

Prince, with percussionist Sheila E. back in the fold, performs on *The Tonight Show With Jay Leno* in December 2002.

IN SOME WAYS, *ONE NITE ALONE …* IS THE SOLO-PIANO COUNTERPART TO *THE TRUTH*, THE ACOUSTIC GUITAR-BASED ALBUM INCLUDED WITH PRE-ORDERED COPIES OF *CRYSTAL BALL*. PRINCE ISN'T STRICTLY ALONE ON THE ALBUM, AS DRUMMER JOHN BLACKWELL FEATURES ON A HANDFUL OF TRACKS, WHILE OTHERS ARE OVERDUBBED BY SYNTHESIZED SOUND-EFFECTS, BUT IT IS CERTAINLY ONE OF THE MOST INTIMATE-SOUNDING ALBUMS HE HAS MADE.

One Nite Alone …

One Nite Alone … Live!

(MAY–DECEMBER 2002)

Released to NPG Music Club members in May 2002, *One Nite Alone …* was recorded at the tail end of the *Rainbow Children* sessions. The result is a 35-minute oddity that feels intimate but never quite lets you decide whether or not you're listening to the 'real' Prince. Although it's a joy to hear him singing and playing so intimately, and without layers of overproduction, the overall effect is somewhat contradictory. One minute he's extolling the virtues of a loving relationship on a cover of Joni Mitchell's 'A Case Of U,' the next he's raging bitterly against a former lover on 'Have A Heart' and 'Pearls B4 The Swine.'

One song that breaks the happy-sad tension is 'Avalanche,' a return to the dubious themes of *The Rainbow Children*'s 'Family Name.' After branding Abraham Lincoln a racist who was "never in favor of setting R people free," he makes the groundless claim that the legendary A&R man John Hammond ripped off all of the acts he signed to Columbia Records.

One Nite Alone … was still a welcome treasure for the many devoted fans who relished the prospect of hearing Prince at his most fragile-sounding. However, the live album that shares its name – Prince's first – is not quite what one might have expected. Given that Prince had played numerous legendary shows over the years, and recorded most, if not all of them, it would have made sense for him to do something in the same vein as Bob Dylan's *Bootleg Series*. Instead he decided to release a three-disc document of his recent One Nite Alone … world tour.

That's not to say that releasing *One Nite Alone … Live!* was a mistake. The first two discs feature a smattering of old hits and rarities mixed with *Rainbow Children* songs recorded across eight nights that do an excellent job of capturing one of the best Prince tours in years. The third disc, taken from a pair of after-show performances, is less successful. Its mix of funk jams, extended rearrangements of old songs, and obscure covers might have sounded electrifying from within the confines of a small venue, but the magic doesn't quite translate onto CD.

One Nite Alone … Live! remains the only official live release in the Prince catalog to date. It will probably never take the place of the bootlegs cherished by hardcore fans, but it's a fine place to start.

Muse 2 The Pharoah

Prince seemed to live out most of his relationship with Mayte Garcia in the public eye, from the highest peaks to the most tragic lows. His union with second wife Manuela Testolini, however, was much more low key.

Eighteen years younger than Prince, Testolini was a fan of the singer long before she met him. She is known to have posted occasionally on the online forum at alt.music.prince, which somehow seemed to lead to her being hired to work for his charitable organization, Love4OneAnother. But such unorthodox assimilation is typical of a man whose world is so insular. Instead of taking the time to seek out a woman in a more conventional manner, Prince gave Testolini a role in his company, making it easier for him to stay close to her, and for her to see what his life was like.

Rumor has it that Prince started dating Testolini, who became his personal assistant in 1999, while still married to Mayte. The fact that she was chosen to appear in his 1998 promo video for 'The One' suggests a certain closeness. Her ascension within the Prince organization coincided with the singer's continued immersion in the Jehovah's Witness faith. It has been suggested that Testolini's religious beliefs were so close to Prince's own that she became almost as important to him, from a spiritual perspective, as Larry Graham.

Testolini became a more visible presence in Prince's life after he finalized his divorce from Mayte in May 2000. The new couple were seen together at basketball games and the annual Paisley Park celebrations, and were married on New Year's Eve 2001 in a Jehovah's Witness ceremony in Hawaii. Testolini remained by Prince's side throughout his conversion and during the promotion of *The Rainbow Children*, and is said to have had a strong positive influence on him, aiding his emergence from a period of artistic and commercial decline.

With Testolini by his side, Prince reopened Paisley Park to fans, and even took to attending Q&A sessions during the annual celebrations. He then followed a period of artistic experimentation with a return to commercial success, beginning with *Musicology*, his most popular album since 1996's *Emancipation*, with which it shares a theme of celebrating monogamy.

The end of the relationship proved to be as inconspicuous as the start. While it is known that Testolini filed for divorce on May 24 2006, her reasons have never been made public, though it's entirely possible that married life with Prince was not quite as idyllic as a fan might have imagined.

In 2013, Testolini married the R&B singer Eric Benét, but Prince's influence on her remained strong. She later recalled how Prince, a "fierce philanthropist" with whom she shared a "magical journey," had encouraged her to start her own charity, the In A Perfect World Foundation. In an official statement following his death, she revealed that she had "reached out" to Prince a few days before he died, in order to let him know that she was planning to build a school in Malawi in his honor. It would subsequently be built in his memory.

Prince never remarried, but when pressed on the subject by *Rolling Stone*'s Brian Hiatt in January 2014, he said: "That's another thing that's up to God. It's all magnetism anyway – something would pull me into its gravity, and I wouldn't be able to get out from it."

Prince and his second wife, Manuela, watch an LA Lakers basketball game on Christmas day 2004.

AFTER MAKING WHAT HE CLEARLY FELT WAS A MAJOR
ARTISTIC BREAKTHROUGH WITH *THE RAINBOW CHILDREN*,
PRINCE THREW HIMSELF INTO RECORDING A SERIES OF
EXPERIMENTAL INSTRUMENTAL ALBUMS.

Xpectation/C-Note/
N.E.W.S.

(JANUARY–JULY 2003)

The move echoed his decision to follow *Parade* by making the first Madhouse record in 1987, but while the Madhouse recordings had a sense of fun about them, the three low-key albums he released in 2003 smacked of pretension. Two of them were even subtitled *New Directions In Music From Prince*.

The first of these albums was made available to NPG Music Club members for download on New Year's Day. It was called *Xpectation*, but any high hopes were quickly dashed upon listening to it. With songs called things like 'Xosphere' and 'Xemplify,' and each one given a patronizing subtitle ('Xotica''s being 'Curiously unusual or excitingly strange'), some wondered whether a more appropriate title might have been *Xcrement*.

Recorded with current bandmembers John Blackwell (drums), Rhonda Smith (bass), and Candy Dulfer (sax), alongside pop-classical violinist Vanessa Mae, the album's ten songs are mostly in the pseudo-jazz vein of Madhouse. The title track in particular could have been lifted straight from 8. There are a few interesting avant-garde touches, but for the most part Prince's jazz explorations show no real progression from his first attempts 16 years earlier. The overall sound is slick and sophisticated, thanks to the quality of the band as a whole (and Mae in particular, who contributes some of the album's most interesting moments), but most of the songs still pass by unnoticed, while perhaps the greatest disappointment is that the impressive, ten-minute long 'Xenophobia,' played live during the One Nite Alone … tour, was left off the final tracklisting.

Two days after releasing *Xpectation*, Prince made *C-Note* available for download. Like it's predecessor, the album is a largely instrumental affair with thematically linked song titles: this time around each song is named for the city it was recorded in during soundchecks, with the first letter of each spelling out *C-Note*. 'Copenhagen,' 'Nagoya,' and 'Osaka' are all instrumental, while the only word sung on 'Tokyo' is the name of the city.

The album closes with a ballad, 'Empty Room,' that was once earmarked for *The Gold Experience*. The rest of the material is very much in the *Xpection* mold, but the fact

that it was recorded live with a seven-piece band gives it a more varied, organic sound.

Both *Xpectation* and *C-Note* can be viewed as test runs for *N.E.W.S.*, the only one of Prince's three LPs from 2003 to be given a conventional release. He perhaps needn't have bothered: this latest set of *New Directions In Music* became his lowest-selling album ever. The cruel irony is that *N.E.W.S.* is probably the most interesting set of instrumentals he has ever recorded. There is still a general air of pretension – the four tracks are titled 'North,' 'East,' 'South,' and West,' and each run to exactly 14 minutes – but the overall effect is much more dynamic and eclectic than previous instrumental efforts, with a sound that blends the most experimental side of Madhouse with the organic feel of *The Rainbow Children*.

N.E.W.S. was recorded in a single day, with Eric Leeds returning on sax alongside keyboardist Renato Neto, drummer John Blackwell, and bassist Rhonda Smith. The album's key strengths stem from the fact that Prince seemed finally to have realized that he didn't have to try to cram his understanding of jazz into five-minute pieces. The four lengthy tracks have a definite ebb and flow to them, taking in everything from Eastern intonations to harsh, abrasive guitar. All in all, *N.E.W.S.* remains Prince's finest jazz-infused album.

Prince didn't tour in support of any of these albums, but instead decided to revisit some of his more crowd-pleasing material on what was dubbed the World Tour 2003/2004, but which actually only entailed one date in Hong Kong, five in Australia, and two in Hawaii during October and December 2003.

Nonetheless, these eight concerts – Prince's first live shows in almost a year – were important in that they gave him a chance to reconnect with his back catalog for the first time since the Hit N Run shows of 2000–01. Cynics might argue that he needed little encouragement to revisit the hits "for the last time" once again, but the singer had genuinely seemed to distance himself from his best-known work on his 2002 tour. Now, away from the media glare he would have faced had he chosen to play in Europe or America, he took the opportunity to have fun with his back catalog, reinventing old songs with new arrangements, while also introducing some of the songs from his forthcoming *Musicology* LP.

Coming at the end of a year in which the only new Prince releases had been three instrumental albums aimed purely at the hardcore, the mini-tour seemed to give Prince the opportunity to reassess his status as a popstar.

Both Xpectation and C-Note can be viewed as test runs for N.E.W.S., the only one of Prince's three LPs from 2003 to be given a conventional release.

Musicology would see him make another grasp for the mainstream for the first time since 1999, while the 2003 live shows seemed to have a similarly invigorating effect. During a break from the tour in November, Prince set about planning a full-scale US tour. It would end up running to 95 dates and be his biggest trek across the country since the one in support of *Purple Rain*. The year just ending might have been one of the quietest of his career, but Prince was poised to launch his biggest comeback yet in 2004.

Prince performs in Melbourne, Australia, in October 2003 as part of a mini-tour that saw him reconnect with his pop hits for the first time in several years.

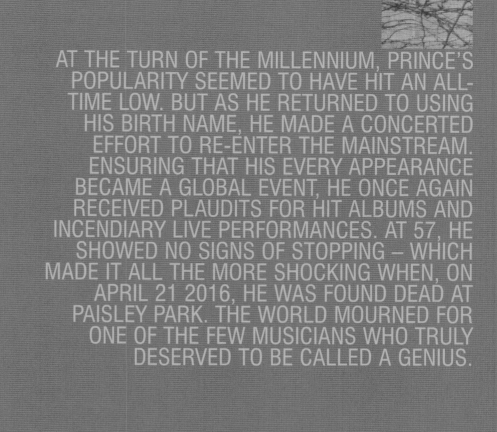

5

AT THE TURN OF THE MILLENNIUM, PRINCE'S POPULARITY SEEMED TO HAVE HIT AN ALL-TIME LOW. BUT AS HE RETURNED TO USING HIS BIRTH NAME, HE MADE A CONCERTED EFFORT TO RE-ENTER THE MAINSTREAM. ENSURING THAT HIS EVERY APPEARANCE BECAME A GLOBAL EVENT, HE ONCE AGAIN RECEIVED PLAUDITS FOR HIT ALBUMS AND INCENDIARY LIVE PERFORMANCES. AT 57, HE SHOWED NO SIGNS OF STOPPING – WHICH MADE IT ALL THE MORE SHOCKING WHEN, ON APRIL 21 2016, HE WAS FOUND DEAD AT PAISLEY PARK. THE WORLD MOURNED FOR ONE OF THE FEW MUSICIANS WHO TRULY DESERVED TO BE CALLED A GENIUS.

THE FINAL YEARS
2004–2016

PRINCE SEEMED TO HAVE ENDED 2003 ON A HIGH WITH
THE COMPLETION OF A SUCCESSFUL MINI-TOUR OF
HONG KONG, AUSTRALIA, AND HAWAII, BUT
THREATENED TO ALIENATE EVEN HIS MOST LOYAL FANS
AFTER AN INCIDENT AT MINNEAPOLIS INTERNATIONAL
AIRPORT IN DECEMBER.

Musicology (FEBRUARY–SEPTEMBER 2004)

According to a report by *Minneapolis Star-Tribune* columnist and long-time Prince-watcher Cheryl Johnson, the trouble started when a fan tried to take a picture of the singer shortly after he landed; Prince's bodyguard then swiped the fan's camera and made off with it in a luggage cart.

A follow-up report on January 15 quoted a number of fans' disgust at their idol's actions. The *Tribune* continued to follow the story until April 7 when the fan involved in the incident, one Anthony Fitzgerald, sued Prince and his bodyguard for "assault and battery, loss of the camera, and intentional infliction of emotional distress." (Reports suggested that it had taken until then for the lawsuit to be put into motion because Prince's people had initially refused to accept it.)

Fortunately for Prince, only his most ardent fans were watching, and most of them quickly forgave him once his busiest and most successful year in recent memory began to take shape. At the end of January he started playing one-off shows in anticipation of the release of a new album, beginning a promotional blitz that reached its pinnacle on February 8 with a duet at the Grammy Awards with Beyoncé. The pair performed a medley of hits from his *Purple Rain* (including 'Baby, I'm A Star' and 'Let's Go Crazy') alongside Beyoncé's 'Crazy In Love.'

For those outside the Prince hardcore, the Grammy performance was a timely reminder of the heights the singer could reach. Dressed in purple and gold, he seemed to have leapt out of the doldrums and onto the front pages almost overnight – just in time to mark *Purple Rain*'s 20th anniversary year.

Not everyone was impressed. Alan Leeds told the *St Paul Pioneer Press* that he found the level of performance "Vegas-y," while Prince himself noted: "I get asked every year to play at the Grammys. This year I did it because I have an album out that I want to promote and a concert tour that I want to promote." But it did enough to draw a large chunk of the world's media to the February 24 press release at which Prince officially unveiled the forthcoming *Musicology* album and tour.

The tour itself promised to be another 'all the hits for the last time' affair, but few of the assembled journalists

seemed to mind. It seemed to most of them that Prince had disappeared completely during the time he spent making records steeped in his Jehovah's Witness faith and releasing instrumental albums over the internet. After giving the wider world a breather, the returning Prince would be gratefully received – as would the news that he would be giving priority seating on the tour to NPG Music Club members – but the singer once again found himself having to challenge the idea that he was making a comeback. "I never went anywhere!" he told *Gallery Of Sound* later in the year. "I've been touring for a while. I took a break to make the *Musicology* project. It hasn't really stopped."

February 24's other big news was that, five years after the disappointment of *Rave Un2 The Joy Fantastic*, Prince was ready to have another go at working with a major label. At the time he had not yet decided which one; given the choice, he said, he would have asked "all of them to release it at once," but was willing to settle for the company "most hyped about pushing the product."

Perhaps the most interesting aspect of all of this was that Prince still planned to make *Musicology* available as a download first, and give copies away free to concertgoers.

"The CD," he noted, "is more or less a companion to the concert." Somewhat amazingly, he was able to convince Columbia Records to agree to promote and distribute the album through conventional channels even while he continued to pursue his own non-traditional methods.

"Sony [Columbia's parent company] has graciously agreed 2 augment the *Musicology* project with worldwide promotion and distribution," he wrote in an email to *Wired* magazine. "They r cool because they do not restrict NPG's ability 2 sell the product as well. It's a win-win situation."

The scheme might have looked like a catastrophe in

the making, but it worked. On April 20, three weeks after Prince had started giving copies away on the accompanying tour, *Musicology* appeared on record-store shelves as a combined Columbia/NPG release. According to Sony President Don Ienner, "With the first copy shipped, we started making money."

By then Prince had filled up further column inches after being inducted into the Rock And Roll Hall Of Fame

> *"Maybe we could put a [CD] sampler on every seat. Or give them the whole thing and build it into the ticket price."* PRINCE, SPEAKING IN 1996

and leading an all-star rendition of 'While My Guitar Gently Weeps' alongside Tom Petty and Jeff Lynne in tribute to the recently departed George Harrison. (Prince played the famous Eric Clapton guitar solo.) He had become a hot property once again. "There are many kings," Alicia Keys gushed in her introductory speech at the induction ceremony, "but there is only one Prince."

The singer himself then took to the stage to note: "When I first started out in this music industry, I was most concerned with freedom: freedom to produce, freedom to play all the instruments on my records, freedom to say anything I wanted to. After much negotiation, Warner Bros granted me my freedom, and I thank them for that." The event put Prince firmly back on the map. "After a decade spent tending only to his faithful," wrote *Time* magazine, "Prince has had a revelation: He's supposed to be a rock'n'roll star."

The American Musicology tour opened to ecstatic praise, with the initial run of 26 dates gradually expanding to include 96 shows in 69 cities – his longest run since the days of *Purple Rain*. Performing in the round, as he had done on the Lovesexy tour, Prince took to an X-shaped stage in the center of the arena and played a hits-based show with a smattering of *Musicology* songs. The highlight for many was the acoustic section, during which he treated rapt audiences to solo versions of 'Raspberry Beret,' 'Little Red Corvette,' and other early classics.

Prince tried to push *Musicology* as the tour's equal, telling interviewers that "school is back in session." Most of the reviews were suitably positive, with *Billboard* noting that the album "focuses on a fun and playful Prince, whose turns of phrase and instrumental dexterity call to mind why we embraced him in the first place," and *Rolling Stone* finding it "as appealing, focused, and straight-up satisfying an album as Prince has made since who knows when." The *New York Times* was one of the few publications to suggest that the album fell short of its early promise, describing it as "a casual exhibition of Princeliness" that could do with some of the "fighting spirit" of *The Rainbow Children*.

The general consensus, however, was that *Musicology* is

a good, solid record, but the *New Musical Express* got closest to the truth with its conclusion that the album offers "a kind of flawed redemption, neither inspired enough to be a true classic nor insipid enough to make it unworthy of your attention." Free from the turgid overproduction that marred much of *Emancipation* and *Rave Un2 The Joy Fantastic*, Prince seemed finally to have worked out how to make a contemporary-sounding record without losing his own style. Some of the songs might be lacking a little in terms of structure, but they work in the context of a concise, easily digestible album. Whereas some of his recent albums had been spoilt by bitterness, excess, or a determination to drive a funk riff home to the

point of banality, *Musicology* is the sound of Prince having fun. He even finds time to poke fun at Michael Jackson with the lines: "My voice is getting higher / And eye ain't never had my nose done."

With the rest of the album's musical and lyrical content pretty tame by comparison, the most controversial aspect of *Musicology* turned out to be the promo video for its third single, 'Cinnamon Girl.' A response to the newly suspicious mindset brought about by the terrorist attacks of September 11 2001, it cast a 14-year-old actress from New Zealand, Keisha Castle-Hughes, as an Arab-American schoolgirl who fantasizes about blowing herself up in airport after being subjected to racial

Prince and Beyoncé at the Grammy Awards, February 8 2004.

harassment. Prince seemed to be making the point that arbitrary suspicion can lead good people down dark paths, but the video was deemed too sensitive and banned by a number of television networks in Britain and America.

Despite Prince's desire for 'musicology' to became a byword for "letting the music come first," the music on his new album seemed to be completely overshadowed by his business practices. Even the Musicology tour, which

"I am violently against this … The charts are supposed to represent what consumers are spending money on. With the Prince album there is no choice." UNNAMED DISTRIBUTOR

ended in September, was reduced to a series of statistics by the end of the year when *Pollstar* magazine put it at the top of its list of the year's biggest concert draws. Prince, the magazine claimed, had earned more than $87 million from the 96 performances – $7 million more than Celine Dion had picked up during 2004 for her residency in Las Vegas. (Reports elsewhere suggested that one-and-a-half million people attended the Musicology tour.)

Perhaps the most amazing aspect of *Musicology* was the fact that it led to another music industry shakeup, albeit unintentionally. After a period of much confusion, Neilsen SoundScan, the organization responsible for counting record sales and compiling charts, decided that it would include copies of *Musicology* given away at concerts from the date of the album's official release (April 20) onward. Industry executives lined up to express their outrage, noting that, while *Musicology* was being presented as a 'free' CD, the cost of producing it had been

incorporated into the price of the concert ticket.

"Nobody can say no to that new CD if they want to see the show," one anonymous executive complained to the *Los Angeles Times*. Another panicked over a hypothetical situation whereby "a dinosaur act that no longer sells records but does great live business can do a stadium tour over the summer and dominate the *Billboard* 200."

Neilsen SoundScan CEO Rob Sisco sought to justify the decision, telling *Billboard* that "the manufacturer was paid by the promoter, who is reselling the merchandise to the customer. Given that there is a sale, with the album ending up in the hands of the consumer … we feel we should count the sales."

As far as Prince was concerned, exploiting the loophole was a masterstroke, as *Musicology* achieved double-platinum status in the USA and reached Number Three on the *Billboard* chart. (It also peaked at Number Three in the UK without any sort of promotional gimmick.) *Billboard*'s chart editor Geoff Mayfield estimated that 25 per cent of the album's recorded sales came from ticket sales, leading most commentators to agree that *Musicology* would have achieved the same success even if Prince had not given it away. But that didn't stop *Billboard* from altering their policy so that all future ticket-and-album bundles had to give concertgoers the chance to opt out of buying the album alongside the ticket.

After completing the tour and maximizing its commercial potential, Prince was content to lay low for the rest of 2004 and enjoy the accolades that came flooding in. *Purple Rain* was given a deluxe 20th anniversary reissue on DVD in August to further rave reviews, while the end of the year brought with it a glut of awards from magazines: Funkmaster Of The Year from *GQ*, Best Use Of Technology from *Billboard*, and Artist Of The Year from his local newspaper, the *Minneapolis Star-Tribune*.

In a year where it had finally been deemed safe to like Prince again, none of this was surprising. More refreshing was the personality shift that seemed to occur within the star, as hinted at on *Musicology*'s more mature material (notably 'If Eye Was The Man In Ur Life' and 'Reflections'). "What we're trying to do is put the family first," Prince told interviewers who commented on the fact that he had put his 'rude' material behind him. "When you come to a certain age, you have certain responsibilities to deal with."

Inevitably, given the recent anniversary of his greatest critical and commercial success, Prince found himself looking back over his career to date. "When I was making sexy tunes," he told *Newsweek*, "that wasn't all I was doing. Back then, the sexiest thing on TV was *Dynasty*, and if you watch it now it's like *The Brady Bunch*." Laughing off the furor over his use of the word 'masturbate' in 'Darling Nikki,' he nonetheless encouraged contemporary acts not to try to emulate the controversies of his earlier career. "There's no more envelope to push," he said. "I pushed it off the table. It's on the floor."

Prince pays tribute to George Harrison after being inducted into the US Rock And Roll Hall Of Fame on March 15 2004.

WHEN PRINCE LET THE WIDER PUBLIC KNOW ABOUT HIS FORTHCOMING *MUSICOLOGY* LP, HE HAD AN EXTRA SURPRISE IN STORE FOR MEMBERS OF HIS ONLINE NPG MUSIC CLUB: TWO MORE ALBUMS OF MATERIAL FROM THE VAULT.

The Chocolate Invasion/ The Slaughterhouse

(MARCH 2004)

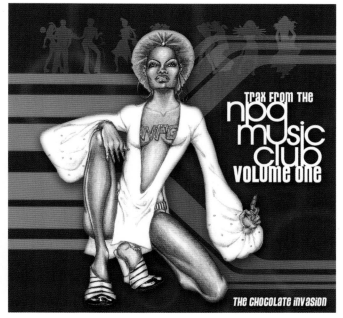

On March 29 2004, Prince celebrated the launch of his NPG Music Club download store by making three new albums available to fans for $9.99 each. Alongside *Musicology*, for which he had just signed a promotion and distribution deal with Columbia ahead of a planned conventional release, were two compilations of 'Trax' previously made available online or on the singles given away during the 2001 Hit N Run tour: *The Chocolate Invasion*, which took its name from a scrapped seven-disc box set originally set for release in 2003, and *The Slaughterhouse*.

Most of the music on both albums seems to have been compiled from material recorded during the late 90s and early 21st century; it seems possible to construct the unreleased *High*, which was once set to come out in 2001, from the two.

The fact that Prince opted not to release *High* suggests that he made a conscious decision not to try to make a commercial hit record in the immediate aftermath of the chart failure *Rave Un2 The Joy Fantastic*. In some ways

> The Chocolate Invasion *and* The Slaughterhouse *might not be groundbreaking, but they did add to the mystery of what else might be locked in* The Vault.

that's a shame, as the best of the material – 'When Eye Lay My Hands On U'; 'The Dance,' which was later re-recorded for *3121* – might well have given Prince the radio hit he longed for at the turn of the millennium.

The strongest track is *The Chocolate Invasion*'s 'Judas Smile,' a stop-start slow-burner with a jittery beat that's not a million miles away from Timbaland's groundbreaking late-90s productions. It's one of the most commercial yet inventive Prince songs of the period, and proves that, while he might no longer lead the charge, he could at least keep up with it.

By contrast, some of the lesser material evokes *Newpower Soul*'s dull funk, notably 'S&M Groove' from *The Slaughterhouse*, so it's entirely possible that Prince scrapped *High* for fear of sending another potential failure out into the world. But by March 2004 he was gearing up to throw his weight behind a new record in a way that he hadn't since the release of *Emancipation* eight years earlier. Releasing two more albums of mostly strong material on the same day that he made *Musicology* available for download served as a reminder that he was still making music as prolifically as ever, but just didn't always want you to hear it.

The Chocolate Invasion and *The Slaughterhouse* might not be groundbreaking, but they did add to the mystery of what else might be locked in The Vault. They also reinforced the idea that Prince could still be funky. But they did so in a way that frustrated many fans who were left wondering why he had not given his most commercial work for some time – *High* – a proper release several year earlier.

AFTER ALL THE EXCITEMENT OF THE PREVIOUS YEAR, 2005 LOOKED LIKE BEING PRINCE'S QUIETEST 12 MONTHS SINCE HE SIGNED TO WARNER BROS IN 1977, AS HE HAD SPENT MOST OF IT JAMMING AND PERFORMING PRIVATE CONCERTS AT HIS RENTED LOS ANGELES HOME.

3121 (DECEMBER 2006–APRIL 2007)

Aside from releasing 'S.S.T.'/'Brand New Orleans' in response to the Hurricane Katrina tragedy, and giving all proceeds to associated charities, he had not issued any new music or given notice of anything forthcoming albums or tours.

To even the keenest observers it seemed that 2005 would end with Prince still trying to figure out how to follow the astounding success of *Musicology*. Then on December 9 a report in *Billboard* claimed that Prince had signed a deal with Universal for the release of his new album, *3121*. Four days later – on December 13, the day picked deliberately to mirror the album's title – the singer held a press conference to make the news official.

"I don't consider Universal a slave ship," he told reporters in response to the usual questions about why he had decided to work with a major label again. "I did my own agreement without the help of a lawyer and sat down and got exactly what I wanted to accomplish … I got a chance to structure an agreement the way I saw fit instead of the other way around."

He also took the opportunity to give those present the first taste of *3121* in the form of its lead single, 'Te Amo Corazón.' There was nothing particularly remarkable about the song, a gentle ballad with a slight Latin feel, but according to Prince it was not representative of the album as a whole. The wider world would have to wait a while to hear the rest, however, as he would spend the first quarter of 2006 acting as a sideman for his latest protégé, Támar, and making a series of high-profile television appearances. The most notable of these was a show-stopping performance at the BRIT Awards in February, for which he was reunited with Wendy Melvoin, Lisa Coleman, and Sheila E. for the first time since the mid 80s.

There was no way that Prince could top the *Musicology* marketing campaign, and no point in giving away 'free' albums with concert tickets now that *Billboard* had changed its chart-eligibility rules. Instead he launched a *Willy Wonka*-style search for the handful of 'Purple Tickets' that had been slipped into random copies of *3121*. The lucky few who found a ticket were invited to attend An Evening With Prince on May 6 2006. A different set of chart regulations meant that Britain was exempt from the

Prince plays in disguise as his own support act at the 2004 Essence Music Festival.

"There's definitely a throwback vibe to 3121, a mostly one-man-band effort that favors the musical minimalism and reliance on synthesizers of early-80s Prince." **MINNEAPOLIS STAR-TRIBUNE**

promotion, but a small band of fans from the USA, Mexico, and the Netherlands were flown to Los Angeles, given $250 spending money, and treated to an intimate performance in Prince's rented '3121' house.

The house itself had become something of a thorn in Prince's side. According to the *Minneapolis Star-Tribune*'s favorite Prince-watcher, Cheryl Johnson, the singer had moved to Los Angeles in 2005 after demolishing his purple home in Chanhassen, Minnesota. His first LA residence actually had the street address 3121, but in September of the same year he moved to a rented property at 1235 Sierra Alta Way, for which he paid $70,000 per month, and which he subsequently renamed '3121.'

The setup seemed perfect until it was reported in March 2006 that Prince was being sued by his landlord, the C Booz Multifamily I LLC, for redecorating the property without consent. His dream home had become a legal nightmare. Papers filed with Los Angeles Superior Court on January 13 2006 reveal that the landlord took exception to the fact that Prince had painted purple stripes and the 'Prince' and '3121' logos on the exterior; removed carpets and baseboards and cut a large hole in a bedroom wall; installed "plumbing and piping in downstairs bedroom for water transfer for beauty salon chairs"; and used "unlicensed carpenters and contractors."

News of the lawsuit was still trickling out when Prince performed at Sunset Boulevard's Tower Records at the stroke of midnight on March 21 to launch the album. The title was officially explained as a reference to the singer's current home, but there were a number of suggested Biblical links, not least Psalm 31:21: "Blessed be the LORD, for he hath showed me his marvelous kindness in a strong city." (The fact that *3121* was subtitled *The Music* also led to speculation that there had once been a movie project attached to it.)

With no 'comeback' story this time around, *3121* was given a slightly more muted welcome than its predecessor. Most of the reviews were positive: *Billboard* praised "one of those rare artists who can remain relevant without compromising his eccentric style"; *The Times* enjoyed the sound of "an artist learning to make peace with his past without turning into his own tribute act." *Entertainment Weekly* was a little more measured, noting that some of the tracks are not quite worthy of "Prince's prodigious gifts," suggesting that he "hasn't figured out how to reach back into his 80s bag of tricks and create something that feels contemporary" in the way that "disciples" such as OutKast and The Neptunes have.

Nonetheless, *Billboard*'s prediction that the record "could well return him to the top of the charts" rang true. Amazingly, *3121* was the first Prince album to debut at Number One in the USA, and his first chart-topper at all since 1989's *Batman*. Interestingly, while *Musicology* had sold 191,000 copies in its first week but only reached Number Three, *3121* sold slightly less – 183,000 – but still claimed the top spot. (Further accolades would follow later in the year when he won a Lifetime Achievement award at the Webbys, made a surprise appearance on the season finale of *American Idol*, and contributed the Golden Globe-winning 'Song Of The Heart' to the *Happy Feet* soundtrack.)

Like its predecessor, *3121* is competent without showing off many new tricks, aside perhaps from the modern electro-funk of second single 'Black Sweat.' There's nothing wrong with the guitar rock of 'Fury,' the jazz-infused 'Satisfied,' or the upbeat, funky 'Get On The Boat,' but there's nothing particularly challenging about them either. It might be slightly more eclectic than *Musicology*, but *3121* is largely self-referential, right down to the way 'The Dance' references the screaming conclusion to 'The Beautiful Ones,' or even the fact that it was another album with a four-digit title. This, the *Minneapolis Star-Tribune* noted, "only leaves you wanting."

Prince himself was happy to have returned to the top of the charts with an album he acknowledged was "a trip back," and set about putting the next stage of *3121* into promotion. Having made a guest appearance with Morris Day & The Time at the Rio Hotel's Club Rio in Las Vegas on May 12, he set about planning his own Vegas engagement, and by October had moved into the hotel's top suite.

The news that Prince would be staging an indefinite run of Friday and Saturday shows at the newly renamed Club 3121 caused consternation. The man who once broke down so many barriers now seemed to be settling into one of rock'n'roll's biggest cliches, the fat Elvis decline, in an attempt to emulate the success Céline Dion had achieved in recent years with her own Vegas residency.

"It's pretty much the Prince world brought to Vegas!" one of the singer's backing dancers, Maya McClean, said in

Gett Off: Prince & Támar

Prince might have rediscovered his own muse during the early 21st century, but he didn't seem to have very much to offer anyone else. The last time he looked beyond his own work was when he attempted to bring Chaka Khan and Larry Graham back into the spotlight in 1998. Eight years would pass before he chose to take another artist under his wing. But although the album he produced for Támar was probably his mostly satisfying R&B disc in a decade, it ended up going almost the same way as Rosie Gaines's long-delayed Paisley Park album, and hardly anyone ever got to hear it.

Prince brought Támar Davis with him when he signed to Universal in December 2005, and originally planned to release her *Milk & Honey* LP on March 21 2006, the same day as his *3121*. But after being postponed for "various reasons," as stated in an official statement made by Támar a month later, it never saw the light of day, except for a hastily withdrawn Japanese release. (Leaked copies subsequently sold for up to $800 on eBay.)

Prince must have believed in Támar at one point. Asked by *Billboard* about what he had been listening to recently during the *3121* promotional run, Prince named Támar, describing her as "a brilliant writer and a kind soul," and noting that her album would now be coming out in May. "Prince has a willingness to promote *3121* because of Támar," explained Universal marketing executive Ted Cockle, adding that she is "basically his musical muse at the moment. She is with him at all times."

Prince's warmth of feeling for Támar was such that he gave her top billing on the short promotional tour in support of both of their forthcoming albums during January and February, and on the duet 'Beautiful, Loved And Blessed,' which featured on both *3121* and *Milk & Honey*, and on the B-side to Prince's 'Black Sweat.' "Who the bleep is Támar," the *Minneapolis Star-Tribune* asked, "and why is she getting top billing over Prince for Saturday's quickie concert at the Orpheum?"

Given that Támar seemed to have appeared out of nowhere, the newspaper was perhaps right to question the decision. But as the tour wound on, with dates and venues announced only a few days before each performance, Prince and his band continued to back Támar for what were mostly hour-long nightclub shows during the early hours of the morning.

Most of the reviews still focused on Prince, whom the *Washington Post* described as a "superb wingman," but he seemed content to play guitar and keyboards while Támar belted out a selection of her own songs and well-known soul covers. That's not to suggest that the headline act was poorly received. "If audience reaction counts for something," the *Chicago Sun Times*

concluded, "then Támar impressed."

But what looked like the start of a promising career ended up coming to nothing. No sooner had Támar appeared than she disappeared, and despite all the effort Prince put into promoting it, *Milk & Honey* never actually made it into record stores. After being postponed from March to April to May to August, the album was finally, quietly shelved. No official reason was ever given, but it was once suggested that the media's 'lying' over the release date had something to do with it.

Milk & Honey's disappearance has left fans wondering about what might have been for both Prince and Támar. Had it been released, it could well have been a breakthrough release for the younger singer, and one that served as further evidence of the creative resurgence of her mentor. The album's 12 tracks are a masterclass in contemporary R&B, with a fresher, more modern sound than anything else Prince had attempted to do with the genre in recent times. Several of the funkier tracks, such as 'Milk & Honey,' 'Closer To My Heart,' and 'Holla And Shout,' would almost certainly have made themselves at home on commercial radio.

Of all the missteps and disappointments of Prince's later career, *Milk & Honey*'s failure to launch serves as one of the great lost opportunities. The *Minneapolis Star-Tribune* saw the initial emergence of Támar as proof that Prince knew when to share the spotlight, but subsequent events seemed to suggest the opposite. It's unlikely that Prince would end up riding anyone else's coattails, but when it came down to it, it seemed he didn't want to risk Támar getting in the way of his continued commercial resurgence.

Prince and Támar perform at New York's Bryant Park on June 16 2006 for Good Morning America.

his defense. "The fans can come and really experience what it's like to be in Prince's home." To that end Prince even brought his own personal chef, Lena Morgan, to run the adjoining 3121 Jazz Cuisine restaurant, where he performed early-hours after-show jams for VIP ticket holders. (The $312 ticket also included dinner and a complimentary bottle of champagne.)

In fact Prince's shows were something of a break from the tacky Vegas tradition. Instead of presenting a glitzy, Barbra Streisand-style revue, he was playing modest, stripped-down sets in a relatively intimate 900-seater club. The shows included a mix of classics ('Kiss'; a truncated 'Let's Go Crazy'), *3121* material, loose funk jams, and jazz/soul standards. He even let his band stretch out on an instrumental version of 'Down By The Riverside,' just as he had done with his 1987 group for renditions of Charlie Parker's 'Now's The Time.' The shows proved so successful that they ran until April 28 2007, with 'normal' tickets costing $125 each. Local news reports suggested that Prince was spending his days off pursuing his love of photography, and was planning to put a *3121* magazine into print to show off the results of his new hobby.

For the man who had previously undertaken massive international engagements, perfected the Hit N Run style mini-tour, and hosted numerous concerts in Paisley Park home, the 3121 residency gave Prince another option when it came to live performance. He still seemed to have an almost pathological compulsion to play music, but had long since grown tired of long jaunts, as evidenced by two

decades of cancellations, curtailments, and complete refusals to tour certain albums.

Playing in Vegas proved to Prince that could make just as much money by staying in one place as he could by taking an entire stage show and entourage across the country. Although he played a few more Club 3121-style

> "I think in a lot of ways I still sound like I did before, so with this new album, it helps make the connection." PRINCE

shows in the middle of 2007, including four dates at the Roosevelt Hotel in Los Angeles in June, he had for all intents and purposes finished promoting *3121* after his final night at the Rio on April 28. Despite launching a 3121 perfume in July with three performances in Minneapolis, Prince had already moved onto his next scheme, appearing in London in May to announce the Earth Tour.

Lisa Coleman, Sheila E., and Wendy Melvoin joined Prince on stage together for the first time in 20 years at the 2006 BRIT Awards.

Prince & The Internet Revolution

DURING THE MID 90S, WHILE BATTLING WITH WARNER BROS, PRINCE LOOKED TO BE DEAD SET ON DESTROYING HIS PUBLIC IMAGE. BUT HE WAS ALSO IN THE PROCESS OF PIONEERING A WHOLE NEW WAY FOR MUSICIANS TO GET THEIR MUSIC OUT INTO THE WORLD.

It took quite a few years for the dust to settle and everyone else to catch up, but Prince was one of the very few people on the planet then trying to harness the potential of the internet. "Once the internet is a reality the music business is finished," he told the *New Musical Express* in 1995. "There won't be any need for record companies. If I can send you my music direct, what's the point of having a music business?"

All of this might have been news to the world at large, but not to Prince. "As early as 1989 he was envisioning a cyber world," Alan Leeds told housequake.com in 2007. "I know because he told me so, teasing me – and everyone else on his payroll – for not completely co-signing his vision."

It wasn't until 1997 that Prince found himself in a position where he could advertise his new album, *Crystal Ball*, over the internet, checking online orders to gauge how many fans were interested in the record before he started manufacturing it. As he explained to *Guitar World* a year later, he was just "testing the water to see if people would buy music over the internet … since the album was a success, it leads me to believe that the whole interactive thing offers great possibilities."

Prince's experiment was also a landmark event for the music business as a whole. *Crystal Ball* was the first full album to be released online by any artist on the planet. And he did it all without anyone else's help. By then he had already opened and closed at least one website, thedawn.com, and would continue to set up others throughout the late 90s, including love4oneanother.com, which on occasion offered individual tracks for download; mail-order site 1800newfunk.com; and npgonlineltd.com.

While groups such as Metallica worked themselves into a frenzy over Napster, the illegal file-sharing program, Prince took a more measured view. "File-sharing seems 2 occur when people want more QUALITY over quantity," he wrote in an email interview with *Wired* magazine in 2004. "One good tune on a 20-song CD is a rip. The corporations that created this situation will get the fate they deserve 4 better or 4 worse … An MP3 is merely a tool. There is nothing 2 fear."

Rather than trying to fight the spread of music on the internet, Prince sought to give his fans high-quality music on his own terms. But it took him a while to get there. In the late 90s, just as the man himself was beginning to cultivate his presence on the internet, some of his more forward-thinking fans started setting up their own Prince websites. In February 1999, Prince filed lawsuits against fan-run magazines and websites, claiming they were making money from bootlegging his music, creating unfair competition with his own activities, and, most ridiculously, breaching copyright laws by using the symbol he had changed his name to.

Most of the sites buckled under the pressure, but a few managed to stick around. The most notable of these was the print fanzine *Uptown*, which defended its right to continue in court with the help of lawyer and future Prince biographer Alex Hahn. The two parties eventually agreed an out of court settlement that allowed *Uptown* to stay in business provided it refrained from discussing bootlegged albums (individual songs were fine), stopped using the 'love symbol' glyph, and added a disclaimer stating that it was not an official Prince product.

Even so, most onlookers were bemused. The most forward-thinking man in music was now suing his own fans. "From a public relations standpoint," Alan Leeds told prince.org, "the situation was badly bungled." Further criticism came in from David Bowie, who had launched his own BowieNet portal a few years earlier and was making similar strides in harnessing the power of the internet. "To understand your presence on the net you have to be a part of it and work within it," he told *Shift* magazine. "I thought it looked so reactionary, for instance, of someone like Prince to clamp down on everything in terms of the lawsuits. You can't stop the sea from coming forwards."

For Prince, it seems, it was important not just to have a presence on the internet but to be in charge of it. In 2001, having recently issued his latest single, 'The Work Pt 1,' through Napster – one month after the site was legally ordered to prevent the sharing of copyrighted music – he made another breakthrough, launching npgmusicclub.com on Valentine's Day.

As Alan Leeds later put it, the internet was "the ideal invention … for a somewhat reclusive artist, who enjoys contact with fans under the guise of anonymity." For a one-off subscription fee of $25, members of the NPG Music Club (NPGMC) were offered exclusive merchandise, priority concert tickets, and previously unreleased music from The Vault, delivered in the form of digital downloads and members-only CDs. (The membership fee was originally set at $100, but lowered when Prince's release schedule slowed.)

In an interview with Yahoo! Internet Live, Prince described the NPGMC as "the experience for those who know better," claiming it as an antidote to the "packaged pop stars" then dominating mainstream radio. "Sometimes," he said, "I want to ask those people, 'Do you even know a D Minor chord?'"

Whether 'those who knew better' were attracted to the club is unclear, but it was certainly a success with fans. In March 2004 Prince built on his internet empire with the launch of the Musicology download store, which was named after his latest album. He made his recent internet-only albums available to download for a fee, and put *Musicology* itself on the site a month before it went on sale in stores.

To Prince, this was just one more way of getting his music direct to fans as quickly as possible. "We didn't create r club to make other labels nervous," he explained in a email to *Business 2 Magazine*. "We make a lot of music and needed a worldwide distribution service that works as fast as we do … U can get music from r club in the time it takes 2 open an emale. 4 once, eye have a distribution service that actually works FASTER than eye do."

Prince's pioneering efforts were given the recognition they deserved on June 12 2006 at the 10th annual Webby Awards, where the singer was given a Lifetime Achievement Award. "Prince is a visionary who recognized early on that the web would completely change how we experience music," Webby founder Tiffay Shlain noted in her official statement. "For more than a decade he has tapped the

power of the web to forge a deeper connection with his fans and push the boundaries of technology and art."

Within just a few weeks, however, the NPG Music Club had been shut down. On July 4 a statement was sent out to members claiming that, in the wake of the Webby victory, "there is a feeling that the NPGMC [has] gone as far as it can go. In a world without limitations and infinite possibilities, has the time come 2 once again make a leap of faith and begin anew?" Prince seemed to be taking it upon himself to answer these questions, and put the club on hiatus until further notice.

Fans were dismayed. Not only had they lost their direct route to Prince, but also the music they had downloaded from the site, thanks to the encoding software used on it.

Prince might have claimed to be taking time off to come up with ways to push the internet further, but it seemed that his boundary-breaking run had come to an end. It was then revealed that, on the day that the website shut down, a trademark infringement lawsuit had been filed by the Nature Publishing Group against Prince's use of 'NPG.'

On December 19 Prince launched another internet venture, the 'online magazine' 3121.com. It didn't have the benefits of the NPGMC, but it was a start as, the following year, Prince began offering news reports, photos, and a weekly Jam Of The Week in streaming audio. It didn't hang around for long, however, as another round of lawsuits led to Prince removing himself from the internet entirely.

The Super Bowl XLI Halftime Show

Over the years, Prince perfected the art of using one high-profile television appearance to herald the release of a new album. Having performed at the Grammys in 2004 and the BRIT Awards in 2006, it made sense that he would one day fill the halftime spot at the biggest US sporting event of the year.

Much had been made of recent halftime performances by The Rolling Stones, whose set was something of an anti-climax, and Janet Jackson, whose 'wardrobe malfunction' in 2004 led to widespread condemnation and an investigation by the FCC. (Even Prince felt compelled to chime in on the controversy, telling *Entertainment Weekly* things had gone "too far" before asking, "What's the point?")

Three years after the Jackson incident, and after more than six months of negotiations, Prince was given the chance to show how these things should be done. On February 4 2007 he took his 'love symbol'-shaped stage to the Dolphin Arena in Miami, Florida, to play a 12-minute set of *Purple Rain*-era tracks alongside covers of 'Proud Mary' and 'All Along The Watchtower,' complete with a full marching band. A few tetchy criticisms aside – some observers felt that Prince had deliberately thrown a phallic pose with his guitar while his silhouette was projected onto a large sheet – the show was a resounding success. Despite having to perform in torrential rain after a storm threatened to ruin the whole event – prompting Prince to ask the organiers: "Can you make it rain harder?" – it was deemed

the most successful halftime show in years.

According to former manager Alan Leeds, Prince's Super Bowl show was "a landmark appearance that will be remembered for years to come." Perhaps the most notable aspect of it, Leeds noted, was that Prince "hasn't had a genuine hit record in many, many years [but] is still viewed in the fickle world of pop music as a major force."

With more than 140 million Americans watching – and plenty more viewers tuning in around the world – Prince's Super Bowl XLI appearance was probably the biggest promotional opportunity of his career. Not only did it mean that all eyes were on him in advance of a new album release, it also raised the bar for future halftime shows. The comparatively lackluster Tom Petty had no chance of competing in 2008.

In January 2004 the singer had forced guide2prince.org to close because of the fact that it allowed discussion of his bootlegs (the implication being that it facilitated the sale of them as well). In October of the same year he also went into battle with the owners of housequake.com, who subsequently came to an agreement with Prince's lawyers, who allowed the site to continue as long as its bootleg trading forum was closed and no 'illegal' photos from the Musicology tour were posted.

In December 2006, princefams.com was told to stop using images of the singer altogether. That particular matter was dealt with fairly quickly, but things took a turn for the worse the following summer when fans began posting photos and video clips from Prince's 21 Nights In London residency. The end result was the start of a full-scale war on the internet that threatened to rival Prince's battle with Warner Bros a decade earlier.

Teaming up with Web Sheriff, an organization set up to help defend artists' intellectual property rights, Prince set his sights squarely on some of the internet's most prominent websites. He challenged various BitTorrent portals to remove links to downloads of live recordings, YouTube to remove all videos containing his image and music, eBay to remove all auctions of counterfeit Prince material, and all other websites to remove his images, likenesses, and music.

"The Warner Bros battle left its scars, but it also made him a lot more savvy in terms of protecting his rights," Web Sheriff's John Giacobbi explained in an interview with *The Register*. "That dispute was about records and CDs, and now that we're into the digital age, he's fighting for his online rights."

A particularly un-savvy move, however, was sending Universal Music Corp's lawyers after Pennsylvanian mother Stephanie Lenz. In June 2007, just before the start of Prince's London residency, Lenz was ordered to take down 29 seconds' worth of footage of her 13-month-old baby dancing to 'Let's Go Crazy.' Lenz in turn sued the company for acting in bad faith, invoking the same 1998 copyright law that Universal had cited.

On August 28 2008, San Jose's District Judge Jeremy Fogel ruled that "copyright-holders can't order one of their songs removed from the web without first checking to see if the excerpt was so small and innocuous that it was legal." Still the case dragged on, until February 25 2010, when Fogel ruled in Lenz's favor, allowing her to recover legal fees incurred while fighting the takedown, and also paving the way for her to make a further claim to recoup the cost of seeking damages in her follow-up litigation against Universal.

The whole case was emblematic of Prince's emergent approach to the internet. In a replay of his actions of February 1999, he sent cease and desist letters to fan websites, including prince.org, princefams.com, and housequake.com, ordering them to remove all copyrighted images, including album sleeves and even fan tattoos of his 'love symbol.' This time, however, the fan sites grouped together. Forming the Prince Fans United (PFU) coalition on November 5, they took a stand against what they saw as an attempt not to "enforce valid copyright" (as Prince had claimed) but to "stifle all critical commentary." Negotiations between the two parties continued well into 2008 – ironically, after Prince shut down his own 3121.com website – but a draft agreement between them was left unsigned.

Eventually, Prince won most of the battles. The much-loved housequake.com shut down on February 24 2009, during the run-up to the release of *Lotusflow3r*. One complaint in a long line of final attacks was directed at the site's homepage banner. Although it celebrated – and indeed promoted – the forthcoming album, Prince deemed its imagery too similar to his official artwork. The site disappeared without a trace, leaving behind only a holding page reading "38:11," a Biblical reference to Job 38:11: "And I said: 'Thus far you shall come, but no farther; And here shall your proud waves stop.'" (Fans also noted that Psalms 38:11 would have been just as apt: "For your arrows have pierced me, and your hand has come down upon me.")

But Prince himself was unable to provide a better service. His own site, lotusflow3r.com, fell far short of providing the promised Vault recordings – and, in many cases, couldn't even deliver on its offer of a free T-shirt for

> "The Warner Bros battle left its scars, but it also made him a lot more savvy in terms of protecting his rights." WEB SHERIFF'S JOHN GIACOBBI

each subscriber. Having paid their $77 fee on March 24 2009, many were still chasing the site's customer support into 2010. After looking into the situation, the prince.org fan site reported that lotusflow3r.com's telephone helpline had been disconnected, while its attempts to contact customer service were being ignored. Disgruntled fans began emailing lotusflow3r.com's team, stating that they did not want their subscription to be automatically renewed after the 12-month term ran out; on March 25 2010, however, many fans awoke to find that a further $77 had been deducted from their bank accounts.

An unsurprisingly speedy response from the website's development team claimed that this had only affected "the earliest adopters" of lotusflow3r.com – who were, of course, going to be refunded. The message also went out of its way to remind fans that "Prince had no hand in this ... the error was due to lack of thoroughness on our part." (Speaking to the *Wall Street Journal* online shortly after the fiasco, Prince's lotusflow3r.com developer, Scott Addison Clay, admitted that "a few hundred" members had to be reimbursed.)

Lotusflow3r.com marked Prince's final attempt to

launch an interactive website for his fans. Though, much like his approach to record labels, he would continue to use the internet whenever he felt it would benefit him, Prince would largely limit his engagement to simply getting word out about his latest project, or selling downloads to fans. Several months after the lotusflow3r.com fiasco, he told the *Daily Mirror* newspaper, which was giving away his *20Ten* album for free in the UK: "The internet's completely over. I don't see why I should give my music to iTunes or anyone else. They won't pay me an advance for it and then they get angry when they can't get it."

Unsurprisingly, these comments shot around online message boards and blogs by the end of the day, with most commentators decrying such a lack of vision – especially from a musician who had once pioneered internet distribution. Many felt that denouncing the internet in order to strike deals with a print media whose future was uncertain was little short of madness. In addition, the idea of making a new album available for just one day via a newspaper seemed to go against Prince's ethos of ensuring that his music reached as many people as possible. For Prince, however, what seemed more important was the fact that, for him, a newspaper advance would be more profitable than an internet release, where the number of paying customers could not be guaranteed.

Prince remained resolute the following summer. In an interview with the *Guardian*, the man who had once said there was "nothing 2 fear" about an MP3, declared: "I personally can't stand digital music … it affects a different place in your brain. When you play it back, you can't feel anything." In 2014, he claimed that he meant the internet was "dead to us – dead energy." He returned to the subject the following year, while announcing his Piano & A Microphone tour from Paisley Park: "What I meant was that the internet was over for anyone who wants to get paid, and I was right about that. Tell me a musician who's got rich off digital sales."

Not that Prince stopped trying. Despite bemoaning the music industry's increasing focus on singles streams over album sales (joking via email with the *Melbourne Herald*, in May 2012, that we "usually buy books by the chapter" and "when we rented *Avatar*, we watched 5 scenes every weekend til it was finished"), in early 2013 he re-entered the fray. After first catching fans' attention with a series of staged song leaks from an enigmatic Twitter user known as 3rdEyeGirl, Prince launched yet another new website on January 22. The eminently un-googleable 20pr1nc3.com (which was later renamed prince2013.com), offered little at first, save for a trailer for a live DVD release of his 2009 Montreux

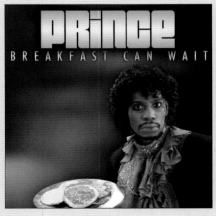

Jazz Festival performance (which never materialized), and a lyric video for his latest song, 'Screwdriver.' Soon, however, Prince would offer a string of new songs, largely through sister site 3rdEyeGirl.com; their wide-ranging styles showed that he was not only testing the internet's efficacy but trying to determine what he wanted to do next, musically. In February alone, he released a remix of the previous year's 'Rock & Roll Love Affair'; a 'single version' and remix of his main focus, the bratty guitar stomp of 'Screwdriver'; songs that tapped into the Minneapolis sound ('Boyfriend,' later renamed 'Boyfriend (Demo),' and 'Breakfast Can Wait'); and an acoustic ballad, 'That Girl Thang.' "I don't do albums anymore," he told *Billboard*. "If my fans want this, they will tell me what to do and how much they want to pay."

Prince, however, set the payment terms, opening a PayPal account and charging 88 cents for WAV file downloads. Many fans were happy to comply, though when Prince charged $1.77 for the 'Screwdriver' live video, some thought that expecting payment for what was essentially a promo shot at Paisley Park was an ask too far.

He might have been back on the internet, but Prince remained as vigilant as ever when it came to what was online, and who was posting it. His band members were permitted, at select times, to share an assortment of songs and rehearsal videos via social media; everyone else was subject to his stringent policing. "I have a team of female black lawyers who keep an eye on such transgressions," he told *Billboard*, joking, "And you know they're sharp." On 22 March, Prince sent a cease and desist letter to Vine, the Twitter-owned internet app which allowed users to share videos limited to six seconds in length, demanding that they remove eight highlighted videos, "as well as all other occurrences," on the platform.

Yet he seemed aware that he had a global fanbase who were unable to catch his US-only club shows with his new all-girl rock band, 3rdEyeGirl. Once they returned to Minneapolis, Prince investigated the Livestream platform, offering glimpses of rehearsals and official concerts, and teasing new songs and remixes in a series of short-notice broadcasts. Though he appears to have considered charging for pay-per-view access to his 3rdEye TV channel, the streams ultimately remained free. Though they were perfect for a man who, when it came to the internet, favored impermanence, the live streams barely lasted into the fall – by which point Prince was once again on the rampage against websites and alleged bootleggers.

In mid August, Prince himself finally embraced social media and set up a Twitter account, initially under the @3rdeyegirl handle. His initial string of tweets included a picture of a salad with the question "DID EYE ADD 2 MUCH PEPPER?" and a live performance video of 'Let's Go Crazy Reloaded,' with the suggestion that fans "CATCH THIS NOW B4 MY LAWYERS DEW." It was an all too knowing statement. Ten days later, fan website PurpleHouse2.blogspot.co.uk shut down "in respect to Prince's wishes … [and] will not be coming back this time." Further sites followed, including the highly popular DaBang blog. While Prince continued to search for the online model that best suited him – allowing a fan to disseminate a rehearsal of The Soul Children's 'The Sweeter She Is' via Twitter; releasing the remix EP *The Breakfast Experience* via iTunes; and selling, among others, the loosey-goosey funk revisit of 'Bambi,' 'Da Bourgeoisie,' ("I guess a man's only good for a rainy day / Maybe you're just another bearded lady at the cabaret") on what was now 3rdEyeTunes.com – he simultaneously targeted bloggers who were sharing live bootlegs.

True to form, Prince's rampage came at a time when he

between fans. Not one of his targets was a known bootleg company profiting from selling live performances or studio outtakes.

Having toyed with various online platforms through 2013, Prince fully embraced social media in 2014. Twitter was perfect for spreading last-minute news of Hit N Run shows to a growing number of followers. (It wasn't foolproof, though: one 3rdEyeGirl post, "4th day of November, we need a purple high: OTNOROT CALLING…" led fans to queue for hours outside Toronto's Massey Hall, only for there to be no gig after all.) He joined Facebook on September 30, taking part in a fan Q&A during which he answered just one of the 4,000 questions sent his way (poster Dee J FoGee requested that Prince "address the importance of all music being tuned to 432hz sound frequencies," and received in reply a link to an article titled 'Here's Why You Should Convert Your Music to 432hz'). Official concert footage was posted to YouTube after almost every gig; his Instagram account was playfully dubbed 'Princestagram' at Jimmy Fallon's suggestion (Prince won the 'rights' to use the nickname after mercilessly defeating the talk show host at ping-pong).

In parallel with his relationship with the music industry, Prince's love-hate relationship with the internet revolved around artists' rights. Guesting on *The Arsenio Hall Show* on March 5 2014, he described

> "He may not have specifically envisioned a Spotify or iTunes, but he damn sure did envision a world where artists would retain more control of their work and how it is marketed." ALAN LEEDS

was gearing up for a new announcement. In advance of a promo push for 3rdEyeGirl in the UK, on January 16 2014, he sued 22 blog owners (only two of whom he could name, the rest appearing as "Does") for $1 million each in what Techdirt described as a "laughably confused complaint" arising under the Copyright Act and the Anti-Bootlegging Laws. Noting that Prince "might have been the first musician to 'get' the internet," the site then lamented how "rather than blame his lack of execution," he had simply started lashing out "in almost every way possible." Techdirt picked over the lawsuit in detail, highlighting how "sloppy" it was, particularly when it came to calculating the alleged $22 million in damages, and in failing to actually describe the direct copyright infringement incurred from websites posting links. But the individual bloggers lacked the resources to fight back. Inevitably, they buckled under pressure, and Prince filed for a voluntary dismissal without prejudice (thereby ensuring he could make the same claims in the future).

Once again facing criticism for the treatment of his most ardent supporters, Prince claimed, "Nobody sues their fans." In a London press conference held on February 5 at the home of British soul singer Lianne La Havas, he admitted that even he owned bootlegs – of his host – before denying that he would ever sell them. "But fans sharing music with each other," he added, "that's cool." The irony was that the 22 defendants named in his lawsuit were doing just that – simply sharing music for free

the internet as "a black hole." "A lot of artists aren't getting paid full scale for their art," he told his host. "It's hard to audit. It's hard to get accounting." A little over a year later, he signed a deal with Tidal, the digital streaming service owned by Jay Z. Happy to be in business with a fledgling, artist-owned company, he allowed it to stream his Warner Bros recordings – all of which he'd removed from Spotify in April, in a dispute over how much the company was paying him. "Nobody can just come up and just start selling the Statue Of Liberty," he told *Ebony* in December, likening the idea to giving away his own music. "The catalogue has to be protected … Spotify wasn't paying, so you gotta shut it down."

In the wake of Prince's death, the internet was awash with live performances and unreleased songs that fans had uploaded in tribute to their hero. Though Prince doubtless would have attempted to shut all of those down too, it was perhaps fitting that he was so deeply honored in the virtual world. Writing in memory of his friend and one-time employer, Alan Leeds noted: "Once the technology caught up with HIS visions, and fundamentally changed how the music industry operates, it seemed like Prince had been a prophet." Fully grasping the scope of Prince's pioneering work on the internet, The Prince Online Museum opened in July 2016. Created by the webmasters who had collaborated with Prince on each of his online ventures, it dedicated itself to presenting working versions of the websites that he had launched in a 20-year timespan.

THE RELEASE OF *PLANET EARTH* LOOKED, TO BEGIN WITH, LIKE IT WOULD FOLLOW THE STANDARD PRINCE MODEL OF RECENT YEARS. AFTER SIGNING A PRESSING AND DISTRIBUTION DEAL WITH A MAJOR LABEL (COLUMBIA AGAIN), HE MADE A ONE-OFF APPEARANCE IN THE MARKET HE INTENDED TO FOCUS ON (A 1AM PERFORMANCE AT LONDON'S KOKO CLUB, HIS FIRST UK CONCERT IN FIVE YEARS), IN ANTICIPATION OF A 21-DATE RESIDENCY AT THE O$_2$ ARENA.

Planet Earth (MAY 2007–OCTOBER 2008)

Prince also planned once again to include a copy of his new album in the ticket price. So far so normal. Then, a few weeks before *Planet Earth*'s planned UK release date, July 16, he announced that he would give the album away free a day earlier, with the July 15 edition of the *Mail On Sunday* newspaper.

Free CD and DVD cover-mounts were not a new phenomenon. They had been used as an incentive for customers to buy magazines and newspapers for years. (The *Mail On Sunday* had already caused a minor stir in April when giving away a copy of Mike Oldfield's *Tubular Bells*, with the artist himself complaining that it devalued his already well-worn music.) The difference with *Planet Earth* was that it marked the first time any artist had given a brand new recording away, and seemed to carry with it a damaging message: screw the expensive middleman, have the album for free instead. Not surprisingly, the industry was outraged, with Sony BMG reportedly tearing up its UK contract with Prince immediately. "It was ridiculous to have a UK deal," a spokesman told Yahoo! News, "when two million copies are going out free with papers."

Record retailers – already losing revenue to online sales and digital downloads – were similarly incensed. "Retailers figure that he owes them because they supported him in his early days," a *Billboard* columnist remarked, "but Prince probably figures he's paid them by providing multiplatinum sales throughout his career." But as far as Entertainment Retailer's Association chairman Paul Quirk was concerned, the artist formerly known as The Artist Formerly Known As Prince was in danger of becoming known as "The Artist Formerly Known As Available In Record Stores."

The battle didn't stop there. It also stirred up trouble between the UK's two major music retailers when HMV decided to stock copies of the *Mail On Sunday* for the first time ever, despite having already publicly criticized Prince's marketing coup. "We're stunned that HMV has decided to take what appears to be a complete U-turn," Simon Douglas of the Virgin Megastores chain told the *Guardian*. "Only a week ago they were so vocal about the damage it will cause." As far as HMV was concerned, stocking the newspaper was simply a way of making the most of a bad situation.

Prince knew that signing the deal with the *Mail On Sunday* would destroy his contract with Columbia, but he probably didn't care. Rumor has it that he was paid somewhere between £200,000 and £500,000 for the giveaway, which is much more than he was likely to have made from a record-label advance. (It was also reported

"*Prince gave up on the industry a decade ago. He's made his millions so all he cares about now is getting his music out to as many people as possible. If he could drop them out of a helicopter over London, he would do.*"

STEWART WILLIAMS, MANAGING DIRECTOR, Q MAGAZINE

that, while the *Mail On Sunday* sold more copies than it had since the death of Princess Diana, the newspaper ended up losing money on the deal because of the cost of promoting the scheme.)

Cynics have since suggested that Prince might well have needed to give *Planet Earth* away anyway. It was received well by fans, some of whom felt it to the best album he had made since his commercial resurgence, but the media response to it was decidedly lukewarm. "By no means terrible" was about the best the *Guardian* could find to say about it, while *Rolling Stone* called it "one of those albums he makes when he's trying a little harder than usual."

Planet Earth's opening title-track plays the same wrong-footing game as 'Sign "O" The Times' did 20 years earlier. It begins with the sense that Prince is about to make his important statement about global warming, but the overall message is as naive as ever, and soon gives way to yet another round of commercially minded funk'n'ballads. 'Chelsea Rodgers' is a tired disco-lite affair; 'Somewhere Here On Earth' another uneventful, jazzy ballad; lead single 'Guitar' a rock riff in search of a song that recalls U2's 'I Will Follow.'

In any case, Prince had bigger plans than just putting out a new album. He knew that he had a captive audience of 200,000 for his 21 Nights at the O_2 Arena, for which he was charging £31.21 for standard tickets, as well as offering VIP passes for the hardcore fans, and playing after-hours shows at the smaller IndigO_2 venue for a further fee. Casual fans who enjoyed a hits-based live set might also decide to seek out his past work in record stores. Instead of touring to promote an album release, he was using the album release – and the attendant controversy – to promote his live show.

Given the amount of money he stood to make from ticket sales, merchandising, and back catalog sales, it was something of a masterstroke, and a sign of things to come. Within months a number of other high-profile acts,

including Madonna and Jay Z, had followed Prince in stepping away from the traditional music industry toward '360 degree' deals with concert promoters.

As with the Jam Of The Year shows, Prince quickly dropped material from his new album in favor of old hits on what started out as the Earth Tour but ended up becoming known as 21 Nights In London. In doing so he seemed almost to be admitting that his new music had no hope of matching his best work from the past. Nobody seemed to mind. Performing in the round on a symbol-shaped stage, he treated his audiences to a wide range of full-band classics, adding a solo-piano section midway through the residency for intimate versions of songs such as 'Sometimes It Snows In April.' He would often end the night alone in front of a synthesizer, teasing the crowd with instrumental riffs from some of his raunchier songs, including 'Erotic City' and Vanity 6's 'Nasty Girl.'

Replicating the success of the previous year's Las Vegas residency, Prince earned far more money from his 21 Nights In London stint than he would have done from a lengthier tour of different venues. Even the event's promoter, AEG's president of international touring, Rob Hallett, was amazed at its success, joking that he wished Prince had moved to a house numbered 9494, rather than 3121. Recalling the initial negotiations for the residency, Hallett noted Prince's insistence that they stage 21 nights at the capital's largest venue. "We said: 'OK, let's do 21

Prince hides his "embarrassment" with a towel after an over-enthusiastic fan ran on stage and kissed him during his 'secret' show at Koko in London, England, in May 2007.

nights in London,'" Hallet told the BBC, "'just as long as you're prepared for the last 10 days to be in Ronnie Scott's'" (a tiny jazz club in the center of town). Prince, of course, knew better, and "wouldn't even consider the possibility of anything else."

During the high-profile launch parties for his *21 Nights* book the following year – at London's Dorchester Hotel, Prince's place of residence during the 21 Nights stint, on October 1, and a two-concert performance at New York's Ganesvoort Hotel on October 10; tickets cost $1,000 and $300, respectively – Prince told reporters: "I couldn't have sold out 21 nights in London in the peak of my career, it would have been an impossibility." Entering his 50th year, he seemed happy to trade on live performances of past classics rather than studio renditions of new songs. "His bands may seem more anonymous with every tour," said Alan Leeds, "but the general public probably couldn't care less as long as Prince remains capable of tearing up a stage."

The Earth Tour never moved outside of London, but its repercussions lasted throughout the year, as Prince was once again embroiled in a lengthy battle with fan websites who had posted pictures of the shows online. Legal threats flew from all directions, with the websites forming the Prince Fans United (PFU) coalition to defend themselves. With no clear resolution in sight, on December 23 2007, Prince took his 'online magazine,' 3121.com, and all of its multimedia content offline, followed by the rest of his web portfolio. By the end of the year his official web

presence was nothing but a blank screen.

One good thing did come of the clash between Prince and his fans. On November 8, three days after the formation of PFU, Prince sent out 'PFUnk,' a seven-minute funk extravaganza allegedly recorded in one night. "I hate to let you know that it's on," he sings, seemingly in reference to the tensions, before reminding his fans that "digital music disappears in a day … I love all y'all / Don't you ever mess with me no more."

The song was greeted as one of his best recordings in years, confirming some fans' assertions that Prince's best music is driven by aggression. Many even felt that it was better than his three recent albums – *Musicology*, *3121*, and *Planet Earth* – put together. It was so good, in fact, that Prince renamed it 'F.U.N.K.' and released it as a digital-only single via iTunes later in the month.

After such an explosive end to 2007, Prince kept a low profile during the early part of 2008, during which time he took up residency in a rented Beverly Hills Park mansion, known as the 77. He stayed in Los Angeles for the rest of the year and made a series of low-key appearances around the city, turning up at various parties, guesting on stage at clubs with the likes of Blind Boys Of Alabama, and performing low-key early-hours concerts at the 77 and the Green Door.

By spring, Prince was ready for a more public unveiling. A one-off April 25 appearance on *The Tonight Show With Jay Leno* saw him unleash a new song, 'Turn Me Loose.' It might have been a slice of James Brown funk that Prince could write in the time it took to perform, but it was notable for its return to more carnal matters. "Whatever's holding up this bed / Won't be here when I'm through," he sings to an unnamed woman who could also look forward to something that's "against the law in 13 states." It was the most straight-up funky Prince had sounded in years, but he ended up confining the recorded version to The Vault (perhaps having had second thoughts about the lyrics). It took LA's KJLH radio station to turn it loose after a resident DJ begged Prince for a copy on the promise that he wouldn't play it, only to fail to resist his own urges.

The Leno appearance was a precursor to Prince's headlining performance at Coachella the following evening. Despite the rave reviews, a rumored $4.8 million fee, and onstage reunions with both Sheila E. and Morris Day, the highpoint – an unexpected cover of Radiohead's 'Creep' – served only to reopen old wounds. Having forced all performance footage off of the internet, Prince then found his reasoning challenged once more when Radiohead's Thom Yorke questioned his right to do so. "Surely we should block it," Yorke said. "Tell him to unblock it. It's our … song."

A minor spat between artists was nothing compared to what Prince had coming later in the year. Despite being one of his quietest, in terms of releases, since 2003, he would find himself on the receiving end of three lawsuits before the year was out. An October 2007 case brought against him by video editor Ian C. Lewis resulted in the ruling, on November 5 2008, that Prince should pay Lewis $58,000 in damages for unpaid work, unreturned equipment, and the breaking of a $25,000 computer. (The judge's figure was at least a significant reduction of Lewis's claim for $1 million.) Later that month, on November 17, Revelations Perfume & Cosmetics Inc. sued both Prince and Universal for their alleged failure to promote the *3121*-branded perfume, claiming a loss of $2.5 million. The case would follow Prince into spring 2013, when, after a 2011 court ruling that he pay $3.9 million to the company, the two parties finally settled over an undisclosed amount.

Even the live arena – which was usually where Prince raked in the dollars – brought legal problems. Just ten days before he was due to perform, Prince canceled a high-profile one-off performance at Dublin's Croke Park stadium (for which he was to receive $3 million). In turn, Promoters MCD sued the artist to the tune of 1.7 million euros, seeking to recoup the financial losses of promoting the show and having to refund 55,126 tickets. Despite Prince's lawyers' claim that "not one line" of an artist's contract had been drafted for the performance (a somewhat hypocritical defense from a man who once boasted of not needing a "CONtract" when he signed Larry Graham to NPG), MCD countered that Prince's booking agents, William Morris Endeavor Entertainment, had made it clear via email that Prince was due to perform.

During the court case, which finally began on February 23 2010, it emerged that, when MCD's founder Denis Desmond grew alarmed at the lack of information coming from Paisley Park just weeks before the gig, Prince had ordered his WMEE contact, Keith Sarkisian, to "tell the cat to chill, I'll figure it out." The warring parties eventually did just that, and the case was settled out of court for an undisclosed sum on February 26 2010. (That same day, Prince unveiled a new song, 'Cause And Effect,' with the lyrics "Leave no enemies / Leave no debt.")

In 2008, with such negativity surrounding him, it's no wonder that Prince sought to remind the world of his recent glories. On September 30, he released *21 Nights*, a hardback photo book chronicling his stay in London the previous year. A luxurious leather-bound edition followed in April 2009: *The Prince Opus*, housed in a velvet box and boasting a Prince-branded iPod Touch featuring 40 minutes of 21 Nights live footage. If the $2,100 asking price seemed steep, the cost of the one-off 'Number One' edition, wrapped in alligator skin and sporting a platinum 'O{+>' symbol encrusted with 21 diamonds (five of them purple), is likely to have been astronomical. According to the publishers, Opus Kraken, the book was due to "globally tour 12 major cities and be finally auctioned in late 2009."

The winner of the auction would also enjoy a private performance by Prince in LA for up to 50 guests, and receive the spray-painted '21' jacket he wore for the final London show. Its fate remains undocumented, perhaps because interest in the ridiculously expensive Kraken artifact enjoyed only a short, early peak. Kraken's CEO and founder, Karl Fowler, boasted of having sold a third of the 950 standard editions in the first weekend, claiming: "We always knew that we would get to a sellout position within a few months." (The *Opus* was, however, still being sold through Kraken's website in 2016.)

Enjoying more longevity was the live recording *Indigo Nights*. Included with all editions of the book, it's a sizzling document of the after-show sets Prince had played almost every night in London in the O$_2$'s intimate IndigO$_2$ club. While many commented on the airbrushed, fashion-catalog feel of the photos (even down to the itemizing of every piece of clothing), photographer Randee St. Nicholas asserted that this is how Prince's life really looked. "It may be glamorous to others," she said, "but that's his comfort zone. It's not like he changes to go out and be Prince. The guy looks amazing 24 hours a day."

Prince at the O$_2$ Arena on August 28 2007, midway through his run of 21 Nights.

AS 2008 DREW TO A CLOSE, PRINCE INVITED A SERIES OF CAREFULLY VETTED JOURNALISTS TO HIS BEVERLY HILLS HOME FOR ADVANCE PLAYS OF HIS NEW WORK: A THREE-DISC SET FEATURING THE PRINCE ALBUMS *LOTUSFLOW3R* AND *MPLSOUND*, PLUS *ELIXER* BY HIS LATEST PROTÉGÉ, BRIA VALENTE.

Lotusflow3r/ MPLSound

(DECEMBER 2008–FEBRUARY 2010)

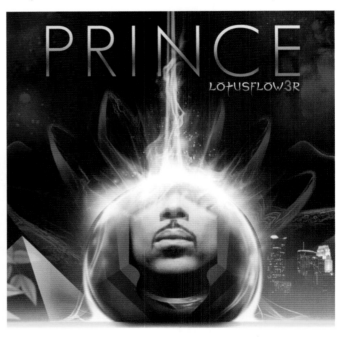

Prince would give them personal listening sessions of *MPLSound* while parked in his sports car (a dark black model he christened 'Miles Davis'), move to the bedroom to unveil *Elixer* (which he introduced as "nasty, but not dirty"), and drive around Hollywood in his limo listening to *Lotusflow3r*. The first the public got to hear of this new music was on December 17, when local rock radio station Indie 103 was given the honor of premiering *Lotusflow3r*'s 'Crimson & Clover' (a Tommy James & The Shondells cover), followed by 'Colonized Mind,' 'Wall Of Berlin,' and *MPLSound*'s '4Ever.'

After spending most of December 2008 shipping the album around Los Angeles in an attempt to find a satisfying method of distribution, it wasn't until early 2009 that Prince revealed the business model for this new venture. His repeated claim was that "the gatekeepers must change." Having decided that it was no longer "realistic to expect to put out new music and profit from it … and keep it from being [exploited]," he went straight

to the distributors themselves. Eschewing the major labels that he'd recently dealt with for *Musicology*, *3121*, and *Planet Earth*, he struck a deal with the Minneapolis-based retailer Target. The company sold the *Lotusflow3r/MPLSound/Elixer* set exclusively (and only in the USA), buying wholesale from Prince – and presumably had to keep unsold copies as part of the agreement. "The beautiful thing about the relationship," Prince told Tavis Smiley, while noting that 30 million people went through Target's doors each week, "is that they're treating us like any other record company. They buy the same amount and they pay the same price, so we've done quite well already." (The Smiley appearance was just one of several return visits to chat shows that Prince had favored while promoting *Musicology*. He also staged a three-night run on *The Tonight Show With Jay Leno* and stopped off at Ellen DeGeneres's syndicated daytime show.)

Then came the launch of yet another new website. Having decided that the cyber war was over, Prince

envisioned a 3D virtual playground for himself, where each of the three new albums was represented by a different world. "Prince wanted Lotusflow3r to function like a videogame in its interactivity," Scott Addision Clay, the site's designer, revealed shortly after its launch on March 24. He was quick to add that this didn't mean "you control Prince with jujitsu moves – that wouldn't be appropriate."

Prince himself was so excited about the new website that he invited six journalists and three 'Purple Ticket' winners to the 77 for an intimate concert and personal tour of the site. (Writing for nme.com, the ever-observant Emily Mackay – the only British journalist present – seemed most amazed that, among the Tuscan designs, pink granite, and Turkish rugs, Prince's house was stocked with something as normal as Bounty kitchen paper.)

Despite Prince's years of running his own label – and pioneering internet distribution – lotusflow3r.com was beset with problems. Just hours before the site was due to go live, at 7:07pm, blogger Dr Funkenberry posted advance warnings from Prince's camp. Among the advice given was: "If anyone has trouble downloading stuff, try later tonight and just listen to what is on the player … you may not get email confirmations for tickets until tomorrow."

Confirmation emails weren't the only things that failed to arrive. In an echo of the distribution issues surrounding *Crystal Ball* in the mid 90s, most of the fans who paid the $77 membership fee didn't receive the free *Lotusflow3r* T-shirt they were promised. (Unsurprisingly, complaints sent to Paisley Park were still being ignored a year later, and the website eventually closed in March 2010.) As the year progressed, much of the promised catalog of unreleased concerts from The Vault ended up being largely culled from a handful of 2009 appearances.

Even logging in to lotusflow3r.com was a chore – and this before fans had even signed up. For all its 3D splendor, the site was initially inaccessible from Europe, and failed to recognize underscores or other non-alphanumeric characters in subscribers' user names. Fans even had to crack a code, filling in the blanks in "Mar 07 _____," and "_____, California" before they could access the registration page. (The answers were "1986" and "Los Angeles.")

Those who finally found their way in – or simply waited for the three-CD set to be released through Target on March 29 – received a trio of albums that saw Prince asserting the various aspects of his work. *Lotusflow3r* showed off his guitar chops; *MPLSound* returned to the electro-funk that had launched the Minneapolis sound over two decades before; and *Elixer* demonstrated his ability to write unremarkable music for a characterless female singer.

The albums' gestation stretched back to 2006, when Prince backed Támar on tour and fell in love with his guitar again, and continued until late September 2008. (An early take of 'Feel Good, Feel Better, Feel Wonderful' was emailed to NPGMC members on June 29 2006;

MPLSound's 'U're Gonna C Me' was even older, having first appeared on 2002's *One Nite … Alone*.) Much of *Lotusflow3r*'s organic feel can be credited to the fact that Prince enlisted long-term cohorts – including Michael Bland, Renato Neto, Greg Boyer, and Maceo Parker – to help record his most artistically questing release since *The Rainbow Children* (though most of its psychedelic effects came courtesy of Pro Tools).

"I'm interested in the inner workings of music, the effect on the body. I'm trying to understand why we respond to beats differently." PRINCE

Musically, when not invoking his jazz muse, Prince seemed keen to pay his dues to rock heroes such as Jimi Hendrix, as on 'Dreamer' and 'Crimson & Clover,' the latter of which included a Hendrix-invoking 'Wild Thing' refrain. But while *The Rainbow Children* had a unifying (albeit heavy-handed) vision, *Lotusflow3r*'s erratic flits from instrumental jazz to state-of-the-world commentaries and personal pleas such as 'Love Like Jazz''s wish to "feel like I've been hypnotized" fail to make it a cohesive artistic statement. 'Wall Of Berlin' muddies the message further, with Prince using the politically charged image of the title as a springboard for a litany of playful double entendres such as "She went down … like the wall of Berlin." (Tantalizingly, Prince once alluded to a *Lotusflow3r* song called 'The Divine' that was so "mind-blowing" he doubted he would ever release it; when the "harmonies hit," he told *USA Today*, he decided to "put it away.")

The most heartfelt moment on the album (and the one for which Prince earned a Grammy nomination) is 'Dreamer,' which required a typically Prince-like 'explanation' for its message to disseminate. Speaking to Tavis Smiley in the first of two interviews to promote the albums, Prince revealed that it was inspired by comedian Dick Gregory's speech at Smiley's recent State Of The Black Union convention. "He said something that really hit home about the phenomena of chemtrails," Prince recalled. "When I was a kid, I used to see these trails in the sky all the time … and the next you know everybody in your neighborhood was fighting." In referencing the conspiracy theory that chemtrails left in the wake of airborne planes were actually biological agents sprayed across the earth at the government's behest, Gregory made Prince realize that he was living in a place that "feels just like a plantation" – in, as he sings, "The United States Of The Red, White, And Blue."

MPLSound is more upbeat, but Prince's overt adoption of Pro Tools-style digital recording results in a cold, distant feel. While the likes of '(There'll Never B) Another Like Me' and 'Chocolate Box' bounce along pleasantly enough (the latter perhaps featuring Prince's first wholly successful rap interpolation, courtesy of Q-Tip), the overall effect is all too one-note. The likes of 'Ol' Skool Company' and 'No More Candy 4 U' – on which Prince bemoans two other modern-day pet concerns: how much better music used to be, crossed with some commentary on the recession; and the numbers of "haters on the internet" – sound like their creator is enjoying himself much more, in the studio, than any listener could via their stereo. However, he wasn't completely devoid of wit. At 51, the one-time sexual omnivore uses 'Valentina' to send a message to Salma Hayek's daughter: "Tell your mama she should give me a call."

The two Prince offerings seemed be the first for some time to unify reviewers, who generally accepted that he remained an adept musician even if there were no new tricks on display. The only real differences in opinion came over whether they preferred guitar-god Prince or electro-funk Prince. Most agreed with the *LAist*'s observation that *Lotusflow3r* is "faintly psychedelic with big gobs of distorted guitar thrown around liberally," while *MPLSound* was neatly summed up by *USA Today*, which noted that Prince was "revisiting the synth vibe of the 80s with his outsize ego intact." A review by Pitchfork's Jess Harvell graciously decided that assessing a new Prince album "all but demands forced objectivity and willfully ignoring his own first decade as a recording artist" – even if she conceded that *MPLSound* found Prince "pastiching his own 80s sound as a profitable parlor game."

Despite a lack of radio play – and thanks no doubt to the fact that the triple-album package sold at Target for a recession-friendly $11.98 – *Lotusflow3r* found itself peaking at Number Two on the *Billboard* chart in its first week of sale. Unsurprisingly, Prince refused to tour the

Bria Valente: Elixer

As Prince noted at the time, Bria Valente's *Elixer* was nasty – but not dirty. Valente wasn't "promoting promiscuity," he said, but singing about "her lover, who could be her partner for life." But if the most Prince himself could say about *Elixer* was that it was "one of those sleeper records," recorded because they got tired of waiting for Sade to make a new album, it's difficult to know what he expected his fans to see in a singer who was better than Carmen Electra but still no Rosie Gaines. Indeed, Prince seemed to be most interested in Valente because of "how rapidly she picked up understanding of scripture." This hardly tallied with her being someone who could record a convincing steamy New Age soul album designed for "a whole lotta people [to] get pregnant off of."

Tacked on at the end of two bona-fide Prince releases, Bria Valente's debut was never going to have much luck with the critics. Even Jon Bream, writing in her (and Prince's) hometown paper, the *Star-Tribune*, couldn't shake the feeling that it was "a throwaway, done as a favor for a friend." (He probably wasn't far off, as Prince had been introduced to the Minneapolis-born Valente by keyboardist Morris Hayes.) It's telling that the closest Valente ever got to performing live was when Tavis Smiley interviewed her immediately after speaking to her mentor and she claimed that she and Prince were "just trying to make some stellar elevator music." She was never invited on tour with Prince, instead becoming another in a long line of acts to release one album with him before fading away.

Curiously, three years after *Elixer*'s release, Prince gave '2Nite' to the Swiss imprint Purple Music. Aimed at the club market, the single boasted a number of remixes, but it, too, failed to make much of an impression.

album, especially as it was initially only available in America. Instead, he performed three full concerts at LA's Live Nokia Center, each at a different venue inside the complex, before making his first high-profile international appearance of the year when he played two sets at the Montreux Jazz festival on July 18. When *Lotusflow3r* eventually saw a European release, in France, Prince undertook a mini-jaunt through Paris, performing another two sets in one day at the Grand Palais on October 11 (billed as All Day/All Night and marking the first time that the historic venue had been used for a full-concert performance). He also recorded a mini-acoustic set for radio broadcasters RTL and made an appearance on Canal+'s *Le Grand Journal*.

Come the end of the year, with Prince's enthusiasm for *Lotusflow3r* having wilted, he returned to try his luck in the hometown whose sound he had sought to reinvigorate on *MPLSound*. A court case followed when 3121 Rep Inc. sued the owners of his $150,000-a-month Beverly Hills property for the return of a $300,000 security deposit, claiming that they had brokered the rental deal for Prince. (The owners of the property claimed that Prince made the payments himself, so the money should go to him; it was faintly reminiscent of the April lawsuit brought against the star by a literary agency seeking its 15 per cent fee for "the negotiations of a publishing deal" for *21 Nights*, in which the company alleged that he had finished the book in secret in order to avoid paying.)

Back home, Prince seemed determined to make up for lost time; to give something back to Minneapolis, and ensure that it remained on the map. On October 24 he played his first concert at Paisley Park since 2004 in support of a Love 4 One Another coat drive. Then, in November, the longtime basketball fan was seen hanging out at Minnesota Vikings football games with Larry Graham – a new pastime, and one that would result in one of the oddest Prince releases yet.

Openly engaging with the local community was clearly invigorating. Having seen the Vikings beat the Dallas Cowboys 34–3 on January 17 2010 – a victory that enabled them to get through to the NFC Championship Game – Prince decided that he "saw the future" in Vikings quarterback Brett Favre. Rushing home with the sports team as his muse, he wrote 'Purple And Gold,' a new song designed to be roared from the terraces as fans cheered the home team on.

However, when it was unleashed via the Vikings' official website on January 21, Prince's "fight song" sounded more like an outtake from a Disney movie. With its thinly veiled religious references ("The veil of the sky draws open / The roar of the chariots touch down") it was more high-school pledge than cavalry call. The fans were dismayed; the song was quietly dropped. But Prince had succeeded in doing what the Vikings themselves hadn't: generating worldwide publicity.

A week later, after spending much of his time in Minneapolis visiting the local clubs, Prince turned up at First Avenue – not to perform, but to attend the fifth birthday party for local public-access radio station 89.3 The Current. As February 2010 drew to a close, he contacted the station again with another new song, 'Cause And Effect,' which premiered at 7:40am on February 26. A much more revealing – and enjoyable – affair than 'Purple And Gold,' its message was simple: Prince is back, and he's happy with his lot. Given the chance to do it all again, he declares, he wouldn't change a thing. "If I could talk to myself back then right now / I'd say, 'Son, you might wanna stick around / Something amazing is about to go down.'" The man who had spent much of the previous decade trying to eradicate the more outrageous side of his past finally seemed to have come to terms with his pre-conversion self. "If you stamp your passport full of regret," he sings, "You'll have nothing to remember but a lot to forget."

AFTER RETURNING HOME TO MINNEAPOLIS, PRINCE WAS SOON BESET WITH PROBLEMS. JUST A FEW MONTHS INTO THE NEW YEAR, THE *STAR-TRIBUNE* REPORTED THAT HE OWED "THOUSANDS OF DOLLARS IN BACK TAXES, INTEREST, AND FINES ON VARIOUS PROPERTIES," AND THAT HE WAS RUNNING THE RISK OF FORFEITING THEM IF HE DIDN'T PAY HIS BILLS ON TIME. ACCORDING TO REPORTS IN THE *CHASKA HERALD*, PAISLEY PARK ALONE WAS $221,891.88 IN ARREARS, WHILE PRINCE'S TOTAL DEBTS WERE IN EXCESS OF $500,000.

20Ten (FEBRUARY 2010–SEPTEMBER 2012)

COMPASSION
BEGINNING ENDLESSLY
FUTURE SOUL SONG
STICKY LIKE GLUE
ACT OF GOD
LAVAUX
WALK IN SAND
SEA OF EVERYTHING
EVERYBODY LOVES ME

Produced, Arranged, Composed & Performed by Prince

©2010 NPG Records

It was an inauspicious start to the year. On August 3, Prince – now almost perpetually court-bound – would find himself sued by his former lawyer, Ed McPherson, for an alleged failure to pay $49,987.74 in legal fees. Ironically, the fees were for services "in connection with a real-estate transaction" for his old Beverly Park home – probably the return of the $300,000 deposit he put down on the 77 – and for defending Prince's "alleged failure to pay agency commissions" for his *21 Nights* book deal. Even worse, however, was the fact that, as the one-year anniversary of lotusflow3r.com rolled around, there were alarming signs of fiscal mismanagement (though Prince did manage to clear his tax and legal debts by the end of September 2010).

Despite attempts to send out positive signals, Prince seemed to be in need of some serious cash. Teaming up again with The Current, he publicly acknowledged his birthday for the first time in years, giving the local radio station 'Hot Summer,' which debuted on June 7, his 52nd birthday. *Rolling Stone* guessed that the song was inspired by Minneapolis's record-breaking May heat wave; Prince told program director Jim McGuinn he thought it had "a B-52's feel to it." Such lowly ambitions would once have been unthinkable. The disappointment was writ large in a review on stereogum.com, which concluded: "At least the lyrics are positive."

Inevitably, rumors began to circulate about a new album. Dr Funkenberry soon revealed that Prince's next release – the unashamedly backward-looking *20Ten* – would be given away by a selection of European print publications on July 10. But while Prince's representative, Kiran Sharma, boasted that the release marked "a world first of delivering the new album across multiple territories, through complimentary distribution channels," the method was merely a wider-ranging variation of Prince's *Planet Earth* giveaway. More intriguing was Dr Funkenberry's claim that Prince had met with his old nemesis, Warner Bros, on June 22 – not only to discuss

US distribution for the album, but also to talk about "something else."

Such a tantalizing promise was all but ignored in the UK, however, where the media whipped itself into a frenzy over the giveaway. The *Daily Mirror* had the honor of receiving *20Ten*. The day after its release, respected music journalist Paul Morley noted how Prince's work "unfold[s] with fertile, otherworldly, Dylanesque consistency." In Scotland, *20Ten* was released by the *Mirror*'s sister newspaper, the *Daily Record*, before being unveiled by Belgium's *Het Nieuwsblad*, France's *Courier International*, and the German edition of *Rolling Stone*.

Equally consistent was the media campaign to accompany the album's release. The *Mirror*, German *Rolling Stone*, and *Het Nieuwsblad* were all given access to Paisley Park in order to interview Prince, who pulled the strings as masterfully as ever in order to get what he needed. The published interviews had enough similarities to suggest that each paper's writers were treated to carbon-copy experiences. (Sitting in on drums with Prince and the band, only to get fired for poor timekeeping, seemed to be a particular favorite for both musician and journalist alike.) Despite the hype, the UK freebie managed only to shift 379,000 additional copies of the *Mirror* and *Record* – a far cry from the *Mail On Sunday*'s claim that *Planet Earth* upped sales by 600,000 in 2007. On July 12, the *Mirror* began offering free copies of the album to anyone who ordered the newspaper online.

Being able to demand up-front payment for his work put Prince in a remarkable and enviable position. With *20Ten*, however, he failed to provide the quality product that ought to reward somebody else's advanced outlay and risk-taking. Unsurprisingly, the *Daily Mirror* trumpeted the album as Prince's "best album in 23 years" and put it "on a par with Elvis's 1968 comeback," singling out individual tracks as his "most soulful," "most spiritual," or "most romantic" for some time. For many listeners, however, *20Ten* proved to be Prince's most disappointing record of the 21st century.

Whereas *1999* still sounded like a futuristic masterpiece, *20Ten* struggled even to sound relevant in the year of its release. The production is slightly warmer and more organic than that of *MPLSound*, but the album still left fans cold. 'Compassion' sounds like a watered-down version of 'Let's Pretend We're Married,' while the irritatingly breezy 'Everybody Loves Me' wholly fails to grasp what made 'All The Critics Love U In New York' such an enjoyable piece of tongue-in-cheek arrogance. There might be a nice quiet storm ballad in 'Walk In Sand,' but Prince had been churning those out for years. And when he sings of taxes helping to build bomber planes "supposedly to keep us safe from Saddam" on 'Act Of God,' it's as if Prince is unaware that Hussein had been hanged in December 2006. The level of disconnection between the artist and the real world was alarming. Typically perverse, he buried the most interesting cut, 'Laydown,' on track 77 of the CD, after 68 silent tracks. The only *20Ten* offering to hint at past glories, it features murky, disconcerting guitar, complex synth lines, and a convincing rap in which Prince crowns himself "the Purple Yoda."

Prince himself seemed aware of the album's failings. He played only one *20Ten* track ('Future Soul Song') during the eight-date European tour which he undertook to promote the record, and even then only during an after-show gig at the Viage in Brussels. Perhaps sensing the lackluster response to the album – even as he talked-up a planned deluxe edition for stores, with the disappointingly lukewarm addition of 'Rich Friends' – Prince began to drop hints that the copyright on his Warners albums would soon revert back to him, and that

> "Someone told me they saw me at my peak, but how do they know when my peak is? I think I'm improving all the time. When I listen to my old records I'm ashamed of how I played them." PRINCE

he had already remastered a number of them. Neither the remasters nor the deluxe *20Ten* ever came to pass.

On October 14 – the day 'Rich Friends' leaked online – Prince announced a new live residency, Welcome 2 America. Launching on December 15 at the Izod Center in New Jersey, the residency would set the pace for Prince through to the fall of 2012, as the initial US dates gave way to the following summer's Welcome 2 America Euro Tour 2011, that December's Welcome 2 Canada jaunt, and eight nights of Welcome 2 Australia in May 2012. Welcome 2 Chicago rounded things off in September 2012 with a three-night stand at the United Center, with which Prince raised money for the Rebuild The Dream organization founded by a former advisor to President Obama, Van

Prince announces the Welcome 2 America tour at the Apollo Theater, New York.

Superconductor: Andy Allo

Cameroonian singer-songwriter Andy Allo rose quickly through the ranks of the NPG. After providing guest vocals during Prince's two performances at LA's Troubadour in May 2011, she became a fully fledged band-member the following month, playing guitar during the Welcome 2 America Euro 2011 shows. "She's great," Prince told the *Irish Sunday Independent* that July. "Soon I'll be backing her up!"

The comment wasn't entirely unfounded. As Dr Funkenberry teased in October, Prince had taken "a musical liking … and perhaps other likings" to the 22-year-old talent. After the European tour ended in Switzerland on August 17, Prince and Andy holed up in Powerplay Studios in Zürich for just over a week, working on what would become Andy's second album, *Superconductor*. Hints that Prince had high hopes for the record came when he registered a new trademark for her, '&Y,' in November, but it would be another year before *Superconductor* finally saw the light of day.

Work on *Superconductor* continued into June 2012 before Andy set out to hype its release. Her official solo debut came on September 24 when she performed at Prince's Welcome 2 Chicago after-party at the House Of Blues; this was followed in October by a high-profile appearance on

Jimmy Kimmel Live! As executive producer of the album (and co-writer on three of its songs, 'Long Gone,' 'The Calm,' and the title track), Prince continued to support Andy up to *Superconductor*'s release, premiering the video for its lead single, 'People Pleaser,' on the same night that he unveiled his 'Rock And Roll Love Affair' promo at LA's Sayers Club, October 24 2012.

As with many NPG-label projects, however, distribution issues seemed to affect the release. Having been trailed as early as March 2012 (for early June), *Superconductor* was finally made available for download on November 20. Not that the delay caused any harm. In Andy's short time with Prince, she had become popular among fans who, within hours of the album's release, sent it to the top of Amazon's Soul/R&B charts in the US, UK, and France.

It was a much-deserved success for Allo, who, though working closely with Prince, made *Superconductor* undeniably her own. Lead track 'People Pleaser' is a catchy pop-funk number that quickly became a live favorite; 'Story Of You & I' is a ballad that proved she had more depth than many before her. While she undoubtedly benefitted from the presence of her NPG bandmates (among them drummers John Blackwell and Michael Bland, keyboardist Morris Hayes, plus Maceo Parker, and The Hornheadz – the latter making their first

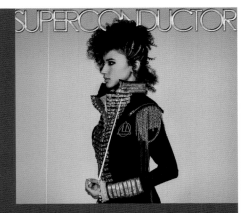

appearance on a Prince-related project since *The Rainbow Children*), Andy's confidence and natural charisma more than carry the record. It's a testament to her drive that two of the three Prince co-writes, 'Long Gone' and 'The Calm,' make for two of *Superconductor*'s most restrained moments.

Perhaps Prince's talk of supporting independent artists had rubbed off. "He gave me that space to blossom and grow," she told Billboard.com in March 2013, by which time she appeared to have been out of Prince's orbit for several months. There exists a professionally shot photo of Andy, drummer Hannah Ford Welton, and bassist Ida Nielsen, grouped behind Prince, suggesting that he might have earmarked her for guitarist in 3rdEyeGirl. (Andy can also be seen playing alongside Hannah and Ida in the 'Rock And Roll Love Affair' video.) But, as Andy put it herself, "Being an independent artist, you have freedom," and it seems as though she wanted to extend that freedom beyond Prince's world. When physical copies of *Superconducter* emerged, she was selling them through her own website, while her follow-up release, the *Hello* EP, had no Prince involvement at all.

Yet it's undeniable that the pairing worked. When Prince teamed up with Tidal in late 2015, he allowed the company to stream the previously unreleased *Oui Can Luv* for a mere half-day in November. An eight-track acoustic album credited to Andy, with Prince on guitar, it features covers of his 'I Love U In Me' and 'We Can Funk,' along with Amy Winehouse's 'Love Is A Losing Game,' Roxy Music's 'More Than This,' and Bob Marley's 'Waiting In Vain.' The latter seemed to have struck a particular chord with Prince, who played it often throughout his Piano & A Microphone shows in early 2016, performing it as a medley with his 1987 classic 'If I Was Your Girlfriend.'

Prince and Andy Allo on stage in Rotterdam, The Netherlands, during the Welcome 2 America Euro Tour 2011.

Jones. In an email interview with *Time Out Chicago*, Prince called the fund-raising "a necessary endeavor," noting that, after Jehovah's Witness meetings, the congregation is asked to clean up for whoever is using the building next. "We feel the same way about this country," he said. "Shouldn't we try 2 leave it in better shape than when we found it?"

In a telling remark to *Ebony* in June 2010, Prince claimed, "Self-interest is on the back burner for now. There is too much at stake." He also mentioned a need "to get back to localized music distribution on all levels" – a stance reflected in the way he released much of his new music throughout this time.

In September 2012, Prince acknowledged that it had been two years since his last full-length release, telling the *Chicago Tribune*, "We're in a singles market again. It's crazy for me to walk into that with a new album." Throughout 2011–13 he gave new songs to local radio stations in cities where he was playing, and he would also allow band members to post rehearsal jams on their Facebook pages, by way of drumming up interest in the live shows.

In October 2011, Prince inked a deal with the Switzerland-based Purple Music imprint, run by dance music entrepreneur Jamie Lewis. Prince had discovered the label at the end of his European tour, while recording in a Swiss studio with his then protégé, Andy Allo. When Purple Music released a remix single of the *MPLSound* track 'Dance 4 Me' at the end of the year, it managed to hit Number One in the British dance charts. A year later, Purple Music was also the beneficiary of a bona-fide new track, 'Rock And Roll Love Affair,' which Prince had initially gifted to iHeartRadio in Chicago to promote the United Center shows. Despite having a high-budget promo video, the frothy pop-rock affair made negligible impact, charting solely in the UK at a lowly Number 121.

Just before Prince embarked on Welcome 2 Canada, a re-recording of one of his most popular outtakes, 'Extraloveable,' was released on the Canadian iTunes store, on 23 November. Yet while Prince wisely removed the threat of rape from the original lyrics, the update paled in comparison to the unreleased version recorded in 1982 during the *1999* album sessions. Though attempting to stay faithful to the original, the remake fails to capture the raw immediacy of its predecessor, while Allo's rap is an incongruous addition. Prince would often insist that many songs hidden in The Vault remained there because they were "unfinished," but comparing the 1982 and 2011 versions of 'Extraloveable' reveals only that starting again

ABOVE **Prince serenades ballet dancer Misty Copeland during a Welcome 2 America show at Madison Square Garden, New York, in February 2011.**

30 years later does not necessarily make for the best result.

With few new offerings in 2012, a number of rehearsals eked out through NPG band-members' Facebook pages, or via Dr Funkenberry's blog. (In lieu of an official web presence, Funkenberry had become something of a mouthpiece for Prince, disseminating information as and when he was instructed to do so.) A rehearsal of the 1984 outtake 'The Dance Electric' (later given to André Cymone) primed fans for Prince's Welcome 2 Australia shows in April 2012, while an epic 20-minute jam on 'Days Of Wild' – incorporating a number of other tracks, including 'America' and The Time's 'Wild And Loose' – was titled 'Days Of Wild And Loose' and announced Prince's return to Paisley Park that June.

"Come early and come often," Prince had said when announcing the Welcome 2 America residency at Harlem's Apollo Theater on October 14 2010. "Because every time we play it's always something new." However, as the Welcome 2 concept stretched out over two years, it began to show signs of fatigue. Across April and May 2011, a planned residency at the 17,500-capacity LA Forum, billed as the '21 Night Stand,' failed to replicate the success of Prince's 21-night venture in London four years before. After sluggish ticket sales, he ended up playing only 15 shows at the Forum, with the remainder taking place elsewhere in the LA area, somewhat stretching the original definition.

As the Chicago concerts brought the Welcome 2 shows to a close, *Rolling Stone* went so far as to call the opening night "lackluster," noting that Prince was all too keen to cede "choruses, verses, entire songs to his trio of backup singers and the audience." Pitchfork was far kinder, calling the show a "giddy party" but nevertheless commenting that Prince appeared to be fashioning himself as "a wedding singer, a leader of a cover band, a DJ, and a director."

In sporadically throwing out songs online, Prince was clearly testing the market. But with no new album, and a live show that, for possibly the first time in his career, was receiving less than across-the-board praise, he clearly needed a change. The following year would provide an electrifying shake-up.

3rdEyeGirl

ON DECEMBER 31 2012, A MYSTERIOUS YOUTUBE ACCOUNT BELONGING TO SOMEONE – OR SOMETHING – CALLED 3RDEYEGIRL POSTED A NEW PRINCE SONG, 'SAME PAGE DIFFERENT BOOK.' RELATED TWITTER, YOUTUBE, FACEBOOK, AND SOUNDCLOUD ACCOUNTS QUICKLY SPRUNG UP AND, THROUGHOUT THE FIRST WEEK OF JANUARY 2013, SHARED REHEARSAL FOOTAGE AND EXTENDED REMIXES OF PRINCE SONGS.

Despite Prince's own band members pointing fans toward the Twitter account, 3rdEyeGirl, a self-professed "international art thief," soon posted a photo of a cease-and-desist letter, supposedly sent from Prince's lawyers, before removing all the "leaked" material.

The following week, Prince's bandmates, Hannah Ford Welton, Ida Nielsen, and Donna Grantis, appeared in separate videos, each denying that they were the culprit. "We were just goofing around," Ford Welton told the author in September 2014. "At that time we didn't really know that we were a band," Nielsen added. "We were just trying to make these mysterious videos … and didn't know that it was actually maybe part of a plan."

After learning 150 songs, Danish bassist Nielsen had been invited to join Prince as part of The New Power Generation in 2010. Hannah, a Texan, was recruited to fill in on drums in late 2012, after Prince found her on YouTube. She received an email while at church, and, after initial skepticism that it was actually Prince who had contacted her, flew out to audition at Paisley Park. Prince's first question concerned whether she played ping-pong – the group's favorite way to wind down. Subsequently proving her musical worth with performances of 'Purple Rain,' 'Cause And Effect,' 'F.U.N.K.,' and 'Get On The Boat,' Hannah was invited on board – and soon tasked with finding a female guitarist. Canadian Donna Grantis fit the bill. ("When I first saw a clip of Donna, what struck me was her hair," Prince later recalled. "She can play better than anyone and she can look better while doing it.")

Soon the three of them were rehearsing with Prince, for up to 12 hours a day, six days a week, at Paisley Park. Noting that "time exists in a different way" at the complex, Donna would explain: "Every day there are things to accomplish but it's not related to the hour. It's just: before the next resting period, we need to get this done."

The group's public unveiling took place on January 18 2013, the final night of a three-night residency at Minneapolis's Dakota Jazz Club, for which Prince performed two shows each evening. With the first two (promoted as a "Soundcheck" and a "Jam," respectively) showcasing an assortment of musicians, the third – a "Surprise" – was given over to his newest band. Not that they had an official name yet.

"I thought: Prince is 3rdEyeGirl, or is it us?" Donna later told the author. "Or is it a random pseudonym for something? I mean, we had no idea." Later that month, Prince continued to insist that 3rdEyeGirl was "indeed a bootlegger." When *Billboard* journalist Gail Mitchell pointed out that Hannah's drum kit was emblazoned with the image from 3rdEyeGirl's Twitter profile, he claimed that it was the girls "poking fun" at the situation. Fans had – rightly – long assumed otherwise, though the band weren't officially christened until their national television debut on *Late Night With Jimmy Fallon* on March 1. After the host introduced the group, Donna recalled, "We were like, 'I guess that's our name!'"

If the charade had lost its novelty by then, the music they were making sounded box-fresh. Like his hero Miles Davis, Prince had recruited a younger band that could give his music some vitality: with a twin-guitar setup on stage,

Prince and 3rdEyeGirl hit upon a funk-rock sound that was part Jimi Hendrix, part hard rock, and total cocksure swagger. The first new music they released was 'Screwdriver,' a riff-driven romp that asserted 3rdEyeGirl's garage-rock credentials. Properly connecting with the electric guitar as a lead instrument for the first time in years, Prince also revamped old classics such as 'Let's Go Crazy,' giving it a slow, bluesy makeover (christened 'Let's Go Crazy Reloaded') that became a standout of the group's live shows.

(Keeping it a surprise from the girls, Prince taught them the song as if he was writing a new one. "He was sneaky about it," Nielsen recalled. "He could have just said: 'Hey, play that song half-time.' But he didn't." It was only after he gave each musician their parts, building it piece by piece, that they realized what they were playing.)

More new songs followed, among them 'L.O.L. (Live Out Loud)' and 'Fixurlifeup,' all available for purchase on the (now official) 3rdEyeGirl website. On April 15, Prince and the group set out on an 18-date club tour, dubbed Live Out Loud and confined mostly to the US West Coast. The band mostly played two shows a night, grafting in smaller venues like any other new act (albeit one that could charge $250-plus a ticket for the honor of standing within touching distance of Prince). "The lack of sleep has been the biggest challenge," Ida later said. "But the thing is, when you play, even if it's late, you forget that you're tired. The adrenaline kicks in and we feed off the energy of the crowd."

Initial reviews switched between amazement at Prince and Hannah's guitar pyrotechnics and indifference to their tendency toward lengthy, indulgent jams. Yet with setlists that mixed rockier deep cuts such as 'Endorphinemachine' and 'She's Always In My Hair' with some of the finer selections of new 3rdEyeGirl material (not least 'Plectrumelectrum,' an instrumental written by Donna Grantis, and which some reviewers would mistake for a cover of Led Zeppelin's 'The Ocean'), long-term fans were largely thrilled by what seemed to be a reinvigorated Prince engaging with his music in a way that he hadn't for quite some time. Night after night, the group improved. Catching them toward the end of the tour at Denver's Ogden Theatre, Prince biographer and Star-Tribune journalist Jon Bream declared it the most exciting Prince

In July 2013, prior to headlining slots at the Stockholm Music And Arts Festival and Denmark's Smukfest, Rolling Stone declared the girls Number Two in its 50 Greatest Live Acts Right Now list. But 3rdEyeGirl arguably never had the chance to reach their full potential. By 2015, though Donna remained on guitar, longtime Prince sideman Kirk Johnson was sitting in for a pregnant Hannah during a handful of early-hours performances at Paisley Park, while Judith Hill's bassist, Dywane "MonoNeon" Thomas Jr stood in for Ida.

Although 3rdEyeGirl continued to play fiery live shows through the summer of 2015 (including an invitation-only performance for President Obama at the White House, in celebration of African-American Music Appreciation Month), it's possible that the world never got to hear them at their best in the studio. Plectrumelectrum had been recorded a year before its release, and, as Ida noted the week before it came out, their sound had "really evolved" in that time. "We've recorded some stuff that's not on the album that I think is so beautiful," she said, but that material remains unreleased. (In an interview with Rollingstone.com, Prince's string arranger, Michael Nelson, suggested that Prince had been working on 3rdEyeGirl studio material in the months before his death. Of a batch of "songs with symphonic guitar solos" to be orchestrated, he received a piece with the working title 'New 3rdEyeGirl String Session.')

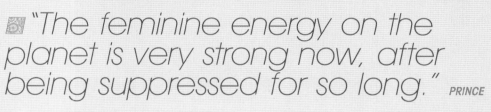

"The feminine energy on the planet is very strong now, after being suppressed for so long." PRINCE

show he'd seen since the Sign "O" The Times tour, with "the most rip-roaringly ferocious four-song opening Prince has probably ever put together."

A rumored run of UK club dates would have to wait until early 2014; before that, Prince and 3rdEyeGirl holed up in Paisley Park, where they recorded and rehearsed incessantly – sometimes broadcasting portions of the sessions on the internet, via the video streaming platform Livestream. One notable event was billed as The Breakfast Experience – Pajama Dance Party. Open to the public, it started at 2am on October 19 2013 and ended around five hours later. During that time, Prince performed two sets, introduced the video and remixes for 'Breakfast Can Wait,' and put on a spread of pancakes for $1 each. A handful of appearances, including one at the Montreux Jazz Festival and three consecutive December shows at Connecticut's Mohegan Sun Arena, saw 3rdEyeGirl take the stage as part of a large, 20-plus-member ensemble with the NPG.

"At the Academy of Paisley Park, you learn everything in a week, or else," Prince told Mojo in 2014. And music's rich history was part of the syllabus: "I'm passing it on to these kids because it's their turn." 3rdEyeGirl duly saw it as their job to pass it on again. "The young kids in this generation need music," Hannah asserted to the author. "Real music." But what Prince taught them, she said, also went beyond that and into "production, the lighting and the sound. All of what goes into a show … he's got so much wisdom that he just willingly shares."

Prince's generosity had a cause. "I'm trying to get these women's careers started," he told V magazine in 2014, "because they're all so talented."

Ida Nielsen, Hannah Ford Welton, and Donna Grantis of 3rdEyeGirl at a *Dazed & Confused* magazine event in London, England, September 2014.

PRINCE MADE TWO VERY DIFFERENT BUT EQUALLY IDIOSYNCRATIC APPEARANCES IN FEBRUARY 2014, AS HE SOUGHT MAXIMUM EXPOSURE FOR HIS NEW MUSIC ON BOTH SIDES OF THE ATLANTIC. ONE FOLLOWED THE MOST-WATCHED TELEVISION EVENT OF THE YEAR, THE OTHER TOOK PLACE AT THE HOME OF AN UP-AND-COMING BRITISH SINGER.

Art Official Age/ Plectrumelectrum

(FEBRUARY 2014–NOVEMBER 2014)

It was always going to be difficult to find a bigger audience than the Super Bowl halftime show, but with 111.5 million viewers tuning in to watch the game on February 2 2014, Prince did the next best thing. Broadcast on Fox directly after Super Bowl XLVIII, the 14th episode of the 3rd season of the sitcom *New Girl* was simply titled 'Prince.' Beamed into the homes of 26.3 million viewers – over five times the number attracted by the second-most-watched episode of that season – it was a light-hearted romp that saw the show's main characters, Jess, Cece, and Nick, attend a party at Prince's mansion. On hand to dispense love advice and serve pancakes, Prince also couldn't resist commandeering the show to debut a new song, 'Fallinlove2nite.' Closing the episode and also featuring guest vocals from *New Girl*'s lead, Zooey Deschanel, the song's heavy EDM influence pointed toward some of the work Prince would unveil later in the year.

Two days later, Prince made a far more modest – but no less newsworthy – appearance at Lianne La Havas's home in east London. Prince had been dropping La Havas's name as early as 2012, when he claimed that the then 23-year-old singer was his favorite live performer. After receiving an invite to Paisley Park in 2013, La Havas joked that she would put Prince up next time he was in London – not expecting him to accept.

Following a *Plectrumelectrum* album preview in New York, in the early hours of Monday, February 3 2014, Prince flew to London. By the evening of February 4, he was sipping tea and seeming relaxed before a handpicked audience of about ten in La Havas's living room. Casually brushing off the approaching 30-year anniversary of *Purple Rain* ("I hadn't even realized. Everything looks different to me, because I was there. I wrote those songs, I don't need to know what happened"), Prince performed a few acoustic songs and announced his UK Hit And Run tour with 3rdEyeGirl.

Promising to play "iconic" venues the likes of Ronnie Scott's, Prince was ready to introduce 3rdEyeGirl to the UK just as he had to the US the previous year: via a series of club shows, only this time the pricing would be less prohibitive for fans. "We want to charge about $10 a ticket," he told the handful of journalists (allegedly as few as three) invited to the event, which he playfully dubbed The Living Room Experience. "This is a new band, people are getting something new," he said. Noting that the visit was open-ended, he said they planned to "work our way up, if people like us, to bigger venues."

Shortly after the press conference, Prince & 3rdEyeGirl performed an "open soundcheck" at the 1,100-capacity Electric Ballroom in London's Camden Town. Beginning just after midnight on the morning of February 5, the brief set was another showcase for an exclusive audience, this time about 300 people, though such a large queue of fans gathered outside that Prince invited them in for the final few songs. Promising to come back the following night (actually later that same day, given the show's start time), "a bit earlier and a lot funkier," Prince was true to his word, charging £10 entry to fans who had queued up all day – despite the freezing cold, rainy weather, and a

London Tube strike – to catch one of two shows he performed that evening.

It was the beginning of a love affair with the UK that would last most of the year. Having earned their chops in the States, 3rdEyeGirl were a tighter unit by the time they crossed the Atlantic, and reviews of their UK debut were ecstatic. *Clash* magazine likened the "all-girl blitzkrieg" to "the primordial sludge of Black Sabbath," albeit with Little

"If you want to be great, get a sidekick. Whoever's your greatest rival, put them in your band. You'll push each other." PRINCE

Richard as the frontman. The *Guardian* reveled in the "wonderfully dissonant" feeling of watching "a galaxy-class showman playing like a band with a residency in a local bar." Equally enrapt was London's *Evening Standard*, which marveled at the group's "savage, monstrous noise" and wondered, with more shows to come, who would end up tiring first: Prince or London.

And so Prince had set the template for the first UK Hit And Run tour of the year: last-minute announcements, small venues, often two sets a night. With no advance booking, fans had to queue all day to ensure entry. Yet the

lengthy queues guaranteed yet more hype, as hardcore devotees panicked over gaining entry and casual onlookers were drawn to the spectacle, even if long-time supporters old enough to have serious jobs or families weren't able to drop everything in order to wait in line all day. Perhaps Prince didn't mind – the shows arguably saw him play to a younger demographic that he might not otherwise have attracted. But that group had less disposable income to spare. When 300 or so hopefuls arrived at Shepherd's Bush Empire in the early afternoon of February 9, within an hour or so of 3rdEyeGirl announcing that night's concert on BBC 6 Music radio, many left after security announced that tickets were going to be £70 on the door. Others launched a Twitter campaign asking that Prince keep his word from several days before. Those who queued for five hours in yet another bitterly cold February day were amply rewarded. Prince sent a delivery of takeout hot chocolate along the line, before announcing a cover charge of £10. The audience got more than its money's worth: in an

iconic music festival or at AEG Live's British Summer Time Hyde Park event. The *Independent* claimed that Prince had been promised "every penny" from the 100,000 tickets sales in return for two greatest hits sets at BST Hyde Park, estimating that he would have taken home £8 million in revenue. In the event, however, Black Sabbath and Neil Young were among the 2014 BST Hyde Park headliners, while Michael Eavis later claimed that he had been close to striking a deal with Prince, but that negotiations broke down once his appearance was announced on social media. Although Glastonbury's organizers hadn't leaked the news, Prince "got really upset because he thought we had advertised that he was playing."

Returning to the US for a handful of surprise shows, Prince attempted to keep the momentum up with the official release of 'Fallinlove2nite.' Released digitally on March 17, it marked Prince's first return to a major label since he signed with Columbia for the release of *Planet Earth* in 2007. Distributed by Epic (which, like Columbia, was owned by Sony), the song was a download-only release that limped to Number 113 in the UK charts. Epic CEO L.A. Reid told *Essence* that the deal he had with Prince was "a handshake" founded on Reid's boast over how quickly he could release music. "Hand it to me," he told Prince,

> ▨ *"When I'm on stage, I'm out of body. And that's when something happens. You reach a plane of creativity and inspiration."* PRINCE

electrifying set, Prince played for two and a half hours, noting at one point that he used to pay £10 for concerts "back in the day."

Subsequent announcements were careful to clarify the £70 ticket prices in advance, though the first show in this new price bracket was unique: a largely acoustic affair, broken up with Q&A segments, staged on Valentine's Day in the 420-seater Hall One at Kings Place. From thereon in, though, it was largely back to business, with a few on-the-spot tweaks. A planned trio of back-to-back shows at Koko ended up becoming two shows with an extended encore, during which the several hundred fans who'd queued for the final, midnight concert were let in for free. Two concerts at legendary jazz venue Ronnie Scott's saw Prince play guitar during the first and restrict himself to keyboard during the second. Though Prince took to the stage with 3rdEyeGirl in tow at the BRIT Awards, held on February 19, it was largely to announce two forthcoming shows in Manchester (presenting the British Female Solo Artist award almost seemed to be an afterthought).

This was all excellent PR, but fans were beginning to wonder what it was for. Though 'Pretzelbodylogic' had been released as a download single on February 3, Prince still hadn't announced the long-awaited 3rdEyeGirl album – which had been largely finished the previous year – nor did he confirm or deny rumors that a second album was on the cards. By the time he headed to Manchester, however, the reason for the trip became clear. While in London, Prince had met with Glastonbury founder Michael Eavis, as well as tour promoters AEG Live, to discuss a summer festival appearance – either at Eavis's

"and then go out to your car and turn on the radio." It was also evidence of Prince shopping around to find a large label to work with again, but the song's disappointing performance must have led him to cross Epic off the list of potentials.

With his publishing deal with Universal Music ending on March 31 2014, and having just regained the rights to his Warner Bros back catalogue, Prince launched his own publishing company, NPG Music Publishing. He then surprised everyone by re-signing with Warner Bros in a deal that promised at least one new album and a long-awaited deluxe reissue of *Purple Rain*. Back in the UK in May to capitalize on the hype, Prince staged the Hit And Run Part II tour. With a bit more notice (and allowing for advanced bookings), he and 3rdEyeGirl performed arena shows in Birmingham, Manchester, and Glasgow, before branching out into The Netherlands, Belgium (where he played three shows in one night at the 400-seater Botanique), France, and Austria. An exclusive appearance at London's Hippodrome Casino, in the 180-seater Matcham Room, rounded out the jaunt. The event was an after-party celebration for the London premiere of the movie *Belle*, and saw Prince provide entertainment for the likes of Bryan Ferry and supermodel Kate Moss.

News of the *Purple Rain* reissue was quietly dropped as the album's anniversary, June 25, came and went. Prince marked the anniversary of the movie the following month, however, with a surprise show at Paisley Park, by which point it was clear that Warner Bros would have to make do with releasing a second new album rather than the promised reissue.

Having issued a string of download-only releases throughout 2013 and into 2014, Prince tried to embrace the "singles-driven market" he felt he was now working in, but conceded, in an interview with Arsenio Hall, that "I come from the old school of making albums, and that's what I'll always do." Though he'd spent the entirety of 2013 and most of 2014 laying the groundwork for the long-delayed 3rdEyeGirl album, by June 2014 he'd turned his attention to a new project. Inviting the *Star-Tribune*'s Jon Bream to Paisley Park to hear previews of a new solo album, Prince enthusiastically told Bream – by phone, from somewhere else in the building – that he'd "finally got something that is a cohesive statement."

The late-September release of *Art Official Age* and *Plectrumelectrum* was officially announced on *Good Morning America* on August 25. A Warner Bros statement followed, promising that the albums would "express the incredible range and depth" of Prince's talent. As Prince's 3rdEyeGirl shows had long suggested, *Plectrumelectrum*, credited to Prince & 3rdEyeGirl, was a guitar-driven affair largely – though not entirely – given over to the funk-rock sound that Prince and the girls had worked up on stage. *Art Official Age* owed more to the Minneapolis sound but still saw Prince working collaboratively; for the first time ever, he gave a co-producer credit, having allowed Joshua Welton, the husband of 3rdEyeGirl drummer Hannah Ford Welton, to update his sound with contemporary touches.

As 3rdEyeGirl told it, they weren't even aware they'd been recording album. Prince had made reference recordings of everything they'd been rehearsing since 2012, and pieced most of the album together throughout the following year. "At the time we didn't really realize what we were doing," Hannah revealed to the author days before the album's release. "And then all of a sudden we had this long list of all these songs we had recorded, and

Brothers Once More

Ever on the hunt for new business partnerships, in 2013 Prince briefly signed with Kobalt Label Services, part of the Kobalt Music Group, a self-proclaimed "alternative to the traditional music business model." A press release trumpeted the deal as a "groundbreaking venture" that would allow Prince to "release a slate of music by new artists, as well as Prince recordings," while Kobalt president Richard Sanders boasted of their ability to give Prince "the flexibility and freedom he's always sought in a label partner." On paper, the arrangement seemed perfect for Prince: Kobalt Label Services allowed artists to keep their master tapes – one of Prince's main points of contention throughout his battle with Warner Bros. It was a surprise, then, when he signed with his old nemesis the following year.

Eighteen years after his acrimonious split with Warner Bros, and according to the terms of the Copyright Revision Act Of 1976 (which came in effect in 1978, the year that Prince released his debut album), Prince seemed to acquire the rights to

terminate his master-recording copyright deal with Warner Bros, thereby blocking them from ever again releasing his old music. The situation was untested and, as *Billboard* noted, many label execs were "unsure how copyright terminations and ownership reversions would play out." The paper speculated that, rather than risk a costly legal battle, Prince decided to cut a new deal with the label. On April 18 2014, it was announced that he had signed a "landmark" agreement that saw him retain ownership of his catalog while allowing Warner Bros to distribute it.

Speaking to the author shortly after, 3rdEyeGirl drummer Hannah Ford Welton praised the deal. "What's cool and different this go-round is that it's not a signed deal – contract – where Warner owns everything," she said. "It's more like a partnership. We give them the contents and then they do what they do with it."

The timing was fortuitous. With *Purple Rain*'s 30th anniversary looming, the official announcement promised the release of "long-awaited, previously unheard material" from The Vault. First of all: a remastered, deluxe edition of *Purple*

Rain. Yet Prince dismissed it as the "same album, just state-of-the-art sound," adding, "It's nice that it sounds better for the fans but I live in the now. I don't have to go backwards to celebrate." And, ultimately he didn't. The reissue never materialized. As far as Ford Welton knew, the remaster had at least been delivered to Warner Bros, leaving speculation as to whether Prince refused to turn over the promised bonus disc of unreleased material.

Warner Bros did, however, issue *Art Official Age* and *Plectrumelectrum*. Both were released on September 30 2014, and comfortably entered the Top 10 in the US – a testament to both parties' ability to bury the hatchet. "I don't deal in history, nor should they," Prince asserted, shortly after the albums were released. Almost 40 years after initially signing with Warners, Prince was not unaware of the boost the label gave to his career. "Warner Bros granted rights unheard of at the time," he told Australian website The FIX in 2011, adding that the label had "allowed him the freedom to produce music unencumbered … thus, music became a real job, not a hobby."

started laying some vocals down." Almost casually, it seems, Prince then suggested they "pick the songs that all go good together and then put 'em in an order that works, and then we'll have an album."

Whether by accident or design, Prince had been canny in touring 3rdEyeGirl for so long before releasing *Plectrumelectrum*. By the time the album came out, it was the best part of a year old; despite having been recorded in analog, live in one room ("It keeps you on your toes," bassist Ida Nielsen said, "because if one person messes up, we have to redo it"), it failed to fully capture 3rdEyeGirl's powerful stage presence. 3rdEyeGirl themselves noted the difference, with guitarist Donna Grantis acknowledging that "a lot of the songs on the album were recorded pretty early on," while Ida rightly felt that their sound had evolved since then. Prince, too, was aware that their live sound packed a stronger punch, telling journalists gathered at the Living Room Experience press conference that, though he loved the record, "live is a different thing with these musicians. There's a certain feeling that we get when we play – this is perfect. This is just perfect."

Even so, the *Telegraph* gave the album five stars, praising "audacious and brilliant" music in a review that seemed to use the album to vicariously relive concert glories. Certainly, *Plectrumelectrum* has its moments, most notably the title track, an instrumental written by Donna and arranged by Prince – an honor the guitarist felt was "totally insane." "What he did with that arrangement was epic," she observed, noting that the song gave each band member's personality the chance to shine, plus her and Prince the opportunity to solo together. "It always warms my heart." But while 'Pretzelbodylogic' benefits from a dynamic arrangement, 'Whitecaps' reveals an often overlooked West Coast-tinged Crosby, Stills & Nash side to the group, and 'Funknroll' trades on memories of 3rdEyeGirl's powerful performances, very often the album fails to capture what made them such a thrilling live proposition. Its thin production at times makes the group sound more like radio pop-rockers Wheatus than the

"All you do is grow and change. A lot of things I don't do [anymore]. And some things I do more of." PRINCE

ensemble that, on stage at least, legitimately reinvigorated Prince's sound. At the furthest extreme to the *Telegraph*'s gushing review, Pitchfork dismissed it as an "anonymous" record that "merely duplicates the sounds and politics of rock'n'roll's stodgy past." A more measured appraisal came courtesy of the *New Yorker*, which noted that, while it's not "subpar, exactly," it is "easier to understand and easier to dispense with" than *Art Official Age*.

That's not to say it did poorly in comparison. Both albums comfortably entered the Top 10 in the US, with *Plectrumelectrum* nestling at Number Eight behind *Art Official Age* at Number Five (in the UK, the same album

came out on top, but peaked at Number Eight, with its sister release hitting Number 11). Doubtless, *Art Official Age* both contains better individual moments and hangs together as a more cohesive album – sometimes despite itself. Speaking proudly of her husband's co-production role on the album, Hannah praised its "radio-friendly and mainstream-sounding approach" as "urban and pop at the same time."

Welton had moved to Minneapolis with Hannah, in 2012, supporting her as 3rdEyeGirl got off the ground. About nine months after relocating, Joshua, the girls, and Donna's husband, Trevor Guy, then Prince's manager, had a meeting to discuss finding a new producer. At first, Prince didn't know Joshua made his own music, but after hearing him working on something in a "tiny studio room" in Paisley Park, Prince "walked in one night and just handed me a hard drive." The drive contained stems – separate vocal and music tracks – "from a famous artist." Prince had installed two other potential candidates in Paisley Park's Studio B, and effectively set them in competition with each other. After several days, Prince, whose personal kitchen backed onto the room that Joshua was recording in, walked in and told him, "I've been hearing the funk through the walls!"

Yet while Joshua was talented, his most obvious contributions to *Art Official Age* also make for some of the album's weakest moments, indebted to a contemporary EDM style that sounded dated almost as soon as the album was released. It makes the opening track, 'Art Official Cage,' an early disappointment. After that, however, the

Prince performs with the NPG Horns at the Hollywood Palladium, Los Angeles, March 2014.

album quickly settles into a short run as assured as any late-period Prince album could hope to have been. Noting that he had spent the past few years leaking songs that seemed to be "less about paving the way for a new album and more about trolling the internet" ('This Could Be Us' appeared to have been written in response to an internet meme that used a picture of *Purple Rain*-era Prince and Apollonia on a motorbike), the *New Yorker* also praised *Art Official Age* for "easily" being his "most coherent and satisfying album in more than a decade."

Not that it wasn't devoid of confusion. Its fuzzily defined concept has Prince being placed in suspended animation for 45 years; Lianne La Havas voices the assurance that "where you are now is a place that does not require time." Later, Prince receives an "affirmation": "there are no such words as 'me' or 'mine.'" Though these moments ultimately distract from, rather than add to, the effect, they do tap into emergent themes in Prince's work over his last few years. In interviews, both he and 3rdEyeGirl would insist that time moves differently in Paisley Park – with Prince stating, in his press conference at La Havas's home, that he was trying to "slow time down." On 'The Breakdown,' one of *Art Official Age*'s high points (notwithstanding the incongruous laser-beam sound effects), he sings, "Give me back the time, you can keep the memories" – a rare, affecting moment where Prince openly faces his own mortality.

Meanwhile, on the likes of 'Breakfast Can Wait,' Prince is as playfully sexy as he would allow himself to be at this stage in his career; 'The Gold Standard' sees him admonish younger stars who, he felt, pushed things too far. "You don't need to be rude, you don't need to be wild," he sings, in a nod to Robin Thicke's controversial 2013 hit 'Blurred Lines,' as if he'd entirely forgotten the first 20 years of his own career. Moments like this – insisting upon the inherent superiority of back-in-the-day music, and more

spoken-word passages about a "memory temple" that can be uploaded on to a hard drive and "review[ed] at your desire" – might not see Prince thinking about his age, but they do have him acting it: a man in his mid fifties trying to come to terms with his place in the world, his legacy, the technological landscape, and how to adapt to it.

"It's especially hard to live in the moment today," Hannah Ford Welton told the *Guardian*. "Everything is planned and scheduled, so when you step out of that … it keeps things fresh and interesting. Tomorrow we could be on the other side of the world." True to those sentiments, a week before the albums were due to go on sale, there seemed to be little plan to mark their release. Trevor Guy and Joshua Welton told the author of a vague idea to be in Paris for the release date, but, having toured for much of the year, Prince ultimately seemed reluctant to hit the road again. Instead, on September 30, he live-streamed a launch party from Paisley Park, during which he brought Kendrick Lamar on stage for a performance of 'What's My Name,' a mid-90s outtake that appeared on the *Crystal Ball* collection, and which Prince had dusted down for 3rdEyeGirl's live shows.

After that, Prince was remarkably quiet for a man who'd just released two Top 10 US albums. His only other notable attempt to keep momentum going was a November 1 appearance on *Saturday Night Live*. His last ever TV performance, it comprised an eight-minute set featuring *Art Official Age*'s 'Clouds' along with *Plectrumelectrum*'s 'Marz,' 'Anotherlove,' and its title track. And then he once again withdrew from the internet. Only a few months before, Hannah noted that Prince had become "a little more social media savvy – but in a fun way, not a dependent way." Appearing to have lost interest in promoting either of his new albums, Prince once again pulled his internet presence, seemingly feeling he had no need to use social media for anything else.

THOUGH HE HAD NO FRESH MUSIC TO RELEASE (IN JANUARY 2015, PLECTRUMELECTRUM'S 'MARZ' RECEIVED A LYRIC VIDEO, AND ART OFFICIAL AGE'S 'THIS COULD BE US' WENT ON RADIO ROTATION, BUT NEITHER MADE MUCH IMPACT), PRINCE SEEMED TAKEN WITH A NEW IDEA: OF HIMSELF AS AN ELDER STATESMAN WITH A MESSAGE TO IMPART.

HitnRun Phase One/ HitnRun Phase Two

(JANUARY 2015–DECEMBER 2015)

On January 11, Prince appeared at the Golden Globe Awards to present John Legend and Common with the Best Original Song trophy. A few weeks later, on February 8, he presented Beck with the Grammy Award for Album Of The Year (for *Morning Phase*.) Though he turned up simply to present the winners with their statuettes, his appearance at the Golden Globes had a deeper significance. Legend and Common had won for their song 'Glory,' used in the film *Selma*, which, in recounting Dr Martin Luther King's fight to secure voting rights for black citizens, brought the civil rights movement of the 1960s back to life. At the Grammys, Prince was more vocal, prefacing his announcement with the declaration, "Like books and black lives, albums still matter."

It was one of the few times that Prince had directly supported a political movement. Formed in 2013, in response to the acquittal of George Zimmerman, the neighborhood-watch coordinator who fatally shot 17-year-old African-American Trayvon Martin in February 2012, the Black Lives Matter movement quickly became part of the public consciousness. In August 2014, activists staged a Freedom Ride; in December, several thousand gathered just twenty minutes from Paisley Park, at the Mall Of America in Bloomington, Minnesota, to protest the murders of unarmed black men by police. Prince would certainly have supported their cause.

He was in a charitable mood, performing a secret gig in London's Koko on February 2 to raise money for Autism Rocks, before playing at the organization's inaugural concert in Dubai two nights later. Back in the US, he performed at a party held in honor of Michael Jordan, then appeared at *Saturday Night Live*'s 40th-anniversary celebrations in the early hours of February 16. His attempts to kick-start a Hit And Run tour of the US seemed half-hearted, though, with Prince and 3rdEyeGirl making it to just a handful of cities in several months (ticket-buyers in each city were awarded downloads of recordings such as 'What If,' a cover of a song by Christian singer-songwriter Nichole Nordeman, and 'The X's Face').

It was as if Prince were awaiting inspiration. Throughout March, most of his energy went toward promoting Judith Hill, a former Michael Jackson backing vocalist and one-time finalist on *The Voice*, whose album he produced and initially sent out for free download to subscribers to Live Nation's Prince email list.

Unfortunately, it would take the death of another young black man for Prince to reconnect with his muse. Arrested on April 12 and dead a week later from injuries to his spinal cord, 25-year-old Baltimore native Freddie Gray was one of a depressingly long line of black youths to have died at the hands of the police in the preceding years. As the Black Lives Matter movement sprang into action across the US, Baltimore citizens staged a number of protests that, perhaps inevitably, erupted into riots that lasted through to the end of the month.

On April 29, Prince recorded 'Baltimore' in response to Gray's death and its aftermath. Inviting a Fox9.com journalist over to Paisley Park to witness the live 3rdEyeGirl rehearsal turned recording session, he made reference to both Joni Mitchell's recent health scare and the events in Baltimore, admitting, "With everything going on there this week, I had a lot I needed to get out." Revealing that it was "the first time we have ever recorded a song live on the soundstage," Prince later recorded a second version on his own that same night, before asking fledgling singer Eryn Allen Kane to add a vocal turn.

Prince gave the song to Tidal to release and started raising money for Baltimore, first via a Dance Rally 4 Peace party and concert held at Paisley Park (during which attendees were asked to donate $30 and wear something gray), before heading to Baltimore a week later, on May 10, to stage a Rally 4 Peace event at the 14,000-capacity Royal Farms Arena. Prince allowed Tidal to live stream an hour of the concert, further cementing his burgeoning relationship with Jay Z's company. Fans who logged in to listen donated a total of $17,323, a figure that Tidal matched in order to give $34,646 to the Open Society Institute Of Baltimore. An undisclosed amount of concert proceeds also came from Prince, who donated to NAACP's Afro-Academic, Cultural, Technological And Scientific Olympics and Baltimore's YouthWorks and OneBaltimore programs.

Strangely, 'Baltimore' did not appear on his next album, the first taste of which came with 'Hardrocklover,' which was streamed via SoundCloud on July 1. Picking up where *Plectrumelectrum* left off, the song did nothing new with its phallic guitar metaphors, but it was at least a fiery return. The *NME* greeted it as the best song he'd released since his 2014 UK Hit And Run shows, adding that it was good to have "filthy, bombastic" Prince back.

Yet it was hardly representative of *HITnRUN Phase One*, an album that was hyped by Hannah Ford Welton as

having "a lot of experimental sound" and "hit after hit" that would cater to "those fans who just love to hear what Prince has to say." Another co-production with Joshua Welton, the album was released on September 7, via Tidal, and saw Prince looking around Paisley Park for things he had to hand. As with 'Art Official Cage' before it, 'Million $ Show' is a disposable EDM-infected opener, used earlier in the year as the intro music for the few Hit And Run

> "When was the last time you were scared by anyone? In the late 70s, there was scary stuff then." *PRINCE*

shows of 2015. Remixed by Joshua Welton, a slightly renamed 'This Could B Us' does the rounds again, as does 'Fallinlove2nite,' which, though shorn of Zooey Deschanel's vocals, remains an *Art Official Age* reject. By the time Prince cannibalizes 'Clouds' for 'Mr. Nelson,' much of the album feels more like one of his remix EPs from the 90s, such as *The Beautiful Experience*, rather than a bona fide new work.

That didn't stop the *Guardian* praising *HITnRUN Phase One* as "more like it" following *Art Official Age* and *Plectrumelectrum*, claiming that the album could be "the enduring classic we've been waiting for." The similarly

positive *USA Today* awarded it Album Of The Week and assured fans that it was worth subscribing to Tidal for. Pitchfork, however, found only one true highlight, '1,000 X's & O's,' on which Prince "sings in an environment unmolested by contemporary cliché" (the fact that the song dates back to 1992, and Prince's aborted sessions with Rosie Gaines, doubtless also helped). Elsewhere in Pitchfork's assessment, even the songs that most other reviewers praised, such as 'The X's Face' and 'Hardrocklover,' were, in turn, deemed "initially promising" but "too thin on development," and "strangely bored with itself."

Pitchfork also noted that Prince's "urge to over-promise" (the album was hardly experimental by his standards) extended to the title, which suggested "the possibility of a concept worth serializing." If Prince's album titles have always defined the theme of each new work, *HITnRUN Phase One* suggested that, this time around, he was more concerned with process than content. Yet while 'hit and run' worked as a live concept (Prince could take to the stage, unload a selection of songs – many of them genuine classics – and move on to the next show), it didn't extend so well to the album format, where recordings may sometimes have benefitted from more thought. Prince had always been a legendarily fast worker in the studio, but Joshua Welton's description of the recording process was telling: "When I have a beat ready that I think is funky, I'll send it to him and then he'll send it right back with vocals or a whole new arrangement for a crazy string section. Sometimes he'll even come in and plug his guitar right up here by the soundboard and just lay something down while I'm staring at him!"

Clearly, Prince's first idea wasn't always his best. "You can't hold

something like that back!" he exclaimed of a new song in late 2015, though he was seemingly more taken with it being "the sound of someone not restricted by anything," rather than the quality of the work. And, as co-producer, Joshua didn't seem to be offering any creative guidance.

Prince announced his new deal with Tidal to a group of ten journalists who were in Minneapolis to attend the National Association Of Black Journalists Convention, and, once again, likened record contracts to "slavery." Praising Jay Z for spending $100 million of his own money to build Tidal, he asserted, "We have to show support for artists who are trying to own things for themselves … once we have our own resources, we can provide what we need for ourselves." Prince also allowed Tidal to stream his old NPGMC download albums, among them *C-Note* and *The Chocolate Invasion*, while also starting a series of 'Purple Picks,' in which he highlighted songs from his own catalogue, along with selections from artists he wanted to boost.

A week after streaming *HITnRUN Phase One*, Tidal released CD copies of the album, suggesting that the subscriber uptake was less than expected. When *HITnRUN Phase Two* duly followed, on December 12, it came with far less hype than its predecessor. Prince simply tweeted a link to a Tidal bundle offering both albums for download for $14.99, accompanied by the request, "Please everyone purchase the product after listening." (In early 2016, Prince sold stock of CD copies to local fans, encouraging them to sell the album online to other fans. The decision was partly made because, according to Prince, Amazon wouldn't pay him quickly enough. What he didn't foresee was that some fans would take the opportunity to charge shipping rates that exceeded the cost of the CD itself.)

Prince and 3rdEyeGirl at the Sony Centre, Toronto, Canada, May 2015.

Rock'n'roll Love Affairs

Having seemingly accepted that NPG Records lacked the infrastructure necessary to launch artists, Prince still sought to help new talent in an ever-shifting industry, and went out of his way to name-check musicians he admired. Even while launching two of his own albums in 2014, he invited the likes of Kendrick Lamar and FKA Twigs to perform at Paisley Park. (Sadly, the tantalizing prospect of a collaboration with Lamar never happened: the pair were so engrossed in conversation that they ran out of time for Prince to record a vocal for *To Pimp A Butterfly*'s 'Complexion (A Zulu Love)'). As Prince saw it, "Paisley Park is an academy any which way you look at it." Speaking to *Ebony* in 2015, he boasted of its being a "storehouse of great music to learn from, productions and arrangements you can study."

After focusing mainly on Andy Allo throughout 2011 and 2012, Prince sought to give exposure to a host of young female talent. During 2013, in the run up to the release of her second album, *The Electric Lady*, Janelle Monáe was invited to open several Prince concerts, while Prince later sent her a singing telegram to celebrate the release of the album (on which he guested on the track 'Givin Em What They Love'). He mentored female

soul trio King during their early days, and, even before meeting British singer Lianne La Havas, had made a point of telling the press she was his favorite live performer.

New Power Generation bandmates were also given support in their solo careers. While Prince largely focused on launching 3rdEyeGirl, he let vocalists Liv Warfield and Shelby J. make live appearances with the NPG. He also co-wrote Shelby's 2012 single 'North Carolina' and performed an executive producer's role on Liv Warfield's second album, *The Unexpected* (to which he donated the title track, before reworking it as 'Wow' for the 3rdEyeGirl album *Plectrumelectrum*).

In 2014, Kandace Springs and Rita Ora caught Prince's attention. The latter was invited to appear on *HITnRUN Phase One*'s 'Ain't About 2 Stop,' and also received her very own Prince song, 'The Single Most Amazing Thing In The Room,' which ultimately remained unreleased as her second album went into limbo. Springs, meanwhile, had received a social-media message from Prince promising that her dreams were "about to come true." They, too, recorded unreleased music together, though when Prince sought to hold her hand in the cinema, Springs shyly demurred, ensuring that at least one of the couple's dreams were left unfulfilled.

Prince did take one more shot at launching a protégé through NPG Records when he released Judith Hill's debut album, *Back In Time*, in 2015. Hill, who previously featured in the documentary *20 Feet From Stardom*, became one of Prince's closest friends in the months leading up to death. For his part, Prince seemed to truly believe in her talent, asking Minneapolis record store Electric Fetus to treat her record as they would his own, and even deflecting a legal threat from her former rep in order to produce the album. "Her voice sounds analog to me," Prince boasted of Hill's authenticity, urging reporters at Paisley Park to ask questions while they could, because Hill was "about to become a superstar."

Crediting the album to Prince And The New Power Generation (the band's first album credit since 2007's *Planet Earth*), Prince noted that he only played "keyboards a little" on the record, adding, "I'm getting in the habit of that now. I love schooling musicians on just one track." ("You are gonna do a masterpiece today," he would tell them. "You just gotta listen.") It's perhaps notable, then, that many of the songs date to the early 2010s, when reviewers noted that Prince was relinquishing many aspects of his stage show to his band.

Like its predecessor, *HITnRUN Phase Two* was once again largely a smash-and-grab on Prince's recent past. 'Rocknroll Loveaffair' and 'Screwdriver' had been given single releases just three years earlier, while 'Groovy Potential,' though pleasantly slinky, was one of the deluge of songs Prince issued for download through ThirdEyeTunes.com in 2013 (along with another inferior remake of 'Extraloveable,' suffocating beneath an overly enthusiastic brass section). A clutch of songs dated to 2014

and 2015, though of these, 'Stare' had already received a Spotify release, on July 30.

Noting that the record's throwaway nature was perhaps "what happens when you start pumping out two albums a year," the *LA Times* was nonetheless content with the way Prince had seemingly settled into the routine of releasing a brace of records that broadly represented his

> "These days I can get more done. I'm far more respected than I was before, when I say something [about] the music industry." PRINCE

two extremes: the more electronic, studio-reliant excursions on the one hand, and more organic, full-band outings on the other. Describing the album was "overlooked," *Vanity Fair* agreed with *Rolling Stone*'s assertion that Prince was "back on top form," and concluded that it was worth fans' time. Citing the "casual-seeming virtuosity" that drew audiences to Prince in the first place, *Vanity Fair* praised *HITnRUN Phase Two* for ranging "much more widely" than its predecessor, and saw it as "a grab bag tribute to black music of the 1970s."

Yet as Prince's string arranger (and Hornheadz trombonist) Michael Nelson would later reveal, the album also contains hints of where Prince was headed next. Though his efforts were ultimately cut short, Prince

"A lot of the time I don't talk about the past because you can't do it without naming names." PRINCE

claimed that he and Michael were "going to redefine the Minneapolis sound." With 'Baltimore' – the song that, in April, had rekindled Prince's creativity – Prince had Nelson orchestrate his guitar solo for strings, woodwind, and brass instruments. When Nelson finished the arrangement, Prince told him they were "on to something special"

(though he also moved the orchestration around, making it "completely different than what was intended"). "At 2:28," Nelson noted to *Rolling Stone*, "you actually hear the guitar play with the strings into that string section which originally continued as the guitar solo."

Enthused by the process, Prince sent more songs with solos for Nelson to orchestrate, including unreleased material by 3rdEyeGirl and a track they worked on together just three months before his death, on which Prince wanted "an Earth Wind & Fire thing." Of around 35 songs that they worked on together, Nelson said that only a small number were released. Somewhere in The Vault there remains a song called 'Pangaea,' named for a Miles Davis live album and sung by an unidentified female singer. "I don't know if it will ever come out but it's one of the most incredible things I ever worked on," Nelson claimed. Prince agreed. His simple response to the arrangement was a note in all capitals: "'PANGAEA IS MAGNIFICENT."

THOUGH THE MAJORITY OF HIS ALBUMS CARRIED THE ICONIC "PRODUCED, ARRANGED, COMPOSED, AND PERFORMED BY PRINCE" CREDIT, IN THE 37 YEARS SINCE HE RELEASED HIS DEBUT, *FOR YOU*, PRINCE HAD NEVER SET OUT ON A SOLO TOUR. IN FEBRUARY 2016, HOWEVER, HE GAVE FANS THE CHANCE TO SEE HIM AT HIS MOST INTIMATE WHEN HE EMBARKED UPON THE PIANO & A MICROPHONE TOUR.

Piano & A Microphone

(JANUARY 2016–APRIL 2016)

P rince had initially planned a string of 16 solo dates across Europe, starting on November 21, in Vienna, closing on December 22, in Brussels, and taking in Denmark, Sweden, Spain, Norway, The Netherlands, the UK, Italy, Germany, and France. Announcing the tour to a selection of journalists flown out to Paisley Park, Prince, sitting with the media at his feet, in a room decorated to look like a nightclub, noted that, having perfected his live show over three decades, he rarely got bad reviews. Undertaking the solo tour was, he said, "to challenge myself, like tying one hand behind my back, not relying on the craft that I've known for thirty years." Setlists would change nightly, he claimed, as he wouldn't know what songs he would play before he went on stage.

Europe would never get to see some of the most surprising shows Prince ever played. Ticket sales were postponed when, the day before they were due to go on sale, secondary sales websites were found offering seats for up to £5,000 a pair. On the evening of November 13, the planned on-sale date, terrorists killed more than 130 fans at an Eagles Of Death Metal gig in Paris, in a senseless attack. Prince was quick to cancel the European dates.

Seeking to combat ticket touts, he subsequently hinted that he might just stage Piano & A Microphone as a Paisley Park residency. For £5,000, he reasoned, fans could fly to Minneapolis, book a hotel, and see him in his iconic complex. "Better experience too!" he quipped on Twitter. On January 21 2016, he staged the Piano & A Microphone Gala Event, setting the pace for the remainder of the tour with two intimate shows at which, as promised, Prince played completely

solo. Describing the first performance as "one of the extraordinary oddities of Prince's concert career," Jon Bream, writing in the *Star-Tribune*, praised it as "the most revealing, intimate and personal show he's ever given."

Taking a roughly chronological journey through his career, Prince opened with the first tune he ever learned to play, the 'Batman Theme,' before stopping off at key songs from his Warner Bros albums – 'Baby' (from *For You*), 'I Wanna Be Your Lover' (*Prince*), 'Dirty Mind,' 'Do Me, Baby' (*Controversy*), 'Something In The Water (Does Not Compute)' (*1999*), 'The Beautiful Ones' (*Purple Rain*), 'Raspberry Beret' (*Around The World In A Day*), and 'The Ballad Of Dorothy Parker' (*Sign "O" The Times*). After bringing things up to date with 'Baltimore' and 'The Breakdown,' Prince ended on a rarely performed 'Anna Steisia,' from *Lovesexy* – its first live outing in 13 years.

Throughout, he took the time to explain his development as a musician and songwriter – how his dad, a jazz pianist, wouldn't let him touch the piano at home, but that, after his parents divorced, he became determined to out-perform his father. 'Dirty Mind,' another song that hadn't been played live since the *Lovesexy* tour, marked, Prince said, the point where he was "on my own, trying everything I could to find out who I was." Later, praising Wendy and Lisa for their contribution to his music, he also took a moment to acknowledge David Bowie's recent death, revealing: "I only met him once and he was very nice to me." Closing the show, he seemed to sum up in one sentence how he viewed his career: "Throughout it all, remaining free, I found out that God was love."

Dedicated to Prince's father, "4 all he taught his musical son," none of the remaining Piano & A Microphone

shows were quite as revealing as this first one, but they were nevertheless full of surprises. Despite Prince's self-imposed handicap, they also received rapturous reviews to rival any from his past. The official opening night, in Melbourne, Australia, coincided with the news of Vanity's death, and saw Prince perform one of the most heartfelt shows of his career. As the tour wound on, through Sydney and New Zealand, back to America and up to Canada, his performances took on the feel of a gospel revival. The setlists became more structured, but with Prince digging deep into his catalogue to pull out songs such as 'The Ladder,' 'Joy In Repetition,' and 'Thieves In The Temple,' fans could never be sure what rarities they would hear on any given night.

"You have to try new things. With the piano it is more naked, more pure. You can see exactly what you get.'" *PRINCE*

While Prince was of a mind to embrace his past and share music he had long consigned to history, the famously reticent artist also announced that he was writing a memoir. On a break between Piano & A Microphone shows, he appeared at Avenue, a club in New York, to perform a short set and tell journalists that he had received an offer he couldn't refuse. "We're starting right at the beginning with my first memory, and hopefully we can move all the way to the Super Bowl," he said of the book, which was to be called *The Beautiful Ones*. Three years earlier, Prince's then manager, 23-year-old Julia

Ramadan, had advised him: "When it comes to your life story, don't let anyone hold the pen." It seemed that, after years of closely guarding not only his past but also his back catalogue – from Warner Bros, from bootleggers, and perhaps even from himself at times – Prince was determined to reclaim it all.

Back on tour, in Canada, Prince continued to thrill with the likes of 'Little Red Corvette' (in a playful medley with 'Dirty Mind' and Vince Guraldi's 'Linus And Lucy' theme, from the animated *Peanuts*), 'Girl,' and 'I Love U In Me.' Appearing to have made peace with his more salacious songs, he turned them out anew. When announcing the tour the previous November, Prince felt "it was a pretty good move" to have stopped playing such material: it allowed fans to bring their families to his shows, so a bigger audience could "experience the same thing." His very final performances, however, seemed to be for himself as much as they were his fans; it was easy to imagine that this was how he spent the late evenings and early hours in Paisley Park. ("This last year he was always working. Almost always playing piano," Prince's personal chef, Ray Roberts, recalled, adding that he would hear Prince play just three seconds of a song, dozens of times in a row, in order to get it right.)

Hearing Prince pay tribute to his entire body of work, not just the hits, was a joy. Often closing shows with 'Free Urself,' a song he had released on Tidal and iTunes in September 2015, Prince would lead the audience through the titular chant, reveling in being where he'd fought to be his entire career: free.

PRINCE WAS SCHEDULED TO PLAY TWO SHOWS IN ATLANTA ON APRIL 7 2016. THAT MORNING, PROMOTER LUCY LAWLER-FREAS RECEIVED A CALL FROM TOUR COORDINATOR KIM WORSØE. "WE HAVE A MAJOR PROBLEM," WORSØE SAID. "PRINCE IS REALLY SICK." THE STAR HAD "THE FLU," HAD JUST RETURNED FROM THE DOCTOR, AND COULD BARELY SPEAK. "HE'S NOT GOING TO GET ON THE PLANE AND HE NEEDS TO POSTPONE THE SHOW."

Sometimes It Snows In April...

Two days later, the concerts were rescheduled for April 14. Taking place at 7pm and 10pm, respectively, both lasted around an hour and a half each. Though Lawler-Frees recalled that Prince "wasn't feeling well" when he arrived, she described the shows as "phenomenal. He gave it his all." Prince, too, is said to have claimed they were his best ever. However, rather than stick around to perform an after-show, he immediately went to his private jet, taking off for Minneapolis at 12:51am in the early hours of Friday, April 15. But just a little over an hour after take off, and only 48 minutes away from their destination, the pilot radioed air traffic control to report an unresponsive passenger. In order to make an emergency stop at Quad City International Airport in Moline, Illinois, the pilot landed the plane in a little over fifteen minutes, taking the 45,000-foot descent at a rate of 3,000 feet per minute – over three times faster than an average landing time.

Judith Hill, one of only two other passengers on the plane with Prince, later recalled that, in the middle of talking and eating dinner together, Prince simply lost consciousness. "His eyes fixed," she told the *New York Times*. "We knew it was only a matter of time; we had to get down. We didn't have anything on the plane to help him." Kirk Johnson, Prince's long-term aide and sometimes sideman, carried an unresponsive Prince to waiting emergency personnel. Soon after, they gave him a short of Narcan, a medicine commonly used to reverse the effects of an opiate overdose. Within twenty minutes, Prince was rushed to the nearby Trinity hospital, where he remained for several hours. However, after allegedly being refused a private room, he was back in the air, en route to Paisley Park, that same morning.

After Kirk Johnson informed the *Star-Tribune* that it was merely a case of "bad dehydration" and that "all is good," Prince announced that he was throwing a party at Paisley Park that night. In a brief appearance, he showed off his new guitar – a bespoke purple-and-gold teardrop-shaped model that he'd had made by UK-based guitar maker Simon Farmer of Gus Guitars – but told fans that he had to "leave it in the case or I'll be tempted to play it." He was, he said, still focusing on improving his piano. On another newly acquired instrument, a purple Yamaha piano, he threw off a rendition of 'Chopsticks,' along with another short instrumental passage, before treating fans to a half-hour recording taken from his Atlanta shows – earmarked for a live album he was working on.

The brief appearance was intended to show that he was in fine health; fan Nancy Anderson would note that he looked "pasty, weak, and frail," and had trouble climbing the steps to his piano, but she assumed that was related to the reports of flu. "Wait a few days before you waste any prayers," Prince told the crowd.

In the days that followed, Prince was seen publicly in and around Minneapolis. On Saturday, April 16, Record Store Day, he visited his local store, Electric Fetus, where he bought six albums, among them Stevie Wonder's *Talking Book* (which he blasted in the car on the way home), Joni Mitchell's *Heijira,* and Santana's *Santana IV*. A

In the wake of his death, fans quickly began to leave tributes alongside Prince's star outside the First Avenue club in Minneapolis.

local resident spotted him looking "free and happy" as he cycled along a Chanhassen bike path on April 18. The following evening, he made a brief visit to the Dakota Jazz Club to catch a performance by singer Lizz Wright.

These appearances seemed to be part of a wider effort to show the world he was fine, but at around 7pm on April 20, he was also spotted visiting a local Walgreens pharmacy near his home following a doctor's appointment. About an hour later, Prince was dropped off at Paisley Park. He skipped dinner – the roasted red pepper bisque with kale salad that personal chef Ray Roberts had prepared for him. This didn't appear to be too alarming. Prince was a light eater who, according to Roberts, would sometimes only have "one bite" of dinner. In recent months, Prince had had "the flu or a cold, always," Roberts told the local *City Pages*. "He was off his game and needed to rest. I had to be careful about what I was serving him."

More worrying was that Prince missed an appointment scheduled for the following morning, April 21. Kirk Johnson and assistant Meron Bekure went to Paisley Park to check on him, accompanied by Andrew Kornfeld, a representative from the California-based outpatient medical clinic Recovery Without Walls, who had flown to Minneapolis the night before. They found Prince lying unresponsive in the elevator that led to his private living quarters. With Johnson and Bekure too distraught to act, Kornfeld, a man who'd never visited Paisley Park before, or even met Prince, phoned the emergency services at 9:43am. Less than half an hour later, at 10:07am, medical personnel, having attempted CPR, officially declared that Prince Rogers Nelson, aged 57, was dead. (It later emerged that rigor mortis had already set in, and that, tragically, Prince was likely to have died in the middle of the night.)

Following an autopsy, Prince was cremated at First Memorial Western Chapel, on the afternoon of Saturday, April 22, in what was described by his publicist, Yvette Noel-Schure, as a "private, beautiful ceremony" attended by "a small group of his most beloved: family, friends, and his musicians." In keeping with Prince's Jehovah's Witness faith, the ceremony took place within a week of his death. Many memorials and tributes also took place around the world: fans decorated the fencing outside Paisley Park with flowers and purple balloons, and left a shrine by his star at First Avenue; global landmarks such as the Eiffel Tower, Melbourne Arts Center, and Empire State Building were lit up in a purple hue. Fittingly, NASA looked to the stars and released a photo of the purple-hued Crab Nebula. Even the casts of Broadway musicals included Prince tributes in their performances, while, on June 13, he was added to the Apollo Theater's Walk Of Fame.

Yet closure would be a long time coming. Prince's closest living relatives – sister Tyka Nelson, and half-siblings Sharon L., Norrine P., and John R. Nelson, along with Alfred Jackson and Omarr Baker – failed to find a will expressing his wishes. Fans were shocked that the man who had been so protective over his life's work – not just the released music that he'd so doggedly fought for ownership of, but the countless hours of unreleased material in The Vault, not to mention Paisley Park, which stood as a structural testament to his creations – had failed to leave instructions concerning what would happen to it after his death. That responsibility fell in part to Carver County District Court Judge Kevin Eide.

The authorities also had to be relied upon to provide an official cause of death. Having performed a four-hour autopsy on Prince's body, the Midwest Medical Examiner requested a full toxicology scan, while rumors spread as to Prince's dependence – or not – on prescription opiates. When the official results were released, on June 2, they recorded a verdict of accidental death by overdose of fentanyl, a prescription opiate known to be up to 100 percent stronger then morphine, and up to 50 percent more potent than heroin. (Nonetheless, fentanyl is approved for controlled use by the US Food And Drug Administration, though it is also often illegally manufactured.) A slow-release drug, it is sometimes used in conjunction with oxycodone, an immediate-release opiate found in Percocet, a painkiller that many people alleged Prince had taken.

Once again, fans were left shocked and wondering how a man so vehemently anti-drugs – and a devout follower of the Jehovah's Witness faith, which prohibited their use – could find himself in a position where he was taking lethal amounts of a prescription drug that had begun to cause nationwide fatalities at an increasingly alarming rate. Almost equally distressing was the knowledge that, even accounting for Prince's closely guarded privacy, the situation had gone unchecked for so long.

Despite the incident on his private jet, it took five days before anyone in Prince's camp sought professional help. After his hospitalization, Judith Hill, before travelling back home to LA, let insiders know how serious the situation was. The day before Prince died, an aide contacted Dr. Howard Kornfeld, father of Andrew and director of Recovery Without Walls, which specializes in treatment for chronic pain and addiction. Speaking to the press following Prince's death, Kornfeld's lawyer, William Mauzy, said that Prince's people had spoken of a "grave medical emergency," and that Kornfeld "set in motion a plan to deal with what he felt was a life-saving mission."

However, Kornfeld was unable to fly to Minneapolis immediately, so sent his son Andrew, whose role at the clinic was to meet prospective patients and explain the treatment to them. After being put up in a hotel overnight, Andrew was collected in the morning and taken to Paisley Park, carrying with him what was later described as "a small amount" of Suboxone, an opioid medication containing buprenorphine, which is used to treat opioid addiction. Though his father is trained in buprenorphine use, Andrew was not legally allowed to administer it. William Mauzy later stated that Andrew had not intended to give the Suboxone to Prince, but was planning to give it to an unnamed doctor who was due to meet them on site that morning.

Mauzy did not confirm who that doctor was, though a local doctor, Todd Schulenberg, did arrive on the scene shortly after Prince was pronounced dead. Like Andrew Kornfeld, however, Schulenberg had not undergone the eight-hour training course required in order to be put on the federal Substance Abuse And Mental Health Services Administration's list of doctors authorized to use buprenorphine. His reason for arriving at Paisley Park, he told police, was to deliver the results of some tests that he had performed on Prince. In the days following Prince's death, Schulenberg also hired a lawyer, Amy Conners, and left his job at North Memorial Medical Center in Robbinsdale, a half-hour drive from Paisley Park, without publicly announcing why.

Schulenberg had, according to a *Star-Tribune* source quoted by the Associated Press, worked with Kirk Johnson in the past, which is possibly how he came to meet Prince. As well as having worked for Prince as both a sideman and manager of various business affairs since the 90s, Johnson taught classes at a local Life Time fitness center, and lived nearby in a house owned by Prince. Johnson, too, declined to release an official statement through his lawyer, F. Clayton Tyler, but, in the days following Prince's death, he did not return to the gym.

Though the Carver County Sheriff's office remained tight-lipped about its findings, it emerged that prescription drugs had been found at Paisley Park. The court subsequently ordered that the search warrants be sealed, until either the beginning of criminal proceedings or 180 days after they were filed. The court also enlisted

"Everything is a hundred percent. I never saw him go on stage and be like, 'OK, let's get this over so we can get out of here.'" IDA NIELSEN, 3RDEYEGIRL

the help of the Drug Enforcement Agency, to help ensure that no fraud or illegal drug dealing had taken place.

A picture began to emerge: Prince, ever the committed artist, had pushed himself to the brink. Following Prince's cremation, his brother-in-law, Maurice Phillips, husband to Tyka, told fans gathered in mourning outside Paisley Park that he'd been with Prince the weekend before, and that Prince had been up for over six days, working for "154 hours straight." But that was just one in a long line of similar stories from throughout his career, such as how, in the 80s, studio engineers worked around the clock in shifts, burnouts being replaced as Prince just kept going.

And then there were the marathon concerts – sometimes several in one day; shows that, right up until Prince's death, earned him rave reviews, and upon which no small part of his legend rests. The Midwest Medical Examiner's post-mortem report noted a scar on his left hip, presumably the long-rumored operation that he'd had in 2010, after decades of wearing high heels while performing vigorous dance routines and leaping into the splits – even as he entered his forties. His incomparable live shows thrilled audiences worldwide, but they took a toll on his body. (The post-mortem also noted a scar on his "right lower leg," though gave no indications as to its cause.)

Prince had taken to wearing wedged trainers in later years, and, in his final months, could often be seen with a cane, but the years of jumping off pianos, pushing himself – and his bands – to perform the best live shows on the planet, had done their damage. Recalling her years on tour with him in the mid-to-late 80s, Sheila E. said: "There was always something kind of bothering him, as it does all of us." Noting that musicians of their caliber were "like athletes, we train, and we get hurt all the time," Sheila added that such grueling shows "messed up his hip and his knee, but he kept doing it because he loved doing it and it was something no one was doing." Looking in from the outside, Alan Leeds felt that "the idea of him medicating himself in order to perform isn't strange to me."

Even in his mid-fifties, Prince pushed himself far beyond the limits of most people his age. "Everything is a hundred percent," 3rdEyeGirl bassist Ida Nielsen told the author in 2014. "I never saw him go on stage and be like, 'OK, let's get this over so we can get out of here.' Every part of him is just in it … it's a beautiful experience, and I think also for the audience."

Preternaturally talented, Prince had a gift for music, for performance – and for cultivating mystique – that made him seem almost immortal. That he wasn't, after all, just makes his achievements all the more astounding.

Fans would have to learn to adjust to life without their idol. For Prince, however, after years of spiritual discovery, there was the possibility of an afterlife. "You ain't supposed to die," he asserted in 2015, adding that faith is "supposed to be like wings. Take you up higher. Now do your work from a higher place, get more done, cover more ground." Perhaps, as he promised in 'Let's Go Crazy,' he didn't let the elevator bring him down. Rather, he may have just gone to a higher floor.

"Wait a few days before you waste any prayers," he had told fans at Paisley Park: words that would come to seem grimly prophetic. But according to Judith Hill, after his near-death experience in the air, Prince became "serious about getting help" because "he wanted to do the right thing for his own body." Perhaps, as he stood on stage for what would be the final time, Prince knew that professional treatment was the only way forward. He needn't have asked for fans' support. They would have given it willingly, as they had throughout his 38-year career.

At the end of concerts, long after the house lights had gone up, one of Prince's favorite stunts was to return to the stage, perhaps with an acoustic guitar, or to sit down at the piano, for one more encore. It was another part of his mystique: the anything-can-happen aura he cultivated. No one knew when Prince might choose to make a last-minute return, but at every show, die-hard fans remained until the last moment – until they were absolutely sure it was over.

But the house lights have been up for long enough now.

Endnotes

CHAPTER 1

8 "He inspired me because" Prince to *Guitar World* (1998)
8 "Listening to white radio" Owen Husney in Liz Jones, *Slave To The Rhythm*
8 "I disliked him immediately" Prince to *Musician* (1981)
9 "Everybody was talented" Pepé Willie to *Prince: The Glory Years* (Chrome Dreams, 2007)
9 "His mother basically walked" Alan Leeds to *Icon* (1998)
10 "When they sleeping" Prince to *Rolling Stone* (1990)
11 "I thought this group" Owen Husney in *Prince: The Glory Years*
11 "I presented myself as" and "I lied my way in" Owen Husney in Alex Hahn, *Possessed*
12 "He didn't want that" Owen Husney in Liz Jones
13 "What we would call" Dez Dickerson in *Prince: The Glory Years*
14 "Because I do all" Prince to the *New York Times* (1996)
14 "Tommy was heartbroken" Owen Husney in Alex Hahn
15 "You're white, you're blonde" Gayle Chapman in *Prince: The Glory Years*
15 "An amalgam of rock'n'roll" Dez Dickerson in Alex Hahn
15 "Sometimes the basement was" Dez Dickerson, *My Time With Prince*
16 "There were some definite" Dez Dickerson, *My Time With Prince*
16 "He thought the show" Charles Smith in Alex Hahn
17 "I knew how to" Prince in Liz Jones
19 "I was brought up in" Prince to *Guitar World* (1998)
19 "I got countless calls" Gary Brandt to housequake.com (2006)
19 "We were all groping" Matt Fink to *Keyboard* (1991)
19 "Loud spandex and bright" Dez Dickerson, *My Time With Prince*
19 "We were young and" Bobby Z in Alex Hahn
19 "I felt sorry for" Rick James, *The Confessions Of Rick James*
19 "He sent his girlfriend" Gayle Chapman in *Prince: The Glory Years*
19 "The simulation of some" Dez Dickerson, *My Time With Prince*
20 "Nobody knew what was" Prince to *Rolling Stone* (1981)
20 "The record company was" Dez Dickerson in *Prince: The Glory Years*
20 "Mo Ostin did what" Alan Leeds to housequake.com (2007)
21 "*Dirty Mind* was a" Bob Cavallo in Liz Jones
22 "He turned Warner Bros" Marylou Badeaux in Alex Hahn
22 "Tidal wave of critical" Dez Dickerson in *Prince: The Glory Years*
22 "André's ego got in" Prince to *Bass Player* (1999)
22 "Prince refuses to play" *New Musical Express* (1980)
24 "He'd come to our" Jimmy Jam to *Performing Songwriter* (2002)
24 "He definitely knew what" Mark Brown in Alex Hahn
25 "I was horrible" Prince to MTV (1985)
26 "I think he is" Jimmy Jam in Liz Jones
28 "We can't let a" Dez Dickerson, *My Time With Prince*

29 "We knew we weren't" Jimmy Jam in Liz Jones
30 "Jesse had a major" Matt Fink in Alex Hahn
30 "I thought it was" Morris Day to thewavemag.com (2003)
31 "They started to lose" Alan Leeds in Alex Hahn
31 "It turned into a" Jimmy Jam in Liz Jones
32 "I was just getting" Prince to *Bass Player* (1999)
32 "He was an unbelievable" Peter Doell to thelastmiles.com (2005)
34 "Prince sauntered over to" Denise Matthews in Liz Jones
34 "He juggled the affairs" Alan Leeds in Alex Hahn
34 "There's something really crazy" Tommy Lee in Nikki Sixx, *The Heroin Diaries*
35 "The *1999* album was" Dez Dickerson in *Prince: The Glory Years*
35 "He yelled at us" Bob Cavallo in Alex Hahn
35 "I did this last" Jimmy Jam on *Top 10 80s Soul* (Channel 4 UK TV, 2001)
35 "Nothing but me running" Prince to *Musician* (1997)
36 "I felt like an" Bobby Z in Liz Jones
37 "I'd better not confuse" Alan Leeds in Alex Hahn
37 "I knew I didn't" Dez Dickerson, *My Time With Prince*

CHAPTER 2

40 "Right at the point" Jimmy Jam in *Purple Rain: Backstage Pass*
41 "There was no precedent" Alan Leeds in *Purple Rain: Backstage Pass*
41 "Casual conversation is not" William Blinn in Barney Hoskyns, *Imp Of The Perverse*
42 "He'd flip right out" Don Amendolins in Liz Jones
42 "In ten minutes I" Albert Magnoli in Liz Jones
42 "She was a competitive pistol" Alan Leeds in Alex Hahn
42 "very sweet and tremendously" Albert Magnoli in *Purple Rain: Backstage Pass*
48 "vitally interested in music" Bob Cavallo in Alex Hahn
48 "What kind of fucking record" Marylou Badeaux in Alex Hahn
48 "He just kind of" Roy Bennett in Alex Hahn
48 "like it was the Marines" Eric Leeds in Liz Jones
50 "The more famous he got" Wendy Melvoin in Liz Jones
50 "Prince was hungry for" Wendy Melvoin in Liz Jones
50 "Prince is an entertainer" Wendy Melvoin on *I Love The 80s* (BBC TV, 2001)
51 "We all needed to" Prince to *Rolling Stone* (1990)
51 "an opportunity to have" Dez Dickerson to nashvillescene.com (2014)
52 "He had a very" Alan Leeds to thelastmiles.com (2005)
53 "Wendy and I flipped" Lisa Coleman in Liz Jones
54 "I think the smartest" Prince to *Rolling Stone* (1985)
55 "I felt it was" Matt Fink in Alex Hahn
56 "I think he really" Alan Leeds in Alex Hahn
56 "The coldest song ever" Prince to *Rolling Stone* (1990)
56 "If there was a" Alan Leeds in *Prince: The Glory Years*
57 "It's important to me" Prince to *Rolling Stone* (1985)
57 "It's a brand new band" Paul Petterson to the *Washington Times* (2015)

58   "We had a whole" Bob Cavallo in *Liquid Assets: Prince's Millions*
59   "I don't regret anything" Prince to *Rolling Stone* (1990)
59   "That three months in" Alan Leeds to housequake.com (2007)
63   "Sending tapes back and forth" Alan Leeds in *Prince: The Glory Years*
64   "He was an engineer's" Alan Leeds to thelastmiles.com (2005)
65   "I started feeling a little" Mark Brown in Alex Hahn
65   "The aftershows were a" Alan Leeds to housequake.com (2007)
65   "I remember the first" Dez Dickerson in *Prince: The Glory Years*
67   "If Michael was the" Stevie Wonder to thewrap.com (2016)
70   "It came at a time" Susan Rogers to housequake.com (2006)
72   "Concepts for albums were" Alan Leeds in *Prince: The Glory Years*
72   "He knew that three" Alan Leeds in Alex Hahn
72   "They came up with" Prince to MSN Music Central (1996)
73   "I hate the word" Prince to *Rolling Stone* (1990)
75   "Half the new console" Susan Rogers in Liz Jones
76   "Prince wasn't taking" Alan Leeds to prince.org (2005)
76   "He failed to disguise" Alan Leeds to prince.org (2005)
76   "A succession of girlfriend" Alan Leeds to housequake.com (2007)
77   "'Girlfriend' stopped radio in" Alan Leeds to prince.org (2005)
77   "The music was first" Alan Leeds to housequake.com (2007)
77   "According to the press" Sheena Easton in *Top 10 80s Soul*
78   "He had no mortgages" Bob Cavallo in *Liquid Assets*
79   "In his mind we" Marylou Badeaux in Alex Hahn
80   "He started to see" Alan Leeds to thelastmiles.com (2005)
80   "I learn things from" Miles Davis with Quincy Troupe, *Miles: The Autobiography*
80   "He just couldn't even" Alan Leeds to thelastmiles.com (2005)
82   "They were odds and ends" Susan Rogers in Liz Jones
82   "Ten kind-of-okay songs" Marylou Badeaux in Alex Hahn
83   "I was very angry" Prince to *Rolling Stone* (1990)
84   "When I talk about" Prince to *Rolling Stone* (1990)
84   "cutting off people in" Prince to *Rolling Stone* (1990)
84   "a turning point" Alan Leeds in Alex Hahn
86   "I don't think Prince" Alan Leeds to prince.org (2005)
86   "a mind trip, like" Prince to *Rolling Stone* (1990)
87   "There was also supposed" Roy Bennett in *Prince: The Glory Years*

CHAPTER 3

94   "He didn't really wanna" Bob Cavallo in *Liquid Assets*
95   "It was one of" Prince to *USA Today* (1990)
96   "*Graffiti Bridge* should be" the *Washington Post* (1990)
96   "take the entire gamut" Albert Magnoli to the *Los Angeles Times* (1989)
96   "Prince wanted a lower-budget" Albert Magnoli in Liz Jones
96   "Not listening to anyone" Marylou Badeaux in Alex Hahn
97   "I like to give" Prince to *Rolling Stone* (1990)
98   "It was non-violent" Prince in Liz Jones

99   "Prince's music in the" Alan Leeds to prince.org (2005)
100   "Rob, you know that" Rob Borm in *Liquid Assets*
101   "Black awareness is really" Tony M to *Details* (1991)
103   "I was brought up" Prince to *MTV* (1995)
103   "I was dismayed" Michael Koppelman to housequake.com (2006)
103   "The 'keep it real'" Alan Leeds to prince.org (2005)
105   "more diverse than ever" Prince to hour.ca (2011)
106   "No one works more" Hans-Martin Buff to *Details* (1998)
107   "His name is Prince" *Rolling Stone* (1992)
111   "Our dispute was not" Bob Merlis to *USA Today* (1996)
111   "Prince would show up" Jeff Gold in *Liquid Assets*
111   "He's finally gone mad" Chris Poole in *Liquid Assets*
111   "Everybody at Paisley Park" Jeff Gold in *Liquid Assets*
112   "He spent more energy" Alan Leeds to prince.org (2005)
113   "Prince wanted to have" Jeff Gold in *Liquid Assets*
114   "If I knew then" Prince to the *Los Angeles Times* (1996)
114   "I know what time" Prince to MSN Music Central (1996)
114   "I never meant to" Prince on *Oprah* (1996)
114   "I've washed my face" Prince to the *Los Angeles Times* (1996)
114   "They gave me a lot" Prince to *El Pais* (1997)
114   "situations where we finally" Prince to *Ebony* (2015)
120   "We had a big graph" Bob Cavallo in *Liquid Assets*
120   "Before we even shot" Rob Born in *Liquid Assets*
120   "I'm not scared of" Prince to *El Pais* (1996)
120   "I was being fired" Heidi Presnail to the *St Paul Pioneer Press* (1995)
122   "I've produced 50 music videos" as reported in *An Evening With Kevin Smith*
122   "I don't do tours" Kim Worsøe to nytimes.com (2016)
122   "She could call him" Marnie Gustavson to the *Hollywood Reporter* (2016)
124   "He has a small" Chris Poole in Liz Jones
125   "A lot of the guys" Prince to British tabloids (1994)

CHAPTER 4

131   "That's what we were" Prince to the *Los Angeles Times* (1996)
133   "I've never been this much in love" Prince to *Oprah* (1996)
134   "I worked for a year" Prince to *Hello* (1996)
135   "The record is important" Prince to *Oprah*
136   "It was all quite" Mayte to fiyamag.com (2005)
137   "all the ingredients were" Prince to *Hello!* (1996)
137   "I haven't had a nightmare" Prince to *El Pais* (1996)
137   "My soul has been" Prince to *Interview* (1997)
137   "I wasn't allowed to" Mayte to fiyamag.com (2005)
137   "We believed he was" Mayte to fiyamag.com (2005)
139   "Some couples are brought" Mayte to fiyamag.com (2005)
139   "We don't plan to investigate" *City Pages* (1997)
148   "This is a poet" Clive Davis to *New York Times* (1999)
148   "When I was at" Prince to *Minneapolis Star-Tribune* (1999)
152   "kept a floor-to-ceiling" Margaret Wetzler to foodandwine.com (2016)
152   "It's fun being in Islamic countries" Prince to the *Guardian* (2011)
154   "Religion, when used properly" Prince to *Ebony* (2015)
154   "We recognise that life God" Larry Graham to the *Star-Tribune* (2016)

CHAPTER 5

164   "I get asked every year" Prince to the *Canadian Press* (2004)

166 "Maybe we could put" Prince to *Forbes* (1996)
166 "is more or less" Prince to the *San Francisco Examiner* (2004)
166 "With the first copy" Don Ienner to *Rolling Stone* (2004)
166 "The charts are supposed" unnamed record executive to *Billboard* (2004)
166 "What we're trying to do" Prince to MTV.com (2004)
172 "There's definitely a throwback" *Minneapolis Star-Tribune* (2006)
174 "It's pretty much the" Maya McClean to clubplanet.com (2007)
174 "basically his musical muse" Ted Cockle to *Music Week* (2006)
175 "I think in a lot" Prince to housequake.com (2005)
178 "copyright-holders can't order" sfgate.com (2008)
179 "hasn't had a genuine hit" Alan Leeds to housequake.com (2007)
180 "The internet's completely over" Prince to the *Daily Mirror* (2010)
180 "I personally can't stand" Prince to the *Guardian* (2010)
180 "dead to us" Prince to the Associated Press (2013)
180 "What I meant was" Prince to the *Guardian* (2015)
180 "I don't do albums" Prince to *Billboard* (2013)
181 "laughably confused complaint" techdirt.com (2014)
181 "a black hole" Prince on *The Arsenio Hall Show* (2014)
181 "Nobody can just come up" Prince to *Ebony* (2015)
181 "Once the technology caught up" Alan Leeds on medium.com/cuepoint (2016)
184 "We said: 'OK, lets'" Rob Hallet to BBC News (2008)
184 "His bands may seem" Alan Leeds to housequake.com (2007)
185 "tell the cat to chill" Prince to the *Irish Independent* (2010)
185 "We always knew" Karl Fowler to the *Wall Street Journal* (2009)
185 "It may be glamorous" Randee St. Nicholas to *USA Today* (2008)
186 "nasty but not dirty" Prince to the *Los Angeles Times* (2008)
186 "the gatekeepers must change" Prince to the *Los Angeles Times* (2009)
186 "The beautiful thing" Prince on *Tavis Smiley* (2009)
187 "Prince wanted Lotusflow3r to" Scott Addison Clay to *Variety* (2009)
188 "I'm interested in the" Prince to the *Los Angeles Times* (2009)
189 "promoting promiscuity" Prince to the *Los Angeles Times* (2009)
189 "one of those sleeper records" Prince on *Tavis Smiley* (2009)
189 "a whole lotta people" Prince to the *Los Angeles Times* (2009)
189 "saw the future" Prince to Fox9 (2010)
190 "thousands of dollars in" *Star-Tribune* (2010)
191 "Someone told me they" Prince to the *Daily Mirror* (2010)
192 "Soon I'll be backing" Prince to the *Irish Sunday Independent* (2011)
192 "He gave me that" and "Being an independent artist" Andy Allo to billboard.com (2013)
193 "a necessary endeavor" Prince to timeoutchicago.com (2010)
193 "Self-interest is on" Prince to *Ebony* (2010)
193 "We're in a singles market" Prince to the *Chicago Tribune* (2012)
194 "When I first saw" Prince to *Mojo* (2014)
194 "time exists in a" Donna Grantis to the *Guardian* (2014)
195 "The feminine energy" Prince to *Mojo* (2014)

195 "The lack of sleep" Ida Nielsen to the *Guardian* (2014)
195 "We've recorded some stuff" Ida Nielson to the author (2014)
195 "I'm trying to get" Prince to *V* (2014)
197 "If you want to be" Prince to *Essence* (2014)
198 "When I'm on stage" Prince to *Essence* (2014)
198 "got really upset" Michael Eavis to nme.com (2014)
198 "Hand it to me" LA Reid to *Essence* (2014)
199 "I come from the" Prince on *The Arsenio Hall Show* (2014)
199 "finally got something that" Prince to the *Minneapolis Star-Tribune* (2014)
199 "At the time we didn't" Hannah Ford Welton to the author (2014)
199 "What's cool and different" Hannah Ford Welton to the author (2014)
199 "same album" and "I don't deal in history" Prince to the Associated Press (2014)
200 "All you do is" Prince to *Essence* (2014)
200 "pick the songs that" Hannah Ford Welton to the author (2014)
200 "it keeps you on your toes" Ida Nielsen to the author (2014)
200 "a lot of the songs" Donna Grantis to the author (2014)
200 "radio-friendly and mainstream-sounding" Hannah Ford Welton to the author (2014)
200 "walked in one night" Joshua Welton on medium.com/cuepoint (2015)
200 "from a famous artist" Joshua Welton to *Ebony* (2015)
201 "a little more social" Hannah Ford Welton to the *Guardian* (2014)
203 "With everything going on" Prince to Fox9.com (2015)
203 "a lot of experimental" Hannah Ford Welton to BBC 6 Music (2015)
204 "When I have a beat" Joshua Welton to medium.com/cuepoint (2015)
204 "You can't hold something" Prince to medium.com/cuepoint (2015)
204 "We have to show" NPR.org (2015)
205 "an academy any which" Prince to *Ebony* (2015
205 "about to come true" Kandace Springs to the *Times* (2016)
205 "Her voice sounds analog" blog.thecurrent.org (2015)
205 "These days I can" Prince to the *Guardian* (2015)
205 "keyboards a little" Prince to *Ebony* (2015)
206 "redefine the Minneapolis sound" Michael Nelson to *RollingStone.com* (2016)
207 "to challenge myself" as quoted in the *Guardian* (2015)
208 "When it comes to your life story" Prince to the *Star-Tribune* (2013)
208 "This last year he was" Ray Roberts to the *Star-Tribune* (2016)
209 "We have a major problem" Kim Worsøe, as quoted in the *New York Times* (2016)
209 "His eyes fixed" Judith Hill to the *New York Times* (2016)
209 "pasty, weak, and frail" Nancy Anderson to the *Star-Tribune* (2016)
210 "free and happy" Heather Hoffmeister to etonline.com (2016)
211 "Everything is a hundred" Ida Nielson to the author (2014)
212 "There was always something" Sheila E. to the Associated Press (2016)
212 "the idea of him medicating" Alan Leeds to the *New York Times* (2016)
212 "You ain't supposed to die" Prince to *Ebony* (2015)
212 "serious about getting help" Judith Hill to the *New York Times* (2016)

PICTURE CREDITS

The photographs in this book are reproduced with permission from the following copyright holders, and we are grateful for their help. Many of the images were supplied by Redfern's (indicated by the initials RF), Rex Features (RX), Retna (RT), Getty Images (GI), and the Kobal Collection (KC). All record jackets reproduced from the author's collection.

Jacket front LA Media Collection/Sunshine, RT; **4–5** Rico D'Rozario, RF; **6** Virginia Turbett, RF; **9** Chuck Stewart, RF; **10** RX; GAB Archives, RF; **11** George Chin, RF; RX; **11** RB, RF; **13, 14, 15** Robert Whitman; **17, 18** Richard E. Aaron, RF; **21** George Chin, RT; **23** Barry Plummer; Ebet Robert, RF; **26** Echoes Archives, RF; **27** Michael Ochs Archives/Stringer, GI; **28** Scott Weiner, RT; **29** Ebet Roberts, RF; **31** David Atlas, RT; **33** Ebet Roberts, RF; **36** Scott Weiner, RT; **37** Echoes Archives, RF; **38** WB/Photofest, RT; **41** Richard E. Aaron, RF; **43** WB/Photofest, RT; **44** Richard E. Aaron, RF; **46** Sipa Press, RX; **47** Ebet Roberts, RF; **51** WB/Photofest, RT; **53** GAB Archives, RF; **55** Ebet Roberts, RF; **56** Richard Young, RX; **59** Ebet Roberts, RF; **60–61** WB, KC; **63** Ebet Roberts, RF; WB, KC; **64** Suzi Gibbons, RF; **65** Sipa Press, RX; **67** Grant Davis, RF; **69** Ebet Robert's, RF; **71, 72** GAB Archives, RF; **74** Cavallo, Ruffalo & Fargnoli, KC; **76** Tim Hall, RF; **79** Erhan Guner, RT; **81** Suzi Gibbons, RF; **83** Ebet Roberts, RF; **84–85** Nils Jorgensen, RX; **87** Brian Rasic, RX; **89, 90** SNAP, RX; **90–91** Kip Rano, RX; **92** Brian Rasic, RF; **95** Paisley Park Films/WB, KC; **96** Mick Hutson, RF; **97** Paisley Park Films/WB/KC; **98** Eddie Boldizsar, RF; **100–101, 102, 103** Araldo Di Crollalanza, RX; **105** Michel Linssen, RF; **106** Paul Slattery, RT; Paul Bergen, RF; **107** Mick Hutson, RF; **109** Echoes Archives, RF; **110** Brian Rasic, RF; **115** Araldo Di Crollalanza, RX; Dave Lewis, RX; **117** Brian Rasic, RX; **119** Sipa Press, RX; **122** Tim Rooke, RX; **125** Mick Hutson, RF; **126** Brian Rasic, RX; **127** Steven Parker, RT; **128** RX; **130** Tim Clary/AFP, GI; **133** David Corio, RF; **135** Clemens Rikken/Sunshine, RT; **136** Sipa Press, RX; **138–139** Paul Bergen, RF; **141** Toby Wales, RF; **143** Paul Bergen, RF; **147** Peter Brooker, RX; **149** Alex Olivera, RX; **150** Fotex Agentur GMBH, RF; **151** Frank Micellota, GI; **153** Brian Rasic, RF; **154** Kieran Doherty; **156** Kevin Winter/Image Direct, GI; **159** T Ikic/Keystone USA, RX; **161** Martin Philbey, RF; **162** JW International, RF; **165, 166** Grant Davis, RF; **167** CBS/Everett, RX; **168** RF; **170** Chris Graythen, GI; **172–173** Richard Young, RX; **174** Debra Rothenberg, RX; **175** JW International, RF; Ethan Miller, GI; **177** Scott Wintrow, GI; **179** Nick Laham, GI; **183** GI; **184** Claire Greenway, GI; **185** Harry Scott, RF; **187** Kevin Winter, GI; **188** Bertrand Guay/AFP, GI; **191** Kevin Mazur/WireImage, GI; **192** Brian Ach/WireImage, GI; **193** Kevin Mazur/WireImage, GI; **195** David M. Benett, GI; **197** Samir Hussein, RF/GI; **199** Kevin Winter, GI; **200, 201** Kevin Mazur/WireImage, GI; **203** Chelsea Lauren, GI; **204** Cindy Ord, GI; **205** Karrah Kobus, GI; **206** Cindy Ord, GI; **209** Mark Ralston/AFP, GI; **210, 212** Scott Olson, GI.

BIBLIOGRAPHY

Bream, Jon, *Prince: Inside The Purple Reign* (Collier 1984)
Davis, Miles, with Quincy Troupe, *Miles: The Autobiography* (Simon And Schuster 1989)
Dickerson, Dez, *My Time With Prince: Confessions Of A Former Revolutionary* (Pavilion 2003)
Hahn, Alex, *Possessed: The Ride And Fall Of Prince* (Billboard 2003)
Hill, Dave, *Prince: A Pop Life* (Faber 1990)
Hoskyns, Barney, *Prince: Imp Of The Perverse* (Virgin 1988)
Lewis (Jones), Jel D. (ed), *Prince – Is Back On Top, The Man, The Artist: In His Own Words* (Xlibris 2006)
Jones, Liz, *Slave To The Rhythm* (Warner 1998)
Matos, Michaelangelo *Sign "O" The Times* (Continuum 33 1/3 2004)
Morton, Brian, *Prince: A Thief In The Temple* (Canongate 2007)
Nilsen, Per, *Dancemusicsexromance – Prince: The First Decade* (Firefly 1999)
Uptown, *The Vault: The Definitive Guide To The Musical World Of Prince* (Uptown 2004)

Plus the following publications, broadcasts, and resources: 3121.com, AOL Online, *An Evening With Kevin Smith*, *An Evening With Kevin Smith 2: Evening Harder*, BBC Magazine online, *BET Tonight: Talk Back With Tavis Smiley*, *Bass Player*, *Boston Globe*, *Business 2 Magazine*, *The Canadian Press*, *Central High Pioneer*, *City Pages*, clubplanet.com, *A Current Affair*, *Daily Mail*, *Details*, *Detroit Free Press*, *Ebony*, *El Pias*, *Entertainment Weekly*, fiyamag.com, *Forbes*, *Gallery Of Sound*, *Giant*, *Guardian*, *Guitar World*, *Harper's Bazaar*, *Hello*, housequake.com, *Humo*, *I Love The 80s*, *Icon*, *Interview Magazine*, *Keyboard*, *Liquid Assets: Prince's Millions*, *Los Angeles Times*, *MSN Music Central*, *MTV.com*, *Minneapolis Star-Tribune*, *Musician*, www.npgmusicclub.com, *New York Times*, *Paper*, *People Weekly*, *Performing Songwriter*, *Philadelphia Daily News*, *Philadelphia Enquirer*, prince.org, prince-live.com, *Oprah*, *Prince: The Glory Years*, *Q*, *Record Collector*, theregister.co.uk *Rocky Mountain News*, *Rolling Stone*, *San Hose Mercury News*, *Shift*, sfexaminer.com, *Spin*, *St Paul Dispatch*, *St Paul Pioneer Press*, *Sunday Times*, *Sweet Potato*, thelastmiles.com, *The Telegraph*, *Time*, *Time Out*, *Top 10 80s Soul*, *USA Today*, *Vibe*, *Village Voice*, *Washington Post*, *Wired*, Yahoo! Internet Live, Yahoo! News.

ACKNOWLEDGE ME

My Darling Nicky and Chota
If I was anything else, I'd be the the water in your bath

Where to start thanking people, but at the beginning? My mum used to play *Diamonds And Pearls* in the car when I was a kid, so who knows what effect that had on me? Years later, Dad would travel up from Plymouth just to watch one of Prince's 21 Nights In London shows – one of many visits to the O2 for me that summer, the one and only time my dad would get to witness Prince live. My brother Matt also travelled up for one. At the time, I was writing the first edition of this book, and it was encouraging to know that younger people cared about Prince too. I thank my family for everything.

This book has had several lives since 2008. While space permits me from once again thanking everyone who contributed to previous editions, rest assured that you are not forgotten. That said, Tom Seabrook and Nigel Osborne at Jawbone also once again deserve special thanks, particularly for making all the right noises when it came to my concerns about deadlines. Tom, especially, went above and beyond in his role as editor. Knowing how hard he was working in order to pull this together at his end only made me want to work harder in return.

My wife Nicola has – as ever – been a constant source of support. Despite, in her own words, having the good sense to like Prince "a normal amount," she has endured more than enough conversations that might start about anything, but usually end in some obscure point of Prince lore. I know I will be soon doing the same for you with your book, and I can't wait. I believe in you.

Knowingly or unknowingly, a number of other people deserve thanks for their support, among them my former editor, Ian McCann, who kindly asked me to write a Prince memorial for *Record Collector*, allowing me to go some way toward getting my head around Prince's tragic death and formulate some thoughts that would later appear in this book. I also thank my current employers and the whole team at USM for their encouragement, among them Giancarlo Sciama, to whom I'll just say: hey, look this over. Tell me, do you like what you see?

Since I had the good fortune to meet Gavin McLaughlin after the publication of *Prince: Chaos, Disorder, And Revolution* (though perhaps he had the ill sense to have asked to interview me about it), he has become a close friend and an invaluable source of information. It seems only fitting that I write this on a day that we're due to see The Time at a Prince tribute in London, though it's sad to think there will be no more actual Prince gigs.

Thanks also to Jerome Tillekeratne, whose enthusiasm and ability to send a new article my way at any time of day was a great help.

Any Prince biographer owes a debt to Per Nilsen's tireless work as an archivist, along with the team behind *The Vault* (now princevault.com) and other dearly departed fan sites, among them housequake.com. Prince might not have appreciated your work, but many of us do.

Finally, this book wouldn't even exist – and our lives would be far less rich – if it weren't for Prince's life and work. As the circumstances surrounding his death made clear, he quite literally gave his life to his art. I will be forever grateful for the part his music plays in my life, and know that there are generations to come who will feel the same. *Life & Times* is a whole book dedicated to his phenomenal career, and yet no words can truly express the impact of his loss. For Prince fans around the world… may you live to see the dawn.

PUBLISHER'S THANKS

Stephen Atkinson at Rex Features; Paul Cooper Design; the Balley Design crew; Philip Grimwood-Jones at Getty Images; Rebecca Pate at The Pictures Desk; Julian Ridgway at Redfern's; Robert Webb; Robert Whitman; Nancy Wolff; Kelly Wong at Retna.

"The problem is getting it all out before another idea comes along."
Prince to *Rolling Stone* (1985)